Advance Praise for *Framed*

"Michael Skakel is fortunate to have a cousin as loyal as Robert Kennedy Jr. In *Framed*, Kennedy presents a compelling, methodical case that Skakel is innocent of murder and is a victim himself. Americans interested in justice should be captivated by this book."

—**Bill O'Reilly**, Fox News anchor,
#1 *New York Times* bestselling author of *Killing Lincoln*

"Robert F. Kennedy Jr.'s new book, *Framed*, is a furious and fascinating condemnation of the persecution of Michael Skakel. This account will shock and astound those who read the press reports of the case at the time, particularly Dominick Dunne's reportage, and believed Skakel to be the monster portrayed there. It is deeply researched, bitingly written, and entirely convincing."

—**Stuart Woods**, #1 *New York Times* bestselling author of
the Stone Barrington series and Holly Barker series

"A brilliantly written autopsy of a wrongful prosecution and conviction, Kennedy's book is a masterpiece that chronicles the Kafkaesque persecution of an innocent man. It is a riveting narrative of greed, hubris, envy and sloth. Michael Skakel's saga is a heartbreaking account of an abuse of power paralleled in infamy only by the Duke Lacrosse prosecutors."

—**Anne Bremmer**, American attorney, television personality,
defense counsel in Amanda Knox's Italian murder trial

"Bobby Kennedy pulls no punches in making the compelling case for his cousin's, Michael Skakel's, absolute innocence. But he goes much further: indicting those who he believes were complicit in what he calls a frame-up by prosecutors, police, and the media. . . . This book is a devastating indictment of our justice system and media for their systemic unwillingness to confront their own errors. It is a must-read for those who care about justice and integrity in our public institutions."

—**Alan M. Dershowitz**, author of *Taking the Stand: My Life in the Law*

"An exciting page turner." —**Morris Dees**, author, attorney, and
co-founder of the Southern Poverty Law Center

"In *Framed*, Robert F. Kennedy Jr., with Capote-like precision, tells his gripping story of an innocent man caught up in a Kafkaesque nightmare between a corrupt prosecution and a disastrously inept criminal defense that resulted in 11½ years in prison for a crime Skakel didn't and couldn't have committed. RFK Jr. lays it all out in a page-turner that will convince all but the most rabid Kennedy haters. Then again, the arguments are so compelling, maybe even they'll be convinced."

—**Michael Shapiro**, Perennial Superlawyer,
Former Queens County District Attorney, New York Special Prosecutor,
faculty Benjamin N. Cardoza School of Law, adjunct Harvard Law School

"*Framed* is the riveting true story of a life turned upside down by unethical prosecutors and irresponsible journalists in a justice system which is anything but. It is both the story of one man's nightmare and a cautionary tale for us all . . . because while it is true that we can ensure that we do not COMMIT a crime, we can never ensure that we are not CHARGED with one. Kudos to Kennedy, not only for writing a page-turner, but for never giving up his quest for the Truth."

—**Shawn Holley**, defense attorney for O.J. Simpson's Dream Team
and in over 60 trials for high-profile clients, including Tupac Shakur,
Snoop Dogg, Paris Hilton, Nicole Ritchie, Lindsay Lohan, and others

"Crime thrillers and true crime stories both aim to explore our notions of justice. *Framed* by Robert Kennedy Jr. combines the best of both with a powerful story that grabbed me in the first few pages and wouldn't let go. Kennedy meticulously torpedoes the case that convicted his cousin Michael Skakel of murder. He chronicles a decades-long horror show of incompetence, prejudice, malfeasance, and outright misconduct. What I didn't expect, though, were the feelings that surfaced while I was reading. Kennedy took me from rage to tears at the injustices suffered by his cousin and family. *Framed* is a must-read for anyone who cares about our judicial system."

—**Libby Fischer Hellmann**,
award-winning author of *Easy Innocence* and other crime thrillers

"An electrifying, meticulous exposé. Kennedy shows how his cousin was wrongfully convicted by a grim yet fascinating cast of characters cruelly assembled, as it were, to thwart justice; corrupt police and prosecutors, an incompetent defense lawyer, a judge who falls in love with the 24 hour news cycle while forgetting his role as neutral arbiter, and the TV "commentators" who directed the outcome of the case for ratings and not justice—all conspiring to convict an innocent man while allowing the real murderers to go free. Kennedy gives the reader a front-row seat, and, unlike the jury, all of the evidence necessary to watch, in horror, the conviction of yet another innocent man. If this book does not wake people up to the terrifying reality of how our criminal justice has become a game not of seeking justice but of winning, I do not know what will. This book is mandatory reading for anyone who cares about truth, individual rights, and the corruption of justice in America."

—**Joe Cheshire**, attorney in the Duke Lacrosse case,
North Carolina's "Top Lawyer" three years running by SuperLawyer.com

"Kennedy exposes the toxic brew of incompetence and sensationalism that led to his cousin's conviction. The 'cold case' had every ingredient that made it an irresistible stew that fed the ambition and corruption by press, prosecutors, and police; the brutal, senseless murder of a privileged teenage girl, a self-seeking prosecutor with 'elastic ethics', a society gossip fabulist who stirred the brew, a crooked cop, sloppy police work, a cavalier defense lawyer, and a 'Kennedy cousin' with an ironclad alibi who nevertheless became the perfect suspect.

"Now, years after a monumental miscarriage of justice, Kennedy, by careful investigation, deconstructs the prosecution's case, convincingly shows Michael Skakel's innocence, and identifies the true culprits who have escaped justice for decades."

—**Dick DeGuerin**, considered one of America's top lawyers,
most notably for his defense of Tom DeLay,
David Koresh, Robert Durst, and others

"An awful, awful story brilliantly told. How many more innocent men and women will be wrongfully convicted and punished with long and terrible jail sentences? This book is a scream for change."

—**Martin Garbus**, legendary criminal and constitutional attorney,
educator, and author of *Courting Disaster* and other books.
"One of the world's finest trial lawyers," according to *The Guardian*

"The definitive account of the perfect storm that led to Michael Skakel's wrongful conviction, Kennedy recounts the blunders of investigators, the misconduct of prosecutors, the perjury of witnesses, the legal ineptitude of judges and defense lawyers, and the failings of a criminal justice system that cares more about defending a conviction, even one that is wrongful, than in delivering justice. And he answers the question that has remained unanswered for more than 40 years: Who killed Martha Moxley?"

—**David Cameron**, Professor of Political Science, Yale University, and member of Connecticut's Eyewitness Task Force

"Kennedy explains with new clarity and detail the pervasive corruption in the Connecticut State Prosecutor's Office that led to Michael's wrongful conviction. He shows, in a persuasive, compelling narrative, of how four writers, pursuing their own craven ambitions, orchestrated Michael's media lynching and wrongful conviction."

—**Randy Wayne White**, *New York Times* bestselling crime writer, author of more than 40 books, including the Doc Ford series, former member of the Florida Judicial Nominating Committee and Florida Bar Association Grievance Committee

FRAMED

ROBERT F. KENNEDY JR.

FRAMED

Why Michael Skakel Spent
Over a Decade in Prison
for a Murder
He Didn't Commit

Skyhorse Publishing

Skyhorse Publishing books may be purchased in bulk at special discounts for sales promotion, corporate gifts, fund-raising, or educational purposes. Special editions can also be created to specifications. For details, contact the Special Sales Department, Skyhorse Publishing, 307 West 36th Street, 11th Floor, New York, NY 10018 or info@skyhorsepublishing.com.

Skyhorse® and Skyhorse Publishing® are registered trademarks of Skyhorse Publishing, Inc.®, a Delaware corporation.

Visit our website at www.skyhorsepublishing.com.

10 9 8 7 6 5 4 3 2 1

Library of Congress Cataloging-in-Publication Data is available on file.

Cover design by Brian Peterson
Cover photo credit: Chris Buck

Print ISBN: 978-1-5107-0177-9
Ebook ISBN: 978-1-5107-0178-6

Printed in the United States of America

To Cheryl,
the wisest person I know

and

To my mother,
who tried to give her children her love for reading and language
and who taught us, through word and actions, to trust in God,
but to be skeptical of dogma and to always question authority.

ACKNOWLEDGMENTS

Andrew Goldman was my invaluable partner and collaborator in researching, writing, and structuring this book. I watched him evolve from a skeptic into Michael Skakel's passionate and energetic defender. Andrew has all the qualities of a great journalist. He is tough, thorough, meticulous, fearless, probing, and hungry for truth. His deep research cracked the code on lawyer Sheridan's key role in framing Michael—a role that the Skakels had long suspected, but were never able to prove. I'm grateful that Andrew cheerfully continued to volunteer his time to this project for three months after completing his work.

I could not have written this book without the aid of Stephen Skakel, who archived tens of thousands of relevant documents and took the leadership role in screening and hiring Michael's new lawyers and orchestrating his defense. His encyclopedic knowledge of Michael's case far exceeds anybody's, including Michael's. Stephen was available to Andrew and me 24/7. Stephen inspired me, both with his love for Michael, and for justice; he spent a decade making grueling personal sacrifices to defend his brother heroically when all the world believed Michael guilty. Stephen has made a career pursuing St. Paul's admonition that we pursue peace, labor for justice, comfort the afflicted, care for the sick, feed the hungry, clothe the poor, and welcome refugees. His devotion to Michael is proof of Emerson's notion that "If a single man plants himself firmly upon his own ideal, and there abides, the whole wide world will come round to him."

Three people—Lori Morash, Dr. Val Chamberlain, and Christine O'Neill—typed this manuscript. All of them worked grueling hours on an insanely tight schedule and somehow managed to unscramble many hundreds of handwritten legal pad pages of my reprehensible penmanship. Dr. Val Chamberlain, a retired archaeologist and professor at the University of Idaho, moved into my home for nearly six weeks and put in 14-hour work days with me as I raced to complete the manuscript. I benefited from her beautiful sense of structure, her impeccable Oxford grammar, her scrupulous fact checking, and her perpetual good cheer. My children loved hearing her dinner-table tales of college days at Oxford when she was the lone woman in her department. We have all relished hunting fossils with Val, learning from her some of the wonders of archaeology and paleontology.

Christine O'Neill typed all of these chapters through their various iterations and edits, while simultaneously managing my complex schedule, supporting my litigation and teaching responsibilities, and fielding phone calls—and doing everything with grace and humor. She often worked until dawn and was up bright eyed and ready for more work after breakfast.

I'm grateful to my children for taking care of each other while I worked on the book—and for always rooting for Michael.

I owe too much to Cheryl to inventory here. She supported me in every way and at every moment as I researched and wrote this book. She was the first to read it and gave me brilliantly targeted notes, all of which are incorporated here.

I owe special thanks to David Michaelis and Nancy Steiner, who provided me my home away from home, wonderful garden-fresh homegrown and home-cooked meals, and who read selective chapters for me. I'm particularly grateful that they hosted Michael Skakel for dinner once each week and gave us all love and support.

To my mother ,who inherited the rich portfolio of Skakel virtues—her humor and courage, her reckless generosity and her competitive spirit, her peculiar combination of faith and irreverence, her love of nature, and her curiosity about everything and everybody—and who tried to give those gifts to her children.

To my best friend, *New York Observer* editor Peter Kaplan, who worked unsuccessfully in 2003 to help me find an independent journalist willing to venture beyond the seductive narratives and write the real story of Michael Skakel's persecution. When those efforts failed, Peter observed, "Every reporter is scared of appearing to have been seduced by your family. You need to write this story yourself." Shortly before his death in 2013, he read my chapter on "The Ghosts" and told me to turn it into a book. I felt his presence every day that I worked on this project. Peter's widow, Lisa Chase, recommended Andrew Goldman to help me with research and writing.

To my agent, Kris Dahl, who I think must be the savviest and coolest agent in the book business, and to my amazing team at Skyhorse—President and Publisher Tony Lyons, Publicity Director Charlie Lyons, Creative Director Brian Peterson, Senior Editor Mike Lewis, Group Editorial Director Mark Gompertz, and Senior Production Editor Stacey Fischkelta—who believed in this project when no one else did and who supported me. Thanks to Mark's supervision and Stacey's furious editing, we managed to produce and publish this book on a world-record crash schedule. Despite daunting setbacks, no one ever lost their cool. With the book done, my hope is that Stacey can do her laundry again.

All men make mistakes, but the good man yields when he knows his course is wrong and repairs the evil. The only sin is pride.
—Sophocles, *Antigone*

CONTENTS

Cast of Characters   *xvii*

Timeline   *xxv*

Introduction   *xxix*

PART I: The Stage

CHAPTER 1   *The Murder*   *3*

CHAPTER 2   *The Prosecutor*   *14*

CHAPTER 3   *Skakels and Kennedys*   *35*

PART II: The Suspects

CHAPTER 4   *The Neighbor*   *55*

CHAPTER 5   *The Brother*   *62*

CHAPTER 6   *The Boyfriend*   *73*

CHAPTER 7   *The Gardener*   *77*

CHAPTER 8   *The Crush*   *81*

CHAPTER 9   *The Tutor*   *104*

PART III: The Victims

CHAPTER 10   *Martha and Michael*   *125*

PART IV: The Frame

CHAPTER 11   *The Caller*   *133*

CHAPTER 12   *The Gossip*   *156*

CHAPTER 13   *The Perjurer*   *163*

PART V: The Witnesses

CHAPTER 14   *The Model*   *179*

CHAPTER 15   *The Bully*   *188*

CHAPTER 16   *The Junkie*   *195*

CHAPTER 17   *The Handyman*   *201*

CHAPTER 18   *The Barber*   203
CHAPTER 19   *The Friend*   205

PART VI: The Lawyer
CHAPTER 20   *The Clown*   215

PART VII: The Ghosts
CHAPTER 21   *The Killers?*   239

Epilogue   273

Index   279

CAST OF CHARACTERS

THE MOXLEY FAMILY
DAVID MOXLEY, Martha's father
DORTHY MOXLEY, Martha's mother
JOHN MOXLEY, Martha's older brother
MARTHA MOXLEY, murder victim, age 15

THE MOXLEYS' FRIENDS AND THEIR ASSOCIATES
VINNIE CORTESE, John Moxley's friend, out with him on night of Martha's disappearance

JOHN HARVEY, John Moxley's friend, out with him on night of Martha's disappearance

LOU PENNINGTON, Moxley family friend who told John that his sister had been killed

JOHN SALERNO, John Moxley's friend, out with him on night of Martha's disappearance

ZACHARY SMITH, Peter Ziluca's Santa Fe roommate

NANCY ZILUCA, Peter's mother
PETER ZILUCA, Martha's boyfriend

THE MOXLEY HOUSEHOLD HELP
THERESA TIRADO, Moxley maid

THE SKAKEL FAMILY
ANNA MAE DECKER SKAKEL, Rucky's wife
ANNE GILLMAN SKAKEL, Tommy's wife
ANNE REYNOLDS SKAKEL, Michael's mother
DAVID SKAKEL, Michael's younger brother
GEORGIE SKAKEL, Michael's son
JOHN SKAKEL, Michael's older brother
JULIE SKAKEL, Michael's older sister
MARGOT SHERIDAN SKAKEL, Michael's ex-wife

MICHAEL SKAKEL, Martha's friend and neighbor
RUSHTON "RUCKY" SKAKEL SR., Michael's father
RUSHTON "RUSH" SKAKEL JR., Michael's older brother
STEPHEN SKAKEL, Michael's younger brother
TOMMY SKAKEL, Michael's older brother

THE SKAKEL RELATIVES

GEORGEANN DOWDLE, Michael's cousin

JIMMY DOWDLE, Michael's cousin

JOHN DOWDLE, Georgeann Terrien's first husband (deceased), father to Johnny, Jimmy, and Georgeann

JOHNNY DOWDLE, Michael's cousin

GEORGEANN SKAKEL TERRIEN, Rucky's sister (Michael's aunt), mother of Jimmy, Johnny, and Georgeann Dowdle

GEORGE TERRIEN, Georgeann's second husband

MARY ELLEN REYNOLDS, Anne Skakel's sister, former nun who lived in the Skakel household

ANN BRANNACK SKAKEL, Rucky's mother, Michael and Bobby's grandmother

GEORGE SKAKEL, Rucky's father, Michael and Bobby's grandfather

GEORGE SKAKEL JR., Rucky's brother, Michael's uncle

JIMMY SKAKEL, Rucky's brother, Michael's uncle

PAT SKAKEL, George Skakel Jr.'s wife, Michael's aunt

THE KENNEDY COUSINS

ETHEL SKAKEL KENNEDY, the author's mother, Michael's aunt

ROBERT F. KENNEDY SR., the author's father, Michael's uncle

ROBERT F. "BOBBY" KENNEDY JR., Michael's cousin

STEVE SMITH, husband of Jean Kennedy Smith, the author's uncle

THE SKAKELS' FRIENDS

FATHER MARK CONNOLLY, Skakel family friend, priest

GINNY FITZGERALD, Anne Skakel's friend

DAN FITZPATRICK, Helen's husband, attorney

HELEN IX (FITZPATRICK), Martha's friend and neighbor, Skakel neighbor

BOB IX, Helen's father

CISSIE IX, Helen's mother

DENNIS OSSORIO, Georgeann Dowdle's boyfriend

ANDREA SHAKESPEARE (RENNA), Julie Skakel's friend

THE SKAKEL HOUSEHOLD HELP

ETHEL JONES, Skakel cook

MARGARET "NANNY" SWEENEY, Skakel housekeeper

FRANZ "FRANK" WITTINE, Skakel gardener

PAULA WITTINE, Frank's wife, Skakel housekeeper

LARRY ZICCARELLI, Skakel handyman, driver

THE BELLE HAVENITES

CYNTHIA AND BOB BJORK, Belle Haven residents, Moxley neighbors

ART BYRNE, Geoff's father
DARYL BYRNE (FLEUREN), Geoff's much older sister
DORI BYRNE, Geoff's mother
GEOFFREY "GEOFF" BYRNE, Martha's friend and neighbor
GREG BYRNE, Geoff's much older brother
WARREN BYRNE, Geoff's older brother

PETER COOMARASWAMY, Belle Haven resident, Michael's friend
MARIA COOMARASWAMY, Peter's younger sister

ED HAMMOND, Belle Haven resident

SHEILA MCGUIRE, Martha's friend and neighbor, discovered Martha's body

JEAN WALKER, Margie and Neal's mother
MARGIE WALKER, Martha's best friend and neighbor
NEAL WALKER, Margie's brother, friend of Geoff Byrne and Tony Bryant

JACKIE WETENHALL, Martha's friend and neighbor (Michael and Jackie shared a mutual crush)
JANE WETENHALL, Belle Haven resident, Jackie's mother
JOHN WETENHALL, Belle Haven resident, Jackie's father

CARL WOLD, Belle Haven resident
JEAN WOLD, Belle Haven resident, Carl's mother

THE GREENWICH BIT PLAYERS

PAUL CZAJA, headmaster, Whitby School

VIRGINIA LIDDELL, Greenwich resident who offered information on John Moxley

CRAWFORD "TRES" MILLS, Tony Bryant and Neal Walker's friend from Brunswick School

CHRIS ROOSEVELT, attorney, Whitby School board member

FRIEDA SAEMANN, Greenwich resident who told police to question John Salerno

MARIE SALERNO, Greenwich resident, John Salerno's mother

JOANNE MALLORY TUCKER, Tony's friend who ran away to New York, Greenwich resident

GRAY WEICKER, Greenwich resident, Martha's admirer, son of US Senator Lowell Weicker

THE NEW YORKERS

BARBARA BRYANT, Tony's mother, film producer
TONY BRYANT, former Brunswick student, moved to Manhattan

ADOLPH HASBROUCK, Tony's friend from high school in Manhattan

BURTON "BURR" TINSLEY, Tony's friend from high school in Manhattan

THE DOCTORS

DR. WALTER CAMP, Skakel family physician

DR. RICHARD DANEHOWER, Moxley family physician

DR. STANLEY LESSE, psychiatrist at New York Presbyterian Hospital

DR. KATHY MORALL, forensic psychiatrist

DR. ALVIN ROSEN, Rucky Skakel's psychiatrist in Florida

DR. NANCY VRECHEK, psychologist, forensic hypnotist

THE LAWYERS

LINDA KENNEY BADEN, defense attorney, brief member of Michael Skakel's defense team, wife of Michael Baden

JONATHAN BENEDICT, Connecticut state prosecutor who tried Michael

DONALD BROWNE, Connecticut state prosecutor before Jonathan Benedict

JOE DONOVAN, Great Lakes Carbon lead attorney

SUSAN GILL, Jonathan Benedict's assistant prosecutor

MANNY MARGOLIS, Tommy Skakel's defense attorney

JIM MCKENZIE, Great Lakes Carbon attorney

JOHN MEERBERGEN, Kenny Littleton's defense attorney

CHRIS MORANO, Jonathan Benedict's assistant prosecutor

JOHN REGAN JR., attorney, Coleman family lawyer

JOE RICHICHI, Mickey Sherman's longtime law partner

HUBERT "HUBIE" SANTOS, Michael's co-lead appeals attorney

STEPHAN SEEGER, attorney on Michael's defense team

HOPE SEELEY, Michael's co-lead appeals attorney

TOM SHERIDAN, Skakel family lawyer and bursar, Margot's uncle

MARK SHERMAN, attorney on Michael's defense team, Mickey Sherman's son
MICKEY SHERMAN, Michael's lead defense attorney

JOHN SMRIGA, Fairfield County State's Attorney after Jonathan Benedict

JASON THRONE, junior attorney on Michael's defense team

THE JUDGES

JUDGE THOMAS BISHOP, Connecticut appellate court judge (Michael's habeas appeal, 2013)

JUDGE JOHN KARAZIN, Connecticut appellate court judge (Michael's appeal, 2007)

JUDGE JOHN KAVANEWSKY, judge (Michael's trial, 2002)

JUSTICE RICHARD PALMER, Connecticut supreme court justice (Michael's appeal, 2010)

JUDGE GEORGE THIM, Connecticut superior court judge (Michael's one-man grand jury, 1998)

THE POLICE

STEPHEN BARAN JR., Greenwich Police chief

TED BROSCO, Greenwich Police detective

STEVE CARROLL, Greenwich Police detective

WAYNE CARVER, medical examiner who testified at Michael's trial

FRANK GARR, Greenwich Police detective, state's chief investigator of Moxley case

MARK GERBINO, Rochester, NY, Police major in homicide division

ELLIOT GROSS, Medical Examiner who performed Martha's autopsy

SERGEANT HENNESSY, Greenwich Police officer who searched the Moxley home

GERALD HALE, Detroit Police chief, hired by David Moxley to consult on the murder

DAN HICKMAN, Greenwich Police youth officer, first on scene of murder

MILLARD JONES, Greenwich Police youth officer, first on scene of murder

PAUL KASEMAN, Ogden, NY, Police inspector

TOM KEEGAN, Greenwich Police captain

JIM LUNNEY, Greenwich Police detective

JOE MCGLYNN, Greenwich Police detective

CHARLES MORGANTI, Belle Haven security officer

JACK SOLOMON, state's chief investigator of Moxley case before Frank Garr

HENRY LEE, state chief criminologist

THE ÉLAN CREW

LIZ ARNOLD, Élan resident with Michael

DANIEL BENNISON, Élan resident who did Michael's intake

GREG COLEMAN, Élan resident with Michael

DR. GERALD DAVIDSON, cofounder of the Élan school, psychiatrist

ALICE DUNNE, Élan resident and counselor

KIM FREEHILL, Élan resident with Michael

CLIFF GRUBIN, Élan resident with Michael

JOHN HIGGINS, Élan resident with Michael

HARRY KRANICK, Élan resident with Michael

SARAH PETERSON, Élan resident with Michael

JOE RICCI, cofounder of the Élan school, racetrack operator

CHUCK SIEGAN, Élan resident with Michael

THE WITNESSES AND THEIR ASSOCIATES

MATT ATTANIAN, friend of Gerranne Ridge, photographer

KENNY LITTLETON, Brunswick football coach, Skakel tutor
MARY BAKER LITTLETON, Kenny's ex-wife

JAMES MANCHESTER, Kenny Littleton's boss, proprietor of Preston's Airport Lounge in Nantucket, MA

MICHAEL MEREDITH, prosecution witness in Michael's trial, son of football great Don Meredith

GERANNE RIDGE, Boston function coordinator

THE MEDIA

TIM DUMAS, Greenwich native, author of *Greentown*

DOMINICK DUNNE, *Vanity Fair* columnist

MARK FUHRMAN, disgraced former LAPD detective, author

LUCIANNE GOLDBERG, Mark Fuhrman's literary agent, Clinton impeachment figure

NANCY GRACE, HLN host

RICHARD HOFFMAN, ghostwriter Michael Skakel hired to pen his memoir

BETH KARAS, HLN reporter

LEN LEVITT, former *Newsday* reporter, author of *Conviction*

THE PRIVATE EYES

JAMIE BRYAN, writer hired by Jim Murphy to write Sutton Associates reports

VITO COLUCCI, Mickey Sherman's primary investigator

GREG GARLAND, Larry Holifield's co-investigator

CATHERINE HARKNESS, Mike Udvardy's assistant investigator

LARRY HOLIFIELD, private investigator hired by Bobby Kennedy

WILLIS "BILLY" KREBS, former NYPD lieutenant Jim Murphy hired for Skakel case

DICK MCCARTHY, former FBI agent Jim Murphy hired for Skakel case

JIM MURPHY, former FBI agent, founder of Sutton Associates

KRIS STEELE, Vito Colucci's co-investigator

MIKE UDVARDY, investigator hired by Hubie Santos to find Barbara Bryant

THE EXPERTS

MICHAEL BADEN, forensic pathologist, former New York City chief medical examiner, husband of Linda Kenney Baden

ROBERT BRISENTINE, US Army polygrapher

ELIZABETH LOFTUS, expert on memory

RICHARD OFSHE, expert on false confession and therapeutic cults

TIMELINE

OCTOBER 31, 1975: Sheila McGuire discovers the body of her neighbor Martha Moxley.

NOVEMBER 1, 1975: Dr. Elliot Gross performs Martha Moxley's autopsy and determines that her injuries were inflicted with a golf club.

NOVEMBER 2, 1975: Greenwich Police remove from the Skakel home a set of Toney Penna golf clubs that appear to match the club used to murder Martha Moxley. Rucky Skakel signs "Consent to Search Premises Without Search Warrant" granting police free rein to search his house and remove "any merchandise, materials, or other property."

NOVEMBER 9, 1975: Tommy Skakel passes a polygraph test.

DECEMBER 9, 1975: John Skakel passes a polygraph test.

DECEMBER 10, 1975: Helen Ix and Geoff Byrne tell police that they recall as they were leaving Skakel house on October 30 seeing Tommy Skakel pushing Martha Moxley into a bush.

DECEMBER 12, 1975: Rucky Skakel furnishes Greenwich Police with a key to his Windham, NY, ski house, and invites them to search it at will.

DECEMBER 13, 1975: Tommy Skakel tells police that around the time of the murder, he was working on a report on Abraham Lincoln, which his teachers say was never assigned.

JANUARY 16, 1976: Rucky Skakel provides Greenwich Police a letter authorizing them to access "any and all hospital, medical, psychological, and school records and/or any and all reports concerning my son, Thomas Skakel."

JANUARY 22, 1976: Rucky Skakel writes to Greenwich Police revoking his previous letter authorizing permission to access Tommy's medical records, and hires attorney Manny Margolis to defend Tommy.

MARCH 15, 1976: Dr. Stanley Lesse performs various psychological tests on Tommy Skakel.

MARCH 25, 1976: Connecticut State's Attorney holds a press conference expressing frustration with the Skakel family's lack of cooperation.

MAY 1976: Greenwich Police present State's Attorney Donald Browne with an arrest warrant for Tommy Skakel. Browne refuses to sign it.

UNDETERMINED 1976: Tony Bryant confides in Esme Dick that the Skakels were not responsible for the crime, and that he was in Belle Haven the night of the murder.

OCTOBER 18, 1976: Kenny Littleton fails a polygraph.

MAY 1977: Kenny Littleton is given 5 to 7 years suspended sentence for burglary charges in Nantucket, MA.

MARCH 5, 1978: Michael Skakel is arrested in Windham, NY, on various charges, including DWI.

APRIL 1978: Michael Skakel is transported to the Élan School in Poland, ME.

NOVEMBER 15, 1978–DECEMBER 12, 1978: Michael Skakel escapes from the Élan School on three separate occasions, is apprehended, and returned.

MAY 1980: Michael Skakel graduates from the Élan School.

DECEMBER 27, 1980: Geoff Byrne dies at 16, reportedly of a drug overdose.

OCTOBER 25, 1982: Michael Skakel enters an Alcoholics Anonymous meeting in Greenwich, never to take a drink or drug again.

MAY 1983: Greenwich Police turn over more than 400 pages of the Martha Moxley case file to *Greenwich Time* reporter Len Levitt.

NOVEMBER 21, 1988: David Moxley dies of a heart attack at age 57.

JUNE 2, 1991: *Greenwich Time* finally publishes Len Levitt's story under the headline "Moxley Murder Case Still Haunts Greenwich" after holding it eight years.

JUNE 1991: Andrea Shakespeare Renna tells investigators that she was under the "assumption" that Michael Skakel did not go to Sursum Corda with his brothers on October 30, 1975.

AUGUST 9, 1991: State investigator Jack Solomon and Greenwich detective Frank Garr announce at a press conference that the Moxley case will be reinvestigated and the Moxley family raises reward money to $50,000.

FALL 1991: Rucky Skakel's attorney Thomas Sheridan engages Sutton Associates to reinvestigate the Martha Moxley murder.

DECEMBER 1991: During William Kennedy Smith's rape trial, Dominick Dunne and *Hard Copy* erroneously report that William Kennedy Smith had been with the Skakels on the night of Martha Moxley's murder.

DECEMBER 1992: Kenny Littleton flunks a polygraph administered by polygrapher Robert Brisentine, and is examined by psychologist Kathy Morall, who reports that his behavior would "suggest involvement or guilt."

APRIL 13, 1993: Crown publishes Dominick Dunne's novel *A Season in Purgatory*, and Dunne states during interviews that Tommy Skakel is Martha Moxley's likely killer.

SEPTEMBER 30, 1994: Frank Garr retires from the Greenwich Police to work full time on the Martha Moxley murder for the State's Attorney's office, replacing Jack Solomon.

SPRING 1995: Rucky Skakel discontinues Sutton Associates' investigation at the urging of Manny Margolis.

JULY 1995: An unknown source provides Len Levitt with Sutton Associates' "purposely prejudicial analyses" of Michael and Tommy Skakel.

NOVEMBER 26, 1995: Len Levitt publishes a story in *Newsday* in which he reports that Tommy Skakel changed his story about the night of the murder to Sutton Associates investigators.

FEBRUARY 15, 1996: Frank Garr appears on NBC's *Unsolved Mysteries*, seeking leads on the Martha Moxley case.

JUNE 1996: *People* magazine reports that the Moxley family has raised reward money to $100,000.

FALL 1996: Sutton Associate's writer Jamie Bryan turns over copies of Sutton's reports to *Vanity Fair*'s Dominick Dunne.

OCTOBER 3, 1996: Mark Fuhrman pleads no contest to perjury for lying under oath during the O.J. Simpson trial about his use of the word "nigger" and is sentenced to three years of probation and a lifetime bar from serving as a police officer in California.

DECEMBER 6, 1996: Frank Garr interviews Michael's fellow Élan resident John Higgins for the first time.

WINTER 1997: Dominick Dunne provides copies of Sutton Associates' reports to Frank Garr.

SUMMER 1997: Frustrated by Frank Garr's inaction, Dominick Dunne turns over Sutton Associates' reports to Mark Fuhrman.

NOVEMBER 20, 1997: Cissie Ix tells Frank Garr that Rucky once confided in her that Michael had told him that he didn't know if he might have killed Martha Moxley during a blackout.

FEBRUARY 1998: William Morrow publishes Mark Fuhrman's *Murder in Greenwich*, which names Michael Skakel as Martha Moxley's likely killer.

SPRING 1998: Leonard Levitt and Frank Garr agree that they will collaborate on a book about the Moxley case despite the fact that the investigation is ongoing.

APRIL 1998: Connecticut State's Attorney Donald Browne abruptly retires, replaced by Jonathan Benedict.

MAY 1998: Jonathan Benedict applies for, and is granted, a rarely used one-member grand jury to indict Michael.

JUNE 1998: Superior Court Judge George Thim starts an 18-month, one-member grand jury review of information gathered by Frank Garr and the State's Attorney's office.

JUNE 7, 1998: Frank Garr receives a call from Rochester NBC affiliate reporting that Greg Coleman called the station saying he heard a confession from Michael Skakel while at Élan.

SUMMER 1998: Coleman family attorney John Regan Jr. tells State's Attorney's office that Greg Coleman should not be trusted as a witness.

JANUARY 20, 1999: Frank Garr illegally seizes a book proposal, tapes, and various personal items belonging to Michael Skakel from the Cambridge, MA, home of writer Richard Hoffman.

JANUARY 19, 2000: Michael Skakel surrenders to Greenwich Police after prosecutors announce that a warrant for his arrest has been issued. He is released on $50,000 bail.

JUNE 20, 2000: Michael Skakel as well as prosecution and defense witnesses appear for a three-day Probable Cause hearing to determine if Michael can be tried as an adult.

JANUARY 29, 2001: Élan founder Joe Ricci dies of cancer at 54.

JANUARY 31, 2001: Juvenile Court Judge Maureen Dennis rules that Michael Skakel will be tried as an adult.

AUGUST 7, 2001: Prosecution witness Greg Coleman dies from a dose of bad heroin at age 39.

DECEMBER 2001: Tony Bryant tells Crawford Mills that he was in Belle Haven the night of the murder and believes that Adolph Hasbrouck and Burton Tinsley likely committed the crime.

JANUARY 2002: Crawford Mills speaks with Mickey Sherman, who fails to follow up on Tony Bryant's allegations.

SPRING 2002: Crawford Mills sends several letters and faxes to Dorthy Moxley and Jonathan Benedict, outlining the allegations, but receives no response.

MAY 7, 2002: Testimony begins in *State of Connecticut v. Michael Skakel*.

JUNE 7, 2002: Michael Skakel is found guilty of first-degree murder.

AUGUST 28, 2002: Michael Skakel is sentenced to a term of 20 years to life in prison.

JANUARY 2, 2003: Rucky Skakel dies at 79 of frontal lobe dementia.

JANUARY 2003: Bobby Kennedy Jr.'s article "A Miscarriage of Justice" appears in *The Atlantic*. Shortly after publication, Crawford Mills reaches out.

AUGUST 24, 2003: Investigator Vito Colucci videotapes an interview with Tony Bryant in the Wyndham Hotel in Coconut Grove, Florida.

OCTOBER 12, 2004: Regan Books publishes Len Levitt's *Conviction: Solving the Moxley Murder.*

MARCH 2005: Dominick Dunne settles the $11 million defamation lawsuit brought against him by former Congressman Gary Condit.

AUGUST 25, 2005: Hubie Santos and Hope Seeley file a petition for a new trial, based on the revelations of Tony Bryant.

SEPTEMBER 1, 2006: Tony Bryant invokes his Fifth Amendment right against self-incrimination when questioned by Skakel attorneys in Miami.

OCTOBER 25, 2007: Superior Court Judge Edward Karazin rejects Michael Skakel's appeal.

FEBRUARY 23, 2008: Tom Sheridan dies at 83 of emphysema.

OCTOBER 6, 2008: Crawford Mills commits suicide at 47.

AUGUST 26, 2009: Dominick Dunne dies at 83 of bladder cancer.

APRIL 12, 2010: Connecticut State Supreme Court upholds 2007 decision to deny Michael Skakel appeal for new trial in a 4 to 1 decision.

JUNE 30, 2010: Mickey Sherman pleads guilty in federal court to willfully failing to pay taxes for 2001 and 2002. Prior to his plea, he pays about $400,000 of the $420,710 he owes in taxes, interest, and penalties owed for those years.

FEBRUARY 8, 2011: Peter Ziluca dies at 51 of an apparent overdose from a combination of vodka, hydrocodone, and cocaine.

MARCH 15, 2011: Mickey Sherman turns himself in to federal prison in Otisville, NY, for a one year, one day prison sentence for tax evasion.

AUGUST 17, 2011: Manny Margolis dies at 85 of non-Hodgkin's lymphoma.

OCTOBER 24, 2012: Connecticut Department of Correction denies Michael Skakel's request for parole.

JANUARY 2013: Prosecution witness John Higgins dies in his sleep.

OCTOBER 23, 2013: Judge Thomas Bishop grants Michael Skakel a new trial based on his habeas corpus appeal, stating the Mickey Sherman's defense was "constitutionally deficient" and so lacking that "the state procured a judgment of conviction that lacks reliability."

NOVEMBER 21, 2013: Michael Skakel is released from prison after posting $1.2 million bail.

OCTOBER 31, 2014: Michael Skakel settles his 2013 slander lawsuit against HLN host Nancy Grace and Time Warner, Inc. The company releases a statement apologizing for erroneously reporting that Michael Skakel's DNA was found at the Martha Moxley crime scene.

FEBRUARY 24, 2016: Prosecutor Susan Gill presents oral arguments to the Connecticut Supreme Court that Michael Skakel should not receive a new trial. Defense lawyer Hubie Santos argues that "the weight of the evidence is that Tommy Skakel killed Martha Moxley."

FEBRUARY 25, 2016-PRESENT: Michael Skakel awaits the Supreme Court's decision about his fate.

INTRODUCTION

*The media's the most powerful entity on earth. They have the power
to make the innocent guilty and make the guilty innocent, and that's
power. Because they control the minds of the masses.*

—Malcom X

On October 30, 1975, someone killed 15-year-old Martha Moxley outside
her home in the swanky Belle Haven section of Greenwich, Connecticut.
Martha was friend and next-door neighbor to my cousin, Michael Skakel, who celebrated his 15th birthday five weeks earlier. At the time of Martha's
murder, Michael was eleven miles away with five eyewitnesses. Prior to 1998, no
police agency had ever considered Michael a suspect in Martha's murder.

Twenty-seven years after Martha's death, the State of Connecticut spent
some $25 million to convict Michael Skakel of murdering Martha. At Michael's
criminal trial, the State offered no physical or forensic evidence, no fingerprints
or DNA, no eyewitness testimony linking Michael to the murder. Indeed, bungling police investigators had lost many items of physical evidence that might
have exculpated Michael, including a bloodied section of the golf club used as a
murder weapon; vaginal and anal swabs and slides from the victim made by the
Connecticut medical examiner; blood-stained, size-13 Keds sneakers; the bloody
pants of a large adult male, shown by police to witnesses following the crime;
several hairs removed from Martha's body; and beer cans taken from the crime
scene. With no evidence linking Michael to the killing, the State tried him based
on the perjured testimony of three confession witnesses suborned by a crooked
and malevolent cop obsessed with winning his career case. Despite Michael's
ironclad alibi, and the State's obvious evidentiary defects, a Connecticut court,
nevertheless, convicted him of Martha's murder in 2002 after a six-week jury
trial. The trial court judge, John F. Kavanewsky Jr., sentenced Michael to a term
of 20 years to life in prison.

Because of the dearth of evidence against him and his airtight alibi, a number of people had to commit selfish, malicious, or illegal acts in order to convict Michael, who found himself in a confluence where the pooled ambitions of several unscrupulous men and women intersected to sweep him away. Among these scoundrels were a craven family bursar and lawyer, Tom Sheridan, who leaked selective lies to incriminate Michael, a boy whose legal troubles represented to Sheridan a permanent gravy train; Dominick "Nick" Dunne, a nationally published gossip columnist who minted his long campaign against the Skakel family into lucrative books, TV shows, and the celebrity he craved; Mark Fuhrman, the disgraced LA policeman, convicted perjurer, and racist, who wrote a shoddy and inaccurate account of the Moxley murder, pointing the finger at Michael in an effort to rehabilitate his own damaged reputation; Frank Garr, a morally corrupt Greenwich Police officer who rescued his failing career by cajoling, harassing, intimidating, and tampering with witnesses, and suborning perjury to gin up a case against Michael, whose family he despised; Jonathan Benedict, an unscrupulous prosecutor with elastic ethics, who put ambition ahead of truth and justice, and who illegally concealed exculpatory evidence to win Michael's conviction; and Len Levitt, Garr's sidekick and dupe, a starstruck local reporter who penned a secret deal with Garr to split the proceeds of a book and any subsequent movie deals arising out of their efforts to convict Michael. Following their own selfish agendas, these men meshed together a net of lies that would ensnare Michael and put him behind bars for a crime he didn't commit.

Michael compounded his problems by hiring Mickey Sherman, a slick but incompetent, dissolute, and pathologically narcissistic wannabe television lawyer. Sherman, who described himself as a "media whore," drank, gambled, and luxury-binged away the $2.2 million that Michael's friends and family had scraped together to finance his defense.

A cyclone of media malpractice consolidated the perfect storm of greed and ambition that ended in Michael's imprisonment. His conviction was a failure of the legal system. It was also a failure of the press. The prevailing news story crafted by Dunne, Fuhrman, and a conniving prosecutor—of the spoiled rich "Kennedy cousin" using political power and connections to get away with murder—was flypaper to the national media that parlayed the narrative into a cottage industry. In a classic and corrupt loop, the media vultures hungry for ratings egged on Connecticut prosecutors to file scurrilous murder charges against Michael. The 18 satellite trucks and almost 55 reporters attending Michael's trial signified a journalistic obsession with the case that was 10 miles wide and an inch deep. With 401 reporters certified to cover the case, only one, Leslie Stahl, bothered to look beneath the flimsy veneer at the myriad facts undermining the prosecutor's frail parable. A new breed of TV lawyers, led by CNN's Jeffrey Toobin and HLN's Nancy Grace and Beth Karas, stoked the pitchfork brigade and officiated over Michael's press lynching. The media lemming stampede was evidence of a broken system that sacrificed Michael on the altar of ratings and revenue, and compounded the tragedy of Martha Moxley's death with the conviction of an innocent man.

Sympathy for Mrs. Dorthy Moxley, Martha's mother, and the narrative of the Kennedy kid who got away with murder, were ferociously embraced by press, police, and prosecutor. It swayed Connecticut's judicial system, which obligingly dismantled the imposing legal barriers to wrongfully jail Michael for his implausible role in a 27-year-old crime. The courts, which are meant to safeguard individual rights against the volatile tides of public passions, instead capitulated to the mob. The judicial system shamefully bent its own rules and overturned longstanding black-letter precedent regarding its ironclad five-year statute of limitations on non-capital murder in the State of Connecticut.

I am going to show that Michael Skakel did not and could not have killed Martha Moxley; how and why he got framed for the crime; who did the framing; and how they accomplished it. I'm also going to show how I tracked down the likely killers, phantoms who moved in and out of Greenwich like shadows, and whose presence was detected by neither police nor press during 30 years of flawed investigations. Despite overwhelming evidence of their guilt, Connecticut prosecutors and police still refuse to investigate them. Today, those men walk free, as entrenched, ego-bound police and prosecutors stick to their guns and refuse to acknowledge their mistake.

Michael is my cousin, and it would be natural for a reader to suspect I'm in the tank for him. For this reason, I will methodically lay out the overwhelming evidence that supports Michael's innocence. I mean to be painfully honest in telling this story, even relating things that some members of my family will find difficult to read. I will share personal stories and memories that I would otherwise never discuss. I do this because Michael's freedom, reputation, and constitutional rights are more important than the privacy I sacrifice by recounting these anecdotes.

There are broader issues, as well, that need airing, including the abuse of police and prosecutorial power and the role of the media in our democracy. Michael's ordeal is a parable about how mercilessly the flames of passion and prejudice consume even the most privileged individual when democracy's firewalls—police, prosecutors, the justice system, the press—give way to the clamoring of the mob. The inferno that devoured Michael is no anomaly. It feeds every day on the economically disadvantaged and minorities. Only visibility distinguished Michael. Mostly the casualties of their broken institutions are the invisible and discarded—people living in ghettos and fringe communities, from Ferguson to Baltimore.

Michael has spent 11½ years in jail. In October 2013, after a successful *habeas corpus* appeal, a courageous appellant court judge, Thomas Bishop, ordered Michael released from prison based on his claim that his lawyer was so monumentally incompetent that Michael did not receive a fair trial. When Fairfield County prosecutors appealed Judge Bishop's 128-page ruling in favor of Michael to the Connecticut Supreme Court, I hired a private investigator, Larry Holifield, and began working on this book. As of this writing, Judge Bishop's ruling in Michael's favor is on appeal by prosecutors to a six-judge panel of the Connecticut Supreme Court. If the Supreme Court decides against Michael, he will return to prison to serve out his sentence. If the justices rule in his favor, the new Fairfield County prosecutor will decide whether to retry Michael for the Moxley murder. Michael would then face a new trial.

I know that Michael Skakel is innocent. I expect that anyone who reads this book will be similarly convinced, and, if I've done my job in writing it, they will also finally understand how the players and events conspired to jail him. Finally, if prosecutors have the courage to acknowledge their mistake, I will have provided police a blueprint to finally indict, try, and convict Martha's true killers.

This is the story of two crimes: the murder of Martha Moxley and the wrongful imprisonment of my cousin Michael Skakel.

Robert F. Kennedy Jr.
Mt. Kisco, New York

PART I

The Stage

CHAPTER 1

The Murder

Childhood is the kingdom where nobody dies.
                                        —Edna St. Vincent Millay

Sometime between 6:30 and 7:00 p.m., on the evening of Thursday, October 30, 1975, 15-year-old Martha Moxley finished a grilled cheese sandwich and left her home on Walsh Lane to socialize around her Belle Haven neighborhood.

Belle Haven is a well-heeled enclave of 120 houses on Long Island Sound in Greenwich, Connecticut. Eighteen months earlier, the Moxleys had relocated there from Piedmont, California. Martha was a sophomore at Greenwich High School. Her brother, John, was a senior. Martha's father, David, who headed the New York office of Touche Ross, an international consulting and accounting firm, was away that night in Atlanta for a conference.

It was Halloween eve, a popular anniversary that Belle Haven teens referred to as "Mischief Night" or "Hell Night." Neighborhood children played pranks such as ringing doorbells, toilet papering houses, soaping windows, and throwing eggs. As she left home, Martha slipped into her blue winter parka against unseasonable cold; temperatures that night would dip just below freezing.

According to Martha's mother, Dorthy Moxley, Martha and her friend Helen Ix set out from the Moxley property with 11-year-old neighbor, Geoffrey "Geoff" Byrne, who would unwillingly play a pivotal role in Martha's murder and whose life would be destroyed by the event nearly as surely as Martha's. The trio headed for the Skakel house in search of Michael and his older brother Tommy. According to the Skakel gardener, Franz Wittine, all six Skakel children—Rush Jr., 19; Julie, 18; Tommy, 17; John, 16; Michael, 15; David, 12; and Stephen, 9—together with their new 23-year-old tutor, Kenneth "Kenny"

Littleton; their cousin James "Jimmy" Dowdle, age 17; and Julie Skakel's friend Andrea Shakespeare, age 16, were having a 6:00 p.m. dinner at the nearby Belle Haven Club. Littleton, a football coach and teacher at Brunswick, the private day school the Skakel boys attended, had been hired a week earlier by Rushton "Rucky" Skakel Sr., father of the Skakel children and my mother's brother, to help look after the children and to tutor Tommy and Michael. Rucky was away on a hunting trip, and would not return until the following evening. Rucky's wife, Anne Reynolds Skakel, had passed away two years before after a prolonged battle with brain cancer. Littleton was celebrating his first day on the job by drinking with his teenage charges. Rucky, an alcoholic, exerted only anemic parental supervision. A minor household army, including a cook, a housekeeper, a gardener, and, now, Littleton, managed the chaotic homestead.

After leaving the Skakels', Martha, Helen Ix, and Geoff continued, in Helen's words, "messing around" Belle Haven, and then stopped for a short visit at the home of the Moukad family on Otter Rock Drive, where Martha ate some ice cream. There, they picked up another neighborhood friend, Jackie Wetenhall. The group, now a quartet, left the Moukad home and headed back toward the Skakels'.

According to various trial testimony, Littleton returned with the kids from the Belle Haven Club between 8:30 p.m. and 8:45 p.m. For about 15 or 20 minutes they all remained in the house, mostly drinking and playing games. Jimmy Dowdle recalled drinking at least one more Heineken along with Michael and John, with whom he was playing backgammon on the enclosed back sunporch. Michael recalls breaking out two Heinekens for Jimmy and John. As he handed them the bottles, according to his testimony during his 2013 *habeas* hearing, Michael looked down toward the Skakels' backyard chipping tee and saw a group of large boys he did not recognize on the lawn. Michael also shared this detail with author Richard Hoffman in 1997, who was ghostwriting Michael's memoir, four years before the identity of these figures would become a crucial factor in this case. Among those strangers, in all likelihood, was the murderer—or murderers—who would bludgeon Martha Moxley to death 75 minutes later.

On the day Martha's body was discovered, Helen Ix told police that after leaving the Moukads' house the night before, she, Martha, and Geoff appeared at the Skakels' at "about 9:10 p.m." Michael told police that at approximately 9:10 p.m., he saw Martha, Helen, and Geoff come into the backyard. He motioned for them to go to a door between the sunporch and the mudroom where he let them into the house. He told police that he led his three friends through the house and out the kitchen door into the driveway. Michael said he and his friends then climbed into Rucky's Lincoln Continental that was parked by the side kitchen entrance to talk and listen to eight-track tapes.

"Martha was my friend," Michael told me recently. "I would have liked to kiss her, but I would have liked to kiss just about any girl back then." Michael, a virgin in early puberty, had teen crushes on Francie, the daughter of a family friend from nearby Armonk, New York, and on his Belle Haven neighbor Jackie Wetenhall. The runt of the Skakel litter, he was a scrawny kid who was always the smallest person in his class and at summer camp. "I was five foot five, weighed about 120 pounds and looked like a girl," he said. "Martha was my size and could have kicked my ass." The photo of Michael stolen by Detective Frank Garr that prosecutor Jonathan Benedict presented to Michael's jury, without objection from Michael's attorney, Mickey Sherman, depicted a beefy Michael four years after the murder. By then, he had passed puberty and had spent 24 months doing push-ups and bulking up for self-preservation at Élan, a brutal Maine reform school and drug rehabilitation facility he was attending.

Tommy told police that between 9:15 p.m. and 9:20 p.m., he had gone out to the Lincoln to find a tape. He climbed in the front seat beside Martha. Martha's diary revealed that she, Michael, Tommy, and several other teenagers from Belle Haven enjoyed a close friendship, often socializing at each other's homes. Martha and Tommy Skakel had developed mutual crushes.

Around 9:15 p.m., Rush Jr. along with John and their cousin Jimmy, having finished their backgammon game, appeared in the driveway, saying they needed to use the car to take Jimmy back to the Terrien/Dowdle home, a stone gothic fortress known as Sursum Corda (Latin for "lift up your hearts," the opening line to the Eucharistic prayer). Sursum Corda sat on Jimmy's mother, Georgeann Terrien's, sprawling back-country estate 11 miles away, over a narrow, winding two-lane. The boys all intended to watch the 10:00 p.m. American premier of *Monty Python's Flying Circus*. Rush Jr., a Dartmouth junior, had fallen in love with the British screwball comedy when he saw it with a test audience in Hanover, New Hampshire, and was anxious to showcase it for his brothers and cousin.

In the 1990s, Michael told investigators from Sutton Associates—a Nassau County (New York) investigative firm that Rucky Skakel hired in 1992 to re-investigate the Moxley murder—that Martha declined his invitation to come with them to Sursum Corda, citing her 9:30 p.m. curfew. Michael and Martha made plans to go trick-or-treating the following night. With that, Rush Jr. backed the car out onto the street and headed off to Sursum Corda with his brothers John and Michael and his cousin, Jimmy, leaving Helen Ix, Martha, Geoff, and Tommy standing in the driveway. The facts of this departure and the occupants of the car have never been plausibly disputed. Tommy and Jimmy told this to police in 1975. John did as well; on December 9, 1975, he passed a polygraph administered by Connecticut State Police, asking him, "On October 30, from 9:30 to 10:30 p.m., were you with Mike, Rush, and James Terrien?" Georgeann Dowdle, Jimmy Dowdle's sister (of the same first name as their mother, Georgeann Terrien), told police in November 1975 that she remembered seeing John, Michael, Rush Jr., and her brother arriving at Sursum Corda "just before 10:00 p.m." A 1992 police report confirms the approximate time of the Lincoln's departure from the Skakel home, as well as the four occupants of the car.

A few minutes after the Lincoln exited the driveway (around 9:20 p.m.), Helen Ix and Geoff decided to leave. Helen testified in 2002 that she felt like a "third wheel" because Martha and Tommy became "playful . . . flirtatious" at the end of the darkened driveway. Helen also had a 9:30 p.m. curfew. "It was time to go home," she testified. It was the last time she saw her friend Martha alive.

A gentleman at 11 years old, Geoff walked Helen to her door and then disappeared into a nightmare that would not end until his own death five years later. The day after searchers discovered Martha's body, Geoff told the police that, after escorting Helen to her house, he heard "footsteps following him" and bolted home with someone in pursuit. He was too spooked, he said, to turn and see who was dogging him.

At approximately 9:30 p.m., only 10 minutes after Helen and Geoff departed the Skakel driveway, Julie drove Andrea home in the family station wagon, according to Julie's October 31, 1975, interview. While she was in the driveway waiting for Andrea to get in the car, Julie "observed a shadow of a person" running in front of her house in a crouched position. She told police the figure disappeared into the wooded area adjacent to the asphalt. Andrea confirmed to police that she, too, heard the figure running by her. For many years various homicide investigators wondered about the identity of this mysterious figure that both girls saw or heard only 25 minutes before Martha's murder.

On October 31, 1975, Tommy told police that after his brothers and Helen and Geoff left, he and Martha chatted for a few minutes, and said goodnight. He watched Martha walk toward the rear yard, and then he went into the side door of his house. Eighteen years later, Tommy changed his story, telling Sutton Associates investigators in an October 1993 interview that as soon as his sister, Julie, drove off, he and Martha snuck behind the toolshed and engaged in a sexual encounter that lasted 20 minutes, and ended in mutual masturbation to orgasm. Following their dalliance, around 9:50 p.m., the two rearranged their clothes and Martha said goodnight. Just before he ducked in the kitchen door, Tommy watched Martha hurrying across the Skakel rear lawn chipping tee toward her house, 20 minutes late for her curfew. It would have been a three-minute walk but for the savage ambush that extinguished her young life. When police discovered Martha's body, they found that she had written the name "Tom" on her left moccasin.

Julie returned from dropping off Andrea at 9:55 p.m., a fact she has attested to on many occasions, including a March 1993 interview under hypnosis. Julie recounted that when she pulled into her driveway, she was frightened to see a large man, bigger than any of her brothers, "crouched, big, dark, maybe even hooded," dashing across the Skakel property between her car and the front of her house. Julie recalled that the figure was carrying an object in his left hand, and ran across the driveway and into the hedge only feet from the toolshed, where Tommy and Martha had just completed their make-out session. Julie told me that she watched terrified from her car as the figure sprinted south to north the full length of the Skakel home. I believe that this man may have been one of Martha's murderers closing in for the kill.

Connecticut medical examiner Elliot Gross, who performed Martha's autopsy, originally estimated that Martha died between 9:30 p.m. and 12 p.m. the following day when her body was discovered, "but closer to 9:30 p.m." The Greenwich police sought outside help to determine a more exact time of death. They consulted one of the country's preeminent forensic pathologists, Houston's Joseph Jachimczyk. Dr. Jachimczyk established the time between 9:30 p.m. and 10:00 p.m., based on the condition of Martha's bladder and the three ounces of unabsorbed liquid in her stomach. Connecticut police conferred with Detroit's medical examiner, Werner Spitz, and two New York City deputy chief medical examiners, Michael Baden and John Devlin. All of them generally concurred with Jachimczyk.

Non-forensic indicators also suggested a 10:00 p.m. time of death. Martha, who had a 9:30 p.m. curfew, had gotten into trouble the prior weekend for breaking it. In a 2014 interview with investigator Vito Colucci, Helen Ix recalled that it was important for Martha to return home by 9:30 p.m. to avoid further angering her mother. Martha's best friend, Margie Walker, confirmed in a May 2016 interview with me that Martha intended to keep her curfew that night. Margie, who was grounded, told me that Martha promised to call as soon as she got home at 9:30 p.m. to give her the lowdown on Mischief Night. "For her to have broken curfew that night would have been really weird," Margie recounted.

Dorthy Moxley, testifying at Michael's trial in 2002, said she was painting in the master bedroom when, sometime between 9:30 p.m. and 10:00 p.m., she heard a loud "commotion" in the yard on the side of the house where Martha's body would later be discovered. Mrs. Moxley testified that the ruckus consisted of "excited voices" and incessant barking. In 1983, she recalled to both reporter Leonard Levitt and Greenwich detective James Lunney that she heard Martha's screams; she confirmed this memory during a 1993 hypnosis session encouraged by state investigators. Greenwich Police continually ignored her consistent recollection. "I have told people this over and over again and nobody has ever . . . paid much attention to the fact that I heard these voices," she testified in 2002. "I have always been trying to convince them . . . about the voices I heard and

nobody . . . really believed." At Michael's trial, she testified that the racket was so
unusual and disturbing that she stopped painting and ventured to the window to
look outside. Unable to penetrate the darkness, she turned on an outside porch
light. After a few seconds, she switched off the light, fearing that whoever was
there might see Martha's bike on the porch and steal it.

Helen Ix testified in 2002 that, after arriving home at 9:30 p.m., she telephoned a couple of friends. At approximately 9:45 p.m., her Australian shepherd, Zock, began to bark "incessantly." Three days after the murder, Helen told
police that Zock barked until approximately 10:15 p.m. The barking became so
loud and annoying that Helen put down the telephone receiver to retrieve her
dog. She found Zock at the end of her driveway, "frozen" by the edge of the road,
baying in the direction of the Moxleys' driveway. Helen testified that she never
had seen her dog so agitated and that he was "scared" and barking "violently."
Although Zock always came to her when she called him, Helen said that on this
occasion, he refused. After a while, she gave up and went back inside. The dog
barked continuously for about 25 minutes, until the family's housekeeper went
out and horsed him in. In April 1976, the Greenwich Police Department interviewed Dr. Edward Fleischli, a Pound Ridge, New York, vet, who stated, "All
indications given suggest the Ix dog witnessed part and/or all of the murder."
Helen agrees. "I firmly believe the murder happened when the dog was barking,"
she told me in March 2016. "Zock was always very obedient, but he was going
nuts, barking excessively. He was at the edge of the Moxleys' property barking his
head off. I called and called and called him and he wouldn't come in."

David Skakel, who was 12 years old in 1975, testified in 2002 that Zock's
barking was so "distressed and prolonged" that he got out of bed and opened a
window to see what was going on. His bedroom overlooked his family's backyard
with views of both the Ixes' and Moxleys' properties. He could not see the dog in
the darkness, but he said he could tell from the direction of its barking that the
Australian shepherd was positioned near the road at the end of Ixes' driveway.
David recently told me that Zock always barked when there were people or cars
passing. But that night the barking was much closer than usual. "Zock was yelp-
ing and howling. The sound was agitated and forlorn. I had never heard it bark
like that before." On cross-examination, prosecutor Jonathan Benedict mocked
David for his "ridiculous" claim that he could tell where the dog was from 100
yards away, but David says, "The foliage on either side of Walsh Lane acted as
a kind of sound corridor and I could tell that Zock's barking was not coming
from over the hill the way it usually did. He never barked like that before. It
was incessant." All over Belle Haven the dogs were barking madly. One of the
Moxleys' neighbors, Cynthia Bjork, told police in 1976 she heard her springer
spaniel barking wildly beginning around 9:30 p.m. At 9:50 p.m., it dashed over
toward the Moxley property. The day Martha's body was discovered, Mr. and

Mrs. Charles Gorman, who lived one house north of the Moxleys on Walsh Lane, reported hearing multiple dogs barking. Kenny Littleton testified in 2002 that at 10:00 p.m. the Skakels' elderly Irish housekeeper, Margaret "Nanny" Sweeney, asked him to go outside and investigate the "fracas." Kenny divulged to his wife, in a 1992 conversation surreptitiously recorded by police, that he also heard dogs barking when he went outside.

John Moxley, Martha's 17-year-old brother, told police on November 5, 1975, that, when he arrived home between 11:00 p.m. and 11:30 p.m., his mother told him Martha had not returned and that she was "a little worried about her." John testified in 2002 that he reassured his mother that it was Mischief Night, and that Martha probably was out having fun and would be home soon. After watching the evening news, John went upstairs to bed. His mother fell asleep on the sofa in front of the television.

After *Monty Python* ended at 10:30 p.m., Rush Jr., John, and Michael stayed at the Terriens' for "maybe 15, 20 minutes," according to Rush Jr.'s 2002 testimony, and then returned home to Belle Haven. John testified that the Skakel brothers left Sursum Corda at "about 11:00, maybe a few minutes later." The trip home had been a signature Skakel undertaking. Michael recently told me that Rush was drunk and had to pull over for a time in Glennville, Connecticut, unable to drive. Following a group consultation, 16-year-old John, who was somewhat less poached, drove the Lincoln. Under hypnosis in 1993, John confirmed that Rush "gave up the wheel" to him. "I think he said it was better if I drive," John told the interviewer. In the spring of 1976, Rush Jr. told psychiatrist Dr. Stanley Lesse, hired by the family to evaluate Tommy, that the brothers arrived back home in Belle Haven between 11:30 and 11:45 p.m. Martha had been dead for well over an hour. At Michael's trial, Rush Jr., John, Jimmy, and Georgeann Dowdle all gave similar accounts of their activities on the night of the murder to those that they had given to police in 1975. John, Jimmy, and Rush Jr. all maintained from the first time they were questioned that they all left with Michael for Sursum Corda at 9:30 p.m., when Martha was still alive, and returned around 11:20 p.m. As mentioned, the police felt that polygraph test that John passed in December 1975 covered all four boys.

Julie was in her bedroom at the top of the stairs when her brothers rolled in. She testified at Michael's trial that she heard noises downstairs at 11:30, a memory that jibed with a 1993 interview under hypnosis. "I did have a TV in my room; maybe I was watching the news. I definitely got up out of my bed, opened my door," she said under hypnosis. "The noises were downstairs, but I don't think I went any further than the top of the steps and then I went back in my room." Recently, she elaborated on her memories. "They made such a racket that I came out of my bedroom," she told me in May 2016. Michael was making his usual commotion. "He was off the charts hyperactive and he was always bouncing off the walls. He never stopped. It was bedlam—laughing, shouting, and slamming doors. He made his own singular pandemonium." As John and Rush Jr. stumbled into their rooms to retire, she could still hear Michael running around downstairs creating his customary din. Michael briefly came upstairs to the landing near Julie's door. "I saw Andrea was gone and everyone was in bed," he told me recently. Still high on pot and alcohol, he decided to go back outside for a walk, a detail he first disclosed to investigators in 1993, but which he'd told me and many other witnesses beginning a decade earlier, long before police considered him a suspect.

Under hypnosis in 1993, John corroborated Michael's account to an investigator, recalling that he heard someone either entering or exiting the house at this time. "It was changing to 11:33 on the clock radio," John told the interviewer. "Something going on in the mudroom." John reported hearing "the sound of the back door." Julie told me in 2016 that she also distinctly recalls hearing Michael's departure. "I heard him whip the French door open with a loud bang as he left the house." Michael's notion was to peep through the windows of a live-in Spanish housekeeper who occupied a cottage on Walsh Lane. She sometimes obliged Belle Haven teens and amused herself by strolling about nude with the shades cracked. (Michael has told me this story since the early 1980s.) Disappointed to find her house dark, with the curtains drawn, Michael turned for home. Then the thought struck him that he would seek out Martha Moxley. "Martha likes me. Maybe she'll give me a kiss," Michael told Richard Hoffman in 1997. He was already on Walsh Lane, 100 yards north of the Moxley house. "I was drunk and the booze made me bold." At the Moxley house, Michael saw a light and climbed a tree next to a front bedroom he guessed was Martha's. He tossed pebbles to get her attention, calling, "Martha! Martha!" There was no response. It was only in 1992 that Michael would learn from investigators hired by the Skakel family that the room was not Martha's. It belonged to her brother, John, who was at that moment, watching TV in the living room with his mother. Michael repeated to Hoffman a story I'd heard many times over the years: he made a half-hearted attempt to masturbate in the tree before reconsidering the project. Thinking to himself, "What if someone spots me?" he scurried down. On his way home, he sensed a presence in the dark bushes near the Moxleys' driveway. He yelled and threw stones in the direction. "Come out of there, and I'll kick your ass!" Michael shouted with what he now describes as "He-Man bravado." He explained to me, "I was always scared of the dark and something that night made me scared shitless. I ran home from street light to street light." The downstairs doors were bolted, so he climbed through his bedroom window at about 12:15 a.m. He had been out for about 40 minutes. Julie, still awake, was surprised to hear him back so soon. In 1975 Michael omitted this midnight escapade when he talked to the police.

Embarrassed and frightened of his father's wrath, Michael told police he stayed in bed after returning from Sursum Corda. "At that point in my life," Michael reflects now, "I'd rather have had my fingernails yanked out with pliers than admit I was up in a tree spanking the monkey."

Largely owing to the retelling of this story by disgraced Los Angeles police officer—now writer—Mark Fuhrman, it would later become a common assumption that Michael had admitted masturbating in the tree below which Martha's body was discovered. In fact, the two trees are on opposite sides of the Moxley house, nearly 300 feet apart. But Michael's accusers deliberately conflated them. (In 2015 Michael won an apology and a monetary settlement of an unknown amount from persistent critic Nancy Grace, for erroneously reporting DNA evidence linked Michael to Martha's murder; in fact no DNA was recovered from either Martha's body or the crime scene that linked Michael to the crime.)

According to her 2002 trial testimony, at approximately 1:30 a.m., Dorthy Moxley woke up to discover that Martha had still not returned. She roused her son to hunt for his sister, and began calling her daughter's friends, including Helen Ix and Julie Skakel. At Mrs. Moxley's request, Julie woke Tommy. He told Julie that he'd bid goodbye to Martha at the back door at 9:30 p.m. and hadn't seen her since. After phoning various friends and neighbors, Mrs. Moxley rang the Skakel house again and asked Julie to bring Tommy to the phone. Tommy repeated his story. Then, at 3:00 a.m., with still no sign of Martha, Mrs. Moxley telephoned the Skakels a third time. At some point during this period, Mrs. Moxley asked her son, John, to drive his car around the neighborhood to search for Martha. A Greenwich Police report shows that at 3:48 a.m., she called the police a second time to report Martha missing. The October 31, 1975, police report states that Dorthy Moxley expected Martha home "at 9:30 p.m." for her curfew and that Martha "had never been late like this before."

At about 8:30 a.m., according to her 2002 trial testimony, Mrs. Moxley walked to the Skakel house. Martha and her friends sometimes socialized in the Revcon motor home parked in the Skakels' driveway, and Mrs. Moxley hoped that maybe Martha had fallen asleep there. Though Mrs. Moxley testified that Michael answered the door, Michael has long said it was actually the Skakels' cook, Ethel Jones, who answered the door and brought Mrs. Moxley to Michael's bedroom and awoke him. Mrs. Moxley testified that Michael, barefoot in jeans and a T-shirt, appeared "hung over." Michael says that he had slept in the same clothes he had worn the night before to Sursum Corda. Michael told Mrs. Moxley that he didn't know where Martha was. At Mrs. Moxley's request, Franz Wittine checked the Revcon motor home and Michael scoured the house and the barn behind the tennis court.

By mid-morning, the entire community was searching for Martha, as were Greenwich youth officers Dan Hickman and Millard Jones, who, starting at 9:45

a.m., spent an hour driving around Belle Haven vainly scouting the streets for Martha. Then, between 11:30 a.m. and 12 p.m., her friend, 15-year-old Sheila McGuire, found Martha's body under a large pine tree in a wooded area on the backside of the Moxley property, 161 feet from the Moxley house. Hickman and Jones rushed over to the Moxley house where Sheila ran toward them. "She's down there," she sobbed, according to Jones's police report. "Don't make me go down there again. I think she was raped." Martha was lying face down with her pants around her ankles. She had suffered multiple crushing blows to her head and impalings to her neck consistent with being stabbed by a broken golf club shaft. Police found remnants of the murder weapon, the blood-caked head of a Toney Penna six iron and an eight-inch section of its steel shaft on the circular driveway, and another shaft segment on the grassy lawn near two large pools of blood. Both Hickman and Jones remember the club handle with its "leatherette grip" protruding from Martha's neck. Martha's doctor also remembered seeing the handle at the crime scene. The three men were either mistaken or the police later lost that instrument.

Subsequent investigation revealed that her killer or killers first assaulted Martha near her driveway, across largely unlit Walsh Lane from the Skakels' backyard meadow (also known as "The Mead"). The murderer or murderers then dragged her approximately 80 feet in a zigzag pattern to a pine tree on the far end of the Moxley property. Henry Lee, the distinguished forensic scientist and former state chief criminologist, said that the erratic drag path suggested the assailant or assailants were unfamiliar with the neighborhood. Lee said the golf club probably had broken into pieces from the extraordinary force with which Martha had been struck. This powerful swing, according to Lee, propelled the head of the golf club, with a piece of its shaft, over 70 feet, from the location of the fatal assault to the center of the circular driveway where police subsequently discovered it. According to Lee, the assailant or assailants stabbed Martha's neck with the broken shaft.

In the hours following the discovery of Martha's body, Greenwich Police canvassed the Belle Haven neighborhood questioning anyone who had been out the night before. At approximately 3:00 p.m., Detective Jim Lunney went to the Skakels' home and interviewed all of the Skakel children except for Rush Jr., who had driven the Revcon bus to a Georgetown University Homecoming in Washington, DC, that morning, not knowing that Martha, whom he had never met, was dead. The children and Kenny Littleton told Detective Lunney that Rush Jr., John, and Michael all had gone to the Terrien/Dowdle home and that Tommy was the last person in the family to see Martha before she left for home.

In the days and weeks following Martha's murder, the police repeatedly interviewed the Skakel children, as well as their cousins, Jimmy and Georgeann

Dowdle. In addition to John, Tommy would also take a polygraph exam administered by police.

Martha's friend Helen Ix has, for more than four decades, been unwavering in her opinion that Michael went to Sursum Corda with his brothers, and that only one Skakel brother remained behind at the house. "I think they all left with the exception of Tommy," she testified under oath in 2002.

Michael's cousin Georgeann Dowdle also confirmed his account. She told police in November 1975 that Michael spent the evening at her home. At the 1998 grand jury hearing, she added that she was home with her "beau" when Rush Jr., John, Michael, and Jimmy arrived to watch *Monty Python*. Michael's attorney, Mickey Sherman, never bothered identifying her "beau" as Westchester county psychologist and restauranteur Dennis Ossorio. Ossorio did testify at Michael's 2012 *habeas corpus* hearing. The 72-year-old told the presiding judge, Thomas Bishop, that he distinctly remembers watching *Monty Python* with Michael that evening. Judge Bishop faulted Mickey Sherman for failing either to interview or call Ossorio, Michael's only alibi witness who was not a member of the Skakel family. Ossorio had no motivation to cover up anything; Ossorio's brief relationship with Georgeann Dowdle ended more than 40 years ago. Ossorio's testimony at trial would have shattered prosecutor Benedict's baseless theory: that Michael had never left his home and that his alibi was part of a disciplined, 30-year family conspiracy.

On Saturday morning, November 1, the day after Sheila McGuire found Martha's body, Kenny Littleton, according to his testimony at the 1998 grand jury proceedings, made the decision to take the boys up to the Skakels' Catskill Mountains ski house in Windham, New York, to get them away from the morbid scene in Belle Haven, which was lousy with press, police, and curiosity seekers.

Rucky sent a turkey to Mrs. Moxley and went over to give his condolences as Kenny and the three Skakel boys left on their two-hour drive to Windham. That trip, thanks to writer Mark Fuhrman, would become the centerpiece for a far-fetched conspiracy narrative that helped put Michael behind bars.

CHAPTER 2

The Prosecutor

It is better that ten guilty persons escape than that one innocent suffer.
—Blackstone's Formulation

One of the bedrock fundamentals of trial strategy is to pick a "Theory of the Case" around which to organize your trial. Always pick a single unifying theory and then discard all evidence that is inconsistent with that theory.

—Professor Irving Younger,
The Ten Commandments of Cross-Examination

Michael didn't acknowledge me seated in the gallery of the Norwalk, Connecticut, courtroom on June 3, 2002, the day of closing arguments in his murder trial. We had been estranged for several years. Beginning in 1998, stress from the public focus on Michael as a murder suspect began to affect his worldview. Believing the Kennedy family was partly responsible for his predicament, Michael lashed out at my family and stopped speaking to me. On the two days I attended his court proceedings, he was cold and distant. (He resumed communicating with me only when I visited him in prison later, where, let's face it, he had little choice.)

The media played my appearance at Michael's trial with predictable hyperbole: the Kennedy family operated like the Kremlin, and the Hyannis Port politburo had dispatched me to portray the impression of a supportive family. Many people asked me why I would publicly defend Michael—a cause unlikely to enhance my own credibility. I supported him, and continue to do so, not out of misguided family loyalty, but because I was—and am—certain he is innocent.

Like nearly everyone else who knows him well, I love Michael. However, if he were guilty, I would have testified against him. He is not.

I know my first cousin Michael Skakel as well as one person can know another. He helped me to get sober in 1983 and over the next 15 years, we attended hundreds of addiction-recovery meetings together. We spent many weeks on wilderness trips and many nights around campfires. In those contexts, and others, we have shared our deepest feelings and probed each other's characters.

Michael was also close to my younger brothers, David and Michael. With Michael Skakel's support, my brother Michael got sober in 1994. After my brother Michael's death in a skiing accident in 1997, life began to crumble for Michael Skakel. In 1998, Mark Fuhrman, striving for his own resurrection after being disgraced during the O.J. Simpson trial, published a book purporting to solve the Moxley murder by pinning it on Michael. There was talk that a grand jury might indict him.

Michael's teenage ordeal at the brutal drug treatment program in Maine left him severely afflicted with post-traumatic stress disorder (PTSD). The relentless public attacks naming Michael a murder suspect darkened his worldview and aggravated his PTSD. His paranoid suspicions about our family were a symptom. That paranoid impulse caused Michael to record a fateful series of interviews with author Richard Hoffman in 1998. Michael wanted to write his memoir as a kind of defensive shield against his perceived persecution by the Kennedys. He says that he never intended to publish it. Indeed, he had Hoffman sign three separate confidentiality and nondisclosure agreements to ensure the materials were not inadvertently released. Hoffman would later package Michael's interviews as a yet-unseen and unapproved book proposal that Hoffman tentatively titled *Dead Man Talking: A Kennedy Cousin Comes Clean*. The unpublished transcript was a showcase of Michael's signature honesty all mixed up with his wild paranoid ravings. Michael told Hoffman he believed the Kennedy family had a hand in his misfortune, including the growing clamor—triggered by Fuhrman—to make him the scapegoat in the Moxley murder. He thought the Kennedys were trying to silence him or punish him for Michael Kennedy's death. The tapes were chock-full of this sort of delusion. Two years before Michael's 2002 trial, Connecticut Police Officer Frank Garr illegally seized Michael's tapes from Hoffman, and then illegally leaked them to the tabloids. I knew Michael was innocent and that his wild attacks on my family were a product of his daily emotional agony from a lifetime of abuse, so I showed up to support him. Every family has problems and challenges. Our family problems sell newspapers.

Norwalk, Connecticut, where the trial was being held, was a media circus. The prosecution team had no evidence with which to convict Michael. Their default strategy, from the moment of his arraignment, was to present him to the public as a monster. The press was compliant. Michael's trial became a national bear-baiting exhibition with every new cruelty applauded by the drooling media. Reporters lit off on frantic searches for gossipy tidbits that completed the characterization of Michael as an elitist who got away with murder. Michael's first public appearance for his arraignment was a freezing day in January 2000. Fresh off a plane from Florida, he wore a zip-up yellow sweater under his cotton suit. The media decided that his sweater collar was an ascot—an accessory Michael wouldn't have been caught dead wearing—and Michael became Thurston Howell III, a caricature of the effete, unaccountable wealthy. The prosecution fleshed out that portrait by repeatedly telling the jury that Michael was a "spoiled brat" and "a killer." During the trial, media condemnation of Michael's arrogance amplified because he appeared not to be paying attention as he cast his eyes downward toward the defense table. "My wrists were sore from writing 'Object Mickey! All lies,'" Michael said. During difficult testimony, Michael looked down at the photos of his son, George, and his black lab, Neeta. It was his method for keeping his PTSD symptoms at bay.

Despite the wretched damage to his public image, it still seemed impossible that Michael could be convicted. The case was a prosecutorial dog. The murder had occurred 27 years earlier. Until 23 years after Martha's death, no branch of law enforcement had ever considered Michael a suspect. The prosecution acknowledged the many ways that State and Greenwich detectives botched the investigation. There were no eyewitnesses to Martha's murder. No fingerprints, DNA, or other forensic evidence linked Michael to the crime; cops found only Martha's blood at the scene. Her fingernails contained no biological material. The many hairs police recovered from her body didn't match Michael's.

Without real evidence, the prosecution's only path to conviction was a confession. Michael hadn't confessed, but that didn't stop Frank Garr, an outcast cop—now a State detective—nursing a single-minded hatred for the Skakel family, from ginning up three "witnesses" who claimed he had. A parade of felons, drug addicts, habitual liars, riffraff, and attention seekers looking for reward money or desperate for a part in a celebrity legal spectacle crowded the prosecution's witness list. In the words of his partner, Len Levitt, Garr "had pursued, cajoled, harassed, and threatened" this muster of misfits and liars in order to recruit them to testify. Recorded transcripts of Garr's conversations prove that he actively suborned perjury. The prosecution's pack of scoundrels didn't inspire much confidence in those who wanted to see Michael go to jail.

The morning of May 17, the ninth day of the trial, just four days before the State rested its case, Dorthy Moxley, Martha's 69-year-old mother, stood in the courthouse parking lot speaking to a battery of microphones and cameras. "We're in the middle of the trial but it is still not too late to help," she pleaded. "If you know anything, please call the State's Attorney's office in Bridgeport. I know there are many other people out there who know what happened—who heard Michael Skakel say he murdered Martha." Since her husband, David's, death of a heart attack in 1988, Mrs. Moxley had kept the case alive by periodic media appearances around the October 30 anniversary of her daughter's murder. Understandably, she refused to hear the particulars of the crime, view crime scene photos, or dwell upon the details of her daughter's violent death. But three notable people who had taken an interest in the case—Garr, Fuhrman, and gossip writer Dominick Dunne—had convinced Mrs. Moxley that the cops had finally found the right guy in Michael. "I am positive that he did this," Mrs. Moxley told the cameras. This wasn't exactly true. Garr, Fuhrman, and Dunne were positive, and Dorthy Moxley trusted them.

Mickey Sherman, Michael's flamboyant defense attorney, certainly didn't think losing was a possibility. He assured Michael and his brothers over lunch each day at a local Tex-Mex restaurant, "I know what I'm doing. I have everything under control. There is no way in hell Michael will ever see the inside of a jail cell." Those who weren't paying close attention at that point—and, regrettably, I was in that camp—also assumed Mickey couldn't lose. A middling first-year law student could have won the case. Dunne later told CNN's Larry King that, after sitting through the trial, Michael's guilty verdict shocked him as much as had O.J. Simpson's not-guilty verdict seven years earlier.

Prosecutor Jonathan Benedict was no picture of confidence, either. On May 21, 2002, the day he rested his case, Benedict stood on the back steps of the courthouse, during a recess, shoulder to shoulder with the prosecution's reluctant final witness: Michael's ghostwriter, Richard Hoffman. Benedict had subpoenaed Hoffman after Garr illegally seized the seven audiotapes of Michael's interviews from Hoffman's home in Massachusetts. Benedict and Hoffman looked down at the parking lot where Sherman giddily commanded the gaggle of reporters. The most perilous spot in Norwalk, in those days, was between Mickey Sherman and a microphone. "Well, it's his case to lose," Benedict sighed. "Benedict absolutely knew that he hadn't made a case beyond a reasonable doubt," Hoffman told me. "He knew that."

But Benedict had a trick up his sleeve: he was preparing to cross ethical, legal, and moral boundaries to avoid losing the biggest case of his career. The Moxley case had ended the career of his predecessor, Connecticut State's Attorney Donald Browne. Until he stepped down in 1998, Browne had spent 23 years driving his detectives to build cases against the two reigning suspects: the Skakels' tutor, Kenny Littleton, and Michael's elder brother Tommy. In 1976, Browne's investigators presented him with an arrest warrant for Tommy, but Browne, who knew the case intimately, didn't think the application met legal standards for probable cause. He refused to sign. "I read it," Browne told me some years ago, "and there was nothing in there, other than the fact that he was the last to see her alive and that he'd had some mental problems in the past."

For over a decade, the case remained dormant. Then, in 1991, Dunne's rumormongering triggered a chain of events that would lead to Michael's prosecution. That year, my cousin William Kennedy Smith was tried for rape in West Palm Beach, Florida, a period of great difficulty for my family. During the trial, which was every bit the media circus that Michael's trial would be, Dunne reported the scurrilous libel that Will was in the Skakel's Greenwich house the night of Martha Moxley's murder. Dunne even published in *Vanity Fair* his concocted allegation that Connecticut State's Attorney Browne had asked for a swab of Smith's saliva to compare with DNA from the Moxley murder. Browne denied the Dunne rumor. Once again, police had recovered no DNA other than Martha's from the scene.

Dunne didn't know at the time of Martha's murder—and probably didn't care—that, with the exception of my mother, Will Smith had never encountered a Skakel. In 1975, no Kennedy cousins outside of my immediate family had ever met my Skakel cousins. That libel was emblematic of Dunne's journalistic career: dishy, delicious, and indifferent to the truth. Still, Dunne's fabrications launched a media firestorm that reinvigorated the Moxley case. Dunne's reliable business model was matching celebrities, guilty or otherwise, with notorious crimes. In 1993, Dunne published *A Season in Purgatory,* a fictionalized take on the Moxley case in which he modeled the killer of a Greenwich girl on my cousin John Kennedy Jr. On his press tour, however, Dunne loudly repeated that Tommy Skakel killed Martha Moxley, with the dead certainty of a man in the know. "There are country-club whispers of who the person is who did it," he purred to a reporter. "Everybody" in Greenwich knew who was behind it. Dan Rather's *CBS Evening News* ran a story about Dunne breathing life into a cold case. Dunne told the *Boston Globe* that pressure from the Kennedy family compelled police to let Tommy Skakel get away with murder. "I've said all along, I've said it on Jay Leno and Joan Rivers, that this is either a case of the most inept police work in history or of a rich and powerful family holding the police at bay." Dunne's public chastisements caused the *Greenwich Time* to publish a 5,000-word investigative article by then-*Newsday* reporter Len Levitt that had been gathering dust at his paper for eight years. Using hundreds of pages of police reports he'd accessed through the Freedom of Information Act, Levitt chronicled the Greenwich police's catastrophic mismanagement of the murder investigation.

Responding to the public outcry, Browne held a press conference on August 8, 1991, announcing that he had reopened the case, under the direction of the State's chief investigator, Jack Solomon, and his deputy, none other than former Greenwich cop Frank Garr. Browne provided the number for a dedicated tip line. Dorthy Moxley announced her family's promise of a $50,000 reward for information leading to an arrest.

Solomon believed that the Skakel tutor, Kenny Littleton, had murdered Martha. But despite Solomon's best efforts over seven years to build the case against Littleton, Browne again put his foot down in 1998, ignoring public pressure to make an arrest that did not meet the standards of probable cause.

That same year, Mark Fuhrman published *Murder in Greenwich* from which the public first heard the theory that 15-year-old Michael was the murderer. Michael had never even been a suspect. Despite the fact that just a few years before he'd publicly accused Tommy, Dunne wrote a gushing foreword for Fuhrman's book, now taking credit himself for solving the crime. Using sleight of hand, he substituted Michael's name where Tommy's had been in his earlier statements. "The spotlight was on it again," Dunne wrote of his book's effect on the case. "Nothing happened. But the name Skakel was spoken in louder and louder tones. Tommy Skakel. Michael Skakel."

Fuhrman now invoked a populist theme to summon public outrage over the O.J. Simpson acquittal. On the book's back cover, superimposed over Fuhrman's picture, Fuhrman asked, "Are there two systems of justice in this country—one for the rich, and another for the rest of us?" The book is a diatribe against the corruption in the Greenwich Police, who Fuhrman accuses of coddling the Skakels—and the Kennedys.

The book would prove an embarrassment for Browne, and for every State investigator and Greenwich cop who'd ever touched the case file. In *Greentown,* another book about the Moxley murder released that year, author Timothy Dumas chimed in on Dunne's catchy theme: that powerful dark forces, and deep Skakel pockets, explained police reticence. "Some journalists on this story have wondered," he wrote, critically, "whether Browne has been 'paid off.'"

In the face of this amplifying staccato, Browne finally capitulated. To his great credit, he kept his integrity. Rather than make an arrest he deemed unconstitutional, he quit. He deeded the problem to his succssor, Jonathan Benedict. A month after Fuhrman published his book, and less than a month after he assumed the lead role as State's Attorney, Benedict bowed to an inflamed media and sent the case against Michael to a one-man grand jury.

As someone who grew up revering the American justice system as nearly infallible, I share Dunne's indignation that a skilled defense lawyer, in the service of a wealthy client, can get a guilty defendant acquitted. However, it is even more dismaying that, as every district attorney knows, a skilled prosecutor can persuade a jury to convict an innocent man. Juries make mistakes. As a former New York City prosecutor, I know that media lynch mobs can turn notorious crimes into easy convictions. When the fierce winds of public opinion batter them, weak-willed or opportunistic prosecutors find it simple, even formulaic, to convict innocent defendants.

For this reason, the American justice system entrusts the prosecutor with the special power known as "Prosecutorial Discretion." That doctrine, a bedrock principle of American justice, both allows and requires prosecutors to refuse even a winnable case if they believe that injustice may result. The prosecutor's job is not to win at any cost, but to "see that justice is done." The prosecutor is a buffer against police enthusiasm or corruption, and against the storms of public passion and media goading. Browne honorably performed his duty when he resisted police requests and public clamor to indict Tommy Skakel and then Kenny Littleton. But sometimes political heat prompts prosecutors with weak spines or powerful ambitions to proceed with a case when prudence says to take a pass.

"Notorious crimes have to be very carefully prosecuted," Michael Baden, New York's former chief medical examiner, told me. "With so-called 'notorious' or 'infamous' crimes, it's so easy to get a conviction without physical evidence. This is the very time to be more cautious, not less cautious, so that a bad decision isn't made because of an inflamed public. Look at the five kids in the Central Park jogger case. There was not a trace of evidence—but with notorious cases, jurors can find you guilty anyway."

The Innocence Project, co-founded by my friend Barry Scheck, has freed 333 wrongfully imprisoned convicts, using exculpatory DNA tests. Many of those had resulted from shoddy, crooked, or overenthusiastic police work. A full 25 percent of those freed had provided a confession to cops, often under duress. Fifteen percent had been victims of a corrupt police informant system, whereby prosecutors compensate criminals with perks such as shortened or suspended jail terms in exchange for incriminating testimony against others. (So called "testimony with benefits" proved a useful tool in Benedict's case against Michael.)

The Innocence Project cites studies suggesting that up to 5 percent of all incarcerated people in America are wrongfully imprisoned. Most of them are in prison because a prosecutor failed his ethical duty to make the right call.

Benedict, unlike his predecessor, failed to make the right call. Under pressure, he brought a weak claim to trial. And since he was new to the case when he sent it to a grand jury, he had to give great latitude to the man who professed to know the case inside and out: Frank Garr, a cop whose fingerprints are visible in every stage of Michael's wrongful conviction.

Feeble as the case was, the one-man grand jury's indictment committed the new prosecutor to bring Michael to trial. Benedict had bought Garr's ticket; now he had to take the ride. The slight, courtly 57-year-old with a full head of straight white hair appeared mild-mannered, and unassuming, but he was also tough and ambitious. A Vietnam vet and triathlete, Benedict had been in the State's Attorney's office since 1976, following two years laboring alongside his father in his small Fairfield law firm.

Benedict came to the Skakel case exhausted from a bruising and humiliating loss in *Connecticut v. Adrian Peeler*, wherein he charged Peeler with gunning down an 8-year-old and his mother in Bridgeport to prevent the boy from testifying in the trial of Peeler's drug-dealing brother. In a preview of Michael's case, Benedict's star eyewitness was Josephine Lee, a crack-addled prostitute who suffered hallucinations and who repudiated her own testimony prior to trial. Lee sent a letter confessing that she'd "lied" to police about her role as lookout in the hit. Lee wrote, "I was scared when the police came to the house to get me so I told them that I had something to do with the murder. But I do not know anything." A jury acquitted Peeler on the first-degree murder charge. "There wasn't enough evidence," the jury foreman told the press.

Benedict's failure in the Peeler case must have weighed heavily when he rose from his desk on June 3, 2002, to deliver his summation to Michael's jury. He never had much faith in the Skakel case and was now on his way to losing it. The State had already spent $25 million in its zeal to convict Michael. Benedict had deployed all of the strategies that enable prosecutors to apply their thumbs to the scales of justice, including basing his case almost entirely on three perjuring confession witnesses and—as we shall see—illegally withholding reams of exculpatory evidence from the defense team. Yet, like in the Peeler case, Benedict found himself with a deranged drug addict as his star witness: Greg Coleman, a lowlife junkie with an encyclopedic rap sheet, a reputation for lying, and wildly vacillating testimony concerning the circumstances and content of Michael's supposed confession. Inconveniently, Coleman had recently died from a heroin overdose and would need to be miraculously resurrected to testify if Benedict were to have a prayer of convicting Michael. Worse still, Benedict had to grant full immunity to Kenny Littleton, the State's primary suspect for the previous 25 years, in order to get him to testify.

The prosecution had so little faith in its underlying case that Benedict made a last-minute attempt to add a manslaughter count to the charges, carrying the possibility of no jail time for Michael. The State's prospects of success seemed so hopeless that the prosecutors sent Dorthy Moxley to the parking lot waving a recently increased $100,000 reward to entice new witnesses. But that was all before Benedict's brilliant summation.

"His case was never tied up," says Stephan Seeger, a young lawyer on Michael's defense team, whom Sherman hired three years out of law school to assist on writing motions. "I don't think the jury had enough to piece anything together. It wasn't a winning case until his misleading, fabricated closing argument. I thought the jury would have been able to see right through it. I guess not."

Len Levitt concurred. He quotes Dorthy Moxley on the cover of his book *Conviction* for the proposition that he and his partner Detective Frank Garr "more than any other two people are responsible for solving Martha's murder." Yet Levitt apparently never believed that Benedict had proven his case. "I never thought Michael would be convicted," he reveals in the opening passage of his hagiography of Garr. "I only hoped for Frank's sake the jury would deliberate longer than the few hours it had in the O.J. Simpson case. That way, Frank wouldn't be embarrassed."

Benedict began his summation by cunningly lowering the jury's expectations and preparing them for the prosecutorial dirty pool that would follow. "While I am sure Mr. Sherman is going to take a great deal of issue with what I am going to say here," Benedict said, "I am going to present to you what I submit is the most reasonable construction of the evidence in this case. Does that mean that the evidence answers every question that could arise? Certainly not. Does that mean that every fact has been proven beyond a reasonable doubt? Of course not."

Then Benedict introduced a motive for the murder: jealousy. Following the theory Mark Fuhrman had first advanced in his book, Benedict argued that Michael killed Martha in a jealous rage after seeing his brother kiss her. "Martha Moxley," he told the jurors, was a "pretty, athletic, flirtatious 15-year-old kid . . . just beginning to come into womanhood. She was . . . clearly drawing the attention of boys. Unfortunately as we learned . . . she was also drawn into the vortex of the competing hormones of two of the young boys who lived across Walsh Lane"—my cousins Michael and Tommy Skakel.

Benedict theatrically pointed his finger at Michael and announced in a stentorian voice, "He murdered Martha Moxley beyond every reasonable doubt." The trouble, Benedict asserted, all began in the Lincoln Continental. Michael had been in love with Martha and he finally found an opportunity for intimacy in the car's dark front seat. "This was the defendant's big moment. Unfortunately," Benedict said, "they were joined by brother Thomas, Michael's nemesis, who wound up with the girl that night, at least for a little while."

Benedict's big problem was Michael's gold-plated alibi: At trial, four witnesses testified that Michael had left for Sursum Corda in the Lincoln at 9:30 p.m., and returned at 11:20 p.m. This meant that Michael would not have been at the Skakels' house to see Tommy kiss Martha (between 9:30 and 9:50 p.m.), nor could he have been in Belle Haven to murder Martha at her 10:00 p.m. time of death. There was simply no way he could have killed Martha.

Even at the brink of the trial, prosecutors apparently had not settled on a theory of the case that could explain how Michael could have committed the crime. During a break in the jury selection at the Norwalk Courthouse, the Moxleys' neighbor Cissie Ix pulled aside Benedict's assistant prosecutor, Susan Gill. Cissie's daughter, Helen, Martha's close friend and a witness in the upcoming trial, had been in the Lincoln with Martha and the two Skakel brothers. She had watched Michael drive off in the Lincoln at 9:30 p.m. After the Lincoln left, she had seen Tommy and Martha beginning to flirt with each other, which had caused her to leave the Skakel driveway in embarrassment. The Lincoln did not return until 11:20 p.m. By that time, Martha had been dead for an hour and twenty minutes. Cissie Ix told Gill she was bewildered as to how the State could believe Michael had committed the 10:00 p.m. crime from 11 miles' distance on the other side of Greenwich. "I told Susan Gill, 'Helen was in the driveway when Michael drove away in the car to the Terriens' with his brothers. How could he possibly have committed the crime?' Susan Gill told me, 'He could have driven around the corner, jumped out, killed Martha, and then jumped back in the car with his brothers and driven to the Terriens.' When I heard that, I thought, 'Oh, Michael's going to win this case, easily!'" Eighteen days later, both sides had rested, and Benedict still hadn't made up his mind about how Michael could have been in Belle Haven to kill Martha.

"Benedict had only the phony confessions," says Seeger. "But he had none of the choreography. There was nothing in evidence to explain the mechanics of how Michael could have been in Belle Haven to commit the murder."

Benedict had two half-baked theories for how Michael killed Martha. Neither of them was supported by evidence, and both were so farfetched even the prosecution couldn't settle on which of these two contradictory hypotheticals to present to the jury. Instead, Benedict went with both of them. He presented a jumble of conflicting evidence during trial, and then offered the two scenarios in closing argument and left it to the jurors to decide how Michael could possibly have accomplished the feat.

It was a daring gambit. The only way to win was to lobotomize the jurors with so much hatred for Michael that they would ignore the huge holes in both of Benedict's theories. He was betting, correctly, that he could poison their judgment and distract them enough to forget about reasonable doubt. Let's look at Benedict's two contradictory theories of the case:

Benedict's Scenario A: Michael never went to Sursum Corda. Having stayed home, he witnessed the assignation between Tommy and Martha from some hidden vantage point, and then killed Martha after she parted from Tommy.

This scenario solved both problems of motive and opportunity by putting Michael in Belle Haven at 9:45 p.m. to witness his brother making out with Martha and also at her 10:00 p.m. time of death. However, it has fatal defects. For Michael to have skipped Sursum Corda, and then covered up that fact, would have required the organization of a monumental conspiracy involving, for starters, Michael, Tommy, John, Rush Jr., Jimmy, Georgeann Dowdle, and her beau, Dennis Ossorio. The cover-up and conspiracy would have had to begin a few hours after Martha's death and then remain flawlessly orchestrated and airtight for three decades. In the hours and days after Martha's murder, Jimmy, Rush Jr., John, and Michael all attested, under repeated police questioning, that they left for the Terriens' house at 9:30 p.m., when Martha was still alive, and returned at 11:20 p.m. John passed a polygraph that the police felt covered all four boys who went to Sursum Corda. Michael also confirmed his recounting to police and in subsequent polygraph and truth serum interviews, administered by Dr. Stanley Lesse at New York Presbyterian Hospital, in the presence of Monsignor (later Bishop) William McCormack, and in interviews with the veteran FBI and homicide detectives at Sutton Associates. Georgeann Dowdle, Michael's cousin, consistently said that Michael had arrived with her brother, Jimmy, in the Lincoln, and watched *Monty Python* at Sursum Corda. Ossorio testified during Michael's *habeas corpus* appeal that he was also watching TV and talking with Michael at the Terrien house at 10:00 p.m.

Any conspiracy would necessarily have to involve not only the five people who saw Michael at Sursum Corda, but also all those witnesses who remained in Belle Haven. On the day after the murder, Tommy told police that Michael left with his brothers in the Lincoln at 9:30 p.m. He confirmed that story over and over to police throughout the next two months during nine hours of intense grilling, without a lawyer present, and during two separate police-administered polygraphs. He repeated the story during two sodium amytal interviews also with Dr. Stanley Lesse at New York Presbyterian in 1976 and in subsequent interviews in 1992 with Sutton Associates. Kenny Littleton, a man with a compelling incentive to inculpate a Skakel, would also had to have been complicit in the conspiracy. Littleton told police that Rush Jr. had checked in with him, minutes before leaving, to let Kenny know that he was driving Jimmy back to Sursum Corda, and Michael was coming along.

After Michael left in the Lincoln, Tommy, David, Stephen, Julie, and Kenny were in the house, up and down the stairs and in and out of the doors, according to their various statements. Julie's friend Andrea Shakespeare told police in 1975 that she went out to the driveway at 9:30 p.m., just after the boys left in the Lincoln. When she dashed back to the house to fetch the station wagon keys, Tommy, Kenny, and Stephen met her at the front door and handed her the keys. (Tommy immediately went back out the mudroom door to rendezvous with Martha behind the toolshed.) Nanny Sweeney and Franz Wittine were also in the house all night. None of them saw Michael after the Lincoln left at 9:30 p.m.

In advancing his fanciful narrative, Benedict never even tried to explain how Michael possibly could have stayed invisible to the eight people who remained in Belle Haven. Furthermore, Benedict never offered any evidence suggesting that Michael would have any reason to hide. He would not have known that Tommy and Martha were going to make out since they started kissing 10 minutes after the Lincoln left. Benedict offered no evidence of any flirtation occurring between the two love birds until after the Lincoln departed.

The veteran homicide detectives at Sutton Associates, hired by Rucky Skakel Sr. to reinvestigate the Moxley murder in 1992, never doubted that Michael went with his brothers to Sursum Corda. Sutton founder and former FBI G-man Jim Murphy told me, "I don't have any reason to think otherwise. He wasn't around. Nobody ever sees him anyplace else around the house."

All five people at Sursum Corda saw Michael there. Not one of the eight people who stayed saw Michael in Belle Haven.

Most damning to the prosecution, in order to cobble together this particular conspiracy theory, Benedict had to commit a grave and unlawful act of prosecutorial misconduct. He had to illegally conceal from the defense a 1975 police report, in which homicide investigators unambiguously stated, "It is known and believed that as that vehicle departed from the driveway, occupied by the Skakel boys (Rushton, Michael, and John) along with their cousin, James Terrien, that both Helen Ix and Geoff Byrne began to walk to their homes, leaving only Thomas Skakel and Martha Moxley standing in the driveway." If the jury had seen that report, they could never have found beyond a reasonable doubt that Michael had somehow ducked out of the departing Lincoln.

This document would have exploded Benedict's entire Scenario A theory. The law requires that prosecutors disclose all exculpatory evidence to the defense. During Michael's 2013 *habeas corpus* trial, Garr acknowledged that Benedict had this memo in his possession. Garr, who was Benedict's evidence manager for the case, acknowledged under oath that it should have been disclosed. He told the court that he was ordered to not disclose it to the defense team. When Michael's counsel Hubie Santos asked Garr who gave him the order, he replied "Mr. Benedict." In 2007, North Carolina State's Attorney Mike Nifong was removed from office, disbarred, and jailed for equivalent misconduct in the Duke Lacrosse rape case.

Benedict's only evidence that Michael didn't go to Sursum Corda was the unsubstantiated hunch of Julie's friend Andrea, who testified that she felt Michael never left in the Lincoln. "Andrea Shakespeare Renna is unshakable in her conviction that the defendant remained behind," he told the jury. But, in fact, Andrea testified that she never saw Michael in the house and she didn't see who was in the Lincoln. She testified that she was "only under the impression" that Michael didn't go in the Lincoln. As we shall see, Shakespeare's testimony contradicted her historical statements to police and investigators during her myriad interviews over 30 years. Shakespeare consistently maintained that she never saw the Lincoln leave the driveway, had no clue who was in it, and never saw Michael in the house or anywhere on the property after the Lincoln departed. Andrea's "feeling," I will show, was what experts characterize as a "false memory," artfully implanted by Frank Garr.

For Benedict to prevail with his Scenario A theory, he needed to persuade the jury that the six Skakel siblings, their cousins Jimmy and Georgeann Dowdle, and Kenny Littleton had all perjured themselves when they testified that

Michael went to Sursum Corda. Prosecutors adopted Fuhrman and Dunne's view that Rucky masterminded a coordinated 30-year cover-up. Both writers proposed that all the Skakels knew from the outset that Michael had committed the murder and immediately circled the wagons. Using Fuhrman's blueprint, Benedict suggested that Rucky had whisked the children up to the family ski lodge before police had a chance to interview them and before concrete hardened on their stories. "Someone has the bright idea to get them out of town," Benedict told the jury. Following Fuhrman, Benedict hypothesized that in Windham the family concocted the entire yarn about Sursum Corda and *Monty Python* and then stuck with it for three decades.

"Why else would the family have traveled to their ski house in Windham, New York, on Saturday, November 1, 1975, if not to reconcile their stories, to rehearse an alibi that put Michael at Sursum Corda at the time of the murder? . . . Not until their return from Windham did the alibi begin to come up." Benedict's statement went unchallenged by Michael's lawyer, Mickey Sherman, even though it was unsupported by any evidence.

First, the Sursum Corda alibi was not hatched for the first time in Windham, as Benedict told the jury. Littleton himself had told the police, before departing for Windham, that Michael had gone in the Lincoln to Sursum Corda. Michael, Tommy, and John had all given consistent statements to police about the Sursum Corda trip, prior to leaving for Windham.

Second, at trial, Littleton testified that the trip to Windham was his idea, not that of any Skakel. Littleton said he wanted to get the children away from the press and police and the morbid conditions at Belle Haven. In truth, the Skakel boys would have gone to Windham anyway. They travelled to the Catskills every autumn and winter weekend to hunt, fish, and ski. Inexplicably, Littleton wanted to drive his own car that weekend. Therefore, Tommy drove his little brothers Michael and John in the station wagon.

Benedict said that all the Skakel family, as well as Jimmy and Georgeann Dowdle, were parties to the Windham trip. However, Rucky Skakel, the so-called mastermind of the Windham conspiracy, did not even go to Windham that weekend. Also not present was Rush Jr., who left for a long-planned Georgetown University Homecoming in the Revcon motor home on Halloween morning, not even knowing that Martha was dead. Twelve-year-old David and 9-year-old Stephen stayed home with Julie, who had little interest in fishing and hunting. Jimmy and Georgeann Dowdle were not there either. In fact, Georgeann Dowdle never visited Windham in her life.

This was a shorthanded conspiracy indeed! The only adult present was 23-year-old Littleton, who would spend the next two decades fending off accusations that he was Martha's killer. Benedict never ventured to speculate how Littleton's interests were advanced by participating in a conspiracy to protect the

Skakels, whom he had met for the first time the previous day. To the contrary, it would have been very much in his interest to expose a Skakel conspiracy, had one existed. After Littleton, the next oldest "conspirator" was 17-year-old Tommy, who had begun a romance with the victim the previous night and was now supposedly helping his 15-year-old brother—his despised "nemesis," according to Benedict—to thwart justice.

Benedict presented no evidence of a Skakel conspiracy, only wildly speculative assertions. Unfortunately for Michael, Benedict and the media had by then primed the jury into believing almost anything. Benedict had the jury teed up to convict no matter how flimsy the evidence of guilt.

Finally, if Benedict had evidence of a conspiracy, he surely would have charged other Skakel family members and friends as co-conspirators. He did not. In fact, he showed no documents, no admissions, no conversations or acts to further the conspiracy theory—no evidence whatsoever. He simply told the jury it was so—and they bought it. That is the power of a prosecutor when trying notorious crimes.

Benedict's Scenario B: Michael went to Sursum Corda and then murdered Martha after returning to Belle Haven after 11:20 p.m.

As he approached the finale of his summation, Benedict made an astonishing pivot that should have signaled to the jury his extreme lack of confidence in his entire case. Benedict shattered that fundamental strategic rule—that litigators should always pick a single "Theory of the Case" and stick to it. In a bold gamble, he offered the jury a hedge: Michael, he posited, could have gone to Sursum Corda, and then returned with his brothers at 11:20 p.m. and killed Martha any time before morning.

Scenario B had even greater problems than the conspiracy theory. For starters, it deprived Michael of motive. In that sense, it obliterated Benedict's entire case. If Michael left for Sursum Corda at 9:30 p.m., he would have never seen Tommy and Martha smooching. (In fact, Michael didn't even know about Tommy's romance with Martha until 1998, when he heard about it on TV.) Michael therefore would have had no jealous rage and no reason to kill Martha. This is a gaping hole in Benedict's theory and yet, astonishingly, Benedict never even bothered to offer the jury a way around it.

Benedict's second problem with Scenario B was opportunity: if Michael got home at 11:20 p.m., he could not have killed Martha at 10:00 p.m.

In 1975, Connecticut law-enforcement officials consulted the nation's preeminent forensic pathologist, Houston, Texas, medical examiner Joseph Jachimczyk, who established the time of Martha's death as between 9:30 p.m. and 10:00 p.m. Jachimczyk based his conclusion on the condition of Martha's bladder and the contents of her stomach. Martha had eaten a grilled cheese sandwich at about 6:00 p.m., Dorthy Moxley told police. She ate ice cream at the Moukads' shortly after 7:00 p.m. The autopsy found no undigested food in her stomach, only three ounces of liquid—probably a Coca-Cola that she drank when she went inside at the Skakels'. The stomach normally clears most food in two to three hours and liquid within 30 minutes. The Connecticut police also consulted Detroit's medical examiner, Werner Spitz, and New York City deputy chief medical examiners Michael Baden and John Devlin. They all generally concurred with Jachimczyk.

Police also relied on non-medical indicators: the barking dogs, Martha's curfew, her appointment to call Margie at 9:30 p.m., and Dorthy Moxley's testimony that she heard Martha cry out and the "excited" voices of men around 10:00 p.m. For 25 years the police operated under the assumption that the murder occurred around 10:00 p.m. In fact, interview records show that when police questioned witnesses and suspects in the aftermath of the murder, they specifically asked about the person's activities and whereabouts between 9:30 p.m. and 10:30 p.m.

Benedict, therefore, had to fudge the time of death. "For Michael's accusers to be correct, the time of death had to be moved back," says Michael Baden, who later served as the chief medical examiner for New York City. While consulting with the Connecticut Police in the Moxley case, Baden had become friendly with the Moxley family. At Dorthy Moxley's request, he acted as a liaison between the Greenwich Police and Mark Fuhrman, who despised each other, while Fuhrman was researching *Murder in Greenwich*.

At the trial, Benedict summonsed Connecticut's former chief medical examiner, Elliot Gross, who had performed Martha's autopsy. But then Benedict did something very telling. He never put Gross on the stand. His decision to subpoena Gross and then not to call him was certainly a tactical maneuver. Clearly Gross was either unwilling or unable to support Benedict's theory that the murder occurred after 10:00 p.m. While the original chief medical examiner cooled his heels in a back office, Benedict called Connecticut's current chief medical examiner, Wayne Carver, to serve as his expert witness. Carver, who had never worked on the Moxley case, evinced a pliancy that Benedict found handy. Based on his reading of Gross's autopsy report, Carver testified that the murder might have occurred as late as 1:30 a.m. Mickey Sherman's cross-examination was reliably languid and stunningly brief. He asked Carver a single question: "Could the murder have occurred at 9:30 p.m.?" Carver answered, "Yes," and Sherman sat down. When Baden read the transcript, he told me, "I was very surprised. He never asked Carver the key question: 'What was the basis of his opinion that the time of death could be both 9:30 p.m. and 1:30 a.m.?'"

And what of the barking dogs? "Frankly," Benedict told the jurors defensively, "the barking dog evidence I think seems silly. Dogs bark," Benedict said. "They bark more on Mischief Night."

The third major problem with Benedict's Scenario B—and it's a mind-boggler—is how Michael might have found Martha after 11:20 p.m. in order to kill her. Let's look at the hurdles 15-year-old Michael would need to overcome.

Benedict himself stated during trial that Tommy "was fast asleep" when the boys returned from Sursum Corda at 11:20 p.m. So, where was Martha hanging out between 9:50 p.m., when Tommy last saw her heading home, and 11:20 p.m.? Why did she decide to violate her curfew? Why was she not seen by anyone during this period? It was freezing outside; none of Martha's friends reported seeing her; she wasn't eating—the only content in her stomach was approximately 3 ounces of unabsorbed liquid. The grilled cheese sandwich had already vacated her stomach. As Martha's diary attests, she was an avid drinker and pot smoker. But toxicology reports showed that she did not have alcohol, marijuana, or any other drugs in her system when she died. And she died with her hymen intact, so she wasn't somewhere in the neighborhood getting high or having sex. Where exactly did Benedict imagine Martha to be? Perhaps she was at home, and Michael somehow coaxed her out—and then murdered her? Benedict never says. But is it plausible that Martha went home and somehow sneaked past her worried mother who was already frantic about her failure to return at curfew? Is it possible that Michael somehow snuck her out again, past her anxious mother and her protective older brother, John, who had returned home at 11:20 p.m. and was still awake? And, after luring her out, is it likely that small, prepubescent Michael, with no apparent motive, beat Martha to death, stabbed her through the neck, and then dragged her body toward, not away from, the Moxley house, all within a few yards of her mother and brother?

Benedict didn't speculate how Michael might have found Martha to accomplish this marvel. He simply pronounced that that mystery was "one of the controversies of the trial. But, as you will see, it is not one that the State necessarily has to resolve in order to convict."

Benedict was perfectly comfortable leaving these questions unanswered. Michael, after all, Benedict averred, had confessed to the crime on three occasions (more about these dubious confessions later). Other than Andrea Shakespeare's strained testimony that she had an "assumption" that Michael may have stayed home from Sursum Corda, and Benedict's unsupported speculation that the figure seen by Julie Skakel running past the kitchen window around 9:30 p.m. may have been Michael, Benedict had offered no evidence whatsoever to support either of his theories. Any of these questions should have constituted reasonable doubt to a jury.

The prosecution seemed to be saying: "Hell, who cares how he did it?" The important thing was that Michael was guilty; how he did it was unimportant. Benedict simply turned over the mystery to the jurors. And he urged them not to be too rigorous about sorting out all the nettlesome details. "As regards time, you must be unanimous that the crime occurred during the time set in the information, 9:30 p.m. to 5:30 a.m. And that's all. For that matter, if half of you were to buy into Zock the dog and figured the crime happened early and not accept the alibi and the other half of you were to accept the alibi and conclude the defendant . . . came by later at night and did it, nevertheless if you all agree beyond a reasonable doubt that the defendant murdered Martha Moxley, you must convict."

Instead of proposing a solid theory and presenting the jury with evidence that established it as true beyond reasonable doubt, Benedict's strategy was to skip quickly ahead to the murder itself and then to hope the jurors' horror over its gruesome details would patch over the yawning gaps in his narrative.

With all his double-talk about those pesky chronologies behind him, Benedict transports Michael and Martha to a patch of grass in the middle of the Moxleys' circular driveway—never explaining how they got there, and before anyone can say "reasonable doubt," Michael strikes Martha with the golf club. "She wasn't knocked unconscious there because we learned that she was somehow able to travel from here to here," Benedict said, indicating with his pointer on a crime scene diagram how Martha staggers 42 feet toward the Hammonds' (a neighbor) house, before Michael belts her again with the six iron. He followed this blow, Benedict theorized, with several others creating a four-foot diameter pool of blood. "At that point," Benedict said, "she was beaten at the blood scene mercilessly. Clearly the first blow or at most the second blow rendered her permanently unable to move." Michael, he said, walloped her so hard, so many times that the club shaft weakened, and then snapped, sending the head of the club flying 100 feet north back to the location of the initial assault, on the grass inside the circular driveway. At this point, Benedict told the jury, Michael stood over Martha in the dark holding only a hollow piece of golf club shaft. "And as a continuation, but not a final step of the hate and humiliation, she was stabbed through and through and through with a piece of broken golf club shaft," Benedict said.

Puny Michael then supposedly hauled Martha's body almost a hundred feet, again toward the Hammond house, then for some reason stopped and took a sharp southeasterly turn back toward the Moxley house. He then dragged the body to the spot under the large pine tree where Sheila McGuire found her. At this point, or some other point—Benedict's not specific—Benedict has Michael pull down Martha's pants and panties. Apparently seconds—at most, minutes—after beating Martha to death, Michael is horny. With two bloody hands, he parts her legs. Benedict projected a crime scene photo onto the courtroom movie screen. The jury saw a red stripe visible on Martha's left inner thigh. "That's not a bruise," he said. "It's not any other kind of injury. Rather it's a smear, as Dr. Henry Lee testified. This is evidence that somewhere in the bloody assault scene, somewhere during the drag episode, but most likely underneath the tree, he administered the sickest of humiliations." Having just murdered his friend and next-door neighbor, Michael purportedly stands triumphantly in the middle of Martha's yard, downs his own pants, masturbates, and ejaculates on Martha's body. Benedict, who lifted this masturbation scene directly from Fuhrman's book, never tried to explain away the fact that the coroner found no ejaculate on Martha's body. But Benedict found Fuhrman's scene too deliciously gruesome to omit. It would, after all, galvanize the jurors' fury and put them beyond the reach of rational thought.

It's now either 10 o'clock or midnight—Benedict gets necessarily vague here—as Michael, in the freezing cold, stands masturbating, while Zock, less than 100 yards away across Walsh Lane, barks furiously. To Benedict, the dog's reaction proved his case (or not). "Of all the players in this case, who was the one that most tormented Zock?" Benedict asked. "Who was the one that Zock hated? Who was the one that would cause Zock to become most agitated in that neighborhood? Michael Skakel." There was no evidence during trial that Michael had ever tormented Zock. Benedict, undeterred, as usual, by Sherman, was on another flight of fancy. (Michael is a dog lover. Children and dogs gravitate toward him. Helen Ix testified at trial that "Zock barked at everybody.")

And then, according to Benedict, Michael disappeared into the night, carrying the golf club handle. The disposal of the murder weapon, he postulated, represented the first step in the 30-year-long family conspiracy to hide Michael's link to the murder. The handle, Benedict said, would be embossed, like some of its sister clubs with "Mrs. R.W. Skakel, Greenwich, CT." The very fact that police never found it at the crime scene, or anywhere else, pointed the finger, he suggested, directly at the Skakels. "The piece that is missing has significance only to somebody named Skakel." Ignoring the science of fingerprint identification, Benedict reasoned, "Now, you want to think about this for a minute? Is there any reason why a stranger . . . would have any reason to hide that label? No. Such a person would have all the reason in the world to simply leave that identifying label right next to the body" (unless, of course, their fingerprints were on it). In fact, Benedict knew that the golf club handle actually had been recovered, then lost, by police. The first two officers on scene reported finding the club's handle, with its leatherette grip, protruding from Martha's neck. The Moxley family's physician subsequently saw the handle lying next to Martha's body. Characteristically, Mickey Sherman never pursued that lead.

Benedict's coup de grâce was Michael's own voice appearing to admit the murder. During his last 10 minutes Benedict unveiled a dramatic and sophisticated multimedia display that legal analysts afterward criticized as deceptive, prejudicial, and unethical. Video PowerPoint presentations were a novel device in criminal prosecution at that time. In recent years, they have become more common, as prosecutors recognize their unmatched capacity to sway juries. According to *Wired* magazine, at least 10 times between 2012 and 2014, US courts reversed criminal convictions because a prosecutor violated the rules of fair argument by using deceptive PowerPoint presentations of the kind that Benedict pioneered at Michael's trial. In many other cases, appellate courts have criticized the device without reversing.

A picture is worth a thousand words and Benedict's video utilized well-known strategies borrowed from the PR industry for subconscious persuasion. An Oregon court threw out a conviction in 2016 because prosecutors used an unflattering security camera photo of the defendant, which the court described as "a calculated device employed by the prosecutors to manipulate the Jury's reasoned deliberation and impair its fact-finding function." Benedict did far worse.

The story of Martha's brutal murder was Benedict's soft-shoe warm-up to his main act. By artfully cutting and pasting Michael's recorded conversations with ghostwriter Richard Hoffman, Benedict transformed Michael's words into a phony confession that would eclipse all the gaping cavities in his two scenarios.

Michael's reedy voice filled the courtroom: "I got home and most of the lights were out. I was walking around the house, nobody was on the porch. I went upstairs, my sister's room, her door was closed, and I remember that Andrea had gone home." It was Michael telling his account of his actions after returning home from Sursum Corda on the night of Martha's murder. I'd heard that story probably a dozen times since we started hanging out in the early 1980s. It was a strange story that Michael probably should have kept to himself. But those who know him understand that Michael is incapable of keeping anything to himself. He's utterly without guile. Everything in his head registers instantly on his huge expressive face and then explodes, volcanically, from his mouth. He's a talker, an over-sharer—oddly, it never gets tedious; Michael's palaver is an overflowing stream of clear and honest emotion and charming, stark, and often awkward honesty.

The account went like this: drunk and stoned, Michael snuck out of the house shortly after returning from Sursum Corda. First, he visited the Walsh Lane cottage to see the "nudie lady," but she had closed shop for the night. Then he got another plan. Benedict played the tape so Michael could be heard saying. "I said, 'Fuck this. Martha likes me. I will be bold tonight.' You know, booze gave me . . . courage again." Michael told me he decided he would see if he could wake Martha. He climbed a tree in front of her house, called her name, and threw a few pebbles at what he thought was her window. He got no response. So he masturbated in the tree for a short period. He did not reach orgasm. He immediately felt foolish, and guilty, and it dawned on him that someone in the house might spy him "playing pocket pool." The thought filled him with horror so he clambered down and sprinted home.

Benedict, in his audio-visual presentation, omitted the context of this story. He removed from his audio Michael's reference to masturbation and instead superimposed Michael's inculpatory statements about feeling guilty on top of gruesome pictures of Martha's slain body, to make it seem that Michael was confessing to murder. For this video finale, the state of Connecticut paid WIN Interactive, a Massachusetts firm specializing in multimedia trial presentations, $67,000 to edit snippets of Hoffman's *Dead Man Talking* recordings to formulate what sounded like a murder confession.

In his 1998 taped interview with Hoffman, Michael had described his reaction when Dorthy Moxley awakened him on Halloween morning. He was asleep in his street clothes, hung over and dazed. Benedict projected a picture of a smiling Martha on a screen in the front of the courtroom, with Michael's words alongside them: "Then I went to sleep and I woke up to Mrs. Moxley saying, 'Michael, have you seen Martha?'" Michael did not know that Martha was dead. In fact, no one then knew except the murderer or murderers. "I . . . was still high from the night before, and a little drunk and I was like, 'Oh my God, did they see me last night?'" But in a bait and switch, Benedict had surgically deleted the contextual words that Michael actually spoke on the tape, describing why he was afraid he had been seen at the Moxley's house: "Oh my God, I hope to God nobody saw me jerking off." Benedict changed the photo from the vital, smiling Martha, to a gory crime scene photo of her crumpled, blood-soaked body, in order to suggest to jurors that Michael was describing his murder of Martha. Suddenly, Mrs. Moxley, seated right behind the jurors, let out a pained wail and doubled over in her seat. She had absented herself from the courtroom during much of the crime scene testimony. Her horror was heart-wrenching. Michael's voice continued: "And I am like, I don't know, I am like and I remember just having the feeling of panic like, 'Oh shit,' you know, like my worry of what I went to bed with, I don't know. You know what I mean? A feeling of panic."

It's been illegal for over 30 years for prosecutors to write across an exhibit in red ink. But Benedict employed new technology to do something far more powerful and prejudicial. As the prosecution played the audiotape, Michael's words appeared on a giant screen, turning red and exploding in size. Each time Michael said the word "panic," the display flashed another crime scene photo of Martha's body. Many observers, including Dunne, credited Michael's conviction to this dramatic summation.

Sherman, who should have been out of his seat objecting to every third line of Benedict's closing, appeared to be as transfixed as the jurors by Benedict's bedeviling horror show. As usual, Sherman didn't move a muscle. As Benedict hit his climax, Michael began to stand, saying to Sherman, "This is bullshit. They are putting words in my mouth." Sherman grabbed his arm and said, "Yes . . . but they can do that. It's legal."

When the courtroom lights went back on, all of the many defects in Benedict's scenarios didn't matter; the lack of evidence against Michael no longer mattered; the conflicting theories of the case didn't matter; reasonable doubt no longer mattered; the fact that Benedict hadn't proven his case didn't matter.

The grieving mother, the ugly portrait of Michael, the gruesome photos, the cut-and-paste audio-video confession provided all the razzle-dazzle that would be necessary to sway the jury into forgetting about reasonable doubt. "Could you ask the defendant to draw you a more incriminating picture?" Benedict asked of the jurors with sly earnest.

In 2008, in a CBS News reexamination of the Moxley case on *48 Hours,* Lesley Stahl confronted Benedict about how he had "rescued" a weak case by slicing and dicing snippets of Michael's innocent yammering into a fabricated confession. "If I did this," Stahl told Benedict, "I'd be fired." Hoffman, the author who'd recorded Michael's words, couldn't believe the deceptive audio editing Benedict had employed. "The prosecution perjured themselves when they spliced that tape," he says. "But that's of a piece with this long media assault on Michael's character, making him the fall guy for the perception of what those rich Kennedys had gotten away with so many times in the past, Chappaquiddick and William Kennedy Smith. The whole thing was an emotional manipulation from the start because they had no facts, no forensic evidence, and no witnesses. So how else can you convict him? You have to just convince people that he's just a fat, smug, rich kid, and murdering girls is what fat, smug rich kids do."

In the grand scheme of the sins committed in this case's history, Benedict's abhorrent closing, I discovered, was actually a minor one. The rot went so much deeper than even I could imagine. The case against Michael was an artifice of lies. And the foundation was the falsehood that Michael Skakel is a Kennedy.

CHAPTER 3

Skakels and Kennedys

The first words he ever said to me was, "I'm going to get away with murder. I'm a Kennedy."
—Greg Coleman, resident of the Élan School
with Michael, heroin addict, and prosecution witness,
to a Rochester, New York, television station in 2001

Michael Skakel likely never would have gone to prison had the press, police, and prosecutors not been able to portray him as a "Kennedy cousin." It was a false characterization from the moment Dominick Dunne and Mark Fuhrman first deployed it in 1997. (Nor did Michael write or approve a draft in 1998 for a book proposal by Richard Hoffman employing the term "Kennedy cousin" in its title.) Building on the Dunne–Fuhrman narrative, prosecutor Jonathan Benedict portrayed Michael as a monstrous fiend using the Kennedy name and connections to get away with murder. However, Michael never identified himself as a "Kennedy cousin" or rode on his relationship with the Kennedys—and for good reason.

The gulf between the Skakel and Kennedy families was always wide and deep; there was so little contact between our families that neither I nor any of my Kennedy siblings or cousins knew Michael Skakel in 1975. I wouldn't even have recognized any of my Skakel cousins at that time. The Skakels never saw themselves as satellites within the Kennedy orbit; they didn't need to. They had a distinctive family history with their own iconoclastic gestalt and greater wealth than the Kennedys. My mother's generation of Skakels prided themselves on being the anti-Kennedys. They were rough and ready carbon Republicans with seasoned contempt for the nanny-state, regulating, soak-the-rich sort of government they imagined the Kennedys promoting. Among their crowd, any association with the Kennedys was a kind of social demotion. "The Skakels and Kennedys were like the Hatfields and the McCoys," recalls Michael.

George Skakel, my maternal grandfather, the second of four children, was born in 1892 and grew up on a homestead near the South Dakota prairie town of Tyndall. George's pedigree was Scotch-Irish and his persuasion was a particularly severe version of Dutch Reform Protestantism. He remained embarrassed by profanity and off-color stories until his death. By all accounts, alcoholism ran through the Skakel clan back to the Neanderthal era. Angry at his father's excessive drinking, Grandpa George ran away from home at age 14, riding the rails to Chicago to seek his fortune.

With his father's example as an admonition, Grandpa remained a teetotaler for most of his life, giving testimony to the old saw that "God invented whiskey to prevent the Irish from conquering the world." Grandpa had ambition, determination, and an entrepreneurial spirit. These qualities, along with a gift for numbers, a photographic memory, and a near-reckless appetite for risk, would make him one of the wealthiest men of his generation. My mother, Ethel Skakel Kennedy, remembers him being grounded emotionally and spiritually, saying he "had a quiet, gentle disposition. His personal humility reflected humble origins. His most striking quality was his generosity. He couldn't bear to see suffering and he always had a hand out for people in need."

After a short stint working for the railroad, he quickly found a job with the William Howe Coal Company, a coal distributor. In 1917 he married Ann Brannack, a tall Irish Catholic from Wabash Avenue on Chicago's tough South Side. Her grandparents on both sides had sailed from Ireland in 1848, at the height of "the starvation" that killed 750,000 Irish and made refugees of millions more. Grandma Ann was loud, brash, and half a foot taller than her husband. She blasted up prayers to the Almighty for hours each day and cheerfully catechized everyone within earshot. She attended daily mass with a fervor that my mother and her brothers would inherit.

My mother described Grandma Ann—using more flattering words—as a striver, who was forever laboring long hours without complaint to better herself and her circumstances. She was an entrepreneur whose many business ventures in later life included the St. Paul's bookstore on Manhattan's Upper East Side and a consignment store under the elevated railroad on the Lower West Side called "Lots O' Little." Out of high school, Grandma Ann attended a secretarial academy she found advertised on a match book. Poor health soon drove her from the febrile Chicago slums to work on a South Dakota Indian Reservation, teaching English to tribal children under Catholic Church patronage. She returned to Chicago a year later "fit as a fiddle" and met George Skakel, who, though initially repulsed by her muscular Catholicism, ultimately surrendered to her garrulous personality and bulldog determination. They married on November 25, 1917, in a Catholic ceremony at St. Mary's Church in Chicago. A decade later, George had seven children, three sons and four daughters, all living at 57th and Wood-lawn, Chicago's most Catholic neighborhood, with his fervent mother-in-law and equally zealous wife.

The drinking flowed from both sides of the family into my mother's genera-tion. Ann's dad, Joseph Brannack, a jut-jawed Irish cop, was a giant with ap-petites to match. His thirst for whiskey scared off his Irish-born wife, Margaret Brannack, who fled soon after her daughter's nuptials and spent the balance of her life with Ann and her son-in-law George Skakel. In her dotage, afflicted by the same genial species of dementia that would ultimately take my Uncle Rucky, she would stuff her stockings with fruit and persuade herself that she was Admi-ral Nelson. The first time my father met her, she shouted from the second story, "Who goes there?" My father, late of the US Navy, answered, "Lieutenant Ken-nedy. Permission to come aboard?" She slid down the bannister to formally greet him with peaches and bananas tumbling from her undergarments.

GRANDPA GEORGE enlisted in the Naval Reserve in 1918 and became an officer, even though he lacked a high school diploma. He trained in Cleveland, Ohio, and served eight months as a Navy ensign during World War I, docking tugboats in New York City. He came home on Christmas Day 1918, so destitute that his only suit was his navy uniform, in which he returned to work at William Howe. St. Ambrose Church provided the neighborhood's social and cultural gravities. My mother, George and Ann's fifth child, still recalls both the poverty and hap-piness of her early youth.

Using his gift for numbers—my mother remembers him easily multiplying seven-digit numbers in his head—George recovered $50,000 for William Howe after discovering that the railroads had been cheating the coal company on haul-ing fees during the war. When the corporate brass refused him his commission for the recovered fortune, he quit, swearing to never work for a boss again.

George persuaded two fellow employees, Walter "Wally" Graham and Rush-ton Fordice (for whom my Uncle Rucky would be named), to cast their lots with his. Each contributed $1,000 to a joint pool and vacated William Howe on the same fateful day to launch their own coal brokerage. They named their ven-ture the Great Lakes Coal and Coke Company and, later, Great Lakes Carbon (GLC). Great Lakes adopted the perilous course of buying and selling only ex-tremely large quantities of the highest quality coal, a strategy for which both the coal sellers and their buyers, the large oil refiners, rewarded them with preferred pricing. Graham's father-in-law was a senior executive at Standard Oil Company, which became their first customer.

Grandpa George spent his career in the world's most polluting industries, leaving, in F. Scott Fitzgerald's words, "foul dust arising from the wake of his dreams." While pollution probably didn't trouble him as a moral transgression, his genius was in reducing it by devising schemes to monetize the industry's abundant waste. Mining companies customarily abandoned coal dust in mountainous heaps around their mines. When the piles of so-called "fines" grew inconveniently large, the companies plowed them into the nearest river. Grandpa foresaw that, during the periodic coal strikes, fines might be profitably marketed to individuals and industries desperate to fire empty furnaces. He contacted mine owners across coal country proposing to buy nuisance fines for five cents a ton. Great Lakes Carbon collected thousands of tons of the stuff and, when the United Mine Workers finally struck, Grandpa sold the fines for over six dollars a ton, a bargain for oil refineries desperate for fuel.

Even though George never made it past grade school, he devoured books on metallurgy and chemistry, geology and business. Browsing through *Business Journal,* he learned of the exploding worldwide appetite for the pure carbon needed to create aluminum for the burgeoning aviation industry. He knew that pure carbon could be gleaned from petroleum coke (petcoke), a waste product of cracking oil into gasoline. As with coal fines, the oil industry's solution for ridding itself of alpine heaps of refinery waste was a bulldozer and a local river. Grandpa signed 99-year contracts with Standard Oil and its competitors to purchase all those companies' petcoke for pennies per ton. In this way he obtained a virtual monopoly on petcoke just as commercial aviation was leaving the runway.

Over the next decade, Great Lakes Carbon sold millions of tons of petcoke in the eastern United States as a substitute for coal in domestic heating, and to the electrochemical and metallurgical industries. In 1935, George and his partners spent $50,000 constructing a giant calcining furnace to refine petcoke, in Port Arthur, Texas. They had the notion to sell the purified version, thereby relieving aluminum companies of an extra step in their manufacturing process and enabling the production of aluminum of unrivaled strength. They quickly persuaded Alcoa, Reynolds, Kaiser, and the other major aluminum companies to purchase their product. They bragged that their Port Arthur oven made $50,000 every six weeks thereafter.

During World War II, George purchased a large region of Moab, Utah, hoping to find uranium. He didn't, but like nearly everything he touched, the venture turned to gold when he struck oil. The easy profits that flowed from his gushing wells prompted my famously laconic grandfather to utter one of the longest sentences anyone recalls him speaking: "Why didn't I get into this racket earlier?"

Despite his lack of formal education, George studied Shakespeare at night. At the breakfast table he commonly read to the children human interest or animal stories from the *Herald Tribune* or the columns of Thornton Burgess. My mother recollects him as "a wonderful dad, always sweet, sensitive, thoughtful, and loving toward his children," and a competent naturalist. He took his kids for long weekend walks and countryside drives, often stopping to identify a bird or a rare tree, or to explain a bit of natural history, his mastery of which was encyclopedic.

My mother's siblings generally inherited their parents' virtues, including Grandma's zealous piety and generosity and Grandpa's driving curiosity about history and the natural world. They espoused highly personalized brands of honor, but despite genuine efforts toward culture and charity, the Skakels never tried to pass themselves off as proper folk. They were carbon nabobs and their roughness showed itself through the generations. All the boys were genuine characters whose only aristocratic pretensions were their robust engagement in clubbing, turfing, golfing, drinking, fishing, and hunting.

My mother lived in Chicago until she was 8 years old, at which time she, with her parents and her older siblings (Georgeann, Jimmy, George Jr., Rucky, and Patricia) moved east, following their father's business to New York, nearer to his customers and bankers. Grandpa's company was on its way to becoming one of the largest private family businesses in the United States. The family settled in nearby Connecticut.

The Skakel house on Lake Avenue in Greenwich was a hybrid of *The Philadelphia Story* and *The Beverly Hillbillies*. Theirs was one of the most enormous mansions, in one of America's wealthiest burbs, with so many bedrooms that it could easily accommodate 30 or more guests in addition to the family. Greenwich at that time was rural horse country with fewer than 6,000 residents, many working or living on large estates. The Skakel home was elegant, graceful, and roomy, with an eight-car garage, a village of outbuildings, an Olympic-sized swimming pool, and a fountain rivaling that at Buckingham Palace. The manse crowned a 10-acre lawn surrounded by 100 acres of woodland and fields. "Even though it was large, it just felt like home," recalls my mother. "There was plenty of land for the kids to hunt and ride horses." Swans preened while the children fished and swam in—and later skated on—a big lake.

Grandma Ann converted their demesne into a farm, a caper that must have struck their swanky Greenwich neighbors as déclassé. She kept horses, turkeys, ducks, 25 pigs, sheep, and two cows. French goats wandered through the house, unchallenged, with 14 dogs. "We had three hundred chickens. I would collect the eggs and milk the cows, which I loathed," my mother recalls.

Grandma Ann's devotion to the Catholic Church was legendary among her friends both in Chicago and in Greenwich. Silver holy water dispensers, religious icons, relics, crucifixes, and saints' shrines with prie-dieu kneeling stations adorned most of the rooms at Lake Avenue. Religious books dominated the collection in the 60-foot-long Skakel library with floor-to-ceiling bookshelves. Ann attended St. Mary's Catholic Church every morning at 7 a.m. The Skakel children grew up praying daily for their father's conversion and Ann always carried a silver rosary and said grace before and after meals. The clan donated lavishly to Catholic charities.

My mother recalls that her mom kept the house thick with clergy and frequently hosted salons for religious societies and assembled a whirl of church groups there for teas. She cultivated a close friendship with the influential Catholic monk, Thomas Merton. The secretive right wing Catholic society Opus Dei launched its American debut at the Skakel house, in keeping with the Society's strategy of aligning itself with wealthy, powerful, and politically conservative Catholics. Ann worked for years on her husband's conversion, with merciless catechizing and regular prayers imploring the Creator's blessings on the enterprise. It was the single request from her that Grandpa resisted.

MY MOTHER was a jock. She was a champion at both sailing and horseback riding and she loved tennis, football, golf, and skiing. My father and mother met during a winter trip to Mt. Tremblant, introduced by my father's youngest sister, Jean Kennedy, my mother's Manhattanville College roommate who had conspired with my mother to unite their families on a ski vacation.

The Kennedys and Skakels dated each other rather furiously after that first encounter. My mother remembers Jimmy and George, a notorious lady killer, dating most of the Kennedy sisters at one time or another. Despite their families' differences, my parents were well suited to one another. They were both competitive, prudish, and pious. My father loved my mother's lively spirit and was intensely proud of her athleticism, her humor, and her peculiar blend of deep religious faith and mischievous irreverence.

After my father and mother fell in love, my mother adopted his family as her own. Historian Arthur Schlesinger described theirs as "one of the great love stories of all time." They married at St. Mary's Church in Greenwich and had a reception at the Skakel mansion on Lake Avenue in June 1950, a year after my mother got her bachelor's degree. It was a lavish affair with 1,200 guests. My father's 27 ushers included his two surviving brothers, John and Edward; the three Skakel boys, George, Jimmy, and Rucky; and several teammates from his Harvard football squad.

With her skepticism toward authority, her self-confidence, humor, and her recklessly competitive spirit, my mother fit right in with her new Kennedy in-laws. And my grandfather Joseph Kennedy and all his children accepted her as one of their own. According to my Uncle John's closest friend, LeMoyne Billings, "She soon forgot she was a Skakel. She became the consummate Kennedy." Lem described her as "more Kennedy than the Kennedys."

When I finally got to know Rucky Skakel's children, in my mid-twenties, I was struck by the tumultuous blend of piety and deviltry. Like all orthodoxies,

Rucky's zealotry was authoritarian and occasionally cruel. I later learned that he beat Michael silly for bringing *Playboy* home from a trove of porn magazines the neighborhood boys found in a covey at Belle Haven Club. Michael laughs, "He told me that masturbation was the equivalent of murdering 10 million potential Christians and that sex was dirty, filthy, and disgusting and I should save it for the girl I loved."

The families seemed ideally matched, with their Catholic piety and love of sports and outdoor adventure. But fault lines soon emerged between the Skakels and Kennedys. At least part of the schism was stylistic. When my Grandpa Joe sent his sons to Europe to work as war journalists or to study under the socialist economist Harold Laski, my mother's brothers George and Jim were working as roughnecks on oil rigs in Utah and in Brownsville, Texas. While the Kennedys were surprisingly chary with their dough, the Skakels practiced a nearly destructive generosity that delighted Catholic charities. Grandpa Joe discouraged his children from riding first class on planes or trains, taking ski trips to Europe, playing polo, or gambling. The Skakel boys, in contrast, were the founders and outstanding players of the Metropolitan Blind Brook and Bethpage Polo Clubs and retreated with the swanks to bet the races at Saratoga every August.

The prevailing narrative of the Moxley murder trial was rooted in the canard pedaled by press and prosecutors that Michael Skakel is a "monstrous, spoiled Kennedy cousin." Putting the "monstrous" part aside, the caricature of Michael Skakel as a Kennedy cousin always seemed strange to me. Our Kennedy parents raised the 29 grandchildren of Joe and Rose Kennedy communally. We spent our summers together in Hyannis Port sailing, swimming, fishing, and playing baseball, football, and tennis. We worked on political campaigns and at Special Olympics. We attended daily mass as a group, took our meals together, and spent every waking moment in each other's company. I am as close to my Kennedy cousins as to my 10 brothers and sisters.

Nevertheless, as I've said, I never knew any Skakels growing up. My mother had turned Kennedy and was estranged from her family. To this day, I have Skakel cousins whom I've barely met and would not recognize.

As Michael had recalled, "the Skakels and the Kennedys were like oil and water." The Skakels were Republican but so little interested in politics that my mother's nuptials into a prominent Democratic family did not set off alarm bells. "When I married Daddy, it wasn't a big deal," she recalls. "They thought I was a little communist, but they all had good humor about it. It wasn't taken seriously." But when she started actively campaigning, she crossed a line. The Skakels were oil and coal Republicans, and like most people in the extractive industries, they were conservative. "Well, my parents weren't bedrock Democrats," my mother says dryly. "Grandpa was neither pro-government nor pro-Democrat." While Grandpa Joe was FDR's top donor in 1932, Grandpa Skakel piped his carbon lucre to the GOP and only rejected an offer to become the Republican Party's national treasurer due to his antipathy for the spotlight.

The only time my mother heard her parents discuss politics was on the subject of "what a bad person President Roosevelt was" and how organized labor was destroying America. She recalls, "The Skakels were very critical of all Democrats, but particularly Roosevelt. They thought he'd be a dictator and they were extremely anti-union." The Skakels were comfortable with people of every station. They often reached out to individuals in need. Grandpa George opened his wallet to children with disabilities and to people suffering deprivation. My Uncle Steve Smith, husband of Jean Kennedy, was unrestrained in his admiration for Grandpa Skakel. "George Skakel was the last great industrialist who really cared about his workers. He made sure all his employees had a safe, dignified workplace and wages that would put them into the middle class. He just seemed to want to share his good fortune with all the people who worked for him."

Personal generosity aside, the principles of representative democracy, or the role of government in protecting the rights of the downtrodden or in fostering an equal playing field, were notions with which the Skakels were not particularly sympathetic. "None of that was ever discussed," recalls my mother. "So it was pretty amazing to come to the Cape and listen to people who cared about the little guy. It was a big change having lunches or dinners with the [Kennedy] family. Well it was just so funny to hear Democrats lauded and admired and what a nice guy FDR was. This was different."

According to Skakel family legend, in September 1955, two years after my birth, Grandpa George reportedly made the momentous announcement to Father Abbott of Thomas Merton's abbey at Gethsemani in Kentucky that he wanted to convert. It was the answer to years of beseeching, imploring, and unctuous supplications by every member of the Skakel clan, and fervent benedictions by their posse of clergy. Grandpa told Father Abbott he wanted to begin the process when he returned from a business trip to the West Coast. He and Grandma took off in a converted Air Force B26 bomber on October 3, 1955. They spent a day in Tulsa and left at 9:45 p.m. the following evening for Los Angeles. Thirty minutes into the flight, both aircraft engines exploded in mid-air. The bomber lit up the sky like a comet and plunged to the ground near Union City, Oklahoma. They were both 63 years old. Police identified Grandma's body by the rosary wrapped around her charred hand.

Uncle George Skakel Jr. had joined his father's business in 1947 and two years before Grandpa's death, he became president of Great Lakes Carbon. By then, the company had 3,000 employees and was manufacturing and selling petroleum coke; carbon and graphite products, including electrodes and fiber; charcoal briquettes; crude petroleum and natural gas filters; and building materials. Its headquarters were at 18 East 48th Street, New York.

In the glow that followed my parents' marriage, Uncle George, an experienced sailboat racer, once agreed to crew for Uncle Jack Kennedy, then a US senator skippering a 28-foot Wianno Senior, in a Cape Cod Regatta. George promptly discovered his discomfort at taking orders from his in-law. He abandoned the enterprise mid-race by jumping into the ocean and swimming to the distant island of Nantucket. It was a signal that George and the Skakel brothers had soured on the Kennedys. There were no more trips to the Cape.

The Skakels supported Nixon in 1960, which stung my mother, but she bore the wound in silence and continued to love her family from a distance. During Uncle Jack's presidential inauguration ceremonies in 1961, George Skakel, for the sake of fun and to show his contempt for the new Democratic president, distributed a pile of coveted, top-shelf family tickets that my mother had acquired for the Skakel family, to some hard-boiled hoboes from Washington's skid row. Uncle Jack's close friend and fellow PT boat skipper, Red Fay, found himself sitting among a dozen pickled winos in the reviewing stand. That, of course, was very funny, but the Skakel brothers became increasingly vocal about opposing my father in his political endeavors, contributing heavily to his opponents. My mother recalls that Rucky was annoyed at my father, then US Attorney General, for bringing an anti-trust suit against Rucky and his business partners when they tried to move their baseball team, the Milwaukee Braves, to Atlanta. The Skakel group eventually prevailed. My father's unwillingness to pull strings felt like treachery to the Skakel brothers, who, in turn, contributed to my father's opponent, Kenneth Keating, during his 1964 New York Senate race. After my father's death, my Uncle Steve Smith, who managed my mother's financial affairs, challenged the management of Great Lakes Carbon by the surviving Skakel brothers. Steve felt that Jimmy and Rucky weren't sharing GLC company revenues among the non-management siblings, including my mother. For years, my mother and her sisters stood on the sidelines and watched Jimmy and Rucky deploy GLC's fleet of company planes all over the world on golf, hunting, fishing, and ski trips that the girls suspected were only tangentially related to business. Uncle Steve hoped he could restore some financial discipline to the company that my mother's father had built. When Uncle Steve's efforts failed, chilly relations between the families turned frigid.

"Let me tell you something," says Julie Skakel. "My father drilled into our heads that we were never to mention the Kennedy name. We weren't even allowed to call Kennedy Airport Kennedy Airport. We had to call it Idlewild." Michael says, "As a kid, it seemed my dad was angry at your family. Remember he and all the Skakel brothers were right-wing Republicans. Dad was furious that Martin Luther King slept around and included all Democrats in his condemnation, particularly your family. He thought King was dragging the nation into an immoral pit of sexual depravity and perdition and that you guys were encouraging him."

Every year my mother's brother Rucky rode in the Rancheros Visitadores, an exclusive, male-only club, on a 60-mile pack trip through the Santa Ynez Valley near Santa Barbara. Ranchero's 600 members were California's oil, gas, and real estate tycoons, the exclusive right-wing aristocracy of the Republican Party. It was one of the macho seasonal musters of the Bohemian Grove's business elite. Members would bond by riding, drinking, dressing in drag or in cowboy costumes, and performing skits. Stephen Skakel showed me a framed picture from the 1967 ride. Then-Governor Ronald Reagan is handing a guffawing Uncle Rucky a mocking cartoon caricature of his brother-in-law—Robert Kennedy—with great Bugs Bunny teeth, protruding ears, and a mop of unruly hair. The Skakels were Kennedy doppelgangers: iconoclastic, irreverent, and unimpressed by the references to American royalty that sometimes attended their in-laws.

The Skakel boys knew that all their devilments came at a price they'd sooner or later have to pay—and they did. Uncle George Skakel Jr. died in an Idaho air crash on September 24, 1966, flying into a remote wilderness airstrip near the Shepp cattle ranch in the Salmon River Valley near Riggins, Idaho. My father's close friend Dean Markham, CIA agent Lou Werner, and two other friends died with him. They were beginning a 10-day pack trip to hunt elk in the Idaho wilderness. The plane, a single-engine Cessna 185 owned by Great Lakes Carbon, became trapped by the nearly vertical walls of Crooked Creek's box canyon and crashed while the pilot was making a desperate, last-ditch attempt to turn. George's friend, Francesco Galesi, who witnessed the crash, recounted to me that, as the plane headed for the wall, George waved goodbye from the co-pilot's seat to his family and friends who had arrived on earlier flights. According to Galesi, George was wearing the broad grin he reserved for moments of extreme peril. The plane nicked some pine trees, hit the palisade wall, and tumbled into the river. George was 44 years old. The crash scene was only a few miles from where my father, my siblings, and I had camped on a Salmon River whitewater trip the previous summer.

In a *New York Times* obituary, conservative icon William F. Buckley Jr. bemoaned his buddy George Skakel's death, which was reported across the nation's front pages. Buckley echoed the Skakels' disdain for the Kennedys, explaining that George was a force in his own right and should not be memorialized for his relationship to the Kennedys. Buckley recalled Uncle George "as a young tycoon and sportsman" of "enormous competence, curiosity, charm" who was "impulsive in mischievous and irresistible ways . . . in the tradition of the total American man," but with the genius for life comparable to that of Leonardo da Vinci.

Following George's death, his brothers Jimmy and Rucky took over management of Great Lakes Carbon. Neither of them had George's interest in the business or his management skills. By 1985, the company was on life support and the family sold it for pennies on the dollar. With competent management, the company quickly regained its value. Ironically for me, a professional environmental advocate, Great Lakes is today one of the shining stars in the Koch Brother's constellation of carbon companies. Bill Koch told my mother that her father's company may be the Kochs' most profitable acquisition.

Funerals were about the only thing that would get my mother back to Greenwich. Eight months after George's death, his widow, Pat Skakel, choked to death on a piece of shish kebab during a dinner party at her home in Greenwich. Their parents' deaths left my four cousins orphaned. Pat's *New York Times* obituary contained a line about my cousins that synthesized the Skakel family gestalt: "Mark, 13, is still in Greenwich Hospital, recovering from cuts and burns he suffered while experimenting with explosives."

Seven-year-old Michael Skakel was among nearly a million Americans who attended my assassinated father's funeral in June 1968. I was 14. Neither of us recalls meeting each other. Michael's mother, age 42, died in an agonizing death from brain cancer a year later.

My mother's youngest brother, Rucky, was confident that he was immune from the dementia that ran through the Skakel family. "I already had that," he once told me, thoughtfully. "And I don't think you can catch it twice." His confidence was misplaced. He died of the disease in 2003, at age 79.

Prior to 1981, I only recall seeing the Skakels once—in June 1965. I have only a distant memory of that day when I briefly visited them at 71 Otter Rock Drive, the house in Belle Haven that became central to the Moxley case. Uncle Rucky bought it in the 1960s with his wife, the former Ann Reynolds. Aunt Ann, another Manhattanville graduate, hailed from the wealthy Chicago suburb of Winnetka, and was as devout a Catholic as Rucky. I was 11 years old when I rode in a trailer from Hickory Hill to join my family in Hyannis Port for summer vacation. We stopped in Greenwich—the halfway point—for the night. It was my first introduction to Rucky Skakel's children. I only recall that there were a lot of them and they seemed wild. Michael would have been 5 years old. I have no memory of him. In 1975—at the time of Martha's murder, I would not have recognized him, and at that time in his life, Michael had no recollection of ever having met a Kennedy.

Politics probably played second fiddle to the Skakels' maverick nature as the force that kept the Skakels and Kennedys apart. "It wasn't just that your family were Democrats," explains Rush Jr. "Even without the political differences, I doubt we would ever have seen you guys. That older generation of Skakels were unbranded iconoclasts. They were right-wing Bohemians—totally individualistic. They liked to keep to themselves. They didn't mingle. They had such huge personalities and they were all so volatile and competitive. Even if they liked your politics, they wouldn't have liked the rivalry. They all seemed to agree to love each other from a distance—and the farther the better. That's why Jimmy moved to California and Aunt Pat to Ireland—to get away from their siblings. They were outsized characters too large to share the spotlight. They needed open range.

"We didn't see you until we all got mobile and found each other," Rush continues. "I didn't know Uncle Jimmy's kids growing up and I never went to the Terrien/Dowdles, even though they lived in the same town. I didn't know them until I was 16 and I started riding my bike over to the fortress at Sursum Corda to see the Dowdle kids. The parents made no effort to put us together."

In the late 1970s and early 1980s, we all began finding each other and discovering that we had a lot in common. My little brother Max met Michael and Rush Jr. by chance in 1978, while skiing at Waterville Valley, New Hampshire. The following year, my brother Michael Kennedy heard he had a Skakel cousin attending the Élan School in Poland, Maine. My brother, who was on his way to run Maine's Kennebeck River with a group of friends, stopped by Élan to meet his cousin for the first time and invite him kayaking. Surveying Élan's vacant-eyed inmates, Michael Kennedy added uncertainly, "You can bring your friends." Michael Skakel remembered the visit with a smile. Shaking his head he said, "He had no clue what he'd walked into! He looked like he'd just blundered into the Thunderdome." It quickly dawned on Michael Kennedy that he had stumbled into some kind of squalid and sinister reform school. Shocked, he asked Michael Skakel, "What are you doing in here?" The visit caused an uproar. Élan inmates and counselors recognized Michael Kennedy and realized, for the first time, that Michael Skakel was some species of Kennedy relative. Despite having been at Élan for months, he had never told anybody of the connection. The counselors accused him of putting on airs. "I took a big pounding after Michael [Kennedy] left," Michael recalls.

We all shared the Skakel sense of fun and a love for the outdoors. At that time, most of the boys from both families were getting sober. Michael has five brothers—all soft spoken, handsome, and athletic. Initially, I became closest to his brother Rush Jr., with whom I share a birthday. The brothers, for the most part, did not adopt their parents' right-wing politics. They were smart, funny, kind, considerate, and unassuming—never ostentatious, even though, in our company, they had a lot they could have boasted about. Each of the Skakel boys was a gifted athlete excelling at the same sports the Kennedys loved.

The first time I remember meeting Michael was in the early winter of 1983. He was recently sober. Michael had graduated from Élan two years earlier, in June 1980, at age 19, with a high school diploma he hadn't earned. "I was hardwired to drink myself into oblivion every day," he told me. "The moment I left Élan, I was back in the bottle with a vengeance. My drinking was worse than when I got locked up. I felt as if my alcoholism had been doing push-ups the entire two years that I was dry in Élan." His discovery that year of cocaine accelerated his free fall. He flunked out of Bradford College and lost his job in the computer room at Great Lakes Carbon. "I was still in denial," he says. "I thought my only drinking problem was that I had two hands to hold bottles and only one mouth."

On October 25, 1982, a month after his 22nd birthday, Michael believes that God spoke to him. He was driving on North Street in Greenwich when he heard a voice ask, "Do you want to keep doing this your way?" A vision of blackness and death flooded his mind, and he watched himself plummeting into a pit. The voice continued, "Or do you want to do it my way?" at which time, a comforting image of a solitary flame replaced the grim spectacle. "I believe it was the Holy Spirit in the car," he says. "I didn't tell anybody for 10 years because I was embarrassed. I thought people would think me crazy." A half hour after seeing the vision, he walked into his first Alcoholics Anonymous meeting. Michael has been drug and alcohol free for the 34 years since.

His life improved immediately. He cofounded and funneled the entirety of his savings—$50,000—into The Serenity Project, a program that helped expose the abuse at Élan and contributed to alumni efforts to finally shut it down. "I didn't want one more kid to go through the hell that I went through." He volunteered for Mother Theresa's men's shelter in the Bronx. When Mother Theresa visited the facility, Michael gave her a bear hug and lifted her off her feet. "I later read that she abhorred being touched," confesses Michael sheepishly. He was also working with the crisis intervention team at Greenwich Hospital and making regular presentations about substance abuse through an outfit called Freedom from Chemical Dependency (FCD) to students, parents, and teachers in classrooms in Darien, New Canaan, and Greenwich. After finally receiving a proper diagnosis for dyslexia, he enrolled in Curry College in Milton, Massachusetts, which offers a special program for students with learning differences. In 1990, he graduated with honors.

I got sober in September 1983, a year after Michael. I lived in Mt. Kisco, New York, only 10 minutes from Greenwich. Michael became one of my closest friends and we spent much of the time over the next 15 years in each other's company. We skied, fished, hiked, camped, scuba dived, and traveled together, often with my wife and children. During that time, I sometimes spent as many as two or three weekends a month with Michael. I brought my children to the Skakels' ski house in Windham, New York, almost every weekend in the winter. We all slept in the bunk room, ate pizza, and skied all day. Together, we taught my six kids to ski, starting when they were 2 years old. My children adore Michael. His natural gentleness, his humor, and his childlike vulnerability give him an easy manner with children. His gift for communicating with kids and making them laugh and his genuine love for playing with them make him a popular favorite among their many fun and funny older relatives. Children appreciate that he is never overbearing, pretentious, or phony.

During that time Michael and I attended hundreds of 12-step meetings together. Every evening at Windham we put my kids in front of a VCR and spent the next hour in some church basement. I got a kick watching Michael inspire laughter reciting his wild stories of addiction and recovery. He shares his experience, strength, and hope with openness and raw, soul-wrenching honesty that melts hearts, cheers program veterans, and encourages newcomers. Michael's natural generosity and openheartedness mesh perfectly with the 12-step formula of service. After nearly every meeting, I watched him seek out and comfort the most shattered or bereft newcomers. He scribbled his telephone number on napkins and AA's big books and then spent hours on the phone comforting fragile and hopeless neophytes, helping them make it through the often despairing days of early recovery. Together, we would pick them up for meetings or sit with them in diners to work through the hard days or nights.

Rather than being bitter or self-pitying over a difficult, often-brutal childhood and his two-year nightmare in Élan, Michael had transformed those years of torture, neglect, and abuse into his greatest capital asset: empathy. Michael is hypersensitive to suffering in others. I've watched his openness about his own struggles alleviate pain and inspire courage in recovering alcoholics. That's not hyperbole. During his sentencing proceedings, 90 people would send letters to the court supporting Michael, with 18 of these attesting that Michael Skakel's moral support and guidance kept them sober. Many of them, including his brother Stephen, said that Michael had saved their lives.

Michael is among the most solidly spiritual people I've ever met. He always carries a rosary and prays it daily. (In prison, he prayed three rosaries on his knees at 3:30 p.m. every afternoon.) During the first decade of our sobriety, we often attended mass together daily. Michael's deeply held religious beliefs and faith in God infuse his every action. He is always trying to do "the next right thing." Yet he lives his beliefs and he practices his religion quietly.

Don't get me wrong; we weren't spending all day in church or meetings. Despite his bulk, Michael, like his brothers, is a graceful and gifted athlete. Like his brother Rush, he is a superb skier. In 1990, Michael qualified for the US World Cup team for speed skiing and earned sponsorships from Swix Wax and Swanee Glove. He was named to the US National Speed Ski Team in 1993 and represented America on the World Cup circuit for the next four years. He landed among the top 10 competitors in World Cup tournaments in Sweden, Norway, and France. In 1997 on the legendary track at Les Arcs, Michael clocked 136 mph. He finished that year ranked third in the United States and 18th in the world. He was 26 years old.

Michael always dresses well. Usually he is in outdoor gear, neat and well-groomed, wearing hunting pants and a sweater, with tweeds that evoke his rustic Celtic heritage. Contrary to the malicious press reports, he has never worn an ascot. He is indeed the opposite of a snob. Humble and hilarious, devoid of pretense or vanity, he is curious about everyone and comfortable in every company. He is nearly always the butt of his own jokes.

Almost nothing the prosecutors said or the press wrote about Michael during the trial was true. No one ever deserved the label of "monster" or "this spoiled brat" less than Michael Skakel. Michael is constitutionally honest and a natural-born gentleman. At all times, he is self-effacing, generous, and unfailingly courteous, as exhibited with his impeccable manners: opening doors for everybody, standing when a woman enters the room, and holding their chairs when they sit or stand. After his trial, jurors complained that Michael had endeavored to ingratiate himself by standing when they entered the courtroom. He wasn't trying to flatter. Courtesy is his nature.

During a visit to Loblolly, Florida, when Michael's cousins and siblings were on the water or playing tennis or golf, Suzanne M. Walsh, a Montessori school teacher from Windham, New York, told me that she spotted Michael crouched in the sweltering 95-degree heat beneath a merciless sun with a bucket of pitch tar and a bale of shingles, putting a new roof on the ramshackle cinderblock home of an elderly lady who once worked for his family. Michael regularly bought her groceries. During a post-hurricane delivery, he noticed a fissure in her roof and returned the next day to patch it. Walsh recalls another day mentioning to Michael that she needed to drain her pond. "Without a word, Michael came over, set up his sump, and did the job."

Michael offered Walsh a ride in Windham in January 1998 only to find an elderly homeless man sitting in front of the car. Michael stopped and talked to the man. With no cash to give him, Michael opened his trunk and pulled out his winter coat, draped it around the fellow and sat down and talked with him for a short while. Then Michael gave him a pat on the back and said, "Keep warm."

In 1991, I was at Michael's Westhampton, New York, wedding when he married Margot Sheridan, whom he met during a Colorado skiing vacation. Margot, a tall, beautiful ski instructor and former racer, had a ready laugh and large, bright, wideset eyes framed by high cheekbones on a broad, open face reminiscent of her great grandfather, Civil War General Philip Sheridan. The two lived in Quincy, Massachusetts, while Michael was finishing college. In the early 1990s they moved to Windham, New York. In 1994, my brother Michael Kennedy, recently sober with Michael Skakel's help, asked Michael to join him in Massachusetts to work on Senator Edward Kennedy's 1994 reelection campaign. Michael and Margot moved to Cohasset, Massachusetts.

After the election, Michael worked briefly as a real estate agent for RM Bradley in Boston and then went to work at Citizens Energy Corporation, the energy nonprofit founded by my elder brother Joe, to provide affordable energy and other services to the poor. Michael Kennedy had been running the company since Joe went to Congress in 1986. In 1995, Michael Skakel became Citizen Energy's international director, supervising projects and assistance to impoverished communities in underdeveloped countries. While employed at Citizens Energy, he helped launch projects in Angola, Ecuador, and Cuba.

In 1997, Michael had a falling out with my brothers. Led by Dominick Dunne and Mark Fuhrman, the wolves were beginning to circle, pointing fingers at Michael as a murderer. Aggravated by his occasionally debilitating PTSD resulting from his time at Élan, Michael partly blamed my family for his woes. Michael became convinced that Joe and Michael Kennedy were promoting his arrest for the Moxley murder. "Michael was mad at your whole family," explains his elder brother Rush Jr. "It wasn't completely unjustified. We all knew that the Skakels had nothing to do with the Kennedys. Yet here he was being persecuted because of this thin, tendentious relationship between our two families. It was like a witch hunt. They were gonna burn him at the stake no matter what the evidence said. That inconsequential link with your family turned out to be this powerful fuel that kept burning and burning 'til it consumed him. It was the Kennedy connection that fed and enriched the press and the whole drama served the interests of the people who hate your family. So they kept fanning the flames. The irony was that Michael never identified himself as a 'Kennedy cousin' and yet that became his epithet. I don't blame him for being angry and suspicious toward your family. Michael doesn't have a drop of Kennedy blood and yet the relationship destroyed his life and destroyed Tommy's life. You could say that it destroyed everyone in our family in one way or another. I made the choice to keep my head down and even to leave the country. [Rush Jr. moved to Bogotá, Colombia, with his family in 1995.] I saw how destructive and toxic that whole relationship between your family and the press was. Between the media and the Kennedy haters, it was like a bluefish feeding frenzy. Innocence and guilt were irrelevant. Everyone in the blood plume was gonna get mangled. Just take a look at Benedict's legal theory as it unfolded. He was not just trying to jail Michael; he was implicating our entire family in a horrible 30-year conspiracy."

Michael left his job at Citizens Energy Corporation and went to work with the International Institute for Alcoholism as a volunteer. He traveled to Russia with the group in order to bring the message of AA to prisons in St. Petersburg. Michael accepted an offer as executive director of the organization, a job that fell through when Mark Fuhrman's book *Murder in Greenwich* named Michael as Martha Moxley's killer. Before long, Michael was under grand jury investigation. Overnight, he became unemployable. The media madness put increasing stress on his marriage; the couple suffered a miscarriage. They sold the Cohasset house and moved to Florida to live with his father and stepmother. While in Florida, Margot gave birth to their son, George Henry Skakel, on December 7, 1998. Michael did housework and took care of the baby while Margot taught golf and worked in school six days a week to get her sports and massage therapy certifica-tion. Michael also took care of Rucky, who was suffering from a long menu of physical and mental health problems. "He'd had prostate cancer," Michael says. "I'd been changing his diaper for two years. I took him to church every day, sometimes twice a day, seven days a week." They lived in Florida for two years.

After Michael was arrested in 2000, the couple moved back to Windham, New York, in order to be closer to Connecticut. Under pressure from the relent-less media pounding and vitriol, Michael and Margot separated in the fall of 2000, and were divorced on September 19, 2001. The divorce decree gave them joint custody of their son.

One Sunday in 2001, after dropping George off with Margot at Windham, Michael saw a broken-down van filled with children on the opposite side of Interstate 287. A man with a military buzz cut stood next to the van helplessly watching traffic pass. A couple miles down the road, Michael did a U-turn and went back. The man, a soldier heading back to West Point, and his wife said they'd been stranded for over an hour. Michael was the first person to stop. Mi-chael called a tow service and waited with the family. When the hooker truck arrived, the driver told him that all the nearby garages were closed. The tow to West Point would cost over two hundred dollars, and the soldier didn't have the money. Michael paid the driver, the kids piled into the tow truck for a fun ride, and Michael drove the man and his wife up to West Point in his car. At this point in his life, Michael spent his waking moments hoping that nobody would rec-ognize him and take him for the monster the media had so effectively convinced the world he was. Nevertheless, and despite Michael's objections, the soldier insisted on taking Michael's address. His wife wanted to send a thank-you note. A few weeks later, Michael received a handwritten note from Major Sean Lewis. The letter would later provide him comfort in prison.

Dear Michael,

I want to thank you for your kindness and true selflessness in assisting me and my family during our time of need. Your actions were far above the call of duty. It took my wife about two seconds to figure out who you were after she read your full name. I wish you had told me. Nothing would have changed in regard to how I would have treated you. . . .

I do not know why you stopped to help us. I do not know why my prayer of "God, please send just the right person to help us" was answered by Him sending you. But what I do know is that God meant for you and my family to come in contact through our misfortune.

Thank you again, from the bottom of my heart.
In God's precious grace

PART II

The Suspects

CHAPTER 4

The Neighbor

Never ascribe to malice that which is adequately explained by incompetence.

—Unknown

Before they decided it was Tommy, and decades before targeting Michael, the bungling Greenwich Police identified a parade of other compelling suspects in the Moxley murder.

Within hours of finding Martha's body, cops fingered W. Edward Hammond as the likely culprit. Hammond, a 26-year-old Yale graduate and army veteran, lived next door to Martha with his widowed mother at 48 Walsh Lane. His bedroom window faced the spruce tree that shadowed Martha's body. The meandering drag trail suggested Martha's killer initially hauled her body toward the Hammond house, then abruptly tacked toward the pine tree. The police surmised that Hammond may have killed Martha and briefly considered bringing the body home before panic and dogs prompted him to reconsider.

Martha's body was still lying beneath a sheet in the grass when detectives Joe McGlynn and Steve Carroll began canvassing the neighborhood. When they rang Ed Hammond's doorbell, they had already pegged him as a spooky loner. Neighbors said he'd been drunk since his father's death two years earlier. The concrete was already hardening on Martha's 10:00 p.m. time of death, and Hammond had no alibi. He claimed he'd been home alone, watching *The French Connection* on television, while his mother was at the Belle Haven Club for a late dinner. While searching Hammond's bedroom, police hit the jackpot. "We thought, 'Oh man, this is him,'" Officer Steven Carroll told author Timothy Dumas in 2001. "There were all kinds of skin magazines. And this was sick: he would masturbate in condoms, then put the condoms back in his closet. Joe and

I were like, 'Let's get somebody down here right now.'" By mid-afternoon, the officers were manhandling Hammond into a squad car as neighbors and press ogled. Confident that they were on to something, the cops returned for Hammond's Mischief Night attire. McGlynn recorded his incriminating wardrobe:

1. One pair men's beige-colored corduroy pants. Blood-stained left upper leg
2. One men's knitted sweater, color red. Unknown type stains on chest area
3. One pair men's brown leather topsider shoes. Moccasin type boat shoe
4. One blue men's shirt, size 17–34 "Alexander" bearing unknown stains on front of shirt

The police had found red knit fabric on Martha's body that was similar to the material of Hammond's blood-stained red sweater.

The Belle Haven rumor factory would become a painful scourge for each Moxley murder suspect in turn, and it took only moments for Belle Haven's minutemen to grab their pitchforks for the Hammond lynching. At 10:00 p.m. that evening, cops got a call from Cynthia Bjork, the platinum blonde who had moved into a home behind the Hammonds five months before. The Bjorks' springer spaniel was one of several Belle Haven canines that yelped, bawled, and bayed at the time of the murder. It then dashed over toward the crime scene at 9:50 p.m. After watching police haul Hammond downtown, Cynthia Bjork couldn't wait until morning to give the cops the lowdown. Hammond, she said, according to police reports, "Always appeared to her as [. . .], a little odd, and a heavy drinker." Hammond had stopped by once when her husband, Bob, was out of the house, with "a very strong odor of alcohol on his breath," asking to borrow a saw. Moreover, Hammond had declined a tennis invitation from her husband claiming his little finger hurt. "Mrs. Bjork could not recall any off-color remarks or sexual advances made by Hammond at this time," although he once chatted about sunbathing. Another time, Hammond called asking to borrow a bottle of Scotch for a party, but never picked it up. The morning after Martha's murder, the Bjorks awoke to discover "a sweet smelling puddle of fluid . . . that smelled like shaving lotion . . . at the base of the main stairs." Since a cellar window in the Bjork home had been left open, the Bjorks felt that Hammond might be the culprit. Greenwich Police recorded these tips and then rushed off to interview Hammond's Yale professors and his college roommates. As a precaution, they called the FBI to check on Hammond's passport to assess his flight risk. Moxley family friend Jean Walker told police that she felt Hammond staring at her from his window when she stood by Martha's body moments after Sheila McGuire reported her grim discovery. Walker accused Hammond of burglarizing his own sister's house and reported that girls had been murdered at Columbia and Yale when Hammond was enrolled in those schools.

Mayo Lane resident James Proctor, former Belle Haven Association police commissioner, confirmed that Hammond "seemed strange in his actions" and "doesn't socialize." Another Walsh Lane neighbor, Jean Wold, reported that Hammond had appeared at her front door at 9:30 a.m., six months before, behaving strangely. According to the police report, "He wanted to see her dog, which she had recently purchased." Neighbors reported that Hammond had been at a cocktail party at the Moxleys on October 25; they seemed to recall him talking to Martha.

Hammond confirmed the police's worst suspicions when he refused their request to take a polygraph. He declined to talk, except through an attorney. Such behavior caused the police to devote much of their investigatory manpower to Hammond in the weeks following Martha's murder. But then the case collapsed. On November 2, the Department of Health determined the blood on Hammond's sweater to be type O, which Hammond said was his type, and attributed to a nosebleed. (Oddly, during Michael's appeals, prosecutors produced Hammond's army records showing Hammond's blood type to be A.) He finally consented to take a polygraph. The first one, on November 13, was "inconclusive." Hammond blamed his subpar performance on his recent ingestion of Antabuse, a drug used to treat alcoholism. Veteran homicide investigators later criticized Greenwich Police for their blind faith in the Delphic powers of polygraphs. That fault was Hammond's good fortune. A week later, he passed the test and Greenwich Police scratched him from their suspect list. "I thought they were hoping that I was a convenient suspect," Hammond told an interviewer decades later. "And if they could wrap it up quickly, that would be great." The police's near-exclusive focus on Hammond during this period may have allowed evidence to vanish, memories to fade, alibis to consolidate, and the trail to go cold on the true killer.

Beginning in 1993 Dominick Dunne began widely broadcasting his toxic canard that "the Skakel family conspired in 1975 to thwart the police investigation." Dunne chastised the Greenwich Police "for its reluctance to challenge the power and wealth of the Skakel family." In 2000, Dunne said on CNN, "The Skakels were able to hold off the police all these years. . . . If this was a family of lesser stature, that simply would not have happened." Benedict, as I've shown, rested his case on his ability to beguile the jury into believing this conspiracy was real. However, even a shallow dive into the case file reveals a more mundane story: a police force out of its depth. Fuhrman, Dunne, and I disagreed on almost everything about this case; but we did all agree that the police fumbled it badly. "The Greenwich Police Department," wrote forensic criminalist Henry Lee, "was quite simply, overmatched by the complexity of this homicide investigation." Even *Newsday* reporter Len Levitt, who would become a cheerleader for

Michael's persecution, told the *Hartford Courant,* "There was no cover-up. There was a screw-up."

From the moment searchers discovered Martha's body, Greenwich cops had to fight the widely held public perception that the 147-member force was unqualified to crack a serious crime. On November 2, 1975, the *New York Times* reported derisively that the Greenwich PD "have not had a murder to investigate in nearly 30 years, and are normally more accustomed to investigating traffic accidents and burglaries." Such ridicule undoubtedly rankled the force's senior brass. They could have handed Martha's murder investigation off to the State Police, which had extensive experience with capital crimes. Instead, they dug in to prove the naysayers wrong. "It was all ego," Sutton Associates' Jim Murphy said later. "It's all that inside fighting that takes place between police station chiefs."

Murphy started his career in the 1960s with the NYPD, and then spent 15 years in the FBI. In 1972, Murphy was the G-man who drove bank robbers John Wojtowicz and Sal Naturale and their hostages from the Gravesend, Brooklyn, Chase Manhattan Bank they had robbed to JFK Airport. The two bandits demanded a plane ride out of the country. (In Sidney Lumet's film *Dog Day Afternoon,* based on the case, Al Pacino played the Wojtowicz character and John Cazale played Naturale.) In the backseat, Naturale held a shotgun to Murphy's head during the ride. At JFK, Murphy swiveled to snatch the shotgun then fatally shot Naturale with a pistol that his comrades had hidden beneath the floor mat, and the crisis ended. Before founding Sutton in 1990, Murphy led the Bureau's Eastern District of New York office, where his team conducted multiple murder investigations. He clearly has the background to state: "The Greenwich Police never should have handled the investigation. They don't do homicide investigations. They should have called in the State Police, someone that had experience in doing homicides. Had someone else conducted it there would have been more thorough searches done at the very beginning that would have picked up other pieces of evidence."

As the case grew colder, cops found themselves increasingly acting as a clearinghouse for Belle Haven's dirty laundry and the wild speculation of its abundant busybodies. Detective Steve Carroll would characterize their targets as "people with drinking problems and violent tempers, oddballs or loners, a lesbian couple, a retarded girl."

On November 6, 1975, Upper East Side, New York, psychiatrist Jane Wetenhall, the mother of Martha's friend Jackie, tearfully told Carroll that her husband, John, might be the killer. John was an unemployed alcoholic living as a hermit in the family attic. He hadn't appeared, even for meals, in five years. "Wetenhall related that there were several sets of golf clubs in the house at this time and this department was perfectly welcome to look at same." After questioning John Wetenhall in his lofty lair, Carroll scratched him from the suspect list.

Carroll's dispatch of the Wetenhall investigation was not typical of other witnesses. As with Ed Hammond's girly magazines, the Greenwich Police continued to treat minor indiscretions as *prima facie* evidence of involvement with the murder. The Greenwich homicide team spent precious days vetting and polygraphing a female Field Point Drive resident, now a Connecticut State trooper, whose villainy was smoking pot. Suspecting a connection to the murder, police dispatched teams of technicians to tap Belle Haven residents' phone lines to trap a prank caller.

Meanwhile, the police often left legitimate leads uninvestigated. For example, the police never investigated a spooky murder-night drama reported by Sheila McGuire, the teenage neighbor who found Martha's body. Sheila recounted the chilling tale to my investigator, Larry Holifield, saying that she drew only blank stares when she repeated the story multiple times to Greenwich Detectives Jim Lunney and Steve Carroll. The Greenwich officers didn't even write it down. The night of her friend's murder, Sheila was out on a blind date with a local boy named David, with whom Martha had set her up. David dropped off Sheila at the bottom of her long driveway on Field Point Drive at around 11:00 p.m. and drove off before Sheila got inside. When Sheila reached the locked front door, she realized she didn't have a key. As she knocked on the door, she heard a loud banging from the unattached garage; it was the entry door slamming. Someone was inside. She describes the incident as the most frightening moment of her life. In a panic, she dove into her father's parked car, locked the doors, and hid on the floor. After an hour, she bolted from the car, and her sister opened the front door, allowing her to rush into the house. The McGuire property was directly adjacent to the Moxleys' property. Their garage was the first structure that a murderer would have encountered fleeing the crime scene south away from Walsh Lane.

On October 31, the morning after the murder, police investigators released the Bjorks' spaniel, hoping it would find the murderer's scent. The dog had barked forlornly at 9:50 p.m. and then dashed over toward the murder scene. That morning the dog led police to the McGuires' house. Pound Ridge, New York, vet Dr. Edward Fleischli told police that the dog had witnessed the murder and was trying to follow the scent. Police never inspected the garage or dusted for fingerprints.

The Greenwich Police were only interested to know if Sheila had tried marijuana, which she admitted. Police pulled Sheila out of class once, and another time woke her at 2:00 a.m. to sweat her into confessing she was dealing weed. She withstood those withering interrogations, but police gravely informed her parents of their daughter's illicit toking, while critical leads evaporated like smoke.

Lack of curiosity and overconfidence in the polygraph were not the Greenwich force's only problems. Shoddy crime scene management and substandard collection protocols for forensic evidence also hobbled the inquisition. The

Greenwich Police possessed no yellow tape to cordon off the crime scene. "We were all standing around, looking over at the body covered up with a sheet," recalls Peter Coomaraswamy, Michael's friend and neighbor. "We couldn't believe there was anybody underneath it, because we were all like, 'Why would they leave someone's body underneath a sheet all afternoon?'" Millard Jones, the first officer to respond when Sheila found Martha's body, watched that afternoon as a neighborhood dog licked the blood trail in the Moxley's grass. Jones's partner, Dan Hickman, was petting the dog. Neither officer had experience or training in crime scene management or evidence collection. Sheila says that Officer Hickman was so distraught that she found herself comforting him. She was only 15.

Dozens of cops would trample the crime scene by 5:30 p.m. that night, when the coroner staff finally removed Martha's body. Police misidentified, mislabeled, or lost critical evidence, including a bloody pair of pants with a 36-inch waist and a bloody pair of size 13 high-top Keds sneakers that police showed to Helen Ix. Police also lost a golf ball found beside Martha's body and beer cans collected from the murder scene that may well have borne the killers' fingerprints. State criminalist Dr. Henry Lee testified at Michael's trial that police found "many hairs" on Martha's body. "We found a lot of hairs." Evidently, police lost all but a few. Lee complained that the police failure to make out laboratory worksheets made it impossible to determine what work had been done and what became of the evidence.

Connecticut's medical examiner, Dr. Elliot Gross, took vaginal and anal swabs and slides and sent them to the Department of Health, run by Dr. Abraham Stolman. Both the swabs and slides disappeared. No one looked at the swabs to determine if they contained DNA material, including Y-chromosome (male) DNA.

Both Hickman and Jones remembered seeing a golf club handle protruding from Martha's neck when they first arrived on the scene. Jones recalled, "You could see the leatherette or vinyl grip (of the handle), and my wife swears that's what I told her when I came home that night." Dr. Richard Danehower, Martha's personal physician, also saw a shiny golf club handle lying next to Martha's body. Police never logged the handle, which also soon disappeared. At trial, Mickey Sherman exhibited monumental incompetence—even for him—by allowing Benedict to persuasively argue that Michael Skakel had disposed of the handle to conceal his mother's name on the grip.

Such police fumbles are normally gold for criminal defense attorneys. Any competent barrister could have minted the mishandled evidence into an acquittal. And for good reason: lost evidence deprives the accused of a fair chance to defend himself. DNA analysis of those lost vaginal and anal swabs and slides could have cleared Michael; both Michael and Tommy Skakel freely offered to provide their DNA samples to investigators. But Sherman didn't know how to capitalize on the blunder. "Mickey Sherman wouldn't know how to make hay, if he were sitting on a hay bale," observes Michael.

In December 1975, Greenwich Police decided that they'd finally identified the real killer. As had been the case with Ed Hammond, everybody in Greenwich seemed to have an anecdote connecting themselves to the suspect du jour, and all of them suddenly became certain of Tommy Skakel's guilt. Dan FitzPatrick, an attorney who in 1985 married Martha's friend Helen Ix, witnessed this odd phenomenon firsthand. "I didn't become familiar with the case until the early 1980s, but for many years, at every social engagement I attended where the topic came up, people would say they knew that Tommy did it," FitzPatrick says. "Then, when Michael became a suspect, the same people claimed—with the same level of certainty—that Michael definitely did it. I was flabbergasted that no one acknowledged the irony of this flip-flop. If that's not evidence of the presence of reasonable doubt, I don't know what is."

In truth, Tommy was a far more compelling suspect than Ed Hammond, and a far, far more plausible culprit than Michael ever was. Tommy didn't kill Martha, and his alibi is nearly as solid as Michael's, but it's understandable why he became the patsy. Tommy was the last person to see Martha alive. Tommy, who had been caught telling lies to the cops, had personality quirks that helped make him a long-term scapegoat. Probably as a result of the suspicion that shadowed him since age 17, Tommy is guarded, enigmatic, and opaque, and therefore less sympathetic than his transparent, cringingly open-hearted and garrulous younger brother. Tommy has been beaten down for so long by suspicion, judgment, and accusations that he rarely bothers to defend himself. For a quarter-century, his criminal lawyer chastised Tommy to never speak about the murder and as a result, silence has become muscle memory. When he ought to explain himself, he doesn't. For that reason, Tommy has never been a good advocate for Tommy. He's likely to meet an accusation with dead air, a response people understandingly interpret as affirmation.

In the early 1980s just after Michael had gotten out of Élan, Michael and Tommy flew with Uncle Rucky aboard the GLC Convair to Las Vegas on a two-day stopover for a little rest and relaxation. Michael found himself alone with Tommy at Caesar's Palace. "Tommy," Michael said, "if you did this, I forgive you, and I still love you."

I asked Michael how Tommy responded. "He didn't say anything to me. He just sat in silence." Tommy's life has been nearly as devastated as Michael's. Although he didn't go to jail, he spent a quarter-century as the police's prime suspect, with even his closest relatives not knowing what to think.

But before they got to Tommy, Greenwich cops had to leapfrog some other compelling suspects.

CHAPTER 5

The Brother

If you tell the truth, you don't have to remember anything.
—Mark Twain

Had some Moxley aunt married into the Kennedy family, Jonathan Benedict could have brought a far more convincing case against Martha Moxley's brother, John, than his confused and wobbly prosecution of Michael Skakel. Benedict would have been able to appropriate the blueprint for his prosecution from a Sutton Associates report like the one he turned against Michael. A 23-year-old Sutton employee named Jamie Bryan wrote a scathing "Worst Case Scenario" report on John Moxley, far more damning than his companion report on Michael that became the basis for Mark Fuhrman's book and subsequently for Benedict's prosecution. The band of bards who cashed in on Michael's misfortune—Dunne, Fuhrman, and Levitt (and his silent partner, Garr)—presumably had John Moxley's "Worst Case Scenario" in their possession, yet none of them has ever acknowledged its existence. The Sutton report, which distills the Greenwich Police files, shows that the police were, after all, guilty of putting the brakes on the investigation of a wealthy Belle Haven family. But that family was the Moxleys, not the Skakels.

Out of solicitude for their tragedy, Greenwich Police gave wide berth to the Moxleys. Anybody can understand why, but veteran detectives consider courtesies to the victim's family one of the most perilous pitfalls of rookie homicide investigators. Department of Justice homicide data show that in incidents in which victims knew their killers, between 24 and 30 percent of perpetrators were family members. While police questioned Ed Hammond and the Skakel children about three hours after Sheila McGuire discovered Martha's body, they did not interview John Moxley until 10:00 a.m. on November 1, nearly 24 hours later. In recounting his Mischief Night timetable, John said that, following an evening with friends, he returned home at 11:20 p.m.

Five days later, Steve Carroll interviewed Theresa Tirado, a housekeeper who had worked for the Moxleys for a year. Tirado told Carroll that she arrived for work at 8:00 a.m. on October 31, 1975, four hours before the discovery of Martha's body. Dorthy Moxley told Tirado not to clean John's room because he was sleeping late. A short time later, Tirado passed by John's room on the second floor; his door was open, the bed empty. "Theresa further related that at 9:00 a.m., while in the living room of the Moxley house, she heard a loud crash in the basement," according to the report. Tirado first saw John at 9:15 a.m., when his friend, later identified as John Harvey, appeared at the house.

Martha now had been missing for 12 hours and Belle Haven was in a state of fearful chaos as neighbors and their children frantically searched for the missing girl. Nevertheless, John and his friend were serenely detached. Tirado related that the pair remained in the living room watching TV until about 11:00 a.m., "and then both left and went out the back door to the wooded area behind the house." This was precisely the area where Sheila would discover Martha's body an hour later. The boys returned to the house a few minutes later and then drove off in Moxley's car. After the two boys left, Tirado cleaned the TV room where she "observed, on one of the tables, what appeared to be smears of blood as if from three fingers," the report read. "She did not think anything of this and cleaned it up." In a case in which police discovered no blood evidence outside the crime scene, the discovery of a bloody handprint in the victim's home was consequential. Remember, police also found blood smears on Martha's thighs, suggesting that the murderer's hands were blood-soaked.

Even after Carroll's interview of Tirado, police did not rush over to inspect the house and search for blood and fingerprints. Instead, Detective Tom Keegan invited John Moxley to the station for an interview. That delay provided plenty of time to hide evidence and wipe the scene. John recounted that he had fallen asleep at about midnight. Around 3:30 a.m. on Friday morning, his mother woke him in a panic that Martha had not come home. After dressing, he went on a two-hour hunt in his Mustang that carried him far from Belle Haven. "His search also took him to Riverside, Cos Cob, and the Bruce Park areas of town," the report read. "He completed his search at about 6:00 a.m." Rather than go up to his room when he returned home, John slept in the TV room where Tirado would later find the bloody handprint. John told Keegan he saw no blood. The smear, he guessed, was probably food, since the whole family used the TV room. It's unlikely, however, that the red handprint was from another family member: John's father was out of town and Martha hadn't been inside the house since late afternoon the previous day. The banging in the basement? John had no idea. Neither he, nor his guest, John Harvey, "were using the weights in the weight lifting room and he could not recall either one of them picking up a weight and dropping it by accident, but added that it could have happened." Harvey, he said, came by at 9:00 a.m. If Harvey had come to assist in the search, the mission was notably devoid of urgency. "Both he and Harvey watched some television, and after securing the TV set, he and Harvey left the house and went to a wooded area at the rear of the residence," Keegan's report read. "Their reason was to check behind an eight-foot wall, directly to the rear of the house, which had a large pile of brush. After checking, they returned to the house."

When they finally got around to checking the Moxley house interior a week after Martha's murder, the search was cursory and slipshod. Greenwich Police Sergeant Roland Hennessy ambled over at 11:00 a.m. and offered this indifferent report: "With the permission of Mr. J. David Moxley the undersigned checked the entire basement of the Moxley residence, with negative results." Hennessey doesn't report even visiting the TV room, where Tirado spotted the blood smears.

John's odd account hiked eyebrows among the distinguished former G-men and other homicide investigators at Sutton Associates.

"John told the police they went out behind the house to look for Martha in a 'brush pile,'" the Sutton report concluded. "On the surface, this is a slightly strange inclination—not to mention an unlikely place to find one's sister. Furthermore, if John was making even a mildly concerted effort at looking around the property for his sister, it borders on the incredible that he never noticed Martha's body, lying only yards away to the side of the house," and a few feet from where the pair had walked during their abbreviated search. His search effort was both strikingly lackadaisical and narrowly specific. John's reconstruction of his morning search suggested to Sutton's Jim Murphy that John might have been leading his friend to Martha's body, a common pattern when one family member murders another. For this reason, trained murder investigators carefully monitor search parties. "Whenever a wife, or husband, or a child is missing and a family member organizes, and then joins, a search party, you often see that family member leading the search party right to the body," Murphy explains. "They can't stand the thought of animals getting to the body. That's what I thought might have been going on here."

John's narrowly targeted brush pile search wasn't the only thing that got Murphy thinking John might have suspicious knowledge. Sutton used hypnosis to clarify dim recollections and ensure truthful responses. Sutton retained world-class forensic hypnotist Dr. Nancy Vrechek to excavate 20-year-old memories. Under hypnosis in 1994, Julie Skakel offered an eerie account of a pre-dawn meeting with John Moxley. After a series of increasingly desperate calls from Dorthy Moxley, Julie answered the ringing phone yet again around

3:30 a.m. Mrs. Moxley told her that John was outside searching, and asked Julie to help him.

DR. VRECHEK: So you went outside and met John. Was that the first time you've met him?

JULIE: I'm not sure. I had seen him. I may have met him once briefly.

DR. VRECHEK: What did you do then? What was John Moxley doing?

JULIE: We started yelling Martha's name at the pool, since we were standing right there. I started feeling ridiculous because John wanted me to go . . . across Walsh Lane onto his property and look for her. And it didn't make sense.

DR. VRECHEK: Because?

JULIE: Because if she were in the area, she would have heard us calling. And if she were with someone, she wasn't about to answer.

DR. VRECHEK: Why would she be with someone? Well, why would she not answer?

JULIE: Well, if she had been with a boy and didn't want her brother to know.

DR. VRECHEK: It didn't make sense that he wanted you to go across to the Moxley property to look for Martha?

JULIE: I just remember going across their front lawn and along the side of their yard. I think I said something like she's not around here. It seems senseless to keep calling her name since our properties were so close.

Julie told me she didn't tell Greenwich Police this story in 1975 because they never asked her. "They just kind of asked the same *pro forma* set of questions to everybody and there was never any probing or any curiosity about anything outside of that framework; they were checking off boxes. There were many things I didn't tell them about that night because they never asked." Julie repeats the story she told Vrechek. "I can remember locating him by the ash on his cigarette," she says. "He was standing on Walsh Lane, which is between our properties, and I remember seeing his lit cigarette coming over to our property, and the pool is right there and very meekly he's like, 'Martha? Martha are you there?' It was almost a whisper. It was spooky. Then he leads me over to his property. He starts bringing me towards the real wooded part. I got really, really scared and I just said, 'I have to go' and I turned and I walked away very fast." In retrospect, I asked Julie what she thought John was doing. "He was leading me right over to the tree," she says. "It was the creepiest thing. He definitely was leading me directly toward that pine tree where they found her body. It was bizarre."

John gave interviews to Sutton investigators in the 1990s. He blew his top when he heard Julie's account, saying that she made it up and none of it took place. According to the Sutton memo: "[John Moxley] was advised that Julie, twice, under hypnosis, stated that she met him at about 3:30 that morning and that they did look for Martha. John is willing to take a polygraph examination on this and other issues regarding the night of October 30, 1975." Julie is similarly adamant. "I'll take a lie detector test, absolutely without a doubt," she says.

I asked Murphy for his thoughts. Particularly, I wanted to know if it was possible that Julie could have imagined or invented this story, and if it is difficult to lie under hypnosis. "If you have a good hypnotist, it is," Murphy says. Vrechek, he said, was the best. "She'd be able to tell when someone is not being truthful." As for the story, he doesn't think it sounds like something a person without a background in criminology would invent. "I think that's pretty sophisticated casting of a doubt for Julie to figure out," he says. "I don't know that she would know that this is typical of somebody who has killed a member of their family."

John's chronicle of his night has varied considerably over the years. On the stand, Dorthy Moxley testified that she woke her son at 1:30 a.m., two hours earlier than John told police in 1975. She said that she only began her frantic telephone calls after he returned from a short search. John was out, she testified, "not too long as I recall." Mrs. Moxley may not have been a particularly good witness. According to the Sutton report, "Mrs. Moxley is alleged to have been intoxicated on the night in question." According to Tirado's recounting of the morning of October 31, Mrs. Moxley told her not to clean John's room because he was sleeping late. John told police that after returning from his search he never went back to bed, and instead collapsed on the TV room sofa. Six days after the murder, John detailed for police an extensive rambling patrol, lasting over two hours, spanning the remote outposts of Greenwich, and ending at 6:00 a.m. When prosecutors questioned him on the stand, however, John's peregrinations had contracted, dramatically, in length and scope. "I got in the car and drove around the neighborhood and, you know, I didn't think it was a big deal so I drove around for 15 minutes and came home and went back to bed." In 1975, he told cops that he'd pretty much been up all night. Now he was testifying to only being up for a quarter-hour and sleeping in his bedroom. Commensurate revisions by Tommy and Michael made them murder suspects.

To police in 1975, John described his early evening on October 30—the period before his 11:20 p.m. return home—as a wholesome evening. He'd picked up his friends John Harvey and Vinnie Cortese. The trio went to the A&P grocery store, then on to Greenwich High School, where they watched preparations for the weekend's pep rally. Next, they went to the Dairy Queen, a local roost for teens. From there, they drove to the Greenwich Civic Center, and then returned to the ice cream parlor. After that, he dropped Cortese and then Harvey at their houses and arrived home at around 11:20 p.m. John acknowledged an alibi gap in this timeline, when he disappeared on a mysterious detour in his own car. "John stated that he had been separated from Vinnie and John Harvey for a short time, when he left the high school and arrived at the Dairy Queen." The Greenwich Police never questioned John Moxley about the specific time of this separation. Police did not seem curious to know if John's alibi gap spanned the 9:45 to 10:15 p.m. period when Martha was bludgeoned to death. Police never determined the duration of his disappearance, or the name of the driver who transported his friends from the school to his alleged rendezvous at Dairy Queen. Later information cast doubt on whether he and the boys went to Dairy Queen at all.

Harvey's recollections of the night were similar to John's, but Harvey switched a detail that signaled John's whole alibi would soon unravel. Rather than a visit to the civic center, Harvey told police they'd gone to a party on Cognewaugh Road in Cos Cob, Connecticut. The Sutton team wondered whether John Moxley wanted to conceal from cops he'd been drinking beer, or something more sinister? The police report noted that Detective Joe McGlynn had reached out to Vinnie Cortese. There are no notes from the interview in the file. My detective, Larry Holifield, reached Cortese, who gave an account of the evening considerably different than Moxley's and Harvey's. He said Moxley, Harvey, and he were among a gang of 10 or 15 guys who started out Mischief Night near the football field. Later, he, Moxley, and Harvey drove around in Cortese's car, engaging in light hooliganism (egg throwing and the like).

By trial, Moxley's account of the evening was vague, shuffled, and incomplete. "I went out with a bunch of friends," John testified. "We used to hang out at the Dairy Queen. Then we went to the high school for a little while. There was a group of people preparing for a pep rally for the weekend for the football game and then I came home." True to form, Sherman let the inconsistencies slide.

John's actions the next morning, October 31, raised suspicions at Sutton. They had already flagged the odd brush pile search as an area for inquiry, but John seemed to dissemble when detectives asked about that morning. "In one of his recent interviews with Sutton Associates, John said, curiously, that it was not John Harvey, but someone named John Anthony who arrived that morning for a visit." The Sutton investigators wondered if Moxley was deliberately altering his friend's name in order to misdirect Sutton out of fear that the trained homicide detective would find and question Harvey with the professional rigor the Greenwich PD lacked. By the time of Michael's trial, both the brush pile search and John Harvey had vanished altogether from John's testimony. "Woke up, had breakfast," he testified. "My mom told me that Martha still wasn't back, started to get nervous about that. We had a walk-through football practice. It was earlier that day than what it would be if we had school. So I left and went to football practice."

Holifield tracked down John Harvey, who confirmed the early-morning brush-pile search. This is from Holifield's report: "He and John spent about

15–20 minutes walking around the Moxley property, mostly in the backyard area. They also walked briefly in the front yard passing by the driveway near the spruce tree where Martha's body was located shortly after noon. Harvey had no explanation for why they didn't see Martha's body, but believed it was there at the time."

John Moxley was at practice when Sheila discovered Martha. Greenwich football head coach Mike Ornato summoned John and told him, "Look, something happened at your home. You need to get there right away."

On December 2, 1975, John passed a polygraph commissioned by Greenwich Police. On his first meeting with Sutton investigators in 1994, he told them that he thought that the police wanted him to take the lie detector not only because of the blood Tirado had seen, but also because when he arrived home from football practice, he yelled out, "That's my sister over there." Sutton assumed that the policeman stationed at the end of the driveway heard John's exclamation when he jumped from the car. At Michael's trial, John testified that he only learned of Martha's death once inside the house. The Sutton team wondered what prompted him to make the statement that had piqued police interest. After all, John had not previously expressed concern about Martha's disappearance and her body was not visible from the Moxley driveway. He told author Tim Dumas that he didn't know the nature of the emergency when he got home. "There was a sea of police cars," he said, describing his arrival home. "There was no question in my mind that this was a major police event that involved us somehow." He told Dumas that he rushed toward his house to see what was happening. According to Dumas's account, on the Moxleys' front steps, his father's co-worker, Lou Pennington, intercepted him to deliver the news that his sister had been "killed." Pennington's words could have described any number of causes of death, accidental and otherwise. Dumas related the exchange that followed:

JOHN: How? Was she stabbed or something?
PENNINGTON: No. Hit with a golf club.

After Fuhrman and Dunne began pushing Mrs. Moxley to condemn Michael, John Moxley became the vocal scourge of the Skakel family. He aggressively promoted his deeply held conviction that Michael was the killer and that other Skakels were co-conspirators. But in earlier days, his preferred suspect was Kenny Littleton.

Sutton's summary of a September 7, 1994, interview reads: "John Moxley stated that, in his view, Littleton is a very, very troubled individual. He believes that Littleton, at one time, had a sexual identity problem and that this belief was based on conversations he has had with several of Littleton's friends. He also volunteered that some of Littleton's friends thought that he may have been gay.

John further volunteered that he thought that Littleton may have been using steroids, although this is only a feeling on his part and he has nothing to support his belief."

Then, in the context of discussing Kenny, John said something that disconcerted the Sutton team. "It was at this point in the interview that John stated that, in his own mind, he made a connection between the manner in which Martha's body was found, with her jeans and underwear rolled down and her buttocks exposed, and Littleton's possible sexual problems," the Sutton report read. "He believed that the body found in this position may have been as a result of Littleton 'trying to fuck her in the ass.' Suffice it to say, the words chosen by John Moxley to convey this scenario struck our investigator as being offensively incongruent with the way one would expect a brother to speak of their deceased little sister."

Sutton would shut down its investigation in 1995 on orders from Tommy Skakel's lawyer, Manny Margolis, before detectives could complete a more thorough investigation of John Moxley. However, John Moxley's name kept popping up in interviews with Frank Garr, who had, by then, taken over the case from Carroll and Lunney. On April 10, 1992, Sheila met with Garr to review her memories. "Sheila reported that she remembered having no fear of Tommy, no fear of Michael, or any of her other friends, and being terrified of John Moxley," Garr typed in his official police report, dated April 10, 1992.

According to Garr, "Sheila reported that on pure speculation, she always suspected John Moxley [as Martha's killer]. Her reason was based on the fact that John really did not like Martha's boyfriend, Peter Ziluca. . . . According to Sheila, Peter had been to Martha's house, and John was furious, and started chasing him around the house with a baseball bat, threatening to kill him. According to Sheila, John Moxley had a drinking problem. She described him as a hostile, tense person, with a hot temper, and reports that ever since then she has feared him. Sheila reported that John had gotten Bonnie Drucker (not her real name) drunk, and date-raped her just after the murder. Apparently, they had been in a car, at the end of Walsh Lane. However, Sheila reports that Bonnie was a bit promiscuous with John, and never reported the incident."

Garr apparently did not follow up on this lead. (Garr refused to talk to me about his work on the case.) But Garr had an uncanny gift for hearing only the evidence he wanted, for filtering out facts and leads that were inconsistent with his theme, and, as we shall see, for inventing evidence when the truth was inadequate. Two years after Garr took Sheila's statement about the rape, a woman named Frieda Saemann, a longtime Greenwich resident, visited Garr with a new take on Moxley's alibi.

Saemann knew John Salerno, who was in John Moxley's senior class at Greenwich High. Saemann told Garr that Salerno had been with John Moxley,

John Harvey, and Vinnie Cortese the night of October 30, 1975. Here was a revelation. Despite intense questioning over many years, Moxley had never mentioned Salerno. Following Martha's murder, Salerno's life had fallen apart. "He was a National Honor Society student, however, according to Ms. Saemann, immediately following the murder, Salerno's grades began to drop and he ultimately did not graduate from high school," the report read. Saemann told Garr that Salerno was working as a carpenter in the US Virgin Islands. She also provided the name of another acquaintance, Virginia Liddell, whose daughter had a friend who attended Ohio Wesleyan with John Moxley. "This friend heard John Moxley confess to murdering his sister in a drunken stupor." Larry Holifield located Liddell and her son and left them many messages, none of which they returned. He was unable to locate Liddell's daughter.

Garr invited John Salerno's mother, Marie, to the station. She confirmed Saemann's story. Her son was with John Moxley the night of Martha's murder, and his life had entered a death spiral after the murder. "Mrs. Salerno reports that in 1975–76, her son's senior year at Greenwich High School, he became disinterested in school, and ultimately did not graduate with his class," according to Garr's report. Salerno said that her son had gone to summer school, then to Boston College, but dropped out after a semester, saying that college was not his thing. "Mrs. Salerno could give no reason for the lack of interest in his school work." She reported that she had been unable to discuss the murder with her son, who immigrated to the Virgin Islands in 1989, where John Moxley would visit him. According to the report, "John Salerno would not talk about the murder, and cautioned his family not to discuss the murder with John Moxley. She reported that another one of her sons had learned of Martha's death and when he told (his brother) John, John cried."

A week later, Garr reached Salerno in the Virgin Islands. During the telephone interview, Salerno confirmed that the rambling trio, described by John Moxley and John Harvey throughout the ages was, in fact, a quartet. He said John had picked him up in his car. They bought a bunch of beers, and eventually made it to Greenwich High for the pep rally preparations. From there, they went to a party; Salerno recalled it as being on either Cat Rock or Cognewaugh Road. In Salerno's account, there were no trips to Dairy Queen.

Holifield tracked down Salerno on December 16, 2015. He was living with his mother in her Lyon Avenue home. Holifield rang the Salernos' doorbell and spoke briefly to Marie, who again lamented that her son had been a straight-A student until Martha's murder. Five minutes later, a white Chevy Suburban backed into the driveway. John Salerno rolled down his window and spoke to Holifield for over an hour without getting out, which Holifield and his co-investigator Greg Garland found peculiar. It was just past 2:00 p.m., and Salerno smelled strongly of alcohol.

Salerno said that he and John Moxley had been close since the Moxleys arrived in Greenwich. They played football for Greenwich High together. Salerno had scored over 1300 on his SAT and had a bright future, but, devastated by Martha's death, he began drinking heavily and smoking a lot of pot. Salerno teared up when he related how he would tuck six packs of Michelob under a bush at the Moxleys for Martha. He said it took years before he admitted this to John, whom he described as highly protective of Martha. Salerno remembered John discovering Martha drinking beer with Gray Weicker, the local Greenwich hockey star and son of then–US Senator Lowell Weicker. Infuriated, John assaulted Weicker with a baseball bat. Holifield's report states that Salerno was "pleasant and talkative although he was extremely evasive when describing the details regarding the night Martha was murdered." Salerno reported that the four boys went to several "keg parties" that night, but his recollection of anything beyond that was suspiciously vague, despite Holifield's probing. Apparently, John Moxley and John Harvey had tapped "Dairy Queen" as a euphemism for keg parties.

Salerno said he was unimpressed by Garr's 1994 phone interview. He said it struck him that the detective was just going through the motions. Salerno gathered from the call that John Moxley was a suspect, so he couldn't understand why Garr's interview was so perfunctory. After all, he was one of Moxley's alibi witnesses and Garr asked only a few heedless questions about the night of the murder and did not press him on details. There were a hundred obvious questions Garr could have asked, for instance: What time did John leave the group? How long was he gone? How many beers had he had? Why did neither John Moxley nor John Harvey mention that Salerno had been out with them? Did Salerno accompany John on whatever trip he went on? Did he go back to Belle Haven at any point? Did John witness something that might have set him off? Police reports do not indicate that Garr made any effort to confirm John Moxley's supposed Ohio Wesleyan confession.

Unsurprisingly, Sherman never contacted Salerno.

During Michael's probable cause hearing, Judge John Kavanewsky gave Sherman a letter the judge had received from an Oakland, California, physician, Dr. Mark Knopp, who knew John Moxley and offered his detailed suspicion that John was involved in three bludgeoning murders in Oakland, California. The victims included a friend of Moxley's wrestling teammate, George Zador; a travel agent neighbor of the Moxley's; and a young girl who was Moxley's schoolmate. Dr. Knopp said that John was on the Montera Junior High golf team and he suspected John had two Toney Penna golf clubs owned by the team coach in his possession in Greenwich at the time of the murder. John admitted chipping golf balls in his Belle Haven yard. Police found a golf ball near Martha's body.

It wasn't until December 17, 1975, 50 days after Martha's discovery, that Mrs. Moxley made it to the State Police Crime Lab in Bethany, Connecticut, where so many Skakels had preceded her, to be polygraphed. She received courtesies never extended to Tommy Skakel. "Mrs. Moxley was too nervous," the report read, and the troopers "felt that the test would be futile." The troopers explained this to Mrs. Moxley and her son; she agreed to try again after the holidays. There is no record that the police ever attempted to retest her. The Greenwich Police impulse to treat the grieving Moxley family gingerly is understandable. But it neither advanced resolution of the case, nor served the interests of blind justice.

CHAPTER 6

The Boyfriend

Jesus, if Peter found out, I would be dead.

—Martha Moxley

Greenwich Police also gave a mulligan to Martha's boyfriend, Peter Ziluca. If there is a sinister figure in Martha's diary, it is Ziluca. The month before she died, Martha wrote, "Sometimes I wonder why I go with [Peter]. He's always telling me he hates me." In her September 12, 1975, entry she describes his black moods. "Peter was being his usual self again," she wrote. "Margie talked to him & she said that the reason he wasn't talking to me was because he got really wasted & he felt like everyone was laughing at him." In the same entry, she described a flirtatious driving lesson with Tommy, followed by a chilling hypothesis. "I drove a little then and I was practically sitting on Tom's lap 'cause I was only steering," she wrote. "He kept putting his hand on my knee. Then we went to the Gazeebo [*sic*] . . . Jesus, if Peter found out, I would be dead!!" (Michael appears innocently in the story: "We went to Friendly's and Michael treated me and he got me a double but I only wanted a single so I threw the top scoop out the window.")

Following her drive with Tommy, she wrote that she intended to end her relationship with Peter. It's the closest thing to an actual motive for murder that she offers for anyone in her milieu. "Yesterday I decided I really don't like Peter anymore." Martha's last diary entry is dated a day before her death. She had not yet broken up with Ziluca.

Michael Skakel's childhood friend and Belle Haven neighbor Peter Cooma-raswamy describes Ziluca as a "badass" who wasn't scared to fight. Michael says he was a "tough guy" quick to anger, good with his fists, and possessive about Martha. Martha, Michael says, was Peter's steady girl and he would have been furious to learn that she was dating other boys. Ziluca was a Belle Haven version of the Fonz, but without the laughs. By all accounts, he was an angry 16-year-old kid who was already deep into drugs.

Experienced detectives would have automatically treated Peter as a "person of interest." In 2007, 45 percent of murdered females were killed by intimate partners, about half of whom they'd never married. And Martha's diary provided Peter with a clear motive. Her journal is a catalogue of assignations with other boys during the period she was going steady with Peter. Martha fretted that he was curious about the contents of her diary. "Tyler & Peter came over & took my diary & boy was I pissed," she wrote. "So I ran out of the house & those guys (Margie etc.) were on their way over. So Margie talked to Peter. Well any ways, I am still a little mad but at least he apologized." If he managed to get a look at the journal, he would have been crushed by her fast-paced juggling, often with older boys. Mark, a college freshman, propositioned her on July 4, 1975. "By the way I forgot to say . . . Mark said to me—'Do you want to go for it?' But I said no (not at 14)." Two days later, on July 6, she was with a high school senior. On July 9: "There were 6 FOXES [she wrote her code for desirable boys in capital letters]. There was Mark, Brad, Matt, Larry, Ralph & Skip. Me & Karen got really bombed. Me and Matt were together & Karen & Brad. (We both went to 2nd.)" The following day, she reunited with Mark. "All of a sudden we were making out! El foxo!" she wrote. "Mark & I went downstairs to his bedroom ON the bed. We went to 3rd, he was so fuckin' cute! About 6'2" very dark (tan) dark hair, brown eyes, very foxy!"

Peter seems to have made powerful emotional and psychic investments in Martha as his girlfriend. Peter professed his love for Martha to author Tim Dumas. He both idolized and idealized her. He told Dumas that she was a virgin and that he had safeguarded her virginity, suggesting his aspirations for a long-term relationship. He talked about his "pride" that she was his steady girl because she chose him over Senator Weicker's son, Gray—another suitor. Initially, he "knew" Martha would never go out with him and yet she did. He described his adoration for Martha as "love at first sight." There was a sense of possessiveness when he spoke of Martha. One can imagine the catastrophic blow he would have suffered had he discovered her cavalier ramblings. Adolescent love is a heightened emotional experience—ecstatic and intense. First heartbreak is correspondingly painful and traumatic. Statistics show that people only rarely kill members of the opposite sex without first loving them. A toxic brew of betrayal, lost possession, shattered dreams, and injured pride provokes men to kill their lovers. Neither Michael nor Tommy enjoyed the kind of profound emotional attachment to Martha that might lead a jilted lover to do her harm.

As with so many Greenwich stories, Peter started life as privileged kid with limitless promise before addiction sidetracked him. Peter was the great, great grandson of Giuseppe Garibaldi, a founding father of Italy. A floor broker on the New York Stock Exchange, his father prospered sufficiently to raise Peter and his four sisters in a Greenwich back-country home so colossal that the locals referred to it as "The Castle." Peter's parents divorced when he was 12. By the night of Martha's death, Peter was living in a smaller home with his mother, Nancy, on Old Church Road beside the Greenwich Country Club.

Unconfirmed rumors of Peter sightings in Belle Haven on October 30 abound in the hazy mist of the Moxley murder, but I found no corroboration. His mother, who died in 1992, provided Peter's alibi. Cops first interviewed Peter at 10:30 p.m., five days after Martha's murder. A local matron, Mrs. Barrington Fuchs, called police to say that she had eight of Martha's friends, including Peter, sitting in her living room on Mayo Lane. Greenwich Detective Jim Lunney soon appeared to question the children, including Peter, who told Lunney that he'd last seen Martha at 2:00 p.m., at the end of the school day Thursday, October 30, at Greenwich High. Lunney's notes are characteristically listless, despite Peter's role in Martha's life. "Martha wanted to come to his house on Thursday evening, but he advised her that he was tired and was going to bed early," the report read. "Further stated that he was going to call Martha, but it had gotten late, so he did not call her. Related that he stayed home with his mother."

Two days later, Detective Steve Carroll called Nancy Ziluca by phone. "Mother of Peter related that her son was with her all evening in the house," Carroll's report read. Immediately after hanging up, Carroll attended to more pressing matters—trying to coordinate a polygraph for then–prime suspect Ed Hammond.

Lunney finally visited the Ziluca house on Tuesday evening, November 4, leaving the Zilucas five days to reconcile alibis. Lunney interviewed the mother and son without separating them—a classic rookie blunder. There is an interesting discrepancy between his two interviews. Peter said that on October 30 he couldn't see Martha because he was "going to bed early." Peter and his mom now told Lunney the pair had stayed up until 11:30 p.m. watching TV together, an excruciatingly long marathon date for a self-described "wild" teenaged boy and his mother. Stephen Skakel wonders, "What if, after standing Martha up for dinner, Peter drove the car to Belle Haven only to surprise her leaving Tommy's arms?"

Peter's explanation as to why he skipped Mischief Night is questionable. With no school on Friday, the 1975 Hell Night was billed as a blowout event for Greenwich teens. Peter knew his girl would be out making mischief and that she wanted to be with him. His mother had urged him to go see Martha and loaned him her car. So it's surprising that he chose to spend the night with Mom. He told Dumas that " '[i]t was creepy outside. The branches of the trees were tapping ominously on the windows. For once in my life I was scared I was like, 'No, I'll stay home and watch *The French Connection*. It'll be fine. I'll see her tomorrow.' "

For a strapping 16-year-old with a reputation as a pot hound and a tough kid, fear of venturing out on Halloween Eve seems a labored explanation.

Abandonment and anger were running themes in Peter's life. Like so many others affected by Martha's death, his life took a nosedive after the murder: his mother evicted her wild boy, and she left for Santa Fe. His destructive shenanigans exhausted his father, who—according to consensus—disinherited Peter. Peter skipped college, married, and then divorced a local girl named Randi; they had two children. After working briefly as an options broker in San Francisco, he moved back to Greenwich and scraped by doing landscaping and woodworking. He sold homemade craft goods, including wooden neckties and hand-carved cummerbunds at local fairs, and built a fat rap sheet in the Fairfield County Courthouse. In 2003, for example, police arrested him for third-degree assault and criminal mischief, to which he pleaded guilty. The following year, police busted him for first-degree criminal trespass and criminal mischief. A court convicted him of the latter charge. Following that arrest, Peter moved to New Mexico. His 2009 mug shot is the picture of a desperado. Santa Fe police charged 49-year-old Ziluca with battery for assaulting his sister Gina, knocking her over a patio table and cutting her arms. He stayed in jail for three days; his sister didn't press charges. The photo shows a rough character with long, greasy, graying hair. He would qualify as a scary guy in the grimiest dive bar. Mug shots are never flattering, but Ziluca's hollow-eyed sneer was bracing. I'd only seen pictures of him as a handsome, clean-cut Greenwich teenager. Less than two years later, he'd be dead, overdosed on a cocktail of vodka, hydrocodone, and cocaine. At the time of his death he was with two females and his roommate, 42-year-old Zachary Smith. Smith was a frequent guest at the Santa Fe hoosegow: he'd had 27 encounters with the local police, and had once been interviewed at the scene of a homicide.

Peter was only a footnote at Michael's trial. In the hands of a qualified defense lawyer, he would have provided the basis for a compelling third-party culpability defense, but Sherman never called him. "I saw Peter Ziluca this morning at the gas station," Sherman told Michael one day during trial. "He sent his regards and told you to 'hang in there.' He said he knows you are innocent." This is how Michael learned that Sherman represented Peter on his Connecticut criminal matters. Characteristically, Sherman never disclosed that conflict to Michael.

In fairness, Tommy Skakel had a different take on Peter than his brothers. Tommy never regarded him as a menacing, mean, tough guy. Tommy was friendly with Peter's sister—"the most beautiful girl in Greenwich," according to Tommy—and saw Peter as a shy, sweet, preppy kid with a kind and generous heart. Peter may have been just another nice kid driven off the rails by addiction but the case against him would have been far stronger than the case against Michael.

CHAPTER 7

The Gardener

We don't know if we live or die, so we rape the women.

—Franz Wittine

During his 1978 to 1980 stay at Élan, the Maine reform school and drug rehabilitation facility, counselors and fellow inmates beat and tortured Michael almost daily in an effort to make him confess knowledge of Martha's murder. No one at Élan believed that he had committed the murder, but the staff considered the accusations and throttlings therapeutic. Nevertheless, the ordeal excited Michael's curiosity about the real culprit. His research convinced him it was Franz Wittine. Following his release from Élan, Michael arduously bird-dogged Wittine to an address in Germantown, New York. "I want you to know, that I know you killed Martha," Michael told him. Wittine's only reply: "I didn't do it." I recently asked Michael whether, in light of his own painful experience with false accusations, he feels remorse now about accusing Wittine. He replied, "Not in the least. Even if Franz had nothing to do with killing Martha . . . he molested my sister. I wish I'd punched him in the nose."

Franz "Frank" Wittine was an odd duck. For decades he worked as Uncle George Skakel's gardener and, after Uncle George and his wife, my Aunt Pat, died in 1966, Rucky hired Wittine and his wife, Paula, who helped clean the house. During the week the Wittines lived together in the Skakel basement and spent weekends at their upstate residence in Walden, New York. Wittine, who was 61 in 1975, was an ethnic German born in former Yugoslavia. He spoke with a thick Austrian accent, was compact and vain, and always slept with a hairnet. He and Paula kept separate beds. The Skakel kids were petrified of Paula, who commanded them to eat all of their food out of respect for starving people and beat them mercilessly when they did not. Rucky finally fired her six months before Martha's murder for belting one of the kids, a prerogative he considered proprietary.

But for Rucky's sustained alcoholic miasma, Wittine would not long have kept his job. Stephen remembers eating carrots with his brother David in the garden as they watched Franz and Paula load Skakel silverware into the bonnet of their Volkswagen Beetle. Young Stephen assumed it a Yugoslavian game. After the couple returned inside, Stephen retrieved the cutlery and buried it in the garden. The Wittines got caught rifling Skakel drawers so often it became a running joke among the older Skakel brood.

Wittine served under Hitler as a soldier during World War II and remained sentimental about the Third Reich. "Frank loved talking about the war with the children," Stephen recalls. Julie and Michael both remember his oft-expressed nostalgia for despoiling women during his soldiering days. "Vee don't know if vee live or vee die, so vee rape zee vimen." He reminisced wistfully about wartime pillaging as he carpooled the boys to school. Michael remembers asking the Skakels' cook, Ethel Jones, "Ethel, what is rape?" The question confounded her. Stephen remembers, "Ethel went bullshit. She said, 'Who the devil told you that word?'"

Wittine didn't entirely change his ways after the war. According to Julie, Wittine earned a reputation for sexual aggression among Belle Haven's belles. Franz was physically powerful with a taste for young girls and a preference for blondes. Franz's lascivious advances toward Julie's girlfriends spooked them from visiting the Skakel house. Julie's cousin Georgeann Dowdle confided that Frank had "attacked" her; Andrea told Julie that Wittine had cornered her and grabbed her breast the year before Martha's murder. Julie says that Wittine was "sexually inappropriate" with her, though she declines to elaborate. Andrea and Julie went to the Greenwich Police following Wittine's assaults. The desk sergeant advised them to forget about it. Stephen heard complaints that Wittine molested at least one other female cousin.

Martha apparently had her own run-in with Wittine. In the days following Martha's murder, Cissie Ix spent hours in the Moxley home consoling Dorthy Moxley. One afternoon, Mrs. Moxley asked her, "Who's Frank?" Ix was nonplussed; she knew no teenagers named Frank. "Because I've been reading Martha's diary," Mrs. Moxley continued, "and in it, she says she's afraid of someone named Frank." When Ix mentioned "Frank" to her daughter, Helen didn't hesitate. "I knew immediately who 'Frank' was," she says. "I thought, 'That has to be Franz the gardener.' We were all afraid of Frank. He was super-creepy."

After Martha's murder, Cissie Ix returned to an earlier memory of Franz Wittine. Anne Skakel was still alive at the time. "I remember one day I went over because Anne was going to give me some tomatoes from the garden," she says. "As we were standing there watching, Franz drove the tractor over a golf club that was lying on the lawn. Franz was infuriated. And Anne said, 'Well Franz, the least you could do is pick up the club!' And he said, 'That will teach the boys not to leave clubs on the lawn.'"

On December 4, 1975, Wittine made a statement to Detective Lunney that police would cite to substantiate their theory that the Toney Penna murder weapon came from inside the Skakel house. He said that on October 29 he walked the entire Skakel property and saw no clubs lying on the lawn. He didn't stop there. According to the police report, "He further stated that he could not remember finding any clubs on the grounds prior to this date." Beyond Cissie Ix's memory, anyone who had ever spent any time at the Skakel house knew this to be lavishly false. The lawn was a virtual sporting goods junkyard. Rucky maintained a chipping tee with two flags in the backyard to practice chip shots. I asked Peter Coomaraswamy if it's plausible that clubs could have been arrayed about the Skakel property on October 30. "It wasn't just plausible; it was a fact." Did he specifically remember clubs lying around? "Absolutely!" he swears. Many other neighborhood kids, including Margie Walker and Michael's Brunswick classmate, Tony Bryant, testified at various times that the yard was perpetually cluttered with clubs, rackets, bats, balls, and lacrosse sticks. Margie told the State's chief detective, Jack Solomon, in April 1992, "There used to be all kinds of stuff lying around, you know, out by the pool area, golf clubs, tennis rackets, balls, all kinds of stuff." Jackie Wetenhall also told police that there were always clubs left around the Skakel yard. Margie's brother Neal Walker affirmed that description.

The question is, why was Wittine lying? Interestingly, he gave the police two other tantalizing items of misdirection, both seemingly intended to cast suspicion on Tommy. Wittine told investigators that Tommy often walked the neighborhood with a golf club. This was another fable: Rucky Skakel carried a golf club to fend off dogs on his daily walk to the beach, one of the reasons he kept a barrel of clubs at the mudroom door. "Tommy never walked the neighborhood, period. He drove," says Michael. Wittine also said that on Mischief Night he heard Tommy walking up the staircase at 10:15 p.m. "Unless he was Superman, Franz would not have been able to hear those footsteps, much less identify their author," observes Stephen. "The staircase was carpeted with deep pile a full story above Franz's basement apartment."

On November 17, the Greenwich Police first brought Franz Wittine down to the station to inquire about his Mischief Night activities. He said that at 8:45 p.m. he was upstairs in the kitchen watching TV when Kenny Littleton and the kids got home from the Belle Haven Club. Annoyed by the racket, he repaired to his basement lair at 9:00 p.m. and listened to the radio until 10:00 p.m. He then slept soundly. However, Michael went down the basement stairs around 8:45 p.m. to access the liquor cabinet next to Wittines' room. The lights were off, which was unusual, and Franz wasn't there. Franz claims he rose the next morning at 6:15 a.m. to let out Max, the Skakels' Belgian shepherd. But, the Skakel siblings say that Max spent that night at the vet. Wittine said that at 8:15 a.m., Mrs. Moxley came over looking for Martha and asked him to check the Revcon motor home. According to the police report, "He related that he checked the camper earlier and no one was in the camper that time." Why was he checking the camper earlier? The Skakels have no idea. But what mystified the family most was that Wittine abruptly quit his job and fled Greenwich shortly after the Moxley murder, abandoning a famously generous Great Lakes Carbon 20-year pension that would have vested in three months had he only stayed on the job.

On October 30, 1975, Wittine's wife wasn't staying in Belle Haven; his only alibi was himself. The back steps leading to his basement room allowed him to come and go without notice. "In most places," observes Julie, "a self-confessed war criminal who's inappropriate with young girls, lives in a basement, and says he was alone all night listening to his radio a couple hundred yards from the crime scene, and only yards from where the victim was last seen alive, would be high on police's priority list in an open murder investigation." But Wittine passed a polygraph and the Greenwich Police moved on. At that point, police were nipping at the heels of their latest suspect, Kenny Littleton. They never looked back at Wittine.

Julie still thinks Franz Wittine is a compelling suspect. She wonders whether Wittine might have witnessed Tommy's assignation with Martha, then followed her home, toting a golf club. It would certainly explain his lie about the clubs on the lawn. Julie recalls his abusive aggression toward young girls and points out the ease of entry and exit; the staircase from his basement dwelling led directly up into the mudroom, allowing undetectable entry and egress. "He easily could have gone in and out and nobody would have known," she says.

Three years after the murder, the Skakels' Belle Haven neighbor, 46-year-old Gloria Sproul, told police she walked into the Colonial Inn in Old Greenwich and spotted Franz Wittine working there. She caught his eye and expected that they'd have a pleasant word or two; Wittine had spent weeks painting her house a few years earlier. He avoided her gaze. She found his behavior so strange, she called Lunney to tell him. Wittine made his final blitzkrieg to that great Reichstag in the sky, or elsewhere, dying in 1997 and leaving more questions than answers.

Finally, Mrs. Moxley also showed Martha's diary entries describing Martha's fear of "Frank" to Margie Walker and Jackie Wetenhall before handing it over to Connecticut prosecutors. Benedict kept Martha's diary in his possession and used it at trial. However, when Michael's team inspected the diary, all the pages about Martha's fears of Franz Wittine were missing, presumably removed by Benedict or Garr.

CHAPTER 8

The Crush

Everyone knows that if you've got a brother, you're going to fight.
—Liam Gallagher

After their mother's death, the Skakel brood went feral, especially Michael and Tommy. Tommy had always been his parents' favorite. Helen Ix remembers, "Tommy was the dapper Skakel brother. He was the suave one. He was the best dressed. He wore Gucci loafers, flew planes, and he was very good looking." But following Anne's passing, even Tommy felt the sting of his father's unhinged despair. Julie says her father adopted an habitual lament: "I have three failures. You're my number one and Michael's number two and Tommy is number three."

To those outside his immediate family, Uncle Rucky was a mensch, a church and community pillar, a generous and kind friend, the life of the party. I experienced him as a somewhat addled but genial bruin with a bald head and prodigious gut who always greeted me at his door with a belly bump and a jovial smile. At his first introduction to my then–brother-in-law, HUD Secretary Andrew Cuomo, Rucky bumped him forcibly enough to bounce Andrew from the front stoop. I loved spending time in Rucky's library, a museum of natural history artifacts—including the giant skull of a loggerhead sea turtle he had found on his travels.

Rucky, a prudish Catholic, attended mass daily and despised pornography. He loved to dance, but unlike his brothers George and Jimmy, he was neither a bar drinker nor a ladies man. Even after Anne's death, he was circumspect and restrained about dating. His best friend was Cissie Ix, a slim and curvy buttoned-down Greenwich matron, with sparkling eyes, a bright smile, and an appreciation for both Rucky's spirit and charming quirks. Ix still lives in the house on Walsh Lane, adjacent to the Skakels' former residence and across the street from the Moxleys. She tells me that almost every day until he moved to Florida in his dotage, Rucky visited an elderly shut-in, Mary Louise Harwood, who shared his loves for God and golf. When Harwood's caretaker found herself without transport, Rucky bought her a car. He hosted regular meals for nursing home seniors and opened his pool each summer to special needs kids from a local camp. Like his brothers, he slept with an arsenal of loaded weapons beneath his bed. I never saw Rucky's angry side, but before he quit drinking in 1977, violent rages were a defining feature of his relationship with his children. "Everyone thought he was just this really great, great guy, and part of him was," Julie says. "He was gregarious and extremely generous anonymously. He helped so many people buy homes and put their kids through college and never wanted repayment. But let me tell you, when that front door closed, it was a completely different story."

My Uncle George's death devastated his brother Rucky, the most sensitive of the elder generation's three Skakel brothers. He idolized George, and relied on his judgment in business, politics, and personal affairs. Rucky flew out to Boise in the GLC Convair and then hiked up the Salmon River to retrieve George's body from the wilderness crash site. According to Tommy, Rucky was never the same. "The experience shattered him and he never recovered." Tommy recalls. "When he tried to talk about it, he would break down sobbing." Rucky lost interest in everything—including his children. "After that," remembers Tommy, "whenever we had a problem, he would tell us, 'See Tom Sheridan.'" Rucky spent the next 31 undistinguished years as chairman of GLC. According to Stephen, his father never showed any interest in running the family company. "My father wanted to be a teacher," he says. "He loved his books. He loved his crossword puzzles and the outdoors. I don't think he ever really gave a shit about Great Lakes." My mother concurs: "Unlike George, Rucky had no talent for business and was the first to admit it."

Sheridan was Rucky's longtime friend and confidant, as well as the Skakel family bursar and lawyer. Sheridan and Rucky's relationship began in the late 1960s. Sheridan and his brother Bob bought a parcel known as the Cave Mountain in the depressed Northern Catskills in 1961 and converted the basin to a ski resort they dubbed the Windham Mountain Club. They cut the land into parcels. Rucky was one of the first buyers. The resort, from its inception, had languished on financial life support and, in 1981, the Pennsylvania-based resort company Snow Time rescued Sheridan from penury by buying the joint. Sheridan redirected his business genius toward managing Rucky's legal and financial affairs. "He was a failed real estate lawyer from the Catskills," says Stephen. "Dad made him the executive VP of the Great Lakes Carbon land business. It's no wonder the company went belly-up." After the leveraged buyout of Great

Lakes in 1985, Sheridan went back to practicing law. "Tom had only a single client—Dad." The Skakel children are unable to name another account that Sheridan had in the thirty years they knew him.

Rucky entrusted Sheridan with a wide-ranging portfolio. He was bursar, money manager, crisis coordinator, family lawyer, and consigliere. Rucky considered him his loyal friend and sounding board. While Sheridan did not have Rucky's wealth, the two men were, in other ways, mirror images: They were ardent Catholics born within a year of one another. They liked to hunt and they were both drunks. Sheridan's capacity to function while blasted gave him ever-increasing power over his client's affairs.

When doctors diagnosed his wife, Anne, with aggressive melanoma in 1968, Rucky took refuge in alcohol and religious zealotry. His drinking, always excessive, degenerated. He started each day with a liquid lunch: Canadian Club on the rocks with milk. As Anne's prognosis bleakened, Rucky's moods darkened and a manic religious fervor possessed him. He spent wantonly on ancient Christian relics. Heirloom shipments arrived daily from the Holy Land and Rucky supervised his household in ritualistic prayer over ancient bits of cloth or bone shards, hoping to cure Anne's inoperable cancer. Rucky presided severely over the seven children as they knelt away painful hours on marble floors at St. Mary's Church, reciting two customized novenas for Anne during double daily prayer sessions, one in the morning and another after school. "Oh my God, it was a nightmare," Julie told me, laughing. "But the afternoon one became a little more fun after Michael, an altar boy, discovered the tabernacle and wine locker in the vestibule. So before mass started, we would grab handfuls of hosts and drink the sherry. It made the prayer marathons bearable."

As is the case with fundamentalism in all denominations, the gravest sins in Rucky's brand of Catholicism were sexual, and his strictures became more rigid, his chastisements more draconian as Anne's cancer metastasized. Michael feels that his father was trying to stem the spread of Anne's cancer through the imposition of strict sexual mores. At age 10, Michael took a memorable beating after Rucky discovered his collection of *Playboy* magazines pilfered from a cache he and his neighborhood chums discovered at the Belle Haven Club. Rucky throttled him, alternating between violently kicking him and slamming him against the wall while repeatedly screaming, "You little slime!" According to Michael, "Sex was the worst sin—even thinking about it. Dad expected Julie to dress no more provocatively than a nun to preserve her from provoking erotic thoughts in strangers."

Rucky tried to shield the children from the awful sight of their mother as the advancing brain cancer blinded her and drove her mad. He moved Anne to Greenwich Hospital and forbade the children from visiting her during the eight months preceding her death. By the end, they prayed that she would die, and when she did, corrosive guilt about those prayers plagued Michael, Tommy, and Julie for years.

The cancer that killed Anne turned Rucky mean, and Michael became the target of his anger. Severe dyslexia had always made Michael a terrible student. But after Anne got sick, Michael's academic failures became a reliable trigger for Uncle Rucky's fury. "I hadn't seen my father in two or three weeks, because he was on a business trip to Japan," Michael told me. "I couldn't wait to see him. When he got home, he came straight up to my room. I sat up in bed, and he looked at me and said, 'You make me sick. If you only did better in school, your mom could come home from the hospital.' It makes me feel like throwing up just repeating it right now."

One Sunday in March 1973, the Skakel kids returned from the family's ski house aboard the Revcon bus that Rucky had purchased to shuttle them on weekend trips to the Catskills. Seeing the line of cars in front of the house, they knew their mother had died. Rucky climbed aboard to tell his kids he expected a Spartan farewell: "You know what happened. If you need to cry, go to your rooms." Then he stepped off the bus and disappeared into the house. "Dad wasn't very good at communicating, particularly about conflict," David remembers. Anne Skakel's name was never spoken again in the house. "[Rucky] had seen so much death in his life," Cissie Ix explains. "First his parents; and his brother-in-law, John Dowdle; then his brother George; then right after, George's wife, Pat; then Ethel's husband, Bobby. There was just so much sadness around that family."

Julie recalls, "Once my mother was gone, everything just went to hell." Rucky's drinking spiraled out of control. "Dad was useless after that," Tommy told me. "He crawled into a bottle of bourbon every day. So he was a complete mess." At the urging of one priest or another, he would periodically check himself into Greenwich Hospital to dry out. Cissie Ix, like clockwork, would scour the house for bottles. Drinking and despair hatched in Rucky a terrible temper. Michael remembers being airborne or smashing against walls on many occasions during Rucky's tantrums. The little boy slept in closets to avoid nocturnal violence should his restless father wander past his bedroom in a nepenthe haze.

As the surrogate mother, Julie, at 16, answered for the behavior of her increasingly rowdy brothers. "Because he had put me in charge, every time the boys would do something he would look at me," Julie says. "I got so scared coming home from school every day. I knew that he had three loaded handguns under his mattress and I knew he'd be drunk. There were two doors I had to go through to get to his bedroom, and I never knew going through them if I was going to be blown away. He was such a nasty alcoholic." Rucky terrorized the boys, but discipline was intermittent and arbitrary. Helen remembers meals of cold SpaghettiOs from a can in the Skakel yard. Between bites, the boys would light M-80s as their elderly Irish caretaker, Nanny Sweeney, smiled through the smoke, calling out "Good show!" But then, in a fit of anger, Rucky burned Julie when he caught her playing with matches, and thrashed Michael with a hairbrush. His parenting philosophy included prophylactic tannings. "A couple days a week, he used to have the cook hold me in the kitchen and he'd spank the shit out of me," Michael recounts. "I have no idea why."

Michael felt himself buffeted between his father's and Tommy's volcanic rages. "Tommy was like milk on a hot stove," Michael recalls. "One moment everything looks perfectly calm and benign. And the next moment the stove had disappeared beneath a flood of boiling milk," Belle Haven neighbor Neal Walker, Margie's brother, told me. "There was something not quite right about him."

There was a medical explanation. When he was 4 years old, Tommy struck his head in a tumble from the back of the family's 1963 Lincoln. Before that, he and Julie had been exceptionally close. "As little kids we were like best buddies," she says. "We were Irish twins; we did everything together." The accident happened on Field Point Road in Belle Haven on their ride home from nursery school. "We had a driver, and of course in those days there were no seatbelts," Julie says. "I'm sitting on the right-hand side of the car near the door. Tommy and I were just fooling around and the next second I knew he wasn't there. He was gone. He fell out of the car. I was so in shock that it took me a little while to tell the driver that Tommy's not here anymore, but I remember by the time he stopped, I vaguely remember seeing a body on the ground. Oh my God, I still blame myself for it." Even though he was only 4, Tommy remembers the accident. "I remember looking down at myself on the side of the road and then looking down at myself in the operating room," he says. "Those are the only two things I remember. And then after that I remember I had to wear a helmet for about a year." Tommy had suffered a linear skull fracture; he was unconscious for a day and in Greenwich Hospital for weeks. The curiously nicknamed James "Bunny" Marr, the Skakel family's driver at the time, told the police he wasn't sure who had opened the suicide door.

Tommy was never the same. Marr said that in the years after the accident, Tommy suffered "fits of anger that would come and go quickly. In the midst of these, Tommy would sometimes destroy his own stuff." He endured agonizing stomach cramps and major memory troubles afterward. "Tommy," he said, had stints "when he would just stare into space for long periods of time and not really remember anything." Julie recalls the change less sympathetically. "He turned mean," she says. "And he had a problem with telling the truth." Julie remembers fielding various queries at school from kids who'd gotten one story or another from Tommy. "People would come up to me and say, 'You have a professional racecar track in your backyard?'" she says. "And I'd be like, 'What? Ah, no.' A lot of stuff like that." Tommy recalls having serious health issues afterward, but can't recall specifics. "I guess it was so painful I just kind of put it out of my mind," he says.

Tommy always fought with Michael, two years his junior, but after Anne's death, he began terrorizing his younger brother, pummeling him fiercely. It went beyond your typical Irish family junior gangsterism, and Michael feels that Rucky tacitly condoned Tommy's violence. Julie shares this assessment. "Absolutely," she says. "He let Tommy do his dirty work." By October 30, 1975, Tommy, 17, and Michael, 15, despised each other.

DOMINICK DUNNE continually accused the Skakel family of using its power and Kennedy connections to intimidate the Greenwich Police "to protect one of their own." In 1991 Dunne wrote in *Vanity Fair,* "It is thought in the community and elsewhere that Kennedy influence was brought to bear." In 1996, he told a UPI reporter, "The [Skakel] family is so powerful that since the first night the police have never been able to question family members."

The rare reporters who investigated Dunne's charges found them false. *Newsday* reporter Len Levitt, who penned the most thorough journalistic treatment of the Moxley case, concluded that, although inept work by a police department that had not investigated a homicide for decades may have let the killer go free, this had nothing to do with intimidation by the Skakels. In an exhaustive 1997 article in the *Hartford Courant,* Joel Lang concluded that Dunne's accusations "probably sprang more from bias than fact." John Elvin, who in 1999 wrote a comprehensive investigative piece on the murder for the magazine *Insight on the News,* described the Skakels as "cooperative—somewhat bizarrely . . . even participating in the search for evidence and serving coffee and snacks to the cops." Greenwich Detective Steve Carroll, one of the first officers on the scene, told the *New York Daily News* that Rucky "was so cooperative and there was the feeling that no one there could have done it."

In the aftermath of Martha's death, everyone in the Skakel house spoke to police investigators freely and without counsel. According to Lunney, "Rushton Skakel had previously stated that anything that the investigators wished to do would be agreeable to him." All the Skakels, including Michael, indicated their willingness to take polygraph tests, and at least two family members, Tommy and John, did take them. In the months after the murder, Tommy submitted to multiple interviews and two lie-detector tests; Rucky gave detectives permission to take hair samples from Tommy and to obtain his school, medical, and psychological records. With the family's consent, the police drained the Skakels' pool, took soil samples from their yard, and searched garbage from the house regularly.

Both Dunne and, later, his friend and protégé Mark Fuhrman complained that the Greenwich Police didn't even dare to obtain a search warrant for the

Skakel residence. "Someone bowed to influence," Dunne declared in the 1991 *Vanity Fair* article. But Rucky gave the police a signed consent-to-search form and full access to the house, and allowed investigators to examine it whenever they chose. Carroll and his colleague Jim Lunney conducted several thorough searches. "It was an open house—he'd never even go with us," Carroll told Fuhrman. Rucky even gave the police keys to both his Belle Haven residence and the ski house in Windham, New York. Carroll explained to the *Hartford Courant,* "People criticize us for not getting search warrants. But the Skakels' attitude was, 'Oh, yes, help yourself.'" He explained to Fuhrman, "We never thought there was any reason to get a search warrant, because we had already been through the house. Up one side, down the other."

Contrary to Dunne's assertions, the Skakels never got a break from the police, who began focusing on Tommy while they were investigating 26-year-old neighbor Ed Hammond. Because Tommy was the last person known to have seen Martha alive, police interrogated him with no adult present for nearly six hours at police headquarters the day that Martha's body was discovered. Detectives Lunney and Ted Brosko first interviewed Tommy and his siblings in the Skakel house on October 31 at 3:00 p.m., at almost the exact time their colleagues McGlynn and Carroll were across Walsh Lane, marveling at Ed Hammond's porn archives. Benedict adopted the fiction of the Skakel family being untouchable from Fuhrman's book as the prosecution's sentinel narrative during Michael's trial. Benedict would later parrot Fuhrman's claim that in the hours following Sheila's discovery of Martha's body, the Skakel house was crawling with "dozens" of lawyers. Actually, at 3:00 p.m. when Lunney and Brosko arrived at the Skakel household, there wasn't a single attorney present. They found only Ginny Fitzgerald, a neighbor and friend of Anne Skakel. Later that afternoon at 5:00 p.m., Great Lakes Corporation attorney Jim McKenzie did show up but promptly left at 9:00 p.m. when Rucky arrived home from his Adirondack hunting trip. Rucky, who considered the Moxleys to be friends (even sponsoring David Moxley at the Belle Haven Club), was in shock from the news and came racing back to Belle Haven. One might assume that Rucky was savvy enough to have ordered a company attorney to monitor his home as press and police flooded Belle Haven. But Julie had summoned the GLC lawyer at Fitzgerald's prompting. "Ginny was concerned and at one point she said, 'Julie, you need to call a lawyer,'" Julie told me. "So I called Great Lakes Carbon. I wanted to speak to Joe Donovan because he was the head attorney and we knew each other pretty well, but he was out of town. But Jim McKenzie was available so I told Jim, 'Look, this is what's going on, I need an attorney here.'"

Before McKenzie arrived, Officers Lunney and Brosko took statements from Julie and Michael, as well as Julie's friend Andrea and tutor Kenny Littleton.

Michael told the detectives that at 9:10 p.m., shortly after returning from the Belle Haven Club, he let Martha, Geoff, and Helen in through the back door of the house. The four of them went out the side door onto the driveway to smoke and listen to music in the Lincoln. The police report includes nothing more from Michael.

Julie was next up. She told the detectives that she and Andrea came out of the house at 9:30 p.m. and got into the station wagon so that she could drive Andrea home. Julie said she saw Tommy going inside the house via the side door. She realized that she'd forgotten the keys to the wagon and sent Andrea back to the front door to fetch them. And then Lunney included this: "While she was waiting, [Julie] observed a shadow of a person, no other description, running in front of her house. She stated the shadow was running in a crouched position, crossed the driveway, and disappeared into the wooded area adjacent to the front of the house. Julie stated that she believed the shadow was a person out for 'Halloween.'"

Detectives interviewed Andrea, but the report only includes her corroboration of Julie's "shadow" sighting: "Shakespeare stated that when she exited the car to get the keys she also heard what sounded like someone running in the area adjacent to the front of the house." A couple days later, the girls would tell the police that, while standing in the kitchen, just before leaving the house for the car, "They observed a figure . . . pass by the window." The police report added, "During this time of occurrence all members and guests of the Skakel household were accounted for." In other words, the runner was not a Skakel. I believe that the large and dark figure dashing through the darkness in a crouched run was Martha's killer. But the two girls' memories about that apparition would fade into the mist until three decades later when they finally emerged as consequential observations during my own journey to track down Martha's killers.

When the police took a statement from Kenny Littleton, "he related that when he returned from dinner, he went to Mr. Skakel's room to watch television. He stated that he watched a movie, *The French Connection,* and during this time he neither heard nor observed anything suspicious." A quiet night with the boob tube was the Alpha and Omega from Kenny—for the time being.

According to Julie, when GLC attorney Jim McKenzie arrived at the house, the police stopped their interviews and left. On the way out, however, the two officers shanghaied Tommy at the front door and put him in the back of their cruiser. "I went down to the police station by myself," Tommy recalls. "And I remember them doing this good cop, bad cop crap and I'm like, 'Come on guys, really? This is just ridiculous.' I told them everything I knew up to the point where we were fooling around, and then they brought me home." According to Greenwich PD's report of the interview, Tommy told detectives that at about 9:15 p.m., he went outside to get a tape from the car then joined the others. At 9:25 p.m., Tommy said that Rush Jr., John, and Jimmy came out of the house and told the group they'd have to vacate the vehicle because Rush had to take Jimmy home to Sursum Corda. Tommy, Martha, Helen, and Geoff got out of the car. Michael kept his seat as Rush, John, and Jimmy climbed in. Just after Rush backed the Lincoln from the driveway, Helen and Geoff started toward their homes through the backyard, leaving Tommy and Martha talking by the side door near the driveway. Tommy said he and Martha continued talking by the door, and said their goodbyes about five minutes later. He told police that he watched Martha walk homeward through the Skakel yard, while, in reality, he had arranged to rendezvous with her behind the Skakel toolshed. Tommy went back into the house through the side door, and heard Kenny struggling with the broken front door. He and Stephen helped Kenny wrench open the troublesome door to find Andrea asking for the station wagon keys. The detectives ended Tommy's interview when he got to the point where they handed Andrea the car keys. The Greenwich cops were already focused on Ed Hammond and didn't appear interested in learning how the last person to see Martha spent the balance of his evening.

The biggest break for police the night of October 31 was finding a Toney Penna four-iron, apparently the sister club to the murder weapon. It was poking from a barrel of sporting gear by the backdoor mudroom. Two days later, Lunney and Brosko returned to the Skakel home. The club hadn't moved. Rucky happily let them take it. He also signed a "Consent to Search Premises Without Search Warrant" form, granting the detectives free rein to search the house and remove, without asking, "any merchandise, materials, or other property" they deemed relevant to the investigation.

"The Skakels were able to hold off the police all these years," Dunne would recount to CNN years later. "If this was a family of lesser stature, that simply would not have happened." Once again, the opposite was true. Beginning that night when Rucky got back from his hunting trip, he opened his home to police. "My father had an open-door policy," recalls Rush Jr. "His attitude was, 'We have nothing to hide. Come on in.'" Police reports echo Rush Jr.'s assessment. "Anything investigators wished to do would be agreeable to him," a November 7 police report read. Rucky, who was something of a law-enforcement groupie, was happy to have his home turned into a makeshift command center. Ethel Jones, the family's cook, served the cops coffee and homemade baked goods; Michael's friend Peter Coomaraswamy recalls going over to the Skakel house during that period and finding the place swarming with cops. David recalls, "The Greenwich Police pretty much moved into our house. They used our kitchen as their headquarters for the investigation. That was their base."

Two weeks after the murder, on November 15, Rucky dutifully brought his kids and his nephew, Jimmy, to the Greenwich police station for formal police interviews. The children all repeated the same stories they told police on Halloween before leaving for Windham.

It was true that Rucky spoke to his family, but not at Windham and not to concoct alibis. "When the boys came home from Windham after the weekend, my father assembled us all in the library," recalls David. "He told us that investigators would be talking to us. You know, we were all kind of in shock about Martha's murder. It just didn't make sense. But that was it. There was nothing else to really talk about. There were only two times that we had family meetings during my entire childhood. The other time was on the bus, after my mother died, and he told us we could go to our rooms and cry." I asked my cousins if there were ever detailed discussions among their siblings about the night of Martha's murder. "Never," Stephen tells me. "No, never," Michael concurs. "We didn't talk about it at first among ourselves because there was no reason to," Rush Jr. tells me separately, "because we were never involved except for being neighbors. By the time they started drilling down on Tommy as a suspect, all the fine details of that night had disappeared." And after that, Tommy's lawyer told them not to talk about it. The Skakels rarely discussed the Moxley case among themselves, and, except for Julie, mostly didn't read press reports about it—first because of family culture and legal advice, and second because most of the press coverage was biased, inaccurate, and painful. "We never talked about it," Julie told me in 2003. "Through all the years we never discussed this. We never compared notes."

When Mickey Sherman first sat the family down together in Florida, soon after Michael hired him as defense attorney, he was stunned to listen as the siblings compared stories from that evening for the first time. "I just remember Julie saying that it was amazing talking about it, because they'd never spoken about it before," Sherman told me in 2002. "That was always a mystery to me after they said that."

Tom Sheridan's perception of the Greenwich Police also contradicted Dunne's. Sheridan told me in 2002, "There was a faction within the Greenwich Police who, from almost the beginning, were not interested in any evidence that did not point to Tom Skakel." Sheridan told me that police investigators violated Tommy's constitutional rights by interrogating him when he was a minor for almost nine hours, without counsel and with no adult present. (When Rucky finally did hire counsel to represent Tommy, the police refused to hand over those earlier interviews to Tommy's lawyer.)

On November 3, 1975, detectives appeared at the Skakel house at dinnertime and told Rucky they wanted Tommy to take a polygraph. Tommy had just gotten home from soccer practice and hadn't eaten dinner. Rather than scheduling the polygraph for a more convenient time, Tommy was in the back of a cruiser a half hour later, barreling up the Merritt Parkway, en route to the State Police's Troop I facility in Bethany, Connecticut, 90 minutes northwest of Greenwich. It was 9:00 p.m. by the time the test started, almost midnight when the State policeman finally pulled the wires and detached the blood pressure cuff from Tommy, and past 1:00 a.m. when Lunney and Brosko deposited him home on Otter Rock Drive. The results: "inconclusive." According to the report, the polygraphers couldn't get an accurate read because Tommy was "in an exhausted state."

Even after this ordeal, Tommy, who still hadn't lawyered up, agreed to a re-test two days later. Knowing that false positive polygraph results often lead to the prosecution of innocent suspects, I never would have allowed a client to consent to one polygraph, let alone two. But it was 1975, and Rucky was flying solo.

Cooperation did not pay off. By early winter, Tommy was the prime suspect. On December 10, 1975, police re-interviewed Helen and Geoff. The two added some new color to their description of the romantic horseplay between Tommy and Martha; as they were leaving the Skakel driveway, they saw Tommy push Martha into a bush. Martha tripped and fell over the embankment encircling the bush and neither of them witnessed her get back up. To cops, it was the first signal that Tommy's horseplay may have galloped out of control.

Detectives Carroll and Lunney went to the Brunswick School to re-interview Littleton about Tommy. Littleton now told them that he wasn't alone for the duration of *The French Connection*: Tommy had joined him around 10:15 p.m. and stuck around to watch the famous car chase scene. But it was another bit of information that started their pulses racing. At 9:45 p.m., Littleton told them, he'd toured the bedrooms to check on the kids who'd remained behind in the house. David and Stephen were asleep in their beds. Tommy's room, however, was empty. If Tommy had said goodbye to Martha at the door at 9:30 p.m., the detectives wondered, where did he go for 45 minutes (from when he handed Andrea the keys to the station wagon and to when he appeared in Rucky's room to watch *The French Connection* with Littleton)?

That's when Tommy tripped up badly. On Saturday, December 13, he appeared at the Greenwich station house for yet another interrogation. As usual, Tommy arrived sans lawyer. Carroll and Lunney took turns pushing and coaxing Tommy to elaborate on the shoving that Helen and Geoff had witnessed.

Tommy initially claimed he didn't remember any shoving. When Carroll and Lunney pressed him, however, Tommy recalled "that he did push her in a joking manner" into the pachysandra patch. But he didn't remember it the way Geoff and Helen had described. "Tom related that he could not remember Martha falling to the ground, and that he believed that he caught her by the arm and prevented her from falling all the way," the report reads. "Tom related that he was not entirely sure about this part of the evening . . . the incident was very foggy and the whole situation was very unclear."

He was, however, more certain about where he'd been between 9:30 and 10:00 p.m., the established time of Martha's death. Littleton, Tommy said, didn't find him in his room at 9:45 p.m. because he was working on an extra-credit history paper. He was across the hall from his own room in the guest room where he'd gone to find a book. "He related that he needed a book, which was on Abraham Lincoln and the log cabin," the report says. Afterward, he "readily agreed" to provide a hair sample, and Lunney cut a lock from his head.

Three days later, Lunney and Carroll drove back to Brunswick School to corroborate Tommy's alibi. Tommy's homeroom teacher was mystified. No Brunswick instructors had offered extra credit for a Lincoln essay. "That was just Tommy being Tommy," Julie tells me. But, to the police, Tommy's stretchers were compelling evidence of guilt. Years later, Tommy told me that he invented the yarn to cover his sexcapade with Martha. But at that time, in the Greenwich police station, all eyes were suddenly laser-focused on Tommy Skakel.

It's tough to imagine what thoughts were ricocheting around in Rucky's head as he pushed his son into harm's way. Perhaps he was so convinced of Tommy's innocence that he sensed no jeopardy, but his paternal alarm bell should have been clanging; he knew the murder weapon was a golf club and that the police had taken clubs from his house. Tommy was the last to see Martha alive. Police had twice polygraphed Tommy, yet they were still questioning him. Even if Rucky was unaware of the Abraham Lincoln fib, it was way past time to lawyer up. Unbelievably, on January 16, 1976, a full month after Tommy's disastrous Lincoln lie, Rucky signed a letter authorizing the police to access "any and all hospital, medical, psychological, and school records and/or any and all reports concerning my son, Thomas Skakel."

Armed with this letter, Carroll visited Dr. Anderson, the neurologist who had treated Tommy's skull fracture when he tumbled from the car. Despite the letter Rucky had signed, Anderson respected Tommy's confidentiality and turned over nothing. However, the Skakels' pediatrician, Dr. Walter Camp, provided a raft of information that further stoked the detectives' interest. According to Carroll, the file contained information on Tommy's longstanding behavior problems, including descriptions of rages so severe that Tommy had required physical restraint.

The inquisitive cops also visited Tommy's elementary school alma mater, the Whitby School. Founded in 1958 by my Aunt Georgeann Terrien, Whitby was the first Montessori school in the United States. The school, which stood on a parcel formerly part of Sursum Corda, was, predictably, protective of Tommy. Paul Czaja, Whitby's headmaster, told police that the school would provide nothing. Lunney reported that he got a call on January 20 from Christopher Roosevelt, grandson of FDR, who was an attorney and a member of the school's board of directors. "During this conversation," the report reads, "Mr. Roosevelt became highly agitated . . . and interpreted the request to be something akin to an actual arrest." Roosevelt, the report said, told them if Tommy were to be arrested and charged, he "would be defended by a battery of lawyers who would claim that Thomas was temporarily insane." In various books about the Moxley case, writers have repeatedly cited this detail to demonstrate the reach of Skakel power in Greenwich. Skakel critics offer the Roosevelt call as evidence that the school was conscious of Tommy's guilt. Lunney and Carroll are both dead, but I called Chris Roosevelt, an acquaintance, who was a onetime assistant district attorney under my old boss, Bob Morganthau. Roosevelt denies the showdown described by Lunney. He said that he advised the Whitby School not to release Tommy's scholastic records, but he says his advice had nothing to do with protecting the Skakels. Educational law was his specialty. He counseled Headmaster Czaja that if he released any student records without a subpoena, Whitby would be in violation of the Family Educational Rights and Privacy Act and open to damage claims. Roosevelt knew none of the Skakel children. He had met Rucky only once—later in Czaja's office to discuss the school's decision not to release records. In that meeting, which followed Lunney's phone conversation with Roosevelt, Roosevelt told Rucky that he might want to reconsider his open-door policy. It was clear as daylight that the authorities were tightening the noose around Tommy's neck. Hearing Roosevelt's words, Rucky wept. It was apparently the first time Rucky considered that Tommy was a suspect. Finally, an attorney was telling Rucky just how reckless he had been by granting police carte blanche.

That afternoon, Rucky went in person to Greenwich Police headquarters to deliver a letter to Chief Stephen Baran Jr., revoking his previous authorization to dig into Tommy's medical and school records. Then he fled to the Ix house in a state of profound despair and agitation. Ix left Rucky in the study to fetch him a drink and when she returned, Rucky was writhing in his chair, holding his chest. He told Cissie that he'd just gotten some bad news. Cissie called an ambulance and the paramedics carted Rucky off to the Greenwich Hospital. Later that day, the cops visited him in his hospital room. Rucky told them that he'd hired Manny Margolis, a seasoned Stamford criminal defense lawyer, to represent Tommy.

The police asked Margolis if Tommy would submit to a psychological profile from a doctor of their choosing. They also requested that Tommy undergo a sodium pentothal—so-called "truth serum"—interview. Manny demurred. According to the police report, Margolis "stated our department has had ample opportunity in the past to obtain the information desired from his client." Margolis was angry at the Greenwich Police, who he said had repeatedly lost or mishandled evidence that might have exculpated Tommy, including the golf-club handle that was found with the body, a white hair pulled by the roots and found on Martha's body, and the vaginal and anal swabs and slides taken by the Connecticut medical examiner and subsequently misplaced. Pledging continued cooperation, Margolis asked investigators to submit to him any further questions for family members. Margolis and Tom Sheridan met and spoke with the police and the State's Attorney's office periodically, conveying questions to and answers from family and household members.

By March 1976, the authorities had disremembered all of Rucky's early willingness to help the police. Fairfield County State's Attorney Donald Browne told the Associated Press that a Greenwich family (whom everyone knew to be the Skakels) "had refused to cooperate with the investigation." He added that the family had "pertinent information" but had taken actions that "clearly impeded" the police.

Margolis didn't flinch at Browne's thrust, but Rucky—who hadn't had a heart attack (anxiety and drinking had landed him in the hospital)—was cracking. Desperate to know the truth, Rucky had sent Tommy to New York Presbyterian Hospital to undergo a battery of psychological exams by Dr. Stanley Lesse. It might as well have been an alien abduction: Tommy came back having been probed, penetrated, tested, tapped, injected, and interrogated; plus strapped to sophisticated lie detectors and a brain wave machine, and grilled during a series of sodium pentothal inquisitions. In March 1976, the doctors concluded, according to Margolis, that Tommy could not have committed the crime. Appearing relieved, Rucky paid Dorthy Moxley a visit. Tommy, he assured her, was innocent. The Skakel family lawyers conveyed the test results to police.

But the stress was taking its toll on Tommy. At the end of April, Greenwich Hospital admitted the boy with excruciating stomach pains and bleeding. His diagnosis was "hemorrhagic gastritis"—a condition generally caused by excessive drinking or stress. "It was from nerves," Tommy says. "I was trying to take care of Dad. He was a mess, dealing with all this and it just got to me. I just remember being really sick. I threw up a lot."

Meanwhile, Martha Moxley's father, David, had recruited Detroit's police chief, Gerald Hale, and his star homicide inspector John Lock to come to Greenwich to reinvestigate the evidence. With Tommy's psychiatric reports in hand, Hale concluded that Tommy was the likely killer. On May 10, 1976, Hale issued a report that focused on Tommy's psychological problems and rages. "He would jump up from the table," the report read, "begin to throw things about, turn over beds, pull phones from the wall or threaten siblings. He would not lose consciousness and the episodes varied from 15 to 20 minutes to as long as 2 to 3 hours. His father was able to control him, but only physically." After just one week spent reviewing the case, Chief Hale was able to conclude, as he told Len Levitt, that, "when it came to the Skakels, the Greenwich Police were treading lightly." Skakel nemesis Frank Garr took issue with this part of Hale's theory. "No one sitting in Detroit or anywhere else for that matter can read a Greenwich police report and know how he would react at any point," Garr told Levitt.

"Hale didn't have the right to criticize anyone. If he wasn't there, he should keep his mouth shut. No one was afraid of the Skakels." Hale also criticized the Greenwich cops for investing polygraphs with papal infallibility. They were using lie detector results to exculpate suspects like Hammond, Wittine, Ziluca, as a substitute for hardscrabble detective work.

In May that year, the Greenwich Police brought Fairfield County State's Attorney Donald Browne an application for a bench warrant charging Tommy with the murder. Browne deemed it inadequate to indict. "The application was based on all kinds of shaky evidence," Harold Pickerstein, the attorney for Jack Solomon, then the chief inspector in the Fairfield County State's Attorney's office, told me in 2002. (Solomon, who, in 2002, was the chief of police in Easton, Connecticut, would not discuss the case.) Solomon and Browne concluded that the application did not meet legal standards for probable cause and refused to sign it. "I read it," Browne told me, "and there was nothing in there other than the fact that he was the last to see her alive and that he'd had some mental problems in the past." Browne remembers the overwhelming pressure from the police to charge Tommy: "There was some suggestion that if you issue a warrant, nobody will accuse you of not doing your job. But I don't do things that way." Despite the suspicious behavior and the circumstantial evidence, the case against Tommy was cold by the end of 1976.

Dispirited Greenwich Police, confident of his guilt, continued to make Tommy's life miserable. When Lunney crossed paths with Tommy on a Greenwich street, he'd yell at him, "You sonofbitch, if it's the last thing I do, I'm going to nail you for murder." Tommy recently told me how traumatic that period was for him. A couple years after the murder, as Tommy drove Andrea to her prom at Sacred Heart, he noticed that they were being followed. Wearing his tuxedo for the special night, Tommy helped begowned Andrea from the car and walked her toward the dance. Lunney rushed up upon them out of the darkness, blocking the couple and fixing Tommy with a menacing glare. "How does it feel to be dating a murderer?" he snarled at Andrea.

Gradually, the police moved on to other suspects, but Tommy was never free of suspicion. It was baked into local lore that Tommy had killed Martha and that the Skakels had paid the police to look the other way. Tommy was the Greenwich boogeyman. Following Martha's funeral, Tommy hugged Dorthy Moxley. "I should have walked her home; she might still be here," he said crying. Mrs. Moxley hugged him back. A few years later, before she moved on to Michael, Mrs. Moxley told Dumas, "I might have been hugging my daughter's murderer."

In May 1989 Tommy married a beautiful, brilliant woman named Anne Gillman, a designer for Banana Republic. The couple moved to Massachusetts and ran a bed and breakfast in the Berkshires, while raising two wonderful girls and trying their hand at a variety of business ventures. But suspicions and public opprobrium toward Tommy continue to dog the couple to this day.

DOMINICK DUNNE would later brag that it was his relentless campaign after the publication of his novel that prompted Rucky to hire Sutton Associates—a move that eventually doomed Michael. In the spring of 1993 at Tom Sheridan's urging, Rucky, who was already suffering from the frontal-lobe dementia that would eventually kill him, hired Sutton Associates, a private-investigation firm founded by Jim Murphy. A cabal of former law-enforcement superstars from the FBI and the New York Police Department staffed Sutton. Sheridan convinced Rucky that the original police investigation had been bungled, to Tommy's detriment, and that hiring Sutton would be the best way to find the real murderers and clear the family name.

Rucky was convinced of Tommy's innocence and believed that an open-ended investigation might finally lift the cloud of guilt from Tommy. By the time the investigation was terminated in 1995, Rucky had paid Sutton upwards of a million dollars.

Rucky's introduction to Sutton came from Sheridan via Dick McCarthy, who was Jim Murphy's fellow former FBI agent colleague. McCarthy, then in his mid-60s, operated a one-man private investigation firm. McCarthy knew Sheridan from the New York Athletic Club. Sheridan had, over several years, inveigled himself into the position as Skakel family crisis troubleshooter, as well as family money manager. From that sinecure, Sheridan would make his own fortune while managing the decline of the Skakels'.

It would be years before all the Skakel brood recognized Sheridan for what he was: a cunning, deadly parasite. His ecological niche was in large gaps of executive control over the Skakels' business and family affairs opened by Rucky's myriad incapacities. Like other parasites, Sheridan would eventually turn on and deplete his host with near-lethal effect. For Sheridan, Rucky's angst at the cloud of suspicion that followed his family after Martha's murder had the aroma of opportunity.

Over lunch, Sheridan told private eye McCarthy his idea for a new gold-plated investigation that would find the real killer. McCarthy said that his own firm was too small for the job but suggested that Sutton Associates could help Rucky solve the case. The two cronies agreed that McCarthy would be part of the package. In the summer of 1991, Sheridan and Rucky had lunch at the Belle Haven Club with Sutton's president, Jim Murphy. Rucky was clear about what he needed: resolution. Rucky never intended his money to buy a whitewash.

Jim Murphy is a straight arrow, an ordained deacon in the Catholic church, who spends his vacations on relief missions to impoverished communities in the Dominican Republican. Murphy says that Rucky genuinely wanted to know the truth. "While Rushton Skakel thoroughly believed his children were innocent, we were told that wherever the chips fall, they, the Skakel family, want to know the truth. I remember very clearly his perspective was that, if we were able to identify who committed this crime, and it if it turned out to be one of his boys, that he would go forward with that and let that information be known to the DA," says Murphy. "Part of the thinking was that he wanted to satisfy Mrs. Moxley because she needed some closure on this. The Skakel family recognized Mrs. Moxley's pain and have instructed that any information that develops which contributes to the solution of Martha Moxley's homicide is to be immediately shared with Connecticut authorities, even if the culprit was one of his boys. Since there hadn't been any similar activity that had taken place with either of the boys since that time, I think the rehabilitation issue would have been an easy one to justify. If we found that one of the boys had done it, they might have done some time in jail, but it would have been minimal if the Skakels themselves came forward and admitted a role rather than them being the subject of a law enforcement investigation."

Both Murphy and Sheridan—who acted as the liaison between Sutton and the Skakel family—told me that they were certain Rucky would have turned any of his children over to the police if he believed them guilty.

When he founded his firm, Murphy had been adamant about two things: he was not going to take divorce cases (he had contempt for the private dicks who make their living snapping pictures of cheating spouses), and he would not snoop for criminal defense lawyers, muddying the reputations of trial witnesses. "I don't do criminal defense work because I don't want to be on the opposite end of the people I worked with for so many years," he says. "It's just not what I do." From Rucky, he got assurances that he was being hired to follow the evidence wherever it led, not to extricate a rich family from trouble. "I believed him," Murphy says. "I wouldn't have taken on the investigation otherwise."

All the members of the Skakel family agreed to talk to Sutton detectives about their memories of that night. It was the first time that most of them had discussed the Moxley murder at any length, publicly or privately, since their original police interviews. Several of them, including John and Julie, underwent hypnosis and sodium pentothal testing. Sutton interviewed hundreds of people, including Kenny Littleton and John Moxley.

Both Tommy and Michael told Sutton detectives details they had not disclosed to the police in 1975. Tommy, for example, described his sexual encounter with Martha on the rear lawn of the Skakel property. Michael told about his late-night pocket pool in the tree outside John Moxley's bedroom.

Murphy believes that Michael is innocent, ironic because a report written by Sutton Associates would convert Michael from a footnote in the Martha Moxley murder drama to its central protagonist. Murphy feels guilty about his firm's role in Michael's predicament. "I've felt a real sense of obligation to Michael for what happened here," he says. "It was my documents that were ultimately responsible for what happened to Michael. It's wrong."

Almost from the outset, Murphy suspected Tommy as the culprit. In the summer of 1992, Sutton investigators Dick McCarthy and Willis "Billy" Krebs, a mountainous six foot, seven inch former NYPD lieutenant, interviewed Tommy in Manny Margolis's office. For 15 years, Tommy had stuck to the tale that he bid farewell to Martha from the back door at 9:30 p.m. Within hours of the murder, Tommy repeated that story twice, first to Julie, then to Mrs. Moxley directly. He told the same tale to police repeatedly in separate interviews. An "unnamed source" (for reasons that will soon become evident, I believe this informant to be Rucky's treacherous "friend" Tom Sheridan) told Len Levitt that before the Sutton interview, Krebs gave Tommy a warning: Henry Lee was going to start testing Martha's clothes for DNA, a scientific process that, at the time of the initial investigation, hadn't been available. "So if there's any reason to believe they'll find any of your DNA," Krebs warned him gravely, "better tell us the truth now." I was unable to locate Krebs after interviewing him in 2002, but this scenario sounds plausible to Murphy. "I don't doubt that Billy would have said that," he says. "There's a lot of things you say to someone you think may be guilty of a serious crime to get them to be completely honest with you."

During the Sutton interview, Tommy divulged his previously untold story, that he hadn't actually said goodbye to Martha at 9:30 p.m. She'd waited for him outside while he fetched the station wagon keys for Andrea. The two teenagers then rendezvoused in a spot behind the backyard shed. There, concealed from the view of those inside the house, they made out and then mutually masturbated to orgasm. The assignation lasted about 20 minutes. Krebs couldn't believe it. Tommy was now placing himself with Martha a few minutes from the time Zock began his plaintive baying less than 50 yards from the Moxley driveway where the killer first struck Martha. Furthermore, he admitted to having pulled down Martha's pants and panties—exactly how she was found.

Why, Krebs and McCarthy asked themselves, if Tommy did not already know Martha was dead, would he lie to Julie and Mrs. Moxley on the night of the murder about what time they'd said goodbye? The two gumshoes detected acute discomfort from Tommy's attorney, Manny Margolis, as Tommy described these new details in the interview room. The tryst was clearly news to Margolis.

"Manny never would have let us talk to Tommy if he had any idea he was going to say that," Murphy says.

Smelling blood, Krebs bore down on Tommy, squeezing him for particulars. Tommy remembered Martha's jeans had a button fly. "What else, Tom?" Krebs demanded. Tommy, 35 and a father of two at the time of this interview, looked like he was about to cry. McCarthy stepped in, suggesting a break. Predictably, Margolis never let his client return to the room with Sutton investigators. "I'm going to kill Dick McCarthy," Krebs told Murphy when he returned to the Sutton offices. "Billy was really upset," says Murphy. "Billy Krebs was by far one of the finest interviewers and knowledgeable detectives that I've ever met. In Billy's mind, he had Tommy right there; he could have pushed him a little bit more and gotten a confession out of him or at the very least come up with more inconsistencies."

When I recently asked Tommy whether Murphy had it right, he laughed. I anticipated his explanation about why he waited so long to tell the full story: Rucky's severe attitude toward sex. Tommy was his father's favorite son. "I loved my father and didn't want to lose his respect," Tommy says. "My father was the most important person in my life. He was a staunch Catholic with strict views about premarital sex. I was frightened of disappointing him." He added that he was, like Michael, physically scared of his father. "Bobby, you understand this," he says. "If Dad knew that you were experimenting with sex, your life was over. You were going right to hell. So for me to even tell the police that I was fooling around, that would have gotten back to Dad and I just couldn't let that happen." This, he says, was the reason he invented the Abraham Lincoln report, to conceal his sexual rendezvous with Martha. "Dad considered fooling around with a girl a mortal sin," he told me. "He thought my soul would be damned to hell for eternity. And it would have made him violent. I just didn't want my father to know what I'd been up to." He says he was emotional because the "big Goliath"—Krebs, presumably—"was kind of a bastard." He says he wasn't close to confessing anything. "Confess to what?" Tommy protests. "I wasn't going to admit to something I didn't do. I had just had enough of holding that sexual encounter in for all those years. But I figured if Dad finds it out at that point I don't care. It was too much."

After he and Martha completed their business, Tommy recalled, "Martha said she really had to get home. She had a hard 9:30 curfew," Tommy continued. "We straightened out our clothes and she just kind of skipped across our front yard toward Walsh Lane." His last sight of her was disappearing into the darkness near the chipping tee just short of the apple trees.

Murphy finds it hard to believe that the sexual liaison happened in the backyard. Tommy says that with the lights on in the house, they were invisible to anybody inside. But Murphy, who shared Rucky's orthodox Catholicism, considered it unlikely that a nice girl like Martha would consent to sex in the shrubbery. Based on his own experience, Murphy speculated that Martha wouldn't like to make love in the bushes. "I don't think there was any way that Martha was going to lay down in the backyard and make out," he says. "He could have taken her into the camper," he suggests. "He could have brought her in the house. They're not going to have their moment of ecstasy lying down in the backyard." My own view is that teenagers, particularly during that era of stricter sexual mores and parental scrutiny, were generally happy for a roll in the bracken.

Michael hasn't spoken to Tommy in more than 20 years. Despite his strong AA program, Michael still can't seem to relinquish the heavy baggage of Tommy's childhood bullying. I can't blame him. The bullying that spawned Michael's PTSD must have seemed to him a long blur of chaotic and arbitrary violence that began with his father, continued with Tommy, and culminated at Élan.

Michael is philosophical about his brother as a suspect. "If Tommy did do this," he says, "he should go to jail. I'm sick and tired of paying for whoever did this." But Tommy killing Martha just doesn't compute with him. Michael says, "Tommy wasn't like that. Tommy could get laid whenever he wanted to. He had an easier time with girls than anyone in Greenwich. He had girls chasing him. And for all his faults, Tommy is a gentleman—that's his shtick. It's constitutional for him. It's not an act. He would never, ever hit a girl." Tommy says essentially the same thing about Michael. "No," Tommy told me. "Other than one incident at Brunswick in eighth grade, Michael never had a fight. It's inconceivable that Michael would have hurt Martha."

Stephen Skakel who housed Michael in his modest rental home in suburban Connecticut following Michael's release from prison, is about as kind and gentle a man as I know. He has devoted his life to an intense brand of service, managing relief efforts for aid organizations in dangerous war zones. His profession requires him to regularly risk his life and welfare on expeditions to the ravaged battlefields of Bosnia, Afghanistan, the Congo, Iraq, Somalia, and Sudan. He helped manage the initial relief at Ground Zero after the World Trade Center bombing. He has spent all his free time for 15 years coordinating Michael's appeals. That effort has nearly bankrupted him. He flashes a very rare moment of irritation when I ask whether there would be any scenario in which he'd want to shield a killer in the family. "If I knew who did this, I'd let them rot in jail forever," he says. "I don't give a shit if they are family. I pissed away 15 years on this. Rush's kids are in college. I've only seen them three or four times in the last 15 years. I've only seen my brother Johnny's kids four or five times as well. That's 15 years I'll never get back."

Stephen's opinion aside, by 1998 Garr and his sidekick, Len Levitt, had eliminated Tommy as a suspect. In their view, Tommy had a perfect alibi: Andrea had accepted car keys from Tommy in the Skakel kitchen at 9:15 p.m. and

Tommy was seated in his father's bedroom, calmly watching *The French Connection* at 10:15 p.m. There was no way, Levitt explained in his book, *Conviction*, that Tommy could have murdered Martha, cleaned up the blood, and changed his clothes during that short interval. "What 17-year-old boy would volunteer to adults that he'd just engaged in mutual masturbation with a girl?" Garr asked Levitt, "Especially if, just after she left him, that girl was murdered?" Garr continues, "Say the murder occurs around the time the dogs are barking. I don't believe Tommy could have killed her, moved her body, discarded the murder weapon, cleaned himself up, and sat watching television with his tutor a few minutes later. No 17-year-old kid could have pulled that off."

Garr asked further, "And you know the strangest indication that Tommy is innocent? It's Littleton's statement that he had noticed nothing unusual when Tommy entered his room after ten o'clock to watch television."

When Levitt told Krebs about Garr's logic, Krebs conceded, "He has a point."

"If you accept that, how can you say that Tommy did it?" I asked Krebs in 2002.

"I can't," Krebs answered.

Benedict concurred. "Tom doesn't fit," Benedict told jurors during Michael's trial. "Tom just doesn't fit. After parting with the victim in the driveway, he was answering the front door for Andrea [Shakespeare] Renna, an independent witness. Shortly after that, he was watching *The French Connection* with Ken Littleton, who, for Tom Skakel, is an independent witness. And later on, when oldest brother Rushton came home . . . Tom was fast asleep." Benedict, in his closing during the trial, continued, "To conclude that Thomas Skakel or Ken Littleton murdered Martha Moxley, you would have to pretty much conclude they were in cahoots with one another. That simply doesn't make sense. The bottom line is, if either of those two people committed this gruesome, horrible, bloody crime and managed so effectively to cover their tracks, he has committed the perfect crime and I submit that's just not possible in this case."

Despite the conviction of police and prosecutor that Tommy's alibi cleared him as a potential culprit, a cloud of suspicion lingered over the entire Skakel clan. The rumors and slander injured every member of the Skakel family. Rush Jr. moved to Bogotá in 1995 to shield his children from the publicity. David and Johnny moved to the Pacific Northwest and Julie to Florida. Tommy moved to the Berkshires but has never succeeded in finding sunshine away from suspicion. The shadow of Martha's murder eclipsed his life since age 17.

"It really cast a shadow over my life," he told me. "I've lived as a pariah since Martha's death. Since November 1975, my life went into a tailspin and it has never recovered. I have not had a decent night's sleep since then and my health has suffered greatly. Ever since I was a teenager, I've had to learn to filter out the constant public disgust I encounter every day, the furtive glances, the hostile stares, the disapproving expressions, the shaking heads and the whispers. I've been under assault for 40 years. I can't list my phone number, because I don't want my daughters picking up crank calls. It's diminished everything I do. My family, my relationships, my career are all truncated. My phone calls go unreturned; my business deals evaporate."

Tommy continues, "When Michael got convicted, it was horrible because I know he is innocent. But it didn't give me any relief. For me, there was never any due process, no chance for me to defend myself, no presumption of innocence. Not one reporter or writer came to me and apologized. Nobody offered to give me back my life, my reputation. They just changed the spin to keep all the rumors alive." At trial, Benedict told the jury that Tommy was part of the conspiracy. Since then, he has continued to say that Tommy helped Michael hide the body. In June 2002, Benedict told the *New York Times* that Tommy helped Michael "clean up" after the brutal slaying and "cover his tracks." At Michael's *habeas* appeal, before the Supreme Court in February 2016, Michael's attorney Hubie Santos told the judges that Tommy was the most "probable killer." For the record, Michael does not agree and was shocked that his lawyer made that statement.

"The worst part is the nightmare for my children and my wife," Tommy relates. "This has almost cost me my marriage and I've had a very difficult time trying to explain to my daughters what took place in October 1975. I can't go anywhere. I never had a chance to lead a normal life and give that gift to my wife and kids. I spent years feeling like I just wanted to cover up and hide and run away from life. I forced myself to hold my head up and walk into those rooms and feel the hostility. And it got worse when I had my family. Before that, I could just cover up and go into a fetal position. Now I had to shield them and it kills me every time they feel the sting. I wish I could take the hit for them. That's the worst part. I'd rather be waterboarded than go through this. It's been an ordeal. Reporters can be soulless, merciless thugs.

"There has been so much evidence pointing toward someone outside of the family and no evidence linking either my brother Michael, or myself, or any Skakel to Martha's murder. But the State had one thing in mind and that was to convict a Skakel. It did not matter which one, just do whatever it took to convict a Skakel, period. I've lost a good part of my life and can't get it back. My brother lost over 10 years in prison; he can't get those back either.

"I'm looking forward to one day being able to go back to Greenwich and someone saying to me, 'Sorry. We are all sorry we put you and your family through hell. You, your brother, and your family just did not deserve this.'"

Garr told Levitt that Littleton gave Tommy a gold-plated alibi by vouching for him during *The French Connection* chase scene. Garr goes on to say, "The strangest indication of Littleton's innocence is that Tommy says the same thing about him. Without intending to, each alibi the other. Believe me, if Tommy or any other Skakel knew Littleton had done this, they'd have given him up in a heartbeat." Levitt was right about Kenny alibiing Tommy. At 10:20 p.m., Tommy was with him in Rucky's bedroom watching *The French Connection* wearing the same clothing he had worn during dinner at the Belle Haven Club and with no visible blood stains. But Levitt and Garr were wrong about Tommy providing a reciprocal alibi for Littleton. From the beginning, Tommy said that Littleton lay in his father's chair with a blanket draped over him from chin to toe, hiding his clothing and body from sight. Kenny never came out from under the blanket. It struck Tommy as odd since it was quite warm in his father's room.

Whether or not he killed Martha Moxley, Kenny Littleton was a natural-born suspect.

CHAPTER 9

The Tutor

Oh my God, this could be the guy who killed my sister.
I had the impression he was crazy enough to do anything.

—John Moxley

In October 1975, Kenneth Wayne Littleton Jr. was a handsome, burly, 23-year-old graduate of Williams College. Littleton was over six feet tall, with flowing chestnut locks, and a solid linebacker's build. Two months earlier, he began a new job teaching science and coaching football at the Brunswick School, the coat and tie Greenwich prep school that the Skakel brothers attended.

Littleton, the eldest of three children, grew up in middle-class Belmont, Massachusetts. His father worked for Western Electric; his mother was a saleswoman at Filene's. Kenny Littleton attended an all-boys private high school, Belmont Hill, on scholarship. He was a good student and a great athlete, with a solid golf game. The captain of his high school football team, he also played varsity baseball all four years. By his own estimation, Littleton was a lady's man. He told a psychiatrist that his high school obsessions were "books, balls, and babes."

Littleton enrolled in Williams College in 1970 with plans to become a pediatric surgeon. He played varsity baseball all four years, varsity football for two, and two years of rugby, but his B average at graduation dashed his dream of a medical career. In the fall of 1974, he landed a teaching position at The Rectory, a private boarding school in Pomfret, Connecticut, but lost the job by spring. He spent the summer on Nantucket cruising the cobblestone streets in his cherry-red Mustang and working as a bouncer at Preston's Airport Lounge, the island venue for visiting rock bands.

In the fall of 1975, he started at Brunswick. Michael's neighbor Neal Walker and Neal's best friend, Crawford Mills, were in Littleton's class. Both of these boys subsequently played pivotal roles in identifying Martha's likely killers. Speaking of Littleton, "He was kind of an odd guy," recalls Neal. "We had him for biology and we never did any work. He'd reminisce about getting laid in college and tell inappropriate stories." Crawford remembered Littleton telling his students how he enjoyed crushing ants with a hammer.

On October 30, 1975, Kenny Littleton and his duffle mustered at Otter Rock Drive for his first night as live-in tutor and companion to Rushton Skakel's seven motherless children.

Michael had a good feeling about Littleton. At dinner at the Belle Haven Club that night, Littleton didn't flinch when the kids ordered drinks. "Here I was having just turned 15 years old, ordering rum and tonic and planter's punch with the football coach. I was already planning to become Littleton's drinking buddy. I would get in good with him, and he would make my life a lot easier by getting other teachers to lay off me and allowing me to drink." The boys were buzzed when they pulled in the Skakel driveway between 8:30 p.m. and 8:45 p.m.

During his October 31 interview, Littleton told Detectives Lunney and Brosko that after arriving home he went directly to the second-floor master bedroom to unpack. Rucky had left instructions that Littleton was to occupy that room while Rucky was away on his hunting trip to the Adirondacks. He said he had remained there until morning. Littleton said he neither heard nor saw anything suspicious. Two weeks later, on November 14, Littleton admitted that he had not stayed upstairs but had wandered downstairs, where he saw Tommy outside with Martha. He said he hadn't set foot outside the Skakel home after returning from the Club. This account stood unchanged in two subsequent interviews.

Then on December 10, Littleton switched his story again. During an interview at Brunswick School, Littleton told Lunney and Detective Carroll that he had gone outside the house, between 9:15 and 9:30 p.m., at the request of Nanny Sweeney, who had heard a "fracas." He told police that he left through the front door, looked around the house to check on the Skakel boys, saw nobody outside, and came back in through the side door. He now said that he never saw Martha. The Lincoln, driven by Rush Jr., had departed at 9:15 p.m. Tommy had been at the front door at 9:30 p.m., handing the wagon keys to Andrea. Littleton was now putting himself outside and a mere three-minute walk from the murder scene. During the December 10 interview, he was vague about the time he went outside, and whom and what he saw, but he volunteered, without prompting, that he had not heard a dog barking:

CARROLL: So when you went out the door, you didn't see Julie in the car, the station wagon? And when you walked around to the side door, you didn't see anything of Tommy pushing Martha or pushing someone?

LITTLETON: No.

CARROLL: Did you see any dogs?

LITTLETON: No, and I didn't hear any barking either! And I didn't hear any barking all night. Unfortunately it was a cold night and I had my window shut. Now my window faced the backyard in the Moxley property and the murder, as I understand it, occurred no more than a hundred yards from the window.

Sutton's Jim Murphy points out that Littleton claimed that after dinner, he'd gone up to Rucky's room to unpack. Rucky's bedroom patio would have afforded a direct line of sight to the spot in the yard where Tommy was making out with Martha at 9:30 p.m. Murphy says that he and Sutton investigators seriously considered the possibility that Littleton had witnessed the teenage sex romp. "Then he goes down and decides he's going to get some for himself," says Murphy, who then lays out how Littleton might have committed the crime.

"If, at 9:50, Martha announced that she was late for her curfew and had to get home, Tommy would have gone inside via the side door, and Kenny could have followed Martha back towards her house, convinced that a handsome, experienced 24-year-old man could certainly get as far with her as a 17-year-old." All the Skakel children attest that there were golf clubs scattered across the Skakel lawn from a Mitsubishi Chipping Tournament a few weeks earlier. Martha had to cross the chipping tee to get home.

Tommy had reported watching *The French Connection* chase scene with Kenny Littleton starting at 10:15 p.m. When investigators checked with CBS in 1976, they learned that the network actually broadcast the scene 10 minutes later, from 10:25 p.m. to 10:32 p.m. Littleton would have had time to kill Martha and still catch Gene Hackman's famous pursuit sequence. Julie reported that when she bumped into Littleton in the kitchen, he was wearing different clothes than he had at dinner. Littleton had a couple beers at the Belle Haven Club and his inhibitions were relaxed. It would soon become apparent how volatile Littleton could be when drinking.

Charles Morganti, a 28-year-old Belle Haven security officer, told police that he saw a white male walking near the intersection of Field Point Road and Walsh Lane at about 10:00 p.m. Morganti accosted the man. "I'm going home," the man told him. "I live on Walsh Lane." He then turned and started down Walsh Lane, which put him 150 yards from the bushwhack spot at 10:00 p.m.

Morganti described the man as: "White male, six feet tall, 200 pounds, late 20s to early 30s, dark rimmed glasses, fatigue jacket, tan slacks, blond hair." At the police station, Morganti helped create a composite sketch of the man. The sketch, which Garr and Benedict purposefully concealed from Michael's defense team, uncannily resembles Kenny Littleton in 1975.

Littleton began to exhibit odd behavior following the murder. On April 10, 1976, Cissie Ix told the police that "girlie magazines were found in Mr. Littleton's room." This, of course, was *prima facie* evidence of guilt in Rucky's house and precisely the sort of tidbit that usually captured the imagination of Greenwich Police's Moxley murder homicide squad. Ix added that Littleton was in the habit of visiting the Skakel gazebo in the nude, after disrobing in front of 80-year-old Nanny Sweeney. Ix urged police to look at Littleton, but the Greenwich Police at the time were preoccupied with building their case against Tommy.

Later that month, Rucky fired Littleton after the police visited the Skakel home to report that he had wrapped Rucky's car around a tree in a drunken blackout and then abandoned it.

When the school year ended and Littleton headed back to Nantucket, he was still not a suspect. There was nothing to prevent him from enjoying a free-wheeling summer like the one before.

But Littleton returned to the island a changed man. His friend Ken Howard told police that after the murder, he noticed a drastic transformation in Littleton's behavior. Howard reported that he had become more aggressive and somewhat outlandish. The previous summer, Littleton had looked like every other island preppy: polo shirts, khaki shorts, and deck shoes. In 1976, he appeared in an all-white disco getup, his shirt unbuttoned nearly to his navel, and a shark-tooth necklace. On occasion he sported a blue tuxedo. He peacocked around town flexing his muscles and adjusting his hair in shop windows. Back at work as bouncer at Preston's Airport Lounge, Littleton practiced calisthenics, drank through his shifts, and brandished his molded musculature for the summer tourists. James Manchester, Preston's owner, thought Littleton was making a nuisance of himself with unsolicited hugging of female patrons and crowding women on the dance floor. When no one else was dancing, Littleton, in his white suit, would leap on deck busting John Travolta moves in preening solos.

Littleton left a trail of mayhem across the island that summer. In July, a Nantucket tourist awoke in her bed to find Littleton lying naked on top of her. He'd pulled off a window screen and climbed in. Shortly after that incident, Manchester fired Littleton for kiting beer from Preston's on his birthday. Littleton threatened Manchester ominously, then returned to bleed the tires on Manchester's brother's car.

With no income, Littleton invited a 22-year-old girl to share his $75-a-week rent. She told police that he repeatedly "forced himself on her sexually and often erupted in fits of violence, smashing things in her apartment." Littleton, she said, was injecting cocaine. Other islanders noticed needle marks on his arm.

Manchester said that Littleton preferred younger girls. A friend of Manchester recounted that Littleton brazenly approached a teenager dining with her father at a local restaurant. He embraced her, provocatively inserted his shark tooth into her ear, and signaled her to follow him. Drunk on Grand Marnier at the Mad Hatter, he cleared the bar with churlish antics. When the bartender cut him off, Littleton smashed his mug, spraying the pub with shattered glass. Police removed him. On the dance floor of the Chicken Box, Nantucket's Dog Officer, Linda Cahoon, accidentally bumped Littleton's dance partner. As she apologized, Littleton backhanded her so hard she hit the floor. "You really shouldn't fool with my woman," he warned.

In early September, Nantucket Police arrested Littleton for a string of burglaries. He stole fresh vegetables from a farmer's garden and sneaked aboard a docked boat to filch a flagon of wine. He pilfered a three-foot statue of Hercules, a fishing pole, a decorative plate, a painting, and other items from gift stores. Littleton heaved a brick through the plate glass window of the wharf-side Four Winds Gift Shop to swipe a scrimshaw basket. He pinched booze from a liquor store and a nude male figure from a lawn. He buried the sculpture in the backyard of his Main Street apartment, then unearthed and reburied it in the front yard. "Ken told me that he intended to sell all these items once he left the island," his girlfriend recounted. She told Steve Carroll that Littleton was always jobless, but never short on cash.

When cops caught him fencing the gift-shop booty, Littleton blamed liquor for his marauding. He directed police to another buried cache of plunder at Swain's Wharf, a half mile from his house, and complained that the elements had destroyed the bulk of his buried loot. They charged him with larceny and burglary and tossed him in the Barnstable County jail. Littleton made bail and returned to Greenwich just in time for the Brunswick autumn semester.

The Greenwich Police, in the doldrums on Tommy's case, were ready to take a fresh gander at Kenny Littleton. In October 1976, Lunney asked John Meerbergen, Littleton's attorney, to produce his client for a polygraph. Littleton confessed to his new Greenwich roommate that he was distressed about taking the lie-detector test; the Greenwich Police were still unaware of his Nantucket arrest.

On the morning of Monday, October 18, 1976, Lunney and Carroll picked up a chatty Littleton for the long ride to Bethany. Tommy, he told them, had seemed relaxed when they watched *The French Connection* together. There was no indication that he was coming in from outside. His cheeks were not ruddy. He wasn't wearing a jacket. Littleton also mentioned that young Rush Jr. had told him at 9:15 p.m. that he was taking John and Michael with him to Sursum Corda. Police recorded this recollection in a case report, which 25 years later, Frank Garr withheld from Michael's defense team. Littleton's admission might have had great significance in Michael's trial, because it was confirmation of Michael's alibi—from a non-family source. Kenny Littleton's statement meant that, if the Skakel family had invented Michael's Sursum Corda alibi—as Benedict contended at trial—they would have had to concoct the plan at least an hour before Martha was killed.

But this fact did not interest police at the time. It would be a decade before Michael became a suspect. During the polygraph exam, Trooper Mike Beal slowly asked the following questions.

1. Do you know for sure who killed Martha Moxley?
2. Did you kill Martha Moxley?
3. Can you take me to the missing section of the golf club used to kill Martha Moxley?
4. Did you strike Martha Moxley with a golf club?
5. Last October, did you participate in any way in the murder of Martha Moxley?
6. Are you withholding any information from the police about the murder of Martha Moxley?

Littleton answered "no" to each query. Beal repeated the questions a second and a third time. The cops disappeared and came back accompanied by Jack Solomon from the State's Attorney's office. Solomon delivered the news: Littleton had failed. Badly. The machine had detected his deception.

At first Littleton fumbled. He was surprised, he said, to learn that the machine thought he was lying. And then he offered a poorly conceived explanation. He'd been arrested in Nantucket for stealing, while drunk. Might his anxiety about that incident, he asked the police, have affected the results? Tell us more about Nantucket, the cops said.

A couple days later, Lunney dropped by to see Tommy's attorney, Manny Margolis, in his Stamford office. He asked to re-interview the Skakel kids. It was good news: the cops had a new suspect. Margolis offered to conduct interviews from questions provided by the police.

In the meantime, Meerbergen, apprised of his client's disastrous polygraph, battened the hatches. Would Littleton submit to another polygraph? No. How about a sodium pentothal exam? Not a chance. Greenwich Police's Captain Keegan ordered a deep investigation on Kenny Littleton.

Back at Brunswick and away from Meerbergen's nettlesome scrutiny, Carroll and Lunney accosted Littleton, pressuring him to take another polygraph. When he refused, the officers told Brunswick Headmaster Norman Pederson about Littleton's Nantucket crime spree, and Littleton was fired. Littleton landed another teaching gig a few miles away, up the road at the St. Luke's School in New Canaan. Within an hour of learning of Littleton's new position, Carroll and Lunney appeared in the office of Headmaster Richard Whitcomb with a lowdown on Littleton's summer escapades. Kenny lost that job, too. He was a hot potato.

The detectives rifled through Littleton's college records in Willamstown, Massachusetts. Sitting in Littleton's parents' house in Belmont, they watched the blood drain from Ann and Wayne Littleton's faces as they explained that their son had flunked his polygraph. They visited Littleton's pediatrician and some old Belmont Hill teachers. Then, in November, Carroll and Lunney took the Hyannis ferry to Nantucket. They crisscrossed the island talking to cops and Littleton's former landlords, boss, and girlfriends, and the woman who awoke in bed beneath a nude Kenny Littleton.

In Williamstown the investigators encountered their first evidence that Littleton may have killed again. Police Chief Joseph Zoito suggested that a local unsolved murder bore similarities to the Moxley homicide. On Halloween 1976, a trapper discovered the body of a 17-year-old white girl named Rocky Krizack in a ravine 20 miles from town—dead from a blow to the head and strangulation. Investigators felt that the motivation was sexual but, as in Moxley's case, she had not been raped. Littleton had spent a lot of time that fall hanging around his alma mater, especially during football season. No arrest was ever made for the murder.

Solomon persuaded the Nantucket Police to offer a deal: if Littleton would agree to a sodium amytal interview about the Moxley murder, Nantucket prosecutors would knock his burglary charges down to a misdemeanor. Littleton refused and plead guilty to the felonies. His decision was consequential. The plea ended his teaching and coaching career. In explaining his crime wave to the Barnstable judge, Littleton said, "When I drink, I flip out." In May 1977, a Nantucket court handed him a 7- to 10-year suspended sentence and five years' probation. He complained that the case had been "rigged by Connecticut investigators . . . Lunney and Carroll," and confessed that he feared that "the Greenwich Police were going to take me back to Connecticut and shoot me in the head."

Solomon was convinced that Littleton had murdered Martha Moxley, but his team lacked the hard evidence needed for a winning prosecution. The many other plausible suspects would give Littleton's defense attorneys ample opportunity to introduce reasonable doubt and sway a jury toward acquittal. The Connecticut police believed that only a confession would win them a conviction. Solomon and Browne resisted the temptation to arrest their murder suspect just to appease public demand for resolution. And so the Moxley murder investigation petered out. It became a "cold file."

In 1982 Littleton moved to Florida, where he lived as a street person. Florida police arrested him for a parade of crimes, including trespassing, disorderly conduct, drunk driving, public intoxication, and shoplifting. He drank a case of beer a day and often blacked out. He once chucked a large rock through a car windshield.

Littleton worked as a stripper for most of 1982, in Orlando and Fort Lauderdale. In north Florida, he met his future wife, Canadian Mary Baker, a fellow alcoholic, in recovery. His stripper gigs dried up as he ballooned to 260 pounds in the mid-1980s. The couple moved to Ontario and married in Ottawa on April 27, 1983. In Canada, Littleton was unable to work, owing to instability and alcoholism. He and Baker played golf and lived off her inheritance. In a 1991 interview with Connecticut police, Baker described Littleton as "going nuts" during that period. Baker said that he liked pornography and would often visit strip bars. In June 1983 his arm was mangled during a knife fight in Hull, Quebec. That autumn Canadian police arrested him for disruptive conduct near the Canadian Parliament. Soon afterward, the couple moved back to Littleton's hometown of Belmont.

In 1984, during a manic period, Littleton serially called former Attorney General Ed Meese. In February of that year, he started railing about the Moxley murder, and then telephoned Martha's father, David Moxley, asking Moxley for money to undergo sodium pentothal testing, offering to give the bereaved father copies of the tapes. Kenny said he thought the testing would give him "peace of mind" and perhaps help him to remember things that happened the night of the murder. He told Moxley that Martha's murder was their "mutual tragedy." Despite his offer to David Moxley, Littleton never took the sodium pentothal test, although, according to his wife, he remained obsessed by the idea.

By 1984, according to Baker, Littleton had begun identifying himself again as "Kenneth Kennedy, the black sheep of the Kennedy family." He told the police that the Kennedys bedeviled him, saying they intended to frame him for the Moxley murder. He believed that he could cause a tornado or a hurricane by flushing the toilet. He ate money, drank toilet water, left golf clubs at synagogues, and collected JFK matchbooks. He was often sick from drinking and occasionally suffered delirium tremens. Baker said that while on a trip through Connecticut in February 1984, Littleton told her that he saw pink elephants and believed that he had magical powers. He was in and out of psychiatric facilities over subsequent years, often arriving in police cars. In November 1984, Belmont cops picked up Baker and her and Littleton's infant child walking the street at 1:30 a.m. on a 35-degree night. A drunken Littleton had locked them out of the house. Belmont police arrested him and found his knife collection. Baker explained that Littleton had carried a knife in his sock ever since his stabbing in Canada. He later described that incident to Michael's grand jury as an attempted hit by the Skakel family.

In April 1985, following another alcohol-induced mental breakdown, Kenny Littleton was admitted to Charles River Hospital. In 1986 he became active in an alcoholism-recovery group, but he slipped repeatedly. The vivid hallucinations and expansive delusions of manic depression plagued him. In October 1988 he was back in Williamstown, attending sporting events, playing golf, and stalking the Williams rugby team. According to police reports, Littleton told security officers at Williams that he was a reformed alcoholic and that drinking and drugs had destroyed his life.

In 1989, Kenny Littleton appeared at the Williams "Old Farts" alumni rugby game where he cornered a young dean and religion professor, William Darrow, to pitch his services as a drug and alcohol counselor to the team. His nightmarish experiences, he argued, could scare the team straight. Darrow told police that Littleton was "nuts, and scared him to death." The hour he spent with Littleton was one of "the most frightening experiences of his life." He recounted that he had "feared for his safety" as Littleton explained the Moxley murder and the Kennedy family's plots to silence him. Darrow later described Littleton to the police as "big . . . and extremely angry." Police reports quoted him as saying that Littleton had started talking about the Moxley murder and "became very intense."

His family found Littleton no less harrowing. Littleton sometimes threatened to kill his wife. He would become particularly depressed, Baker told the police, around Halloween, the anniversary of Martha's murder. In October 1989 Baker threw him out and separated from him. In May 1990 he tossed hot coffee on her and tried to force his way into her house. Littleton moved in with a manic-depressive stripper named Kimberly in Boston's Combat Zone. He aspired to return to erotic dancing and join Kimberly in her act. Baker divorced Littleton on July 12, 1990.

By August 1991, when Dunne's shenanigans prompted Connecticut law-enforcement authorities to reopen the Moxley case, Kenny Littleton was still a prime suspect. He had recently been institutionalized for manic depression and paranoid delusions at McLean Hospital in Belmont. Solomon, Garr, and Detroit homicide detectives, whom the Greenwich police had brought in to help support the investigation (Detroit, at that time the nation's murder capital, was renowned for the cutting-edge expertise of its homicide bureau), all believed that Littleton might be responsible for a string of unsolved killings of young women in Massachusetts, Florida, Maine, New York, and Canada. On September 23, 1991, Garr went to Ottawa to examine the police files on three young women who had disappeared during a 23-day period in 1988. None of the bodies were ever found. Garr's report concluded, "All three women were last seen in the same vicinity . . . within close proximity to where Ken Littleton had resided."

FRANK GARR was new on the Martha Moxley case. His bosses at the Greenwich Police Department assigned him, in 1994, to the State's Attorney's Bridgeport office to work under Jack Solomon to solve the stone-cold homicide. Garr would be the architect of Michael Skakel's wrongful conviction a decade later.

According to Levitt's book, Garr spent his early years just over the New York boundary from Greenwich in gritty, blue-collar Port Chester, where his father, Tony, ran an Italian restaurant. Garr, whose paternal grandfather had changed the family name from Carino, moved his family over the Connecticut border in the early 1970s, paying $62,000 for a place in Glenville, Greenwich's most modest neighborhood.

After an unhappy period selling insurance post–high school, Garr did a tour in Vietnam, and then returned to Greenwich, where in 1967, at age 22, he became a police patrolman. His first assignment was directing traffic on Greenwich Avenue, the town's chichi main drag where boutiques and restaurants catered to Greenwich tycoons and trophy wives. Like many Greenwich cops, he made ends meet by moonlighting for the town's fat cats, providing private airport shuttle service and bartending at events. He worked security at Frank and Kathie Lee Gifford's parties in the back country. When their kids, Cody and Cassidy, were born in Greenwich Hospital, Garr was there to keep the media away. Garr was painfully aware of his place at the bottom of the Greenwich food chain. "I drove. We all drove," he told Levitt. "Did I like it? No. But if my son needed a $350 pair of ice skates each year for hockey, I had to work extra for it." Garr's resentments toward the Greenwich swells may have fed the seething hatred he later espoused toward the Skakel family. He told Levitt that he experienced anti-Italian bigotry on the force. When he grew a mustache, he overheard a superior say under his breath, "That's all we need, another guinea with a mustache." The story may be apocryphal. As we shall see, Garr had a grifter's contempt for the truth and Levitt was his willing pigeon.

In any case, Garr dealt with the snobs by getting up in their grills. Garr presented himself as an iconoclast, an outsider. While the other Greenwich cops were clean cut, Garr concealed the chip on his shoulder with his long, irreverent ponytail, which he wore like an extended middle finger to the elite, straight-laced, and notoriously insular Greenwich constabulary. Writer Richard Hoffman, who was forced by subpoena to help in Garr's office before Michael's trial, recounted, "He had a 100-percent Frank Sinatra–themed office," Hoffman said. "He had a six CD–changer playing nothing but Frank Sinatra and he had one of those novelty phones on his desk with Frank Sinatra with his head cocked a certain way leaning against a lamppost. So I'm listening to 'Strangers in the Night' and trying to read."

Garr had Hollywood daydreams. He got a headshot and took acting lessons in Manhattan at the Weist-Barron School, hoping to find a TV gig. He established the town's first drug unit and went undercover for drug-buying stings.

His bosses plucked Garr from the Greenwich police force to work as an investigator in the office of then–Fairfield County State's Attorney Donald Browne, under Connecticut law-enforcement legend Jack Solomon. The two were yin and yang. While Garr was a rebel, Solomon, then pushing 60, was a by-the-book cop's cop with a three-pack-a-day cigarette habit. Mary Baker told Levitt that Solomon reminded her of John Wayne, "but wearing a brown polyester suit with a bad tie instead of cowboy duds." Solomon had worked the Moxley case from the beginning, back when Garr was still working dispatch. Garr brought his resentment to his new job. He told Levitt that the Moxley murder—by now a 15-year-old cold case—was the booby prize. He had ended up on the Moxley detail because his fellow officers despised him and they wanted him out of Greenwich. The case was 15 years old and hadn't been solved. His new Bridgeport office was the dead-end gulag for an unwanted exile; more punishment than opportunity. Levitt describes a 1997 visit to Garr's seedy Bridgeport digs. At that time, Garr saw himself as a laughingstock, disdained by his fellow officers and boss who regarded him, for reasons Levitt never explains, with acute moral revulsion: "The stillness in the office was unnerving. The phone didn't ring. No clerks or secretaries bustled in or out. Frank was out of the flow of the office's daily activity, estranged from his law enforcement colleagues. 'No one comes in here to speak to me,' he said. 'I walk down the hall, people see me coming and make a sign of the cross, as though to ward me off. I'm the office joke. A royal pain in the ass to everyone.'"

Garr had an easily bruised ego and especially despised his boss, Solomon, who, he felt, disrespected him. "He never considered me an equal," Garr whined to Levitt, who says that the mention of Solomon's name made Garr apoplectic. "Get him started and he could rant. 'You know Jack's problem? He thinks he's smarter than everyone else. He thinks everyone else is stupid. He's in love with the polygraph and with his image and can't admit when he's wrong.'" Garr apparently felt Solomon had poisoned their boss, Donald Browne, against him.

For Levitt, who also despised his boss and felt underappreciated, it was love at first sight. Levitt shared with Garr his own travails working at *Long Island Newsday*, a failing newspaper, where his editor neither trusted him nor valued his work. After all, the paper sat on his article about the Moxley murder for eight years. Now the lonely reporter and the friendless cop had found each other. Levitt describes a blossoming romance between the two wallflowers, "We seemed to enjoy ourselves so much that we arranged a lunch at a pub in Greenwich. Another evening we met for dinner at an Italian restaurant in Stamford. Here we were, two grown men with wives and children, now spending an increasing amount of time together. At each meeting, we'd talk for hours. Our coming together, a reporter and a detective, seemed so unnatural, I said to Frank, 'Jesus, if anyone noticed what was going on between us, they might think we're gay.' 'Who gives

a fuck?' he answered. 'We've developed a friendship. It's the truth.'" Levitt was a
star-struck groupie happy to play crime-fighting Robin to Garr's Batman. Levitt
would later describe Garr as "my mirror image, whose struggles and personality I
saw reflected in my own." The centerpiece of their odd bromance would become
their crusade to nail Michael Skakel for a crime he didn't commit.

Dunne's William Kennedy Smith rumor tripped the wire that ultimately
brought Garr into the Skakels' lives and made him their scourge. Dunne's baseless story that Will had been in Greenwich at the time of the Moxley murder
provoked renewed media hysteria around the case. The *Greenwich Time* finally
printed Levitt's magnum opus attacking the Connecticut police. In response to
the onslaught, Browne held a press conference on August 8, 1991, announcing
that he had reopened the investigation under the direction of Solomon, with
Garr as his deputy. Browne provided the number for a dedicated tip line; Mrs.
Moxley announced a $50,000 reward for information leading to an arrest.

Kenny Littleton had made an impression on Solomon 14 years earlier when
he rejected Nantucket's offer of a reduced sentence in exchange for allowing
Solomon to question him under truth serum. Shortly afterward, Littleton blew
off Solomon and the Greenwich police during a phone interview. "I never want
to see you fucking guys again," Littleton told the cops. "I'll talk to you on the
phone, but you fucking cocksuckers are not going to bother me anymore! Stay
out of my life and leave me alone!"

As the investigation reopened, Littleton was Solomon's favorite suspect by
a mile. Solomon concurred with Sutton detective Jim Murphy as to Littleton's
motive. "He [Kenny Littleton] was drinking," he'd tell Garr. "His horns came
out." Tommy had passed the polygraph. Solomon had been in Bethany when
Littleton failed. Tommy had stayed out of trouble since 1975; Littleton was a
walking crime wave. Solomon saw Littleton's reference to the murder as "our
mutual tragedy" to be a sideways confession offered up to David Moxley.

In late September 1991, Solomon and Garr appeared at Mary Baker's house
in Ottawa to report that they suspected Littleton was a serial killer. She told
the police that Littleton "had frequently and compulsively" made incriminating
statements about the Moxley murder. From the time she met Littleton, in 1982,
he had been obsessed and paranoid about the case, describing the incident as
"a monkey on his back." Littleton had speculated to many that "maybe some
wickedness took him over for five minutes." She said that Littleton was plagued
with "a nagging doubt, because he's not a well man, and [because of] the fact it
was not resolved."

Baker began calling Garr regularly to recount the intimate details of her
ex-husband's private meanderings: his pornography tastes, hospital stays, family
relationships, and his abiding obsession with the murder. Baker carried a heavy
burden. She told the investigators that, when she was 13, her own mother was

murdered. She complained about Littleton's relationship in Florida with a fellow male stripper with whom he sought out free meals and slept in a truck behind a "possibly gay hotel." Baker said that during one of Littleton's various hospital stays, he approached a 15-year-old female fellow patient, in the presence of the girl's mother, and requested oral sex. "It'll do you good to suck me off." Littleton had described to Baker his taste in women as "the younger the better."

Baker began calling Littleton to conduct undercover interviews and report back to Garr. When Solomon and Garr needed a hair sample, she was eager to help. She invited Littleton to visit her in Ottawa. The second he left, Mounties swept in and bundled the sheets off to Connecticut for criminalist Henry Lee to test. Lee found Littleton's hair "microscopically consistent" with a hair found on Martha's body, one of the few pieces of physical evidence that police had managed to recover and not lose. Baker began to see more and more of Littleton, ostensibly to reconcile, but Solomon and Garr treated the reunions as intelligence-gathering missions.

On December 4, 1991, according to the search-warrant request, Baker called Garr to say that she'd just had a telephone conversation with Littleton. He was fretting that the Connecticut State Police might find the missing golf-club handle and trace his fingerprints. "Even if I'm innocent, I could be charged with murder," she said he told her. "Let's say a hunter or someone tripped over them in the woods." He mentioned a pair of pants that he said might have Martha's blood on them. The police knew that Littleton, at his own suggestion, had taken some of the Skakel boys to the family's Catskills cabin the weekend after the killing. Even then, it struck the Skakel family as odd that Littleton insisted on driving his own car the 2 hour and 20 minute ride to Windham. Police speculated that he could have disposed of the evidence on that trip. The police report noted that while in Windham, Littleton had borrowed a shotgun from Tom Sheridan, saying he wanted to go hunting in the woods. Solomon ordered a new-fangled metal detector, cadaver dogs, and a search party to the Skakels' Windham, New York, ski house. Rucky, as per usual, consented. They came up empty-handed.

With Baker's permission, the police began taping conversations between the estranged couple. With the help of the Boston Police Department, Solomon and Garr wired room 1501 of the Boston Howard Johnson's on February 10, 1992. Baker lured Littleton into this ambush with the scent of reconciliation. During the rendezvous, Littleton provided another new detail that sounded to Solomon like a chilling admission. Littleton had long been adamant that he had heard no dogs barking when he left the house that night and he hadn't heard any barking thereafter. He now recalled barking. Baker told the police that Littleton had a peculiar hatred of dogs, "specifically when they bark." She did not say when that hatred began.

"The Irish nanny, she's about 75 years old, half senile, um dogs are barking outside, the German shepherd is barking outside, 'Will you go out and check on what's happening?'" Littleton's voice is audible on the concealed tape. "Um and so the front door is here and there's a circular driveway that goes like that, with another driveway like this, and then . . . there's a row of tall cedars right there." At this point, Littleton was obviously drawing a map, but the details he includes about the Skakel property are curious. Though he places himself in the driveway, at the side of the house where the Revcon motor home was parked, the Skakels had no circular driveway. The Moxleys, however, did, and Martha had first been struck in the grass patch inside of the Moxley's circular driveway. The only line of cedar trees on the Skakel property was adjacent to the tennis courts, at the very southeastern edge of the property, directly across the street from the crime scene. In his story, Littleton mentions the dogs barking several more times, and discloses for the first time that he heard the sound of "leaves rustling" as he stood outside in the pitch black. He also said that he was outside when the dog stopped barking. "So, ah, I, the rustling stops, and I stop, the dog stops barking, and I got into the house," Littleton said.

This was consistent with Solomon's speculation that, after Nanny Sweeney asked Littleton to check on the fracas, Littleton's hatred of dogs prompted him to grab a golf club from the barrel near the door. Outside he heard the rustling of Tommy and Martha in the bushes. Inflamed and in an alcoholic stupor, Littleton followed Martha as she walked toward her house. When she refused his advances, he struck her and dragged her under the evergreen boughs. In Solomon's judgment, the zigzagging path across the yard, first toward a neighbor's house and then back to the pine tree, indicated a perpetrator unfamiliar with the terrain. The tree under which Martha's body was found was adjacent to a path used daily by local children as a shortcut from southern Belle Haven to Walsh Lane, where many of their friends lived. According to Tom Sheridan, "Anyone familiar with the neighborhood would have dragged her another 10 yards into the tall grass, where she might have remained hidden for days."

In June 1992, Baker reported to police that Littleton told her he couldn't have committed the crime because he would have been covered with blood. Baker reported that "Ken made the statement, 'You take a five iron to a girl's head and smash the shit out of it, it's like taking a baseball bat to a tomato, a big tomato: there's going to be a lot of fucking blood.'" Julie Skakel told me that, when she talked with Littleton as he entered the kitchen from the pantry at around 10:00 p.m., he had changed his clothes. His location in the kitchen, at that time, is inconsistent with any of his alibis: when he first described leaving the house, he said he had re-entered through the front door. The door to a mudroom off the pantry was the only place one might expect to enter the Skakel home unobserved. Instead of the plaid shirt he had worn at dinner, Julie said, Littleton was wearing a sweatshirt.

Finally, Tommy told me that he and Littleton had watched *The French Connection* after 10:00 p.m. on the night of the murder, and that Littleton had mysteriously kept his body entirely draped with a blanket—something Tommy had considered odd, because it was not cold in the room.

Six months after the Howard Johnson's operation, Solomon dispatched Garr to talk to Littleton. During that meeting, Garr unleashed the same suite of dirty-pool tactics that he would subsequently deploy on reluctant witnesses to build his case against Michael: lying, intimidation, and psy-ops. "I had to schmooze him," Garr told Levitt. Garr's objective was to get Littleton to take another polygraph and meet with Kathy Morall, a Colorado-based forensic psychiatrist Solomon had seen on *48 Hours.* According to Levitt's book *Conviction,* Littleton asked Garr if he should have a lawyer. "If you get an attorney you'll never clear this up because he won't let you do it," Garr advised. "We all know you didn't do it, but you can't clear this up if you have a lawyer. He won't let you take the polygraph." In December 1992, Kenny Littleton appeared in Greenwich, sans attorney, with Garr's assurance that the cops thought he was innocent. The opposite was true. In Solomon's words, "That meeting would eliminate any residual uncertainty about Littleton's guilt."

Littleton spent a full day with Morall in the Greenwich police library, talking openly about his childhood, his sexual history, his drug and alcohol abuse, and his chronic mental illness. The following day he spent eight hours with polygrapher Robert Brisentine. A heavyweight in the lie-detection field, Brisentine had formerly served as the chief investigator for the army's Criminal Investigation Command. Brisentine had complete confidence in the machine—and his own ability to detect artifice. "You don't fool the instrument. You fool the examiner," Brisentine would tell a reporter. "And I believe that if an examiner does it properly and doesn't have a preconceived idea [of a suspect's guilt or innocence], he will get the truth."

Brisentine asked Littleton the following questions:

Did you have any quarrel with Martha Moxley on October 30, 1975?
Did you have a golf club in your possession on October 30, 1975?
Regarding the matter pertaining to Martha Moxley, do you intend to answer truthfully to each question about that?
Did you cause those injuries to Martha Moxley on October 30, 1975?
Did you have a golf club in your hand on October 30, 1975?

Brisentine approached Solomon afterward. "The man who murdered Martha Moxley is sitting in that room," Brisentine said, according to Solomon.

"Don't ever let anyone persuade you otherwise." Garr told Levitt that Brisentine also took him aside. "Frank, that guy killed that girl," he told Garr. "I polygraphed three convicts in jail that confessed to crimes and their polygraphs were not as good as this guy's." When I approached Brisentine in 2002, he wouldn't specifically own up to saying those things, but he did offer this: "Even if he didn't commit the crime, he definitely had guilty knowledge of the crime and probably knows who did."

If Brisentine's report wasn't powerful enough, Morall's, which arrived in late January 1993, closed the door on any lingering doubts about Littleton's guilt. "The examination of behavior following the crime strongly points to Mr. Littleton," she wrote. "Not only does he engage in violence, much of it is directed towards women. . . . His apparent preoccupation with the crime and his 'theories' of how it occurred would typically suggest involvement or guilt." Morall also downgraded Tommy's profile as a suspect. "In looking at the limited amount of available information about Tommy following the crime, one would have to conclude that, if he committed the crime, he did not follow it with the expected behavior consistent with a person of anger and with a disturbed psychological makeup," she wrote. "The chance that someone would display a one-time-only episode of violent rage is highly unlikely." In his interview, Littleton had once again inched closer to the crime scene. This time, he placed himself at 10:00 p.m. at a line of conifers on the edge of the Skakel property, less than 25 yards from where Martha was attacked. He reported that he heard scuffling in the leaves, like something was being dragged or an animal moving. Kenny Littleton's evolution during the course of the investigation had gone from him not setting foot outside the entire night of the murder, to checking on a "fracas" in the driveway, and hearing no dogs barking, to being less than 30 footsteps from the crime scene, and hearing not only dogs barking, but what was likely the attack or its aftermath.

Kathy Morall reported that Littleton had hinted he sexually abused children, and had been abused himself. At 15, Morall reported, "an older adult male invited him into his home and performed oral sex on him." That same year he began babysitting a 3-year-old boy and a 4-year-old girl. Morall reported that Littleton admitted, "He would periodically pull their pajamas down and view their genitals. He could not explain his motivation for this behavior." He'd had sex with about 60 women, and his type was Martha to a T: "the classic blonde, blue-eyed type." Considering the crime scene, and the amount of blood that certainly sprayed from Martha during the attack, curious imagery popped up in his memory of his first psychotic break in 1981. "I saw pine trees and felt water sparkling over my ankles," he told Morall. "I dashed through it and was going towards a garden. I was doing ritualistic praying in sets of three like the trinity." Littleton was subsequently hospitalized after slashing his forearm with three deep parallel cuts—the mark of the trinity.

Littleton agreed to meet with Martha Moxley's brother, John, in 1994. "When I left there, I felt like I had been in the presence of a true wacko," John told Mark Fuhrman. "And you're standing there thinking, 'Oh my God, this could be the guy who killed my sister,'" he told Dumas, just two years before the State brought Michael's case to the grand jury. "I had the impression that he was crazy enough to do anything."

Solomon, like Morall, believed that whoever had killed Martha would certainly act out again. With Garr, Solomon created a 42-page "Time Lapse Data" report that tracked 15 years of Kenny Littleton's movements, and how his locations corresponded with 20 unsolved murders of white women, beginning with Rocky Krizack in 1976. Many of the connections to serial murder might have been coincidental, but others showed some eerie consistencies. On August 6, 1988, a 22-year-old woman named Jane Boroski, seven months pregnant, stopped at a closed convenience store in West Swanzey, New Hampshire, to get a drink from a vending machine. As she sipped her Coke, a man dragged her from her car and stabbed her 27 times. Miraculously she and her baby survived. She reported that her assailant was a white male driving a golden brown Jeep Wagoneer with wood-grain sides. At the time, Littleton drove a yellow Plymouth Voyager with wood grain-sides. As he buried his knife in her chest and her arms, the man accused Boroski of beating up his girlfriend, which sounded to Solomon rather like Littleton's dance-floor attack of Linda Cahoon years earlier at Nantucket's Chicken Box.

In the years after Michael's conviction, Garr would say that during this whole period he never really thought that Littleton had killed Martha: he was at the mercy of his monomaniacal boss, Solomon. He claimed to have known from the beginning that Michael was the murderer. "I didn't think Kenny did it," he told Levitt in 2003. Unlike Solomon, "My ego wasn't on the line." This statement, like Garr's entire case against Michael, doesn't pass the smell test. Police reports from that period, all signed only by Garr, demonstrate that he was as convinced of Littleton's guilt as his boss. Garr told Levitt that when Fuhrman called him in 1997, he had long since determined that Michael was the killer and that Kenny Littleton was an innocent patsy. But here's what he said to Fuhrman at the time: "It's interesting, in 1976 Littleton submitted to a polygraph examination and failed it, and then 18 years later he takes another polygraph examination and fails again. I mean, that's interesting." Garr not only regularly lied to witnesses and suspects, he also lied to Levitt, his collaborator and hagiographer. Garr's claim that he long suspected that Michael was the culprit was convenient revisionism.

In February 1993 Littleton told the police that he was no longer willing to cooperate with investigators. In 1994 Solomon told Sheridan that Boston authorities had impounded Littleton's car after a run-in with a Boston policeman.

Sheridan told me that Solomon then showed him and Manny Margolis a black three-ring binder containing photos of the bodies of 13 teenage girls fatally bludgeoned within the vicinity of Littleton's various homes. One of them was a 15-year-old blonde girl who looked eerily similar to Martha and whose dissected body had been cleaved in half and thrown in a dumpster across from Littleton's apartment in Boston's Combat Zone. Kenny Littleton was a suspect in those murders, Solomon told him. Solomon said he was trying to assemble an arrest warrant for Littleton in the Moxley murder.

Solomon never got the warrant. In the summer of 1998, Connecticut's attorney general granted Littleton lifetime immunity and removed him from the suspect list in exchange for his testimony before a rarely invoked one-man grand jury called to indict Michael Skakel. Benedict later explained his decision to grant immunity to Littleton in a colloquy with Michael's trial court Judge John Kavanewsky: "Mr. Littleton was given immunity because the State felt it had no evidence whatsoever to prosecute Mr. Littleton. We used his testimony to clear [Tommy Skakel], another longtime suspect."

In July 1999 Kenny Littleton called the *Greenwich Time* from McLean Hospital and said that the Kennedy family was trying to kill him. Shortly after his release, Littleton stabbed himself four times in the chest with a kitchen knife. The police who searched his apartment found the charred pages of a diary, torn from the binding and burned. Littleton refused to talk with the police about the stabbing.

The law requires prosecutors to turn over all exculpatory evidence to the defense prior to trial. This includes evidence that might support a third-party culpability defense. Prior to Michael's trial, Benedict and Garr withheld key pieces of evidence pointing to Littleton's guilt. These included the composite sketch created from descriptions by Belle Haven security guard Charles Morganti of a man seen near the murder scene minutes before Martha's killing. The sketch resembles Kenny Littleton. Michael's lawyers had specifically requested all sketches related to the case. Under oath, in Michael's new trial hearing, Garr conceded that the sketch was both an important piece of evidence and should have been turned over to Michael's defense.

Garr and Benedict also withheld Dr. Kathy Morall's interviews with Littleton. That interview was certainly exculpatory since Littleton had placed himself at the crime scene at the likeliest time Martha was killed. Benedict's office also never turned over Solomon's extensive and inculpatory profile of Littleton, or the 1976 unsigned arrest warrant for Tommy. Those documents demonstrated that the State had compiled compelling cases against two other suspects. But the Littleton profile would have had a far more crucial value to the defense. It showed that on October 30, 1975, before the Skakels had left for Sursum Corda, Rush Jr. had informed Littleton that Michael would be joining them. This seemingly small detail from an interview with Littleton obliterated the prosecution's theory that Michael was in Belle Haven at 10:00 p.m. to kill Martha. Michael's well-documented 9:30 p.m. trip to Sursum Corda was one of the many reasons that police had never considered him a suspect. Unfortunately, at trial the only corroboration for Michael's alibi were family members, all of whom Benedict discredited as participants in the continuing family conspiracy. Littleton's statements were precisely the kind of "independent" corroboration that Benedict told the jury didn't exist. Solomon's "Littleton suspect profile" includes the critical conclusion, "It is known and believed that as that vehicle departed from the driveway, occupied by the SKAKEL boys (Rushton, Michael and John) along with their cousin JAMES TERRIEN, that both HELEN IX and GEOFFREY BYRNE began to walk to their homes, leaving only THOMAS SKAKEL and MARTHA MOXLEY standing in the driveway" [emphasis in original]. Benedict certainly would have known that this one point would have gutted his case against Michael. So why hadn't Garr turned it over? "Uh, I was told not to," Garr said under oath in 2007. "By whom?" Michael's lawyer asked him. "Mr. Benedict," he replied. These are brazen so-called Brady violations, one of the most common forms of prosecutorial misconduct. Courts commonly overturn convictions that have relied on this "convict at all costs" mentality. Judges jail prosecutors for prosecutorial infractions less serious than Benedict's outlaw shenanigans in Michael's case. Connecticut's new prosecutors need to restore the integrity of Connecticut's criminal court system by holding Benedict and Garr to the same standards.

PART III

The Victims

CHAPTER 10

Martha and Michael

Sugar and spice, and everything nice. That's what little girls are made of.
—Nursery Rhyme

Despite his murder conviction, none of Martha's closest friends—not Helen, Margie, Jackie, or Sheila—believe that Michael Skakel had anything to do with her death. The State's flimsy, fabricated, circumstantial case had more holes than Albert Hall. In order to convict him, prosecutors had to make Michael a fiend in the jury's eyes and in the public's imagination. That task called for a marketing job that could paint Michael as a callous, entitled, homicidal brute. Fuhrman, Dunne, and Garr bewitched the elderly Dorthy Moxley to censure Michael even though she steadfastly refused to look at any evidence. Garr even deployed Martha herself to point an accusing finger from the grave.

On January 23, 2000, four days after Michael surrendered to Greenwich Police, a long article in the Sunday *New York Post* previewed the drumbeat of libelous chicanery that would soon make Michael a figure of public loathing. Two years earlier the prosecutor had commandeered Martha Moxley's diary as evidence. Now someone in the State's Attorney's office, presumably Garr, began selectively leaking its contents to the press. The choice to give the story to Rupert Murdoch's down-market tabloid was shrewd. Murdoch, a right-wing media mogul, had made the Kennedys his primary target ever since he began buying US media properties in the 1970s. In 1994, my uncle Senator Edward Kennedy orchestrated a legislative maneuver that forced the Australian tabloid publisher to obey the law and to sell his beloved *Boston Herald*, escalating the fight. Mad as an Australian hornet, Murdoch was ever angling for new opportunities to malign my family. Garr, who shared the media mogul's over-the-top antipathy toward the Kennedys (and Skakels) proved himself a prodigious leaker. The *New*

York Post reported, "In a chilling diary entry, Moxley herself—whose battered corpse was found under a tree behind her home on Oct. 30, 1975—wrote that she liked Tommy but feared Michael." Fuhrman described an almost identical passage from the diary in his book. Martha's fear-filled jottings put meat on the prosecution's bare-bones theory that Martha was entangled in a jealous sibling feud, and Michael, unhinged by envy, had killed her in a green-eyed fury. In his summation, Benedict made much of Martha's journal: "We learned [from the diary] that Michael was infatuated with Martha," and that Martha's daybook described "[t]he jealousy between Tom and Michael over her."

None of this was true, not even a little bit. Benedict, as usual, was misstating the evidence. Sherman, as usual, was snoozing. Michael makes only a handful of cameos in Martha's diary, and never as a courtier. In that respect, he is practically unique. With her baby fat shed and her enchanting smile freshly liberated from braces the previous summer, Martha was swarming with suitors. Seemingly, every teenage boy in Greenwich made a crush-struck foray at Martha, even as she dated 16-year-old bad boy Peter Ziluca. "I think Tom Kovacs likes me now," Martha wrote in November 1974. "I walked into 3rd period and he started calling me Legs." The following month, she wrote, "Ralph Cavello likes me. Maybe not, but I'm pretty sure Tom K does." Six months later, a whole new cast of boys appeared. "I think Rob likes me," she wrote in July 1975. "He's only 12, but he's cute. David Howard called again to ask me out to another movie for tomorrow night or Thurs night boy did I come up with excuses! I really don't want to go out with him!"

Martha, a daily diarist, scrupulously cataloged her impressive intake of beer, liquor, and pot. "I got so stoned 1st block today . . . I put a tea bag in the cup then put coffee in it," she wrote on October 9, 1975. "I could not stop laughing!"

Michael became friends with the buoyant Californian blonde soon after she moved to Greenwich. She was relishing her new power to beguile, but she had lost none of her tomboy charm. She loved catching frogs and candle-lighting worms in the darkness after a storm. "She liked to have fun; she was mischievous, too, like me," Michael recalls. "She used to come over all the time after school. We'd smoke cigarettes, smoke pot, drink beer, be kids. We didn't have a garage so we'd hang out in the big Revcon bus that was parked at the side of the house." Martha carefully cataloged her suitors, indexing appealing boys as "foxes," and the rest as "pervs" or "queers." In the course of a year, over two dozen boys asked Martha out. Martha faithfully gazetted the boys she kissed and the elite who made it to third base. Michael was not in either group.

The only entry suggesting anything less than amicable between Martha and Michael occurred September 17, 1975, following a large gathering of kids at the Skakel house. Tommy was there, as was Jackie, who confirmed to me that, at the time of Martha's murder, Jackie and Michael shared mutual crushes on each other. As usual, there was drinking and weed. "Michael was so totally out of it that he was being a real asshole in his actions and his words," Martha wrote. "He kept telling me that I was leading Tom on when I don't like him (except as a friend) & I said, well, how about you and Jackie? You keep telling me that you don't like her & you're all over her. He doesn't understand that he can be nice to her without hanging all over her. Michael jumps to conclusions. Just because I talk to [Tommy], it doesn't mean I like him. I really have to stop going over there. Then since Michael was being such an ass they all started fighting because he was being such a big He-Man. He kept calling Tom & John fags they were ready to have a fist fight so I said, 'come on Jackie let's go.'"

Benedict suggested the entry showed that Martha sensed danger at the Skakel house. But there is no peril in her musing, only the unfiltered reveries of a 15-year-old girl. True, she described Michael acting the "ass" that day, but Martha's journal spares no one. Elsewhere she refers to her mother as "a royal BITCH." Several people "bug the shit out of me," and she logs a lengthy inventory of "pervs" and "queers," with whom she happily shares her day. Martha's vow to "stop going over" doesn't stick; two days later, she returns. "We went to Skakel's," she wrote. "We had such a good time."

Martha does profile certain boys who seem unhealthily obsessed with her. "Bob S. is still the world's biggest pervert," she wrote on November 11, 1974. "He and Tim want me to go see *The Trial of Billy Jack* on Sat. What excuse can I use to get out of it?" Martha turned down Bob's invitation. "Boy did he get pissed at me!" she wrote. "He went wild. . . . Bob pleaded with me to go out with him. He waited for me after school and tripped me and practically attacked me!" Two weeks later, "Bob" was still nursing his wounds. "Peter and Tony called and so did Tim to tell me Bob is still pissed at me," she wrote on December 1, 1974. "Wowie zowie!"

Martha sometimes appears reckless in exploring her newfound sexuality, particularly with older men. She accepted rides in a Maserati Bora and a Ferrari Dino from "Chris," the salesman at the local Grand Prix Limited sports car dealership. She dodged a stalker during a shopping jaunt on Greenwich Avenue with a girlfriend in March 1975. "We went into Rogers & when we came out there was this guy staring at us," she wrote. "So we did not think much about it. We went to Woolworths' and he followed us & stared at us again so we went in & he watched us through the window. Then we went up to Ann Taylors and we didn't notice but he followed us. So we were looking at the shoes & he was staring at us through the window. Then he watched us through the door & then he left . . . we thought, so we left & he was up by Gengrelly's [*sic*] so we crossed the street & so did he. . . . He was CREEPY!"

The Greenwich of Martha's diary was a parent's nightmare of menacing gargoyles and looming sexual peril, but not from Michael. Michael, like seemingly every other teenaged boy in Greenwich, held a torch for Martha, but it was puppy love. "You know, Martha was a touchy, feely kind of girl, a friendly girl, like a California girl," he told me. "She was the kind of girl that you could talk to. I mean, as a kid I wanted a friend and she was friendly. You know what I mean? She was nonjudgmental. Everyone in my life seemed to be judgmental, including me of myself, and this was one of the few people in the world who wasn't judgmental."

Unlike Tommy, and many of the other boys who were courting Martha, Michael was a virgin. Sherman's long tally of professional malpractice includes his failure to show the jurors a photo of Michael from the time Martha was murdered. Julie describes Michael as "a runt with peach fuzz under his arms and a cute, beardless baby face." His growth spurt didn't launch until he was 16, the year after the murder.

A photo of Michael playing tennis less than one month after the murder captures the absurdity of the State's contentions; Michael obviously lacked the strength to inflict the kind of terrible damage evident in the autopsy photos or summon the savagery to shatter a golf club into three pieces and then drag Martha's body 78 feet. "We do know there's a lot of strength involved, okay," Henry Lee told Tim Dumas in 1997. "Because it is a brutal, brutal murder and you need a lot of strength." Dr. Don Mallard, a physician who knew Michael and who examined Martha's body, told Mrs. Victor Ziminsky, a Skakel family friend, that it was "impossible" that Michael could have wielded a golf club with the savagery or the strength needed to shatter the shaft and drive it through Martha's body. Mallard, who has since died, said it was equally unlikely that Michael could then drag Martha, who matched him in weight, to the tree some 78 feet from where she was first attacked. "Whoever killed Martha should have sufficient amount of bloodstain, and maybe other biological fluid," Dr. Henry Lee observed. In 1995, Lee told Stephen, "I know your brother didn't do it." Michael's photo shows a kid barely sophisticated enough to make it to school on time, let alone murder a girl while drunk and high, clean himself up, conceal the evidence, and then face Dorthy Moxley in his bedroom at 9:00 a.m. Michael does not now, nor has he ever, possessed the kind of executive control—much less the criminal mastermind skills—required for such a sophisticated operation.

Michael's childhood friends remark that he remained unchanged after the murder and they didn't notice any signs that he might be carrying the burden of the crime. "I can tell you that Michael did not withdraw afterwards," his friend Peter Coomaraswamy comments. "I actually became closer with Michael afterwards. He was appropriately upset by Martha's murder." Peter stood next to Michael by the Skakel pool the afternoon that Sheila discovered Martha's body. As news media flooded the neighborhood, the two boys studied the blue sheet displaying the shape of their friend's lifeless body. "We were all stunned," he says.

"None of us could believe it." Peter remembers that, as they stood forlornly near Walsh Lane, a female news reporter shoved a microphone in Michael's face. "Are you Michael Skakel?" she asked. Michael nodded. "I heard your mother was a steak choke victim." She was confusing Michael's mother, Anne, who died of cancer in 1973, with his Aunt Pat Skakel who choked to death in 1967. Michael burst into tears. "This poor kid turns around and we both walked back to his house," Peter says. "I still remember that, years later. I just can't believe that the Michael I remember from that day was a guy that killed his next door neighbor with a golf club." Jackie concurs that Michael's demeanor didn't change following the murder. "He was always the same," she says. She adds, "The fact that he was willing to discuss the case with the reporters in the neighborhood didn't seem consistent with a kid trying to hide anything."

Their mutual friends didn't think Michael killed Martha. He was never a suspect for 15 years. There were far better suspects to put on trial, even among his siblings.

"You can't rule anyone out," says criminal defense attorney Linda Kenney Baden. "The only person they should have ruled out was Michael, but he was the only one who was ruled in."

So why did Michael go to jail for eleven and a half years for this crime? Why is he today facing the prospect of being sent back to prison or being retried for the murder? Like so many human tragedies, Michael's ordeal began with avarice, specifically the greed of a crooked lawyer. This man's villainy caused Michael to miss his son George's childhood.

PART IV

The Frame

CHAPTER 11

The Caller

Gossip and Lies Are the Handmaidens of Treachery
                                    —New England Proverb

O n Sunday, March 5, 1978, 17-year-old Michael found himself in a tight
      spot. Just before dawn that day, New York state troopers arrested him in
      Windham, New York, and charged him with a laundry list of crimes, in-
cluding unlicensed operation of a motor vehicle, speeding, failure to comply
with a police officer, and DUI. He was more than mildly worried. He would
have been frantic if he had known that these misdeeds would lead to two years of
imprisonment and torture in rural Maine and, much later, to a 20-years-to-life
sentence for a murder he didn't commit.

The evening before had started out so promising. Michael spent the day
skiing with his brother Rush Jr. and some of Rush's Dartmouth friends. When
the group lit out that night for Klondike, a disco 10 miles south in Hunter, New
York, Michael made the fateful decision to stay home alone. An hour after his
comrades left, Michael answered the ringing doorbell to find an angel, Debbie
Diehl, a model in her twenties whose family owned a nearby ski lodge. "Where is
everybody?" she asked. "At the Klondike," Michael answered, enchanted. "How
old are you?" she asked. "Twenty-one," Michael lied. "You want to go try to
find them?" she asked. "Sure." Michael didn't mention that he'd swallowed two
"Disco Biscuits"—714 Quaaludes—given to him by one of Rush's college buddies. They hopped in Tommy's brand-new Jeep Cherokee Chief. It was snowing.

Michael had never taken Quaaludes before and was skeptical about their
potential. "Somebody had just given me acid and we took it and it didn't do
anything so I just assumed the same thing would happen with this." While tra-
versing the Catskills back roads on Route 296, Michael noticed that the wintery

mountain landscape had morphed into a pulsating pudding of inky blackness. His legs turned to rubber. "I was really, really high," he says. "Like higher than I'd ever been." Unsurprisingly, they couldn't find the night club. "Well, let's go back to your place," Diehl said. "Excellent!" thought Michael. His driving was sufficiently erratic to win the attention of a roadside trooper who stepped out from tending to a car accident to signal Michael to pull over. Michael ignored the gesture. A minute later, the patrol car's takedown lights appeared in his rear-view mirror. He punched the gas. "Why don't you just stop?" Diehl pleaded. "I don't have a license," he explained. "My father will kill me." Michael succeeded in outrunning the cruiser, but at the Windham town line he found a waiting roadblock. The police report states that Michael "attempted to run down the police officer." Michael objects, "That's not true. I just drove the Jeep around the roadblock." A mile down the road, he crashed into a telephone pole, totaling the vehicle. "Thank God she was okay," he says. "I cut the back of my head open." The police put him in a marked car. "They started taking me to the police station to do a sobriety test and I somehow got the back door open and rolled out of the car at like 30 miles an hour." The police recaptured Michael and, since he was a minor, drove him home after he refused a breathalyzer. Back in Greenwich, Rucky referred the police inquiries to his family lawyer, Tom Sheridan

Hobbled by grief and drink, Rucky had by now abdicated any responsibilities for his kids. Despite his role as chairman of a large, multinational company, he was *non compos mentis*. "When my mother died, he should have just jumped in the coffin with her because he gave up on life totally," Michael says. "He just didn't give a fuck after that." As a kid, Michael never received the attention he badly needed. "I think he definitely would have been categorized as ADHD," Julie says. "At one point he had been on Ritalin. I remember that because it was the first time that I had ever heard of a kid being on medication like that. He was funny, he was loud, but he was like a Ping-Pong ball, just all over the place."

Michael is also severely dyslexic. As the parent of a learning-challenged kid, I echo the experts' assessment: learning differences often manifest as petulance and bad behavior. Michael says, "There's no question at all" that his heavy drug and alcohol abuse was self-medication for his ADHD and learning disabilities. "I would see a 6 as a 9 and a B as a D," he says. "If I knew I had a learning disability back then, it would have been a completely different world for me. My father called me 'stupid.' He told me, 'You are here to make everyone else look good.'"

Doctors wouldn't diagnose Michael's dyslexia until 1985, when he was 25 years old and three years sober. Up until then, he was just misunderstood to be stupid and disrespectful. After Michael's mother got sick, Rucky beat him, blaming his academic shortcomings for his mother's misery. As mentioned, Michael carried a burden of guilt for praying that God would relieve his mother's agony by taking her to heaven. In the year after her death, he said "I killed her" and "It's my fault she's dead" so many times that Cissie Ix told Rucky that he needed to get Michael professional help. By age 13, Michael was an alcoholic.

One episode that preceded his expulsion from Brunswick School nicely sums up his academic career. "I remember this math teacher saying, 'What's the answer to this calculus problem?' Everybody raised their hand but me. I'm in the back of the class, my head on the desk and the guy is like, 'Why don't we hear from the illustrious Mr. Skakel?' I said, 'Look, I don't understand this stuff. Why don't you get off my back?' The guy said, 'What are you, stupid?' and everybody started laughing. I said, 'Why don't you fuck yourself?' The guy said, 'What did you just say?' I asked, 'What are you, deaf?'" Brunswick expelled him in the spring of 1975.

By the time of Michael's 1978 arrest, Michael had been kicked out of 11 schools, mostly for academic reasons. For a fee, Howard Green, a Westport psychiatrist, would place troubled kids in prep schools, and Michael was keeping him flush. But now, Green was scraping the barrel bottom. After the Lowell Whiteman School in Steamboat Springs, Colorado, ejected Michael, Dr. Green arranged for his matriculation to The Vershire School in central Vermont, an institution distinguished for its loose structure and reigning drug culture. Vershire alum Darren Jachts described the school to the *Stamford Advocate* as "a Grateful Dead show without the band every day." State officials closed Vershire in 1988, after staff members complained about drug abuse, dangerously filthy living conditions, and routine sex between students and faculty. Michael lost his virginity to a thirty-year-old Vershire teacher. Alumni boasted that it was impossible to not graduate from Vershire. Tommy, who was barely a better student than Michael, earned a Vershire sheepskin in 1977. Michael flunked out in March 1978.

A week after Vershire booted Michael, Rucky dispatched Tom Sheridan to handle the Windham wreck. "Sheridan spent all of his time dealing with Michael," Julie says. "That and trying to get his hands on my father's money."

In addition to his monthly retainer, Sheridan used Rucky as his ATM. He regularly borrowed large sums. One legal document shows that Rucky loaned Tom $250,000 in 1993 ($413,946 in 2016 dollars). Michael saw a personal check to Sheridan for $300,000. Even though Rucky had a financial planner, Sheridan often proposed investment schemes. He convinced Rucky to buy stud rights to Seattle Slew, the 1977 Triple Crown winner, and pitched him on purchasing the Wauwinet Inn in Nantucket and a 100,000-acre ranch in Darby, Montana. "It took a long time to realize his friend was bamboozling him. He was a flimflam wizard," says Stephen.

The lit cigarette dangling perpetually from Sheridan's lip lent him the aspect of a shady card sharp. His hospitality with the booze went beyond enabling. The Skakel kids saw it as a deliberate strategy to incapacitate and manipulate their father. "I can't tell you how many times as a teenager I brought my father to rehab," Julie recalled. The routine was to drop him at Greenwich Hospital, for trans-shipment to a one-month inpatient facility to dry out. "One of these times, when he was fresh out of rehab, we're up in Windham for the weekend," she said. "It was 10:30 in the morning and I'm trying to keep an eye on dad. Then he just disappeared. I found him at Tom Sheridan's house with a drink in his hand. Tom knew that he had just dried out. That man was evil." Michael reminisced, "We were always trying to get Dad sober and Tom was working to keep him drunk." Stephen, who is solid, even-handed, and equanimous, concurred on this point. "There are very few people in this world I intensely dislike, but Tom Sheridan was one of them," he told me. "Tom Sheridan was a diabolical scoundrel. The guy was Satan, feeding all that disinformation to Sutton. Leaking to Len Levitt. He did everything he could to stab us in the back."

Sheridan wasn't fond of the Skakel kids. He seemed to regard them as needy impediments to the good life he and Rucky could otherwise be enjoying. "The level of his children's behavior disorders is staggering," he complained to Rucky's elder brother, Jimmy Skakel, in a November 1992 letter. "You know as well as I do the level of dysfunctionality that exists." He especially loathed Michael for his big mouth. Julie coined the term "camp followers" to describe the entourage of hangers-on, attracted by her father's easy generosity and epic incapacities. Michael loudly and persistently characterized Sheridan as the worst of the blood-sucking parasites. Characteristically, he said it to Sheridan's face. "I was always the one always saying, 'Man, I don't trust this guy: this guy is stealing,'" Michael recalled, "'He's a lousy bum and a con artist and he's fleecing Dad!'" Julie confirmed the open antipathy between Michael and Sheridan. "Michael had been vocal about it," she said. "It was Michael's nature. If he saw things, he said things, especially when he thought Dad was being wrangled, because there were so many people who were leaching onto him [because of his generosity]. Sheridan was terrified of Michael exposing him for manipulating Dad, and taking money."

A couple days after Michael's accident, Sheridan visited Michael at the Windham house. It was midmorning and Michael was alone. He'd just woken up, so he was drinking his vodka with orange juice and smoking cigarettes. "We found a great place for you Michael," Sheridan told him. "Another place in Maine. They've got skiing, whitewater rafting, rock climbing. It has a great reputation for working with kids like you." When Michael asked for details—Was this a school? Did it have a summer semester?—Sheridan abruptly cut him off. "So you're refusing!" Sheridan declared. "I don't have time for this." He stormed from the house. A few minutes later Michael heard the door swing open violently and what sounded like a squadron of storm troopers barreling into the house. Four brawny men tumbled in followed by Sheridan. It was Élan School's goon squad. Michael scrambled to his feet and dashed up the stairs. Closely pursued, he leapt from a porch balcony and lit out across the Catskill wilderness. The fastest kid in Brunswick School, Michael left them in his dust. They finally ran him to ground in a bathroom of the Windham ski lodge after locating him in the cafeteria seeking sanctuary with family friends. The four thugs tackled Michael, grappled him out the door in a headlock and handcuffs, and pitched him into a waiting van like a feed sack. Michael shouted, "Sheridan, you bastard, you're fired! I'm getting a new lawyer!" he remembered. "The goons slapped me silly in the van," recalled Michael. "They skinned me for running." At a small airfield in Ancram, New York, they heaved him into a twin-engine turbo-prop owned by the school, handcuffed him to a seat, and bee-lined to Poland, Maine, where Hell was preparing for Michael's arrival.

Michael's rendition to Élan proved advantageous to Sheridan. He could claim to have earned his keep as Rucky's lawyer, and he had pleaded away Michael's DUI charges in exchange for a two-year stay in a drug treatment facility. In doing so, Sheridan removed a particularly nettlesome gnat from his own hair. Finally, Sheridan was a sociopath with a vendetta against Michael, and Michael's confinement in Élan would indulge his sadistic streak. He sent Rucky a $60,000 bill in 1978 ($220,178 in 2016 dollars. According to the legal website nolo.com, current legal fees for a first-offense DUI are generally about $2,000.)

Rucky took a long time to realize his friend was bamboozling him. Others knew. "I remember [Rucky] came over one day very upset, very distraught," Cissie Ix told me. "It was after Michael had had his drunk-driving case in Windham. Tom Sheridan had given him an unbelievable bill—I think it could have been as much as $60,000. [Rucky] just couldn't believe it. Tom wasn't even a criminal lawyer," Ix continues. "He said to me, 'I thought he was my friend.'" Rucky was an easy mark. It was less painful for him to sign the checks than to confront his friend.

During Michael's trial, Benedict would have Élan alums Greg Coleman and John Higgins, two longtime drug addicts, lie under oath. Both men testified that Michael told them that he had been placed in the Élan School in Poland, Maine, in 1978 because his family suspected that he had murdered Martha Moxley. The Skakels, Benedict claimed, were stashing Michael in the Maine woods beyond the reach of law-enforcement inquiries. "His family felt a need to put him in that awful place," Benedict told the jury, "because that's what they had to do with the killer living under their roof." Benedict's assistant, Chris Morano, told the court, "[T]here has been testimony produced before the jury that the defendant was there to be hidden from investigators." Benedict knew that this was all invention. Michael was not hiding from Connecticut Police. The family told the police exactly where he was and why he was there. Several Greenwich police reports in 1978 and 1979 detail Michael's Maine ordeal. Jim Lunney heard the story of Michael's DUI arrest directly from Windham Police Chief James Scarey, a close friend of the Skakel family. Sheridan told Officer Lunney that Michael would probably be spending 10 months in the school, to satisfy the Windham traffic court. Greenwich police even traveled up to Maine and questioned him about Tommy and Kenny.

Élan practiced a controversial and now-discredited behavior-modification program, originally developed at Synanon and Daytop Village. That system of violent peer, physical, and emotional confrontation made Élan a fiendish concentration camp for teenagers where Michael endured two years of daily beatings and degrading humiliations.

The school closed in 2011, thanks to an Internet campaign by Élan "survivors" intent on shuttering the barbaric hellhole. Thirty-five years after his internment, Michael was diagnosed with acute PTSD in the late 1980s as a result of the ordeal. (He cannot talk in any detail about his experiences there without breaking down in shoulder-shaking tears.) "For a good 10 years after Élan, I'd have nightmares," said Kim Freehill, a former resident whose tenure overlapped with Michael's. "You wake up in the middle of the night in cold sweats, dreaming of being brutally beaten, or being burned alive. It was horrific, like coming out of Vietnam or something."

Élan's "campus" was a Hooverville of dingy shacks and shabby mobile homes on a retired fishing camp in the mosquito-infested North Woods. Parents of troubled kids shelled out up to $75,000 in tuition for Élan to warehouse their children in the grimy stockade where non-accredited bullyboy counselors would throttle them into mental health. Élan was the brainchild of Joe Ricci, a diminutive, truculent, street-smart entrepreneur whose other Maine business was a third-rate harness racing track called Scarborough Downs. With his silver Mercedes, floor-length leather coat, leashed Doberman Pinscher, and aviator sunglasses, he looked more like a gangster than a mental-health professional. Former resident Liz Arnold told *Details* magazine in 2001, "[Ricci] called himself the God of Therapy, but he looked like a pimp. He was cocky as hell." Ricci was a con artist who never finished high school, but shrewdly identified the burgeoning drug-treatment industry as an underexploited business niche. Born in Port Chester, New York, Ricci was, by 15, addicted to heroin. Police arrested him at age 18 for robbing a mail truck. The court allowed him to choose rehab over jail. His stint at Daytop Village in New Haven, Connecticut, exposed him to the kind of extreme authoritarian therapeutic community that would inspire his creation of Élan. In 1971, Ricci and Boston-based psychiatrist Gerald Davidson founded Élan, which featured Daytop's greatest hits: rigid, boot camp–style discipline; a purgatorial menu of hazing and bullying by other inmates, menial tasks, public shaming, and an idolization of authority figures. Counselors forced residents to wear giant dunce caps or large signs announcing their crimes and personality defects (for example, "CONFRONT ME AS TO WHY I'M A WHORE").

Discipline was corporal and included buzz haircuts and brutal public abasement sessions, in which residents beat, shamed, and heckled fellow inmates for minor infractions, real and contrived.

Élan greeted newcomers by dousing them in "electric sauce"—a mixture of mess-hall trash, ketchup, and mustard. Ricci forced newbies to wear Brillo pad necklaces designed to chafe their skin until it bled. He recruited the largest, most thuggish inmates as "counselors" to coerce weaker colleagues to perform degrading jobs like cleaning a dumpster with a spoon or a toothbrush. Ricci had a love for the theater: his hooligans compelled girls as young as 14 to dress as hookers and drag street signs that said "42nd Street" across a stage. Teenagers deemed "babies" wore giant diapers. Ricci flaunted his own drug use. "While you worthless little fucks sit around here, I'll be home smoking a joint," he'd say. Alice Dunne, a counselor at Élan, recounted, "Joe did coke. He drank. He was out until 2 every morning." Alice arrived at Élan at age 15 and stayed on as an employee until she was 22. "He was popping Percodan, Vicodin, that kind of stuff. He might have been driving a Mercedes and living in a big house in Falmouth but the bottom line was, whatever hole he'd had in his heart was still there." Ricci personally welcomed Michael. "Joe Ricci asked me in front of the whole place why I thought I was there," Michael says. "I said, 'Because I drink too much.' Bam, he punched me in the face. He said, 'You piece of shit, there's no such thing as addiction. You're just a fuckin' asshole.' Élan wasn't rehab. It was a cult."

"Élan was a huge con," said Richard Ofshe, a University of California Berkeley professor emeritus and probably the country's foremost expert on false confessions and therapeutic cults such as Synanon, Daytop, and Élan. "The con was that they could cure drug addiction."

Ricci rewarded devotion to "the God of Therapy" with perquisites and privilege. Compliant residents earned management roles. Big bruisers became "gorilla" enforcers. A draconian reward system put a high premium on harvesting intelligence. "Expeditors" were Ricci's spy platoon, tasked with recording and reporting back rumors and "incidents" they'd observed or heard about. Ricci organized mob paddling; formal beatings of reprobates were a weekly routine, known as "General Meetings," or GMs. Inmates most dedicated to the violent aspects of the program rose quickly through the ranks. "Everybody was involved in the beatings," says Kim. "But Greg Coleman and John Higgins were far more sadistic than the others. Coleman was one of the sickest." Lacking the qualities of guile, sadism, or cunning, Michael had a hard time getting with the program.

Kim's father, a successful Manhattan attorney, dropped her off at Élan on December 7, 1978. She was 16. He had lied when he told Kim they were driving to Maine for a campus tour of Bowdoin College. "I was sent there because I smoked pot and my parents didn't like that," she recalled. She arrived just in time to witness a General Meeting—Élan's most brutal punishment. A noncompliant inmate would don boxing gloves and a helmet and be forced to fight nine rounds. In every round, a new opponent entered the ring. "You never got a break, so you could never win," Alice remembers. "They do that until you're completely beaten down and afraid." Kim was appalled at what she witnessed that first day. "I saw them brutally beating Michael, spitting at him, screaming at him," she says. "There were about 100 people, everyone that lived in Élan at that time. It was like out of *Lord of the Flies*. I found out that if you didn't participate in the beatings, you would be beaten next, so the fear of not doing it created this kind of frenzy." On that day, Ricci's goon squad had put Michael in the boxing ring as punishment for running away. But Michael was always the default target because of his gentle nature and poor academic performance. He couldn't read. For much of his time at Élan, Ricci made him wear a three-foot dunce cap. "Nobody knew what dyslexia was in the eighties," says Kim. "He wasn't doing well in school so they painted Michael up as a clown and made him sit on the stage."

Kim lasted only six months at Élan. She went in relatively healthy, but confinement in the facility caused her to stop eating and drop 30 pounds. "Four people would hold me down and then they'd beat me with a two-inch wooden paddle," she says. Coleman, who was 18 at the time, admitted under oath that he took a lead role in Kim's final stomping. After losing consciousness she was medevaced to Hillside Hospital in Long Island. "When I arrived at Hillside they were absolutely horrified. They had never seen anything like it," she says. "I had open sores all over my body from the beatings. Bruising everywhere. I have a scar on my right buttock that never went away. I had to be taught how to speak and feed myself in a strait jacket for three months until I was well enough or sane enough to leave Hillside."

Michael's experience was no less brutal, but lasted two years. Early in his stay, he asked Ricci if he could go to church. Ricci slapped him in the face. "Church?" he said. "There is no God. I am God. I am the great God of Therapy." For two years Michael never received a letter during weekly mail call. He later learned that friends and siblings had written, but Ricci had hijacked his correspondence. "They'd say, 'Skakel, stand up. Did you get mail?' And I'd say, 'No.' They'd say, 'We want to make everyone aware, Skakel comes from a large family but he's nothing but a piece of shit and nobody writes him. So take shit where shit belongs.' Then Higgins, Coleman, and their goons would drag me to the bathroom and stick my head in the toilet." He spent his days doing pointless tasks: digging holes using only a spoon, polishing a 12-inch-square of linoleum with a toothbrush for 12 hours straight, sweeping sunlight from a cabin floor.

Counselors would hold him over a chair, while inmates took turns beating him with a paddle. "They bored holes in the planks so that they wouldn't catch air," recalled Michael. The abuse was systematic and well documented. The Illinois Department of Children and Family Services accused Élan of abusing 11

Illinois juveniles who resided at the facility in 1975, effectively turning them into "automatons." The same year, the Massachusetts Department of Youth Services launched a similar inquiry. In December 1982, two years after Michael graduated, Élan students, at a General Meeting, beat 15-year-old Phil Williams unconscious in the boxing ring. Phil died the following day of a brain aneurysm. The Maine State Police recently reopened a cold-case murder investigation of Phil's death.

Élan utilized a specific strategy of breaking strong-willed inmates. "Counselors" would identify a psychological crack and hammer it relentlessly. Often, their wedge had no basis in reality. A former Élan patient named Sarah Peterson testified at Michael's trial that she suffered from chapped lips while at Élan. Ricci and others accused her of acquiring the condition while giving blowjobs and made her dress as a hooker. With beatings, humiliation, and relentless pressure, she quickly admitted that she was a "slut." She was a 15-year-old virgin at the time. "They would twist and turn anything just to get at you," said Kim. "The model was that if they broke you down to absolutely nothing, they could rebuild you."

Sheridan made sure to provide Élan with plenty of source material for use in Michael's rehabilitation. "Everything they had about me was from Tom Sheridan," Michael says. "My father hadn't a clue." Shortly after he arrived at Élan, the goon squad gave Michael the sign he wore for the next year: "I'M A SPOILED RICH KID FROM GREENWICH CONNECTICUT. ASK ME WHY MY BROTHER KILLED MY FRIEND MARTHA MOXLEY." It wasn't until the final year they changed the sign to "I'M A SPOILED RICH KID FROM GREENWICH CONNECTICUT. ASK ME WHY I KILLED MY FRIEND MARTHA MOXLEY." When Garr learned of this sign years later, he considered it persuasive evidence of Michael's guilt. "Why would Ricci confront Michael about the murder?" Garr asked Levitt, pointedly. "When Michael flew to Élan in 1978, he had never been a suspect. How would people at Élan have had suspicions about him unless someone in or close to the family had told them?" Garr was right: Sheridan had provided an entire dossier on the Skakel family and the Moxley murder. But Élan's system of psychological domination had no interest in truth. "It would simply be the entry point to pressure him," said Richard Ofshe. "Information would get collected that they could constantly use to put somebody under enormous pressure. But the idea that anyone actually told Élan that they knew that Michael killed Martha Moxley is fantasy. It's wild prosecutorial speculation."

Given Sheridan's manipulative nature and his simmering antipathy, Michael doesn't rule out that the lawyer may indeed have told Ricci that Michael was guilty of murder. We now know that Sheridan had quietly hinted to Sutton Associates that Michael was guilty, though he never had evidence to support his suspicion.

For Sheridan, there was a valuable advantage in Michael being a suspect in the Moxley case. Manny Margolis had firm reins on Tommy's defense so his predicament posed no opportunity for Sheridan. But there was ample upside for Sheridan in making Michael a suspect. "This was standard operating procedure from Tom," says Stephen. "So long as Dad believed Michael might be guilty, Tom was guaranteed a role and a salary. His strategy was to keep Dad in a state of terror, where he was happy to sign checks." Rucky was paralyzed when it came to the boys and the Moxley murder. Michael's status as a suspect represented billable hours to Sheridan whose business plan was to keep Michael under suspicion, but out of jail. "Tom Sheridan fabricated a story to hurt me and keep the gig going," Michael says. "As long as he could keep my father questioning my guilt or innocence he could keep getting paid." Hearing all this, I was skeptical that the family's own lawyer had set Michael up, but that was before I discovered extensive evidence confirming the boys' suspicions.

With the ammunition supplied by Sheridan, Michael got beaten over Martha's murder every day at Élan. He says that in his first months there, the verbal abuse always included mentions of Tommy. "You will never leave here until you admit that your brother Tommy committed this crime," Ricci admonished him.

Michael says the interrogation techniques changed after the first of his three escape attempts. Eight months into his stay—a few days after his recapture—guards dragged Michael over to Ricci's trailer. Michael was surprised to find Sheridan waiting for him, but happy to see a familiar face at Élan, even if it was Sheridan's. "Thank God," Michael thought. "They're going to get me out of here." He soon realized he was mistaken. "Tom dismissed the guards like a mobster," Michael says. "Then turning to me, he snapped 'sit down,' sharply. It was like we were in the military." Michael continued, "And then he said, 'You're a hard bronc to saddle, but we're going to saddle you.' I had no idea what he was talking about." That afternoon, as he scrubbed a linoleum square, Michael overheard two of the Élan goons talking. "We just got the green light to fuck this guy up."

Immediately following Sheridan's visit, the beatings escalated. Michael plotted another escape. In late November 1978, he made it 20 miles from the facility on foot in sub-freezing temperatures. The beating he received as punishment following his capture was the one Kim saw on her first day. "They beat me for eight hours," Michael said. "Kim said when it was finished I had no clothes on. They beat me to the point I could barely see out of my eyes, and they threw me in the kitchen and said, 'Run away now. We're done with you.' I remember my body hurt so much I couldn't get off the floor. And I saw a knife and I thought, 'Well, I'll just slit my throat, but as a Catholic I couldn't, because I knew if I did it, I'd go somewhere even worse than Élan.' I thought, 'Man, am I fucked.'" Michael says that at the end of the stomping Ricci forecast his future. "After they were done with me, Joe Ricci said, 'Your brother didn't murder Martha Moxley.

You did. You committed this crime.'" Michael's torturers adopted a new theme. Michael, himself, was now the killer.

But try as Ricci might, his thugs could not beat Michael into an admission. Michael never broke. "They used me as a punching bag every day for four months," he says. "They made me sleep on a stage. They didn't give me any food. I'd have to go to the bathroom on myself. They said I'd be there for the rest of my life. And the whole time they just kept saying, 'This will not stop until you admit to this crime.' I couldn't admit to something I didn't do, so I figured out if I just said, 'I don't know,' they would stop hitting me." Michael sobbed as he told this story. "So I just kept saying, 'I don't know.'"

Alice's recollection of the Élan torture regime perfectly mirrors Michael's. "I would admit to things too that I didn't do, just to not be beaten anymore, but Michael never, ever said he did it," she says. "He sat up there with 100 people screaming in his face, crying after having nine rounds in the boxing ring, beaten, saying, 'I just don't know.' If he did it, he would have known that he did it. I don't think he did it and I never did. In the time I spent with Michael, he was just so emotional, like a raw nerve. I never saw him as having the capability to ever hurt someone."

Benedict called Alice Dunne as a prosecution witness in Michael's trial in an attempt to convince jurors that Michael's admissions that "he didn't know if he did it" were tantamount to confessions. Ricci, who died of cancer in 2001, the year before the trial, proved an unlikely character reference. "The notion of Michael's confession is just preposterous," Ricci told *Time* magazine the year before his death. "I was there, and I would know."

Even though Michael has spent 11½ years in brutal conditions in Connecticut's toughest prisons, it's Élan that haunts him. "I went to a public AA meeting in Rye, New York, a month ago," he told me. "The whole meeting people stare at me like I'm a killer and I had this visceral reaction to their hostility. I feel like I'm right back in Élan. I can't begin to explain to you what it's like to have a mob of people beat you for hours and hours and kick you and spit on you. It's still with me today."

As horrible as Sheridan's decision was to send Michael to Élan, his 1991 judgment to retain Sutton Associates was even worse. The Skakel kids laugh at the notion that their father dreamed up the idea for an internal investigation of the family. "I loved my father," says Stephen, "but this wasn't a man who was really capable of ordering up anything except dessert." The connection to Sutton Associates came through Sheridan, who broached the idea that Rucky might pay for a grand-scale reinvestigation of the Moxley murder. Sheridan's friend Dick McCarthy, the independent gumshoe, called his former FBI buddy Jim Murphy, whose Sutton Associates annexed McCarthy into the Sutton fold to work as a contractor on the Skakel job. "Tom took care of his friends," says Stephen. "They all made out." Sheridan made the personally lucrative decision to run the investigation out of his Manhattan building. Sutton's offices were in Hicksville, Long Island, and three of the people Sutton planned to investigate—Kenny Littleton, Tommy, and Michael—were all living in Massachusetts at that time. The most economic strategy would have been to find some cheap office space in Connecticut, near Rucky and the crime scene. But Sheridan said the investigation should be close to his office where he kept the family's files. Sheridan owned a brownstone on East 51st Street where he maintained his law office on the first floor, and an apartment on the second. He arranged to rent the third floor to Sutton, a cost he billed to Rucky. Rucky eventually would pay more than a million dollars to Sutton. "There was absolutely no reason for that investigation to be located in Manhattan, except so that Tom Sheridan could get his kickback and act as gatekeeper," says Stephen.

The office deal was only one part of the arrangement that left the Skakel kids scratching their heads. The idea of investigating the family was lunacy from the outset. No experienced criminal defense attorney would have sanctioned the scheme. Tommy's lawyer, Manny Margolis, was in revolt, but Sheridan insisted that Rucky wanted to know the truth.

Sutton's entire report on Michael is colored by Sheridan's loathing for him. Fuhrman and Levitt obtained Michael's Sutton report at a time when police had never regarded him as a suspect, so they were understandably astounded to read this line: "Some feel Michael and other suspects were not thoroughly examined . . . due to a somewhat premature conviction on the part of local authorities that Tommy Skakel was the murderer." The report continues, "It was only later when the spotlight of serious scrutiny was placed directly on Michael. His arrest on drunk driving charges in 1978 probably did as much as anything to renew the police's interest." This demonstrably false statement, which could only have come from Sheridan, lends credence to Michael's and Stephen's belief that Sheridan was guiding the project to smear Michael.

In fact, cops had zero interest in Michael during the period when he was locked away in Élan. The Greenwich Police investigation had all but shut down. Lunney had so exhausted his leads by then that he was spending his days conducting interviews with a psychic who, among many other things, told them she'd had a vision of Martha Moxley swinging a golf club. She offered the words "drugs," "stone wall," and "apparently one parent" to Lunney as clues. The psychic also examined pictures of the suspects. According to Lunney, "She . . . picked Littleton's photo as the subject she sees killing Martha Moxley." She didn't react to Tommy's picture. Michael was so far off the radar that the police didn't bother to show the psychic his photo.

As soon as they ramped up their investigation in 1992, Murphy realized that his team was starting at an extreme disadvantage. Len Levitt, when writing his article that the *Greenwich Time* published June 1991, had succeeded in obtaining the 400-page Martha Moxley police file through a Freedom of Information request. But when Sutton detectives asked for the same file, the Greenwich Police refused. The police explained that the case was reopened. "We were viewed almost as investigators for the defense," Murphy says. "And certainly I think the Greenwich Police Department would have been embarrassed had anybody else come in and solved this." Without those files, they'd get nowhere.

Sutton decided to strike a deal with Levitt. Sheridan brokered a meeting, and he and Murphy went to *Newsday*'s Melville, New York, offices to meet the reporter. Murphy had the impression that Sheridan and Levitt had dealt with one another previously. Levitt says that the meeting was the first time he met Sheridan but does not say whether the two had previously spoken by phone. The men struck a verbal deal: in exchange for the case file, Sutton would give Levitt first crack at reporting Sutton's results once they had wrapped up the investigation. This proposition went beyond dicey: Sheridan's team was heaping insane on crazy. No criminal layer would have ever countenanced this daft project for a client they were trying to protect. Criminal Defense 101 is "Never let your client speak." Yet Sheridan had persuaded Rucky to finance a prosecutorial investigation of his own children. And now he was promising to give the results to a hostile reporter! As we shall see, Sheridan was meanwhile secretly contaminating the report with ginned-up calumnies about Michael. The entire project was a study in attorney malpractice. Sheridan's enterprise, from the outset, wreaked of malice.

Murphy knew he was playing in an ethical Twilight Zone: Sheridan was paying Sutton, with Rucky's dough, to follow the evidence even if it inculpated a Skakel. Murphy realized that if Sutton found some new piece of evidence against Tommy or Michael, no sane defense attorney would want this to appear in a newspaper. Still, Murphy felt they had little choice: "What Levitt had was historical information from day one, and access to information that the police department had that we were never going to get access to." And, Murphy reasoned, Sheridan was speaking on behalf of his client. Murphy's only obligation was to solve the case, not question the client's judgment. Boneheaded though the plan might be, it was supposedly his client's wish. Murphy didn't realize then that Sheridan was manipulating Rucky like a sock puppet. "This deal with Levitt only would have been done with Sheridan's agreement," Murphy said. Still, Murphy was cautious, resolving that he would be especially circumspect in any of his dealings with Levitt. He got Sheridan to agree that, in advance of any communications with the reporter, they would consult each other. Sheridan would repeatedly violate this promise.

Soon after he commissioned the Sutton Report, Sheridan began poisoning it. For example, he provided Sutton a memo about Michael's Windham crash chock-full of editorial slanders. "He was obviously a disturbed person and hooked on either booze or pot," Sheridan wrote. "He showed little or no remorse for having nearly killed the companion in his car, and when confronted with the potential problem of a subsequent conviction for drunken driving, his only comment was, 'Next time I won't get caught,'" an implausible declaration that Michael swears he never said. Sheridan was also providing Sutton investigators with information he professed to have gleaned from Rucky. "Thomas Sheridan also noted being informed by Mr. Skakel that 'Julie is frightened to death of Michael,' and that Michael suffers from enuresis (bed wetting), and has engaged in some transsexual behavior." Julie says Sheridan must have simply invented this stuff since her father never had any reason to think these things. "I was never, ever afraid of Michael," she says. "I wasn't even afraid of Tommy. I was dreadfully fearful of my father because I could see how he would fly off the handle with Michael. I was scared every second in that house when he was there."

Sheridan also provided highly prejudicial impressions he claimed to have heard from Mary Ellen Reynolds, a former nun and aunt of the Skakel children who lived for a period in the Otter Rock Drive house. "Reynolds . . . spent much time eyeball to eyeball with Tommy and she is persuaded that Tommy had nothing to do with the crime," Sheridan's memo reported. "On the other hand, she has 'very negative vibrations with reference to Michael.' Michael is deeply involved in alcohol and not under control—he is capable of anything." Stephen thinks Sheridan made these words up, too: "She loved Michael," he says, "and I find it very hard to believe she would have ever said such a thing." But even if she had uttered those words, it's challenging to imagine how Sheridan deemed these damaging gut feelings helpful to Sutton's investigation, which he had launched, ostensibly, to clear both brothers. Sheridan deluged the Sutton sleuths with an obsessive cascade of gossipy slander, implicating Michael on pure hunches. From the Sutton report: "A Tom Sheridan memo of 6/6/78 stated that it is possible Michael could have committed the murder and doesn't know it, and possibly someone else, i.e., Tommy, could have hidden the body and taken Michael to the Terriens' to provide him with an alibi."

One of Sheridan's contributions stopped me dead in my tracks. "We know that he went after his aunt Ethel with a kitchen knife when she found him stealing liquor," the report reads. "What other incidents haven't we been told about?" The allegation is rank fabrication. Michael was never at our house and had no contact with my mother until after he got sober in 1982. Furthermore, there was a ton of liquor at Hickory Hill and Hyannis Port, and no one ever fought over it. It wasn't even locked up. Because my mother entertained nearly every night, there were huge caches of alcohol in an unlocked walk-in wardrobe beneath the house's central staircase, another liquor closet in the basement, liquor in the living room cabinet, and in glass cabinets in the kitchen. There was always plenty of cold beer and wine in three industrial-sized refrigerators, and cases of Pouilly-Fuissé stacked shoulder high in the laundry room and another in the basement storage room. The idea that Michael would have had to liberate booze at knifepoint is laughable. My mother, who adores Michael Skakel, scoffs at the story. "Nothing remotely like that ever occurred," she said. "Never happened," Michael texts me, when I alert him to the passage: "Another Tom Sheridan frame up. Tom Sheridan had a LONG history of falsifying evidence against me."

Sheridan's subtle campaign to implicate Michael began even before Sutton launched its investigation. In 1992, during his first meeting with Frank Garr, Sheridan told the detective that Michael had lied about owning a stained pair of pants that police recovered from the Skakel garbage. The Wrangler dungarees had come from Camp Pasquaney in New Hampshire, but Sheridan told Garr that Michael denied having ever been to Camp Pasquaney. Police initially believed that stain on the jeans might be blood. It wasn't, but Garr considered Michael's denial significant. "That's when I knew Michael was our boy," he told Levitt many years later. However, Michael said that Sheridan never talked to him about the camp or the pants. "That's Tom Sheridan acting the provocateur once again," he said. "Of course I didn't deny owning those pants. Everyone knew those were my pants and the sneakers that went with them. And everyone knew I'd been at Camp Pasquaney. I threw them out because of the paint stains. Of course I didn't lie."

Two years after his first meeting with Murphy and Sheridan, Levitt reports that he began receiving communications from a source he's only ever identified as "The Caller." The Caller, Levitt wrote, phoned to tell him that Tommy, in his Sutton interview, had changed his story and admitted that he'd been with Martha until 9:50 p.m. The Caller also told Levitt that Michael, too, had changed his story, and confessed to the bizarre masturbation saga. The Caller informed Levitt that Sutton had brought on the Manassas, Virginia–based Academy Group, a consultancy led by two retired FBI agents who had run the agency's behavioral science lab, where they'd studied serial killers. The Academy Group, The Caller said, had determined that because of Martha's lack of defensive wounds and the fact that neighbors heard no screams (conveniently ignoring the fact that her mother heard her screams) she likely knew her attacker. "Martha didn't know Littleton," Levitt told The Caller, wondering if the killer may have been a Skakel. "That's what it would look like," The Caller replied.

In *Conviction*, Levitt writes that, following this call, he tried to get the story confirmed. Murphy stopped returning his calls. Sheridan, however, invited him out to lunch at the New York Athletic Club. Levitt writes that over lunch he told Sheridan that he had heard that Tommy had admitted that he was with Martha later than he'd originally let on. "Oh, so you know about the mutual masturbation?" Sheridan replied. "The what?" Levitt writes, "Poor Sheridan. He had just blurted out something I hadn't known." As soon as he returned to the office, Levitt called Murphy to get confirmation so he could print a story based on the revelations. Murphy was appalled at what Sheridan had done. "First of all, I was surprised he had that meeting with Len and I didn't know about it," Murphy says. "He should have spoken to me about it first. Sheridan just gave up everything to him."

On a Saturday in July 1995, Levitt writes that The Caller visited him at his house and presented him with the mother lode of the work that Murphy and his Sutton colleagues had done in their four years laboring on the case. From his briefcase, The Caller not only passed Levitt a copy of the Academy Group's report, he also provided him with Sutton's summation reports on both Tommy and Michael. After reading Levitt's account of The Caller, Murphy narrows the leaker down to two suspects. "The only people who had access to all that information would have been Jamie Bryan and Tommy Sheridan," he says.

Jamie Bryan is a character Murphy wishes he'd never met. "Jamie proved himself to be deceptive and manipulative," Murphy said. Although he is a minor character in this tragedy, Bryan played a pivotal role in putting Michael in prison. "Given the damage his actions caused, he's a kid whose neck I wouldn't mind getting my hands around," says Murphy.

The Sutton files occupied thousands of pages, filling two file cabinets in Sheridan's home office. At Sheridan's request the company assembled draft "portfolios" that made hypothetical cases against Tommy and Michael Skakel, Kenny Littleton, and John Moxley. These portfolios construct a prosecutor's best case against each one, or a "worst case scenario." The one on Michael was titled "Michael Skakel, A Purposefully Prejudicial Analysis of Michael Skakel and His Testimony." In 2005, Sheridan told me why he had asked Sutton to create a blueprint for prosecuting his client. "My old man told me to always ask for the worst case. That way you know you're not being bullshitted." The explanation was lame. The original purpose of the Sutton investigation was purportedly to clear the boys. Now Sheridan was instructing Sutton to deliberately make the strongest case against each of them. That was beyond crazy. It was malicious.

Murphy and Willis Krebs, the retired NYPD detective working for Sutton Associates, told me separately that they believed Michael Skakel was innocent. However, in order to comply with Sheridan's request for a worst-case scenario, Murphy realized he needed a fresh set of eyes to review and consolidate the information; Sheridan wanted Sutton to marshal all the evidence in a manner that cast Michael and Tommy in the worst possible light, and write it up coherently. Murphy asked his cousin, a textbook editor, to do the job. She was too busy, but her friend's son, Jamie Bryan, had just graduated from the University of Virginia with an English degree. Bryan was an ambitious 22-year-old kid with dreams of being a professional writer. He provided samples of surprisingly strong analytical writing, so Murphy hired him at $75.00 an hour—billed to Rucky, of course—and gave him a desk in Sheridan's office. In a disastrous oversight, neither Murphy nor Sheridan had Bryan sign a nondisclosure agreement.

Bryan's primary assignment was to create Sheridan's worst-case scenarios, "outlining the strongest case against each suspect." Murphy and Sheridan told Bryan to massage all the evidence that a prosecutor might use to make the most plausible case against the Skakel brothers and two other suspects. What species of madman conceived this caper? Certainly not someone interested in exculpating the boys. Only a malicious bastard with a perverse mission of keeping Rucky Skakel on tenterhooks. Bryan was to assume Michael was guilty and to marshal all the evidence according to its most damning interpretation. Bryan labeled his reports "Purposely Prejudicial Analysis," because in them he made wild leaps in logic in order to make even the most innocuous evidence seem darkly sinister, according to Sheridan's orders. If there were ever any good reason to draft such an analysis, it would yield the kind of report that should have been safeguarded with CIA Top Secret–level controls, under lock and key at all times. Instead, it was sitting on the hard drive of a 22-year-old, with no NDA.

By 1995, Sheridan's profligacy had finally tapped out Rucky, who was forced to unload his Windham ski house and sell the family house in Belle Haven. He and Anna Mae, his second wife, moved into a small condominium in Loblolly in Hobe Sound, Florida, in March of that year. Poor management, bad luck, and horrendous lawyers had conspired to obliterate one of America's great family fortunes in a generation. Rucky's family had hit rock bottom only to learn there was a trap door to a subbasin and they were still in free-fall.

In March of that year Tommy's lawyer, Manny Margolis, shut down the Sutton investigation. It had been an unusual lapse for Margolis to allow Sutton to question his client and he was understandingly alarmed by the interview where Tommy changed his story. Margolis thought that the boys' unfiltered chatter to the Sutton flatfoots might feed the ambitions of those police investigators who seemed determined to pin the murder on Tommy. Margolis was a seasoned defense lawyer who had kept Tommy from speaking for 27 years. Margolis had opposed the Sutton project from the outset and had allowed Tommy's participation only reluctantly (Tommy was still the only Skakel represented by counsel as of 1995). Margolis is dead now and one can only speculate that his judgment was skewed by his faith that Sheridan had the best interests of the Skakels at heart. It was a grave blunder. By March of 1995, Margolis saw that nothing good could come of these reports—and Sheridan's unhelpful contributions to them—and ordered the enterprise aborted.

Murphy broke the news to Jamie Bryan that Sutton's investigation was shutting down. Bryan was beside himself to learn that the mission—his gravy train—was over. "We're so close to finishing!" he pleaded. "How can they shut it down?" Murphy told him there was no more money to continue, and he was dropping by his Manhattan apartment to pick up all the material. "Is this everything?" Murphy asked as Bryan handed over his masterpiece. "Yeah, that's all of it," Bryan lied.

The following year, Bryan strolled into Patroon, a stuffy Midtown restaurant, underdressed in a t-shirt and jeans, to meet a man who regularly lunched there: *Vanity Fair*'s Dominick Dunne. "He was 24, but could easily have passed for 17," Dunne wrote of Bryan. During lunch, Bryan turned over copies of his "worst-case" files to Dunne. Why? Bryan didn't return about a dozen of my calls and emails, but all the evidence points to Bryan's ambition for a glitzy career. When Murphy confronted the young writer with his deceit, Bryan explained that he wanted a job at *Vanity Fair* and gave the reports to Dunne as writing samples. Author Tim Dumas reported that Bryan wanted Dunne to arrange for space in *Vanity Fair* for Bryan to write a story pinning the Moxley murder on Michael. Dunne instead screwed Bryan by sending his reports off to Mark Fuhrman. Bryan's worst-case scenario provided the entire architecture for the State's case against Michael. Rucky had spent over a million dollars to get his son falsely charged with murder.

The question remains: Who was the man Levitt labeled "The Caller," who in July 1995 hand-delivered the same documents to Levitt's home? Under oath, Levitt has steadfastly protected his source. Levitt told me that "it never occurred to me" that Sheridan's clandestine transfers of confidential information "violated attorney–client privilege." If, as I suspect, Tom Sheridan was The Caller, then his secret relationship with Levitt not only violated his ethical obligation to his client, it represents a breathtaking act of treachery toward his best friend and lifelong patron. It's noteworthy that Levitt's book consistently paints Sheridan in a flattering light. Levitt erroneously reports that in 1995, Sheridan got one look at the Sutton reports, realized how inculpatory they were to the Skakels, and immediately took action by firing Sutton Associates. Murphy adamantly disputes this account. "It was Manny [Margolis] who told us to stop the investigation," Murphy says.

In December 1995—with the pilfered Sutton reports from "The Caller" in his hands—Levitt reported in *Newsday* that anonymous sources had informed him that both Tommy and Michael had spoken to private investigators hired by the Skakel family and had elaborated on their whereabouts the night of the murder.

Frank Garr and the Connecticut State's Attorney's office publicly called for a full disclosure of Sutton's findings—to no avail. When pieces of the report began to leak, Margolis demanded that all copies of the report and all underlying evidence be turned over to him. Significantly, Margolis insisted that all of the documents be immediately transported from Sheridan's office to his own.

On January 25, 1996, Margolis wrote Sheridan a blistering letter that the Skakel children found in their legal files. "As an experienced member of the bar you are certainly well aware of the gravity of the present situation as well as the extreme seriousness with which any future breach of confidentiality and/or lawyer–client privilege will be viewed by the Skakel family." Less than three months later, in March, Margolis felt the need to reiterate this point in another letter. "I am advised that Leonard Levitt has been poking his reporter's nose," Margolis wrote. "I must remind you of my earlier admonition to have no dealings with Levitt or any other media representative concerning this matter."

Later that year, Levitt broke the news that Dunne had leaked the Sutton reports. Before printing the story, Levitt called Murphy, inquiring whether he had engaged a young writer named Jamie Bryan. The name was obviously new to Levitt. "He didn't acknowledge that he'd ever heard the name Jamie Bryan before," Murphy recalls. When Levitt wrote the story, he named Bryan as Dunne's source. He almost certainly would not have done that had Bryan been his own informant. He has steadfastly protected The Caller. It's easy to see what Bryan thought Dunne had to offer, but an aging *Newsday* reporter held no key to a glamorous career.

Assuming that Tom Sheridan was his source, Levitt has much explaining to do. If Sheridan was The Caller, then Levitt got played by his source in a manipulative scheme to put an innocent man in jail. Levitt needs to reckon with the moral and ethical implications of his actions. He can claim he didn't see through Sheridan, but if Sheridan leaked reports that were overflowing with incriminating innuendos about Michael, sourced to Sheridan, Levitt was on notice that he should have been skeptical about Sheridan's motivations. Remember that Sheridan was violating his ethical obligation by betraying the confidence of his client. If Sheridan was The Caller, then he recruited Levitt as a co-conspirator in a classic frame job to railroad a blameless man. Levitt's participation in this scheme cost Michael more than a decade of his life.

Thanks to the years of abuse at Élan, after he graduated in 1980, Michael himself began to wonder if there was something to the allegations against him. "They got me so turned around at Élan," he said. "Then I came home and flunked out of college because I couldn't read no matter how hard I tried. I'd never heard of dyslexia. I thought, 'There's something wrong with my brain.'" Michael began to question, for the first time, his own memory of the night of Martha's murder. "I'm like, 'Holy fuck, maybe I did have a blackout or something. Maybe I'm blocking something out in my head. Maybe I'm crazy. Maybe that's why I was failing in school.' It was a terrifying thought." According to Richard Ofshe, what Michael experienced is a phenomenon called "persuaded false confession." If a person is put under enough pressure—usually by police, but in this case, by therapeutic tactics—he can begin to believe that he's guilty even if he had no recollection of committing a crime. "They're stripped of the confidence that they have in their memory and then bombarded with false information supposedly linking them to the crime," he explained. "It's a well-established, well-accepted phenomenon. If someone's accused of having done something over and over and over again and there are claims that they did it but their memory is impaired, it's not a stretch to understand why someone could say 'I might have done it. I could have done it, but I was drunk and therefore I don't know.'"

Michael, at that time a broken reed, made the fateful decision to tell Sheridan and Rucky that though he thought he didn't kill Martha, he still wanted to submit to a sodium amytal test to make doubly sure about his activities that night. Sheridan brought him to the office of psychiatrist Dr. Stanley Lesse, who had performed the same test on Tommy back in 1976. Monsignor William McCormack, soon to be auxiliary bishop of New York, was present during Michael's questioning. After Michael woke from the test, Lesse sat down with him. "You definitely had nothing to do with this crime," he told Michael. The episode, however, would come back to haunt him. During a November 20, 1997, interview, Garr reported that Cissie Ix repeated a story that she claimed that Rucky had told her in the period after Michael returned from Élan. "According to Mrs. Ix," the report read, "Michael told his father he had been drinking on the night in question, had blacked out, and may have murdered Martha." Cissie disavowed this statement at Michael's trial saying, "I put words in Rucky's mouth." Nevertheless, Garr felt that he had found his Holy Grail. He considered Cissy Ix's hearsay to be a watershed moment in the case—as close as he would ever get to hearing Rucky blame his own son. Levitt emailed me that this Cissie Ix revelation was for him the linchpin evidence that convinced him of Michael's guilt. "Apparently someone in the family knew something and believed he killed Martha," he emailed me. "I think that person was Rushton." Sheridan's efforts to punish Michael had finally come to fruition.

Cissie Ix, for her part, told me she has no recollection of saying virtually any of the things that Garr attributed to her in the report. "I don't remember [Rucky] ever for a moment thinking Michael had anything to do with it," she says. "[Rucky's] only concern in that regard was Tommy. What Garr wrote in that report is simply untrue."

After Rucky relocated to Loblolly, Sheridan was a regular visitor. The visits were not social; by this point, Rucky's frontal lobe dementia was advanced. His psychiatrist, Alvin Rosen, would testify that Rucky had turned into a child. He would greet women by rubbing noses with them. He would take food off the plate of strangers at restaurants. He'd gotten into the odd habit of mooning his neighbor. "He cannot recall the names of three items after a five minute period," Rosen wrote in a 2002 letter. "He is somewhat paranoid, frequently checking doors and windows, to make sure they are locked. His ability to think in abstract terms is impaired, often resorting to silly neologisms, sticking his tongue out, or making grotesque faces at the other person. His behavior in my office during our sessions is often like a small child. He has several times given money to strangers but is unable to explain why."

"I came to love him during those last years," Michael recalls, "but he was cuckoo for Coco Puffs. Occasionally he would say something coherent and people would think, 'Oh, he seems okay.' But they didn't know that I just changed his diapers and ran a bath for him, then had to go in and turn it off, and stay with him to make sure he didn't drown. In the end, the only thing working in his head was a shit-weasel playing a ukulele and dancing circles on a hamster wheel."

Tommy remembers visiting his father at this point. "He was regularly getting lost on walks; his short-term memory was so compromised that he would spend four hours reading the front page of the *New York Times* because he couldn't remember anything he'd just read." It was during this period that Tommy remembers Sheridan putting paper after paper in front of his father to sign. Tommy trusted Sheridan back then. When Rucky died in 2003, Tommy revised his opinion after learning that, for some unaccountable reason, Sheridan had allowed his father's substantial life insurance policy to lapse a year before his death. "I now think that Tom framed Michael," Tommy tells me. "He was incredibly unscrupulous."

In the 1990s Sheridan repeatedly sabotaged Michael's efforts to find work and start a business. In 1993, at Sheridan's invitation, Michael and his friend Will Vinci submitted a business plan to Sheridan and a request for $10,000. Vinci, an American speed-skiing legend, had bunked with Michael when Michael was on the speed-ski circuit. Will was married and Michael was sober. According to Vinci, "We were the only guys who didn't drink or party, so it was a good fit. We became very close friends. We had deep conversations. He opened his soul. That's why I knew he was innocent when everything went down later."

Vinci, a successful businessman who had already made himself a millionaire in his twenties, wanted to launch a ski business with Michael. Michael needed $10,000 for the venture, which Vinci would match. Sheridan had always told the Skakel boys, "I manage your dad's money. Whenever any of you want to start a business, just get me a business plan and I'll see you get financing." When Michael showed Sheridan the business plan and asked for the $10,000, Sheridan encouraged Michael, "Sure thing. No problem, Michael. I'll get it done." Michael adds, "He said he just wanted to talk to my business partner to button things up." Michael gave Sheridan Vinci's phone number. A few hours later, Michael received a call from a shaken Vinci: "That guy is not your friend and he is no friend of your family." Sheridan had urged Vinci not to go into business with Michael. Vinci recalled to me, "Sheridan told me that Michael was a drug addict and potential murderer and the whole family was dysfunctional." Vinci continued, "I came to believe that Sheridan was a very sleazy man. He was supposed to be the family comptroller, but he behaved as though the family money belonged to him. He was very disparaging toward Michael and open in his contempt for the entire Skakel family." Vinci would go to on to found and operate a string of highly successful North Face ski shops across New England. Sheridan similarly killed financing for Michael's plan to start a sports marketing business with Japan's top ski champion, Naga Kusumi.

Michael believes Sheridan was undermining his other career efforts as well. Michael got his New York real estate license in 1994. He recalls, "I pounded the pavement for work in sports management or commercial real estate, which I had done successfully in Boston. I had a lot of promising interviews, but I never got a call back. Sheridan was always intensely interested in my progress. Where was I applying? Who had interviewed me? There were so many promising interviews, but after talking to Tom Sheridan, I'd never get a call back. In hindsight, I believe he was calling my prospective employers to undermine my prospects."

Sheridan's vandalism against Michael extended through his trial. Sheridan, who had made himself archivist for the Skakel children's lifetime medical records and clothing sizes, refused to hand over records pertaining to the critical issue of Michael's physical size in October 1975. According to Stephen, "Tommy Sheridan slow-walked us. We kept pleading with him to send the information from his files. He kept promising and promising and then, just before the trial, he went dark. We never got the records."

His lifetime smoking habit finally caught up to Sheridan. He died of emphysema in 2008. Not long before his demise, Stephen spied him at a gas station in Windham wheeling an oxygen tank. A lit cigarette was perched in his mouth. Just before the trial, rendered nearly broke by years of poor financial management and the staggering costs of Michael's defense, the Skakel family informed Sheridan that they no longer required his services. Stephen terminated his monthly retainer. Sheridan was incensed. Shortly after she took on his appeal, Michael's new attorney, Hope Seeley, reached out to Sheridan on some matter. She related to the family his shocking words to her. "Michael is finally where he belongs," Sheridan told her.

Sheridan waxed philosophical along the same lines to Levitt, saying, "Going to prison is probably the best thing that could have happened to Michael. It might do him a world of good. Things happen in this life. It might be the making of him. I do feel badly. A sick person has been wrongly accused. But I think that it's for his own good that this happened. He is not the first person to be wrongly accused. He'll probably do a lot of good work in there as a counselor for other inmates and their addiction problems. He is very good at that."

In the acknowegement section of his book, Levitt praises "the unnamed source who provided me with the Sutton report. The world should know how important you were to solving this case."

In 2004, the year after Rucky's children buried their father, Sheridan offered his repayment to the man who supported him for 30 years and who considered him his best friend. Sheridan openly abandoned any pretense of complying with his professional ethical obligations of lawyer-client privilege and granted Levitt yet another interview for his book. To the author, he repeated one of the whoppers that he had fed to Sutton years before, but with some added gore that would earn Levitt a handful of headlines for his book. He told Levitt that while on a visit to Élan shortly after Michael's arrival, a counselor told him and Skakel family priest, Father Mark Connolly, that during his intake, Michael admitted that on the night of the murder he was covered in blood. In a 1979 memo to Sutton detectives, Sheridan recounted the same story, but omitted any mention of blood. He did, however, recite the name of the counselor to whom Michael had supposedly confessed some role in the murder: "Bennison." Years later, the story finally reached Daniel Bennison, a one-time resident and staff member at Élan who had indeed processed Michael's intake. Bennison publicly repudiated Sheridan's lie in a web posting. "I never contacted or was contacted by Father Mark Connolly or Sheridan," he wrote. "I never advised them on anything. Guys, I don't know who came out with this story that I advised Connolly and Sheridan but it just isn't true."

Levitt's final question for Sheridan was about his niece, Margot Sheridan, who had married Michael and was then divorcing him.

"Knowing what you did about Michael," Levitt asked, "did you warn her about him?"

When Sheridan said he hadn't, Levitt asked, "Why not?"

"Lawyer-client privilege," Sheridan answered. "I stared an extra second, waiting for him to smile at what I assumed was a joke," Levitt recounts. "He did not."

In an assessment my cousins found stunningly ironic, Sheridan told Levitt that the entire Skakel clan were "histrionic sociopaths." He explained, "Their interest is only self-interest. . . . They lack empathy for anyone but themselves."

Various Skakel family members struggle with problems including alcoholism. However, they are not sociopaths. To the contrary, they all have guilt-ridden consciences, heavy moral ballast, and deep wells of empathy. Sheridan manipulated them and made a calculated, cynical lifetime effort to strip his best friend and benefactor of his wealth and injure his children. That is the profile of a sociopath.

CHAPTER 12

The Gossip

Gossiping and lying go hand in hand.

—Russian proverb

There's a scene at the beginning of the appalling 2002 television adaptation of *Murder in Greenwich* where Mark Fuhrman, played by the actor Christopher Meloni, in a risible toupee, arrives in Greenwich to research his book on the Moxley murder. "If the Kennedys weren't connected to this, there wouldn't even be a book," Fuhrman growls to his ghostwriter. Those might have been the only true words spoken in that horrendous film. There would be no books, no made-for-television films, no national media coverage, had, say, Kenny Littleton rather than a "Kennedy cousin" been on trial for the murder. Dominick Dunne was the alchemist who poured the Kennedys into the Moxley murder tragedy and minted gold.

Dunne, who successfully transformed his lifelong fascination with celebrity and wealth into a career as a gossip and a novelist, had personal reasons for his attraction to this case. John Sweeney, a Wolfgang Puck restaurant chef, served less than three years in prison for strangling Dunne's daughter in 1982. "I was so outraged about our justice system," Dunne told a reporter in 1996, "that everything I've written since has dealt with that system—how people with money and power get different verdicts than other people."

Dunne's brief career as a Hollywood producer faltered as a result of his alcoholism and drug addiction. At his lowest ebb, Dunne famously sold his West Highland Terrier for $300 to buy cocaine. He fled Hollywood in 1979. Three years later, Dunne's only daughter, Dominique, a gifted 22-year-old actress who'd just made her film debut in *Poltergeist*, was murdered by her ex-boyfriend. Dunne attributed the killer's short sentence to the fact that the jury never heard about

Sweeney's violent history with women. Tina Brown, then the editor-in-chief of
Vanity Fair, encouraged Dunne to keep a journal during the trial, and in 1984
Brown published a feature based on his notes, headlined "Justice: A Father's Account of the Trial of His Daughter's Killer." The acclaimed piece gave Dunne
new life as *Vanity Fair*'s crime columnist. Dunne built his career on linking notorious murders to powerful people, including John and Patsy Ramsey, Claus von
Bulow, and O.J. Simpson. That successful formula gave Dunne his own measure
of celebrity and wealth.

By the time Dunne covered O.J. Simpson's 1995 trial, he may have been the
second most-recognizable person in the courtroom after the defendant. Dunne
was a small man, with a thick white mane. He toddled about Los Angeles County
Superior Court in tailored suits and natty Turnbull & Asser shirts and ties. His
trademark round glasses and scowl lent him the aspect of a dyspeptic owl. Judge
Ito, presiding over the Simpson trial, angered reporters by favoring the similarly
bereaved Dunne with a seat among the victims' families.

In the Simpson trial, Dunne had a clearly guilty defendant to rail against.
But in subsequent trials, his highly speculative, gossipy barbs started to get him in
trouble. In a succession of wildly reckless reporting, Dunne erroneously blamed
innocent, un-indicted people for murders, and for using power or money to
thwart their accusers. Even after a court convicted deranged nurse Ted Maher of
murdering his boss (and my friend) billionaire banker Edmond Safra in 1999,
Dunne continued to speak of a massive cover-up orchestrated by Safra's widow,
Lily. "One day, the whole story is going to get out," he assured a reporter, con-
spiratorially. "I'm so afraid of what I'm saying. I'm going to end up in prison."

The Chandra Levy case was Dunne's Waterloo. In 2001, the raven-haired,
24-year-old intern vanished during a jog in the Washington, DC, Rock Creek
Park. Speculation quickly centered on California Congressman Gary Condit,
with whom she'd had an affair. While police made no arrests, Dunne appeared
on *Larry King Live* and other talk shows spouting fanciful hunches about Condit's role in the crime. Dunne deployed a signature reporting gimmick in his
Vanity Fair stories. He would write that mysterious strangers approached him on
the street to impart jaw-dropping scoops about his stories, and then disappear
without sharing their names. These apparitions were hard to fact-check.

Seven months after Levy's death, Dunne proclaimed that he'd solved the
case. A source Dunne called "The Horse Whisperer" told Dunne that, while
attending a sex party in a Middle Eastern embassy, Condit complained to his
hosts that Levy had become "a clinger" and was threatening to "go public." At
Condit's request, assassins from Dubai murdered Levy then dropped her body
in the Atlantic. Alternatively, Condit's friends in the Hell's Angels whacked
Levy. "She'd gotten on the back of a motorcycle," Dunne said, never to be heard
from again. After Dunne repeated these whoppers on Laura Ingraham's radio

show, Condit filed an $11 million defamation suit. Condit's case outed Dunne's "Horse Whisperer" as Monty Roberts. *Time* magazine had debunked Roberts's memoir, *The Man Who Listens to Horses,* as rank fraud in 1998, three years before Levy's disappearance. The Condit scandal exposed Dunne as a flimflammer and his journalistic reputation suffered. He became a joke. By his own admission, the case shattered Dunne; he settled with Condit in 2005, and died of bladder cancer in 2009, a broken man. In 2010, another man, Ingmar Guandique, who had been convicted of assaulting two other women in Rock Creek Park around the time Levy disappeared, was convicted of Levy's murder. During the Dunne-led media lynching of Condit, Washington, DC, Police neglected abundant evidence against Guandique, the real perpetrator—another painful parallel to Michael Skakel's case.

But all that came later. When Dominick Dunne launched his crusade against my family, he still had both credibility and cachet.

In researching this book, I came across a semi-hysterical diatribe that Dunne lofted against me in the pages of *New York* magazine, after *The Atlantic*, in 2003, published my prize-winning article about Michael's trial. I'd been critical of Dunne. "I don't give a fuck about what that little shit has to say," he responded. (I'm six foot one and weigh 190 pounds.) "That fucking asshole," Dunne continued. "This pompous, pompous, POMPOUS man. I don't care what he has to say. He's not a person that I have any feeling or respect for."

When I noticed Dunne walking toward me on a Manhattan street in 2003, I turned toward him hoping to chat. Seeing me, he swiveled and dashed away with impressive speed. I don't know the source of Dunne's profound love–hate relationship with my family. His friends say that he nursed a grudge against my grandfather Joseph Kennedy for snubbing his father at the Breakers Hotel in Palm Beach. Dunne claimed that when he worked as a producer on *The Howdy Doody Show,* Dunne witnessed Grandpa Joe speaking dismissively to his son-in-law Peter Lawford, the Rat Pack actor whom Dunne admired, and never forgave him. It was not a grudge that my Uncle Peter assumed. Lawford, with whom I was close, loved my grandfather until the end of his life. In either case, neither of these incidents provides a plausible basis for a lifetime peeve. But Dunne was renowned for his snits with friends. Minor slights blossomed into malignancy. His friend Lucianne Goldberg had her own theory. "Nick [Dominick Dunne] identified with the Kennedys," Goldberg told *New York* magazine. "It's not political; he doesn't care about politics. But the Kennedys were glamorous, and the Dunnes weren't. And Nick loves glamour. The Kennedys are taken seriously, and, until recently, Nick wasn't."

Dunne told the *New York Times,* "Ever since I was a kid I wanted a famous person's life." The *Times* observed that covering notorious crimes like the Moxley case gave Dunne the opportunity to indulge "his fascination with celebrities and high society" and "his vengeful streak." Dunne would boast on *Larry King Live,* the week after Michael's conviction, that the case, along with his coverage of previous high-profile crimes, had made him a celebrity. He told King that his new status afforded him front-row seats in the courthouse and acknowledgment from judges and accolades on the street for a job well done, which he said, were what he most enjoyed. "All the people who dumped me years before were now giving dinner parties for me. And I went," he told the *Times.*

Dunne's efforts to connect a Kennedy relative to the Moxley murder formed a decade-long fixation and a profitable enterprise. "The Kennedys," he said "are the greatest soap opera in American history." Michael would get caught in the crosshairs where Dunne's ambitions intersected with his obsessions.

In the fall of 1991, while covering William Kennedy Smith's rape trial in Palm Beach for *Vanity Fair,* Dunne repeated a specious report that Connecticut State's Attorney Donald Browne had requested forensic evidence from Will Smith. Dunne wrote, "Though there have been reports that Willy Smith was a guest of the Skakels [the night of Martha Moxley's murder] no evidence links him to the case." He also wrote that Browne denied the story. Not until two years later did Dunne admit that his absurd rumor was false.

Dunne knew almost nothing about the Moxley murder in 1991. Yet in his initial articles about the Moxley case, his default was already set: Dunne would enlarge the catchy theme that "either the [Moxley] investigation was thoroughly botched or someone bowed to influence" into a best-selling novel, a TV miniseries, and a cascade of articles for *Vanity Fair.* In his novel *A Season in Purgatory* (1993), a thinly veiled John F. Kennedy Jr. murders his young neighbor in Greenwich and gets away with it because of family power. At the time, Dunne was sure that Tommy had killed Martha, and never lost an opportunity to point that out during an extensive national book tour, including appearances on programs such as *Hard Copy* and the *CBS Evening News* with Connie Chung, and also interviews with Jay Leno and Joan Rivers. I and the Skakel family members watched in horror as Dunne publicly accused Tommy of having committed the crime. "I was convinced that [Tommy] had done it," he later explained in *Vanity Fair,* "and had said so on television."

As Dunne liked to say, his book, and the miniseries that followed, dramatically raised the public profile of the unsolved murder. *New York Post* gossip columnist Liz Smith reported in 1993 that the Greenwich Police felt that Dunne had put their department on the spot. Dunne's efforts to tie Will Smith to the Moxley murder prompted the *Greenwich Time* and the *(Stamford) Advocate* to publish Len Levitt's article detailing the sorry performance of the local police. According to Garr and Browne, the publicity generated by Dunne during the Smith trial prompted the State to reopen the Moxley investigation.

If it didn't turn out that a Kennedy cousin had committed the crime, the story would be worthless to Dunne. Dunne ignored the strong evidence against Kenny Littleton; in his many articles and interviews about the case he never mentioned Littleton's five failed polygraphs, his shifting alibis, his call to David Moxley, his statement to the police psychiatrist about whether he could have committed the crime, the physical evidence of hair similarities, Littleton's history of sexual misconduct, and his capacity to deliver the blows. Dunne suggested that Littleton's alcoholism and his criminal activity were the result of stress from unfair accusation, which he blamed on the Skakels. (It mattered little to Dunne that the Skakels never publicly blamed Kenny Littleton for the crime.)

In his *Vanity Fair* article on the murder, Dunne offered a purged and abbreviated inventory of Littleton's criminal and mental-health history and then concluded, "But there is one thing I'm sure he didn't do: he did not kill Martha Moxley." No Skakel ever benefited from the same presumption of innocence in Dunne's writings.

Dunne's M.O. never varied. He began by evoking his daughter's death in a soft-touch approach to the victim's family. Once his nose was under the tent, Dunne launched into reckless accusations; damning denunciation of the accused; anonymous tips; facts bent to fit his theories; and his reliable old chestnut: accusing power and wealth of evading justice.

Soon after Will Smith's acquittal, in December 1991, Dunne wrote to Dorthy Moxley, recounting his own daughter's murder and asking to meet her. Dunne's invocation of their terrible shared tragedies appealed to Mrs. Moxley's trust, and they forged a friendship. "My only motivation in this has been Mrs. Moxley," Dunne said of his interest in the case in 2003. "No one understands the pain she's experienced like I do." Dunne wrote in *Vanity Fair*, "I swore to her that I would help her get justice for her daughter." Mrs. Moxley, who had previously been as judicious as everyone else, now became certain that a Skakel had committed the crime. She acknowledged that her theories about Skakel involvement were influenced by Dunne. She has steadfastly refused to examine the evidence herself and has relied instead on assessments by Dunne, Fuhrman, Garr, and Levitt—all men with mercenary agendas.

In promoting *A Season in Purgatory*, Dunne renewed his needling. "There are only two possible reasons" the murder remained unsolved; he pulled out his well-worn theme to the *Chicago Tribune*, saying, "Either the police are totally inept, or, somehow, power and money have played a part in covering up." Such statements continued to rankle law-enforcement officials. After Dunne's book tour, Garr led several members of the Moxley investigation team on a visit to Dunne's home in Hadlyme, Connecticut, bearing gifts: a State Police plaque, a T-shirt, and a mug. They begged him to stop criticizing their work. Dunne agreed to a truce.

MOXLEY HOUSE

Front view of the Moxleys' home on Walsh Lane in Belle Haven as it looked in 1975.

MARTHA MOXLEY

Sheila McGuire found Martha Moxley's body under this pine tree, center, on the Moxley family property.

ADOLPH HASBROUCK
as seen in the 1976 Charles
Evans Hughes High School
yearbook.

BURTON TINSLEY
as seen in the 1976 Charles
Evans Hughes High School
yearbook.

MICHAEL AS A CHILD

Michael is sitting on his mother, Anne's, lap in a 1967 family photo. Uncle Rucky was never the same after Anne died of brain cancer in 1973.
Front row, from left to right: Rucky, David, Anne, Michael, Stephen, Julie. Back row: Rush Jr., Tommy, John.

Michael as seen in the 1974 Brunswick School yearbook. Undiagnosed dyslexia made him a dreadful student.
Right and Opposite

Michael Skakel, third from right, top row, shown with teammates from Brunswick School's ninth-grade soccer team, 1975. (Courtesy of Greenwhich Library)

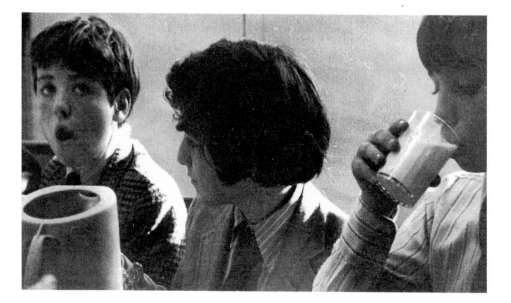

Michael on a sailboat in Nantucket during the summer of 1975, two months before Martha Moxley's death.

Michael playing tennis in Longboat Key, Florida, over Thanksgiving school vacation in November 1975—less than a month after Martha Moxley's murder. Jurors never saw any photos of how small Michael was at the time of the crime.

EXHIBIT 54 SKAKEL HOME FRONT VIEW
Front view of the Skakels' Otter Rock Drive house in Belle Haven, in a photo used at trial.

EXHIBIT 57
The shed behind which Tommy Skakel and Martha Moxley made out on the night of her murder.
Tommy kept the assignation secret for decades.

JOHN AND DORTHY MOXLEY

John and Dorthy Moxley, the brother and mother of Martha Moxley, addressing the media in February 2016. Dominick Dunne, Mark Fuhrman, Frank Garr, and Len Levitt manipulated and misled Mrs. Moxley about Michael's involvement.

THOMAS SKAKEL

Tommy Skakel enters the court in Norwalk, CT, as a jury deliberated his brother's fate in June 2002. (AP Photo/Douglas Healey, File)

DUNNE/FUHRMAN

Dominick Dunne *(above left)* and Mark Fuhrman *(above right)*, the two principle architects of Michael's wrongful conviction. Dunne insisted for years that Tommy Skakel killed Martha Moxley. When his friend Fuhrman wrote in 1998 that Michael had killed her, Dunne immediately got on board. (AP Images)

JONATHAN BENEDICT

Jonathan Benedict at Michael's *habeas corpus* trial in April, 2013. Benedict's illegal suppression of exculpatory evidence was part of a "convict at all costs" approach that cost Michael 11½ years of his life.. (AP Photo/ *The Stamford Advocate*, Jason Rearick, Pool)

MICHAEL IN COURT

Michael cries after learning he will walk free during his bond hearing at Stamford Superior Court, Nov. 21, 2013.

FRANK GARR

Frank Garr testifying during Michael Skakel's 2013 appeal. His friend Len Levitt wrote that Garr "had pursued, cajoled, harassed, and threatened the witnesses" to compel them to testify against Michael at trial. The evidence suggests Garr illegally concealed evidence and suborned perjury to win his career case.

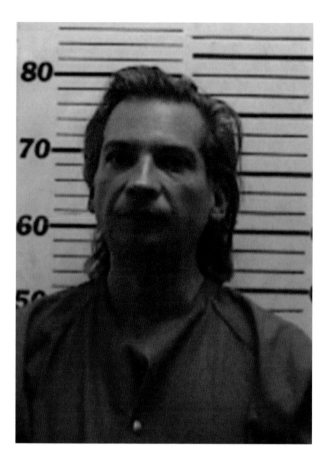

PETER ZILUCA

A mugshot of Martha's then-boyfriend Peter Ziluca, following his arrest in Santa Fe on May 8, 2009 on charges of beating his sister. Ziluca, who lived a short, tortured life, was the only Greenwich kid with any actual motive for killing Martha, but police never seriously investigated him.

LITTLETON/MORGANTI

Side-by-side comparisons of a Brunswick School photo of Kenny Littleton and the sketch of a man that officer Charles Morganti saw near the crime scene at the approximate time of Martha Moxley's death. Prosecutors unlawfully withheld this sketch from Michael's defense team during trial.

TOM SHERIDAN

Tom Sheridan, Rucky's lawyer, in 1982. Uncle Rucky lavished Tom with love, trust, and a rich and cushy sinecure. Tom repaid the favor by robbing Rucky blind and framing Michael for murder. This photo was taken at the Adirondack, New York, farm where Rucky was staying the night of Martha's murder.

FRANK AND PAULA WITTINE

Skakel gardener Frank Wittine sits bottom right in a bowtie. His wife, Paula, sits to his right in a blue dress. Despite Frank's curious behavior and confessions of past sexual violence, Greenwich police never investigated him as a suspect.

SKAKEL FAMILY

Photo from 1979 that prosecutors used in trial that grossly misrepresented Michael's size at the time of the crime.
From top to bottom:
Rucky, Rush Jr., Julie, Tommy, John, Michael, Stephen, and David.

RONALD REAGAN

Ronald Reagan presents Uncle Rucky with a gag gift during the annual Rancheros Visitadores ride through the Santa Ynez Valley. The Skakels and the Kennedys were like "Hatfields and McCoys", says Michael.

Clockwise from top left:

Michael crossing the finish line at Les Arcs in 1978 at 136 mph (a skydiver free falls at 120 mph).

Michael, arms raised, on podium at Mt. Hood, Oregon, 1993. Michael placed third.

Michael in speed ski suit 1991, Silverton, Colorado, with his wife, Margot Sheridan.

Michael, orange jacket, 1992, Stryn, Norway. Michael finished fifth and was top American.

Michael smiling, 1991 Vars, France, during ski training.

In an adult version of the children's game "Telephone," Dunne regularly called Mrs. Moxley during this period to share the kind of reckless gossip that would finally catch up with him in the Condit case. Moxley, in turn, phoned Garr to share Dunne's revelations. Garr then transcribed Dunne's scuttlebutt into police reports. "The Skakels went to their home in Windham, New York, to ski, and buried the clothes," Garr wrote in a May 1993 police report detailing his conversation with Mrs. Moxley. "Andrea Shakespeare is close to someone in the Vatican" read a tidbit in the same report. (Indeed, her father, Frank Shakespeare, went from being head of CBS Television to Ronald Reagan's appointee as Ambassador to the Holy See. In Dunne's world this might have been evidence that Martha was taken out by papal assassins.) "Dunne informed her that he had received information from one Paul Terrien, Essex, Connecticut, who informed him that the murder involved a conspiracy," Garr reported. Paul Terrien, who lived a few miles from Dunne, was the estranged brother of Michael's deceased step-uncle, George Terrien. Prior to his death in 1992, George Terrien had regarded his brother as a deranged oddball. George cut off all contact with Paul a decade before Martha's murder and disowned Paul in his will. No one in Rucky Skakel's family has ever met or talked to Paul Terrien.

In May 1996 Dunne's miniseries *A Season in Purgatory* aired, and Dunne pummeled Tommy in yet another media onslaught. That month he escorted Mrs. Moxley to a press conference to announce that she was raising the reward for information about her daughter's killer from $50,000 to $100,000.

After obtaining the Sutton files from Bryan, Dunne passed the "worst case" portfolios on to Mrs. Moxley. Saying he had landed documents that would crack the case wide open, Dunne swore Dorthy Moxley to secrecy. Too excited to keep mum, Mrs. Moxley shared this news with Garr. The detective, irate, called Dunne. First Levitt had gotten these documents (probably from Tom Sheridan) and now Dunne had them, while the detective assigned to the case was still in the dark. Dunne agreed to give Garr a copy. Garr, however, was underwhelmed. "There was nothing in it," Garr told Levitt of the Sutton report, which Dunne had regarded as game-changing. "It was all theories and speculation." Garr explained to Mrs. Moxley at the time that the Sutton files were just speculative "scenarios."

As the months went by with no Skakel arrested, Dunne grew antsy, and then bitter at Garr's insouiance. In the meantime, Levitt published a story about Dunne having the reports and named Bryan as the leaker. Apoplectic at Levitt for unveiling his informant, Dunne fired off a vitriolic fax to the *Newsday* ink slinger. "After you heard from Dorthy Moxley that I had a copy of the Sutton report, you called your friend at Sutton Associates to tell him that a young man working for him had given a copy of the report to me," Dunne wrote. "The young man had performed a decent act and your call to his boss put him into a state of abject fear for which I felt a responsibility." Then he turned his sights on Garr. "I gave a copy to Frank Garr. That was a total waste of time." Levitt's unveiling of Bryan as Dunne's source had edged the gossip toward DEFCON 1 on the hissy-fit scale. Of Garr's proposed book, Dunne wrote, "Only my innate good manners kept me from saying, 'On what? On how you couldn't solve the case for over 20 years?'" Practically spitting venom, Dunne hinted presciently at his suspicion. "Or maybe he was planning on using the Sutton Report as his plot. Over and out with Frank." Levitt shared the fax with Garr, whose head nearly exploded as he read it.

And so began a juvenile contest of wills between two men who both swore, to anyone who listened, that they only had Dorthy Moxley's interests at heart. After a conversation with his old friend Lucianne Goldberg, Dunne hatched a fiendish plot that would torpedo his two new archenemies, Levitt and Garr. He gave the Sutton files to Mark Fuhrman.

CHAPTER 13

The Perjurer

The Liar's punishment is not in the least that he is not believed, but that he cannot believe anyone else.

—George Bernard Shaw

On October 3, 1996, 44-year-old Mark Fuhrman avoided a jail sentence by pleading no contest to his felony perjury during O.J. Simpson's trial. The court sentenced him to three years of monitored probation. Fuhrman had lied under oath when he told Simpson's "Dream Team" lawyer F. Lee Bailey that he had not uttered the word "nigger" in the past 10 years. The defense produced Fuhrman's audiotaped interviews with screenwriter Laura Hart McKinny. "Nigger," as it turned out, was one of his most cherished expressions. He used the slur 41 times in the tapes, in such contexts as "These niggers, they run like rabbits." He explained how he would often plant evidence on uppity "niggers" to send them to jail. While still with the Los Angeles Police Department, Fuhrman told a psychiatrist that he left the Marine Corps because of his disgust with the laziness of "Mexicans and niggers." The Simpson verdict was, in part, largely an expression by the majority-black jury of its revulsion for Fuhrman, who embodied the notorious institutional culture of violent racism within the LAPD. Fuhrman's virulent bigotry cost the State of California the most high-profile double murder case in its history.

Fuhrman's guilty plea ended his career as a detective. "It is important to understand that, as a result of these charges, this plea and this sentence, Mark Fuhrman is now a convicted felon and will forever be branded a liar," California's Attorney General Dan Lungren told the press at the time. "By pleading to a felony, Mr. Fuhrman will never be a police officer in the State of California again. He is also now the ultimate impeachable witness—a convicted perjurer."

Fuhrman is a liar, a racist, and a bully. It's a great irony that he disgraced himself for his pivotal role in letting Simpson escape justice and then rehabilitated himself by helping to put an innocent man in prison for a murder he didn't commit.

Following his sentence, Fuhrman moved to Coeur d'Alene, just outside of Hayden Lake, Idaho, a notorious mecca for white supremacist militias. He works for Fox News as its "forensic and crime scene expert," but his principal function these days seems to be acting as an antidote to the Black Lives Matter movement. When police abuse and racial killings are in the news, from Baltimore to Ferguson, Missouri, to Columbia Junction, Fox summons Fuhrman in his tailored suit and "in your face" attitude to explain why police brutality is justified.

I happened to catch Fuhrman on Fox News's *Hannity* not long ago, defending a South Carolina police officer who brutally grabbed a black 16-year-old student by the neck, violently body-slammed her, and dragged her across the floor of a classroom by her leg. During the previous 24 hours, that video had horrified the nation. No one defended the police officer. Then came Fuhrman. "I'll tell you why it's not excessive . . ." Fuhrman began, true to form. Fuhrman's unrepentant racism is red meat to a certain segment of the Fox audience who experience civil rights for black Americans as a social demotion. Fuhrman's resurrection proves that, with the correct political alignment, even the most deplorable scoundrels can get a second act on Fox.

In search of a Torquemada to torment the Greenwich Police, Dominick Dunne summoned Fuhrman, whom, Dunne oddly claimed, he had come to admire during the Simpson trial. Fuhrman's reinvention began in earnest in 1997 with his O.J. Simpson book *Murder in Brentwood,* which made him a best-selling author. Now, Fuhrman was looking for an unsolved crime to write about. When Fuhrman answered the phone, Dunne said, "Hey, Mark, I've got just the one for you, and I have a private detective report that's going to knock you on your ass." Dunne provided Fuhrman with the Sutton report—which became the Cliffs-Notes version of Fuhrman's book *Murder in Greenwich.* According to Fuhrman, Dunne also gave him the inspiration to write it. Fuhrman reported that he and Dunne discussed the Moxley case intensely at a Four Seasons lunch in 1997. Dunne hosted a cocktail party for Fuhrman to introduce him to Connecticut law-enforcement officials.

Before Fuhrman launched into the real Moxley case, he immersed himself in Dunne's novel *A Season in Purgatory.* "While it was an entertaining read, the book also angered me," he wrote. "Money, power, celebrity, deceit, corruption. It was the Simpson case all over again." Fuhrman was indignant about a case that Dunne had invented. ("I changed the murder weapon to a baseball bat," Dunne wrote of his process. "I also . . . gave some Kennedy touches to the Skakels, whom I called the Bradleys. I threw in some of my own Irish Catholic family too. All of this was for libel reasons.") Fuhrman's own gift for blending fact with fiction allowed him to craft the Sutton report into a compelling parable invoking Dunne's favorite theme of wealth corrupting the justice system.

To sell the book, Fuhrman partnered with another infamous figure from the 1990s, literary agent Lucianne Goldberg, who first introduced him to Dunne. (The two men saw each other across the courtroom, but never met during the Simpson trial.) Goldberg was the wizard of right-wing conspiratorial fiction packaged as political exposé: she convinced White House executive assistant Linda Tripp to secretly tape-record lurid conversations about President Bill Clinton with Tripp's "friend," White House intern Monica Lewinsky. Lewinsky described to Tripp the details of her occasional sexual favors for the president. Goldberg had previously encouraged Tripp to author a book exposing Clinton as the murderer of his aide Vince Foster. Goldberg planned to market her prospective author as "the woman who served Vince Foster his last hamburger." Before triggering the Clinton impeachment saga, she represented Fuhrman in his Blame-a-Kennedy-Cousin book deal.

Following Fuhrman's 1998 publication of *Murder in Greenwich,* Dunne complained of the continuing public disquiet with the disgraced detective's racism and corruption: "Although Fuhrman's extraordinary work on the Moxley–Skakel case has brought about redemption in his life, there will always be some who can never forgive him."

As previously noted, Dunne wrote the foreword to *Murder in Greenwich,* an unsheathed tirade of naked malice against Frank Garr. "I gave a copy of the files to a detective who had been working on the Moxley case from almost the night of the murder," he wrote. "Time went by. Nothing happened. I began to think that nothing was ever going to happen. Then along came Mark Fuhrman, whom I grew to admire after the fiasco of the Simpson trial. . . . Say what you want, the guy is a great detective." The message was clear: due to the incompetence of the Connecticut cops, Dunne had no choice but to bring in a real homicide detective to solve the case. Dunne was incorrect about Fuhrman being a great detective. Everyone already knew Fuhrman was a bigot, a perjurer, and a thug; but it turned out, he was a sorry detective as well.

The book is a 283-page jeremiad against the Greenwich Police, who, Fuhrman says in his book, angered him by treating him as a pariah. Fuhrman castigates Greenwich cops as "servants of the rich and powerful." Echoing Dunne, he wrote, "Someone killed Martha Moxley and got away with it. And the reason he got away with it was that the Greenwich Police Department . . . didn't have the courage to go after him."

Murder in Greenwich was a quickie, dime-store crime thriller, with an aphorism about wealth and power. Its villain is the "spoiled rich brat" Michael Skakel. The literary enterprise cost Fuhrman and his ghostwriter only three months. In his acknowledgments, Fuhrman thanked his family for tolerating his "stress of doing two books in less than one year." The Sutton report and Dunne's fanciful inventions were Fuhrman's principal feedstock.

The Connecticut investigators, Lunney, Brosko, Solomon, and Keegan, and State's Attorney Browne, all refused to meet with Fuhrman. Only Steve Carroll spoke to the disgraced cop. Carroll pointed the finger at Tommy and told Fuhrman that, after reading the Sutton report, he and Garr had specifically dismissed the idea of Michael as a suspect because of Michael's rock-solid alibi. "He just wasn't there," Fuhrman wrote of Carroll and Garr's conviction. When Fuhrman called Garr to ask for help, Garr rebuffed him. "Well I don't think I could do that. To tell you the truth I've been thinking about writing a book about the case." Fuhrman interpreted Garr's reticence as evidence of an organized police conspiracy to perpetuate the Kennedy–Skakel police cover-up. "I wondered what they were afraid of," he wrote. "I sensed something else was behind Frank's refusal to work with me. Something was starting to smell." Fuhrman is either extraordinarily thick or was being purposely obtuse about why cops wouldn't be happy to help him, given his racist, felonious background. Fuhrman took his revenge by sniping at Garr throughout his book. Invective against the detective is his pervasive theme. He wrote that Dunne had given the Sutton reports to Garr. "Yet apparently Frank had talked to hardly any of the people I interviewed whose names I got from the files. And none of the leads I followed showed any of Garr's tracks."

After years of accusing Tommy Skakel of the crime, Dunne followed Fuhrman's lead, and, without missing a step, he turned his sights on Michael. Dunne explained that an anonymous tip by a mysterious woman had caused him to reassess his original accusations against Tommy. "I felt that this woman, whose name I did not write in my notebook—at her request—and which I subsequently forgot, knew more than she was telling me. But I liked her. I trusted her," Dunne said. "As she was leaving she said, 'It wasn't Tommy.' She repeated it. Up till then, Tommy Skakel had been the major suspect in the case. I was convinced that he had done it, and had said so on television. Her words haunted me." That clue finally gave Dunne mental clarity about the case. "I firmly believe that Michael Skakel killed Martha Moxley," he declared on *Good Morning America* in March 1999. On the CNN program *Burden of Proof,* when asked whether he believed that Michael Skakel did it, he replied, "That is what I absolutely, firmly believe." He made no apology to Tommy for the years of tormenting accusations. To ease his own shift from Tommy to Michael as the designated murderer, Dunne simply made them partners in the crime. In January 2000 Dunne told ABC News, "I firmly believe Michael Skakel killed Martha Moxley and that Tommy Skakel may have helped him move the body."

Fuhrman acknowledges in *Murder in Greenwich* that the Moxley murder attracted him because it reminded him of the Simpson case: "Money, power, celebrity, deceit, corruption." On the day he began investigating the crime, he repeated this formulation to Greenwich police officers when they asked him about his interest in the case. Fuhrman had clearly decided before he began his investigation that the killer must be a wealthy, powerful celebrity who had corrupted the police. Fuhrman exposes this bias by explaining his reasons for rejecting Kenny Littleton as a suspect, which he says he did "early on": "Littleton had no money, no powerful family behind him, no clout. If Littleton had murdered Martha Moxley, he would not have gotten away with it." Being neither rich nor famous, by Fuhrman's reasoning, Littleton couldn't be guilty. Fuhrman might find comfort in this view, which conveniently exonerates him from his central culpability in the disastrous O.J. Simpson acquittal: if Simpson got off because he was rich, then it was not because the prosecution's principal witness was exposed as a perjurer, who bragged about planting false evidence on blacks.

Ignoring the fact that Kenny had changed his alibi five times, Fuhrman boldly concluded, "While other suspects have had trouble with their alibis, Littleton has always stuck to the same story." He explained Littleton's failure to pass five lie-detector tests over a period of 16 years by arguing, "If Littleton is a paranoid, psychotic, bipolar alcoholic, then how could [Greenwich Police] expect him to pass any kind of polygraph?"

Curiously, Fuhrman makes a much stronger case against Tommy than he does against Michael. Fuhrman was directly tracking the Sutton report—which was far more damning to Tommy; the Sutton authors believed that Tommy was guilty and Michael was innocent—but then, Fuhrman pivots abruptly near his book's conclusion and declares Michael the killer.

I have my own theory as to why Fuhrman chose to blame Michael for the murder: Michael made good copy. As Fuhrman himself acknowledged, nobody would buy a book about Kenny Littleton. Kenny wasn't related to anyone famous. No suspect other than a Skakel was bankable. And no Skakel but Michael met Fuhrman's requisites. Tommy was old news. Dunne had already gone down that road. Fuhrman never could have claimed that he had solved the case by rolling out an old retread. The world would not have paid any attention to another book fingering Tommy, who had been the cops' favorite suspect for 15 years. It wouldn't make sense for Fuhrman to write about how badly the police had bungled their investigation if he agreed that they'd identified the correct suspect early in the investigation. For a successful book that would restore Fuhrman as a credible detective, he required a different Skakel to take the rap, one for whom he alone could take credit. Fuhrman needed a spectacular victory to overshadow his disgrace. "While his brother Thomas was a suspect from day one, Michael Skakel has avoided scrutiny and suspicion," Fuhrman began the chapter in which he "solved" the 23-year-old case he'd studied for all of three months. Michael had pulled the short straw.

In his book, Fuhrman introduced and diagrammed all the major elements that Benedict and Garr would subsequently adopt to convict Michael. In order to maneuver around Michael's alibi, Fuhrman moved Martha's time of death to 11:30 p.m. He did this simply by disregarding the professional forensics report and ignoring the barking dogs, the curfew, and Martha's screaming. Voila! Martha was murdered at 11:30 p.m. after Michael's return from Sursum Corda. Fuhrman invented the motive: Michael's supposed jealousy toward his brother Tommy. This was the problem that befuddled Benedict: how would Michael have learned about Tommy kissing Martha if he left for Sursum Corda before the flirtation began? Benedict solved this puzzle by offering the jury the option that Michael never went to Sursum Corda. Fuhrman gave himself more flexibility for flights of imaginative fancy: in order to provide Michael with a motive, he clears out the Skakel homestead to make a honeymoon retreat for Tommy and Martha. Fuhrman extended the couple's 20-minute, back-of-the-toolshed make-out session into a two-hour marathon love fest that moved into the Skakel house. When Michael discovers the blissful sweethearts upon his return from Sursum Corda, he screams at Tommy for stealing his girlfriend.

"Martha is embarrassed and sickened by the confrontation," Fuhrman writes. "The two brothers seem to be fighting over a toy. As they exchange vicious threats, Martha slips out the back door." Fuhrman has Michael, furious at the jilting, grabbing a golf club and pursuing Martha. He beats her to death, and drags her under the tree. "To most people this would be a horror, but to him this is a conquest," Fuhrman writes. "He pulls her pants and panties down below her knees . . . masturbates while staring at Martha's ravaged body. Once he ejaculates, he runs back to his house" to organize the 30-year cover-up.

Having dispensed with the sleuthing, Fuhrman picks up his psychiatrist's pipe and pad. Michael's "psychological profile reveals a severely disturbed youth with violent tendencies," he diagnoses. Hmmmm. Who is he really talking about here? In the 1980s, Fuhrman attempted to earn disability pay from the LAPD by claiming to be mentally unbalanced and homicidal. "I have this urge to kill people, which upsets me," he told a police psychiatrist. Fuhrman admitted that he got into altercations nearly every day of his life and confessed that he needed to be "violent to exist."

And the long-touted role of the Kennedy family in the cover-up? Only more speculation. For example, Fuhrman surmises about what the police might have discovered had they subpoenaed Rucky's phone records for Halloween. "It would have been interesting to see if any of the phone calls had been made to Ethel or Ted Kennedy, or Stephen [Steve] Smith, the Kennedy family fixer," he wrote. "If the phone calls occurred before 12:30 p.m., then someone in the house knew something had happened before Martha's body was discovered."

The phone records probably would have been a lot less interesting than Fuhrman imagines. First of all, Rucky wasn't home; he was in the Adirondack wilderness. But so much for detective work! Second, Fuhrman's idea that Rucky would call my uncles Teddy Kennedy or Steve Smith or my mother to enlist their help in covering up a murder demonstrates that Fuhrman might be just as dense as he is racist. Quite apart from loathing each other's politics, there was no social discourse between the Skakel and Kennedy families. Neither Teddy nor Steve, I imagine, would have recognized Rucky in a crowd; they hadn't spent any time in each other's presence since my parents' wedding 25 years before, aside from Uncle George's 1965 funeral. Uncle Steve's interaction with Rucky was mainly through lawyers, and Steve's regard for the Skakels was particularly severe. His role in managing my mother's finances had pitted him in a pitched battle with the two surviving Skakel brothers since my father's death in 1968. He was annoyed at them for squandering the company's once-immense value, mismanaging its assets, and monopolizing its resources—all to my mother's detriment. For seven years he had fought with them, perennially threatening litigation. The brothers, in turn, were furious at his efforts to wrest control of GLC from them. Steve Smith would have been the last person that Rucky Skakel would turn to in a jam—and particularly if he were trying to conceal a crime. My father had already taught Rucky that the Kennedys placed principle before family loyalty when, as attorney general, he prosecuted Rucky and his business partners for thin antitrust violations. Steve would have called the FBI if he'd ever gotten wind of any kind of crime—let alone murder—perpetrated by the Skakel or, for that matter, the Kennedy family.

Murder in Greenwich was as much a work of fiction as was *A Season in Purgatory.* Levitt told me that Fuhrman "based his conclusions about Michael on intuition rather than fact." Nevertheless, the book got Fuhrman on television talking about something besides his perjury conviction and racism.

Garr dismissed Fuhrman's bestseller to the *New York Daily News* as a cut-and-paste rewrite of old newspaper stories and police files. The Greenwich Police said that Fuhrman's work was "riddled with inaccuracies and contains no new information." Nevertheless, the book lit a fire beneath Connecticut law-enforcement officials, and made Michael their new target.

Fuhrman's book came out in May 1998. Four months later in his own book, former *Greenwich News* editor Tim Dumas speculated darkly and baselessly that Browne may have been "paid off" to take a dive on the Moxley case. In April, under increasing public pressure to make an arrest he wasn't ready to make, State's Attorney Browne abruptly retired. Solomon stepped down soon thereafter, leaving Garr as the senior investigator in Connecticut. Garr was now in charge of the Moxley case. Although Solomon, who was lead investigator on the homicide for 20 years, would not speak to me about the case, a source close to him who wishes to remain unnamed told me in November 2002, "Jack believes that your cousin did not commit the murder. He is absolutely sick and beside himself because he believes an innocent man is in the can. But Jack is a cop through and through, and he will not make any public statement that might embarrass his law-enforcement colleagues."

By May, Fuhrman was still jawboning on the talk-show circuit, shilling his book, patting his own back for solving the case, and telling the press that the only way Connecticut authorities could save face would be to call a grand jury. "I've given them an outline," he boasted on CNN on May 16, 1998. "This book is an outline of a homicide investigation and it's definitely an outline to do a grand jury, the people that you need to call, the questions you need to ask, and the way that the case probably went down." He told anybody who'd listen that if a grand jury were to be called, the world had one guy to thank. "I'm going to take credit for it, along with the Moxley family," he told *USA Today.* He said he'd rescued an investigation that had been thoroughly bungled, most notably by Garr.

On June 17, 1998, one month after the publication of Fuhrman's book, Browne's successor, the new State's Attorney, Jonathan Benedict, convened a one-man grand jury consisting of Judge George Thim, sitting, according to grand jury witness Richard Hoffman, "at a collapsible plastic table from Staples" in Bridgeport. That would be the State's first step in its $25 million effort to imprison Michael Skakel.

A banner on the paperback version of the book advertises *Murder in Greenwich* as "the book that spawned the Connecticut Grand Jury investigation." "I firmly believe," Dunne wrote in the October 2000 issue of *Vanity Fair,* "*Murder in Greenwich,* for which I wrote the introduction, is what caused a grand jury to be called after 25 years."

Levitt's description of his friend Garr during these months is of an emasculated man raging at the gelding Fuhrman was giving him. Garr's new boss, Benedict, was obviously monitoring the press closely and paying more attention to Fuhrman than to the detective in charge of the case. In the midst of this racking humiliation, Garr learned that his nemesis, Dunne, had befriended his new boss, Benedict, and introduced Michael's prosecutors to Garr's tormentor, Fuhrman.

Garr was incensed that Benedict sent two of his assistants, Chris Morano and Dominick Galluzzo, to meet repeatedly with Fuhrman in Manhattan. "I am telling Benedict that Fuhrman is the most notorious liar in America," Garr told Levitt. "I am hearing that Fuhrman is pushing to get himself called as a witness before the grand jury and that Morano and Galluzzo are helping him. I'm telling myself it will be over my dead body." Garr's rage approached apoplexy when he learned that Morano had become friends with his Hadlyme, Connecticut, neighbor and Garr's bête noire: Dominick Dunne. Levitt tried to soothe Garr by telling him the important thing was that a grand jury was finally being called.

But Garr and Levitt both knew the truth: Dunne and Fuhrman had swept into town and stolen their case. By Levitt's own admission, the jealousy and humiliation they both experienced became nearly unbearable. "At our lowest ebb, we resolved to tell our story," Levitt wrote. This was the moment Garr and Levitt struck a deal to write a book that would once again make the Moxley case their own. They agreed to a 50/50 split. Garr now had a vested interest in the case being salable. While Garr had a legal responsibility to practice blind justice, the book deal with Levitt gave him a financial incentive to make sure that a "Kennedy cousin" was on the gibbet.

After indicting Michael, Benedict was legally bound by the US Supreme Court's Brady decision to turn over any information that might exculpate Michael. The Brady law requires prosecutors to keep an "open file"; any evidence collected by police must be available to the defense during the discovery period preceding the trial. Garr, on the stand during Michael's new trial appeal, acknowledged his legal obligation, "basically that everything is available to the defense." Three sources had reported that Garr was working on a book. So Michael's lawyer specifically asked prosecutors if any book deals existed that might prejudice investigators against Michael. Benedict was adamant that no such book deals existed. Garr, who, in addition to his role as evidence manager, was a key witness for the prosecution, never revealed his conflicts to Michael's lawyers or to the Court. His bosses in the police and prosecutor's office apparently knew of his covert deal and urged him to keep it quiet.

There were additional political pressures that narrowed Garr's and Benedict's focus on Michael. Right up until the publication of his book, Fuhrman claimed that both the Greenwich Police and Garr still considered Kenny Littleton a prime suspect. Why, then, did they give him immunity just a couple months later? Benedict and Garr must have concluded that a prosecution of Littleton—especially if it failed, and any prosecution 23 years after the crime stood small chance of success—would not end the public debate over their competence and integrity. The loss would instead inflame Fuhrman and Dunne, who had already accused the police of giving the Skakels a pass by making Littleton the fall guy. The only way to still the criticism was to prosecute a Skakel. To clear Tommy, as Benedict explained to Judge Kavanewsky, they would need Littleton to testify in support of his *French Connection* alibi. The case against Michael was weak, but by indicting a Skakel, investigators could at least quiet Fuhrman's charges that they were sycophants and cowards. Dunne had already sent signals that he would be satisfied short of a conviction, so long as Connecticut indicted Michael. "I just want to see this guy indicted. I just want to see this guy with handcuffs on," he told *Burden of Proof.*

According to Fuhrman, members of Benedict's staff told him that they planned to use *Murder in Greenwich* as the blueprint for the prosecution. In fact, the State followed the book practically line by line. Adopting Fuhrman's theory, the State argued that Michael fabricated the masturbation story during his Sutton interrogation in 1993, after Sutton detectives told him that forensic expert Henry Lee was about to conduct DNA testing (which was not available in 1975) on evidence from the crime scene. According to Fuhrman, Michael concocted his masturbation story to inoculate himself against the possibility that police would find his semen on Martha's body.

There are numerous problems with Fuhrman's theory. First, the tree in which Michael said he had attempted to masturbate was a football field's length in distance from the tree where Martha's body was found. Second, Michael said he did not masturbate to orgasm. The story would therefore not account for his semen on or near Martha's body. Third, Michael did not invent the story in the early 1990s for his Sutton interview; he has been telling it consistently for at least 23 years. Michael told the story to his aunt Mary Ellen Reynolds in 1979; to his psychiatrists, Stanley Lesse and Hyman Weitzen; to Monsignor (later auxiliary Bishop) William McCormack in 1980; and to many friends before the 1990s. I heard him tell it several times, beginning in 1983. The prosecution's own witness Michael Meredith testified that he heard the story from Michael in 1987, long before DNA was widely used in criminal cases, while staying at the Skakel home. Michael's explanation for his failure to tell the story to the police in the first instance—adolescent embarrassment and fear of a puritanical and wrathful father—is plausible. As Jay Leno suggested, referring to the Skakel trial, many people would prefer to be found guilty of murder than be suspected of masturbating in a tree: "I would rather confess to murder. Wouldn't you?" Leno quipped. Characteristically, Michael's lawyer, Mickey Sherman, never defended Michael against the accusation of recent fabrication. I told Sherman several times during the trial that I would testify about Michael's pre-Sutton recounting, but he never called me, or any other witness, to rebut Benedict's claim.

Taking his cue from Fuhrman, Benedict argued that Michael had killed Martha in a drunken, jealous rage after seeing his older brother kiss her. But Michael says, and other Skakels agree, that he was a virgin with crushes on a family friend, Francie, and his platonic "girlfriend," Jackie Wetenhall. "Martha was cute," he told me when I visited him in prison in September 2002, "but every girl was cute to me." Michael says that he was unaware of any romance between Martha and his brother. "I never knew about Tom and Martha," he told me during the same prison visit, "until I heard it on TV in 1998." This claim is tenable. None of the Skakels ever saw the Sutton reports, which first reported Tommy's romance with Martha. Sheridan, for obvious reasons, prevented the Skakels from reading the report, which he kept under lock and key in his office. Nor did the Skakels discuss Martha's murder among themselves. Because of his dyslexia, Michael doesn't read much. He has still never read my article in *The Atlantic* defending him. He steers clear of news reports about the murder. "I don't want to spend my life in the fetal position," he explains.

Benedict would also ape Fuhrman's scam for moving back Martha's long-established 10:00 p.m. time of death in order to get around Michael's alibi. To support a later time of death, Fuhrman quotes renowned forensic pathologist Dr. Michael Baden, who had only limited access to the case file in 1998. Fuhrman suggests that Baden believed the time of death could have been as late as 1:00 a.m. Baden told me that he was surprised to learn of Fuhrman's assertion. "I'm sure I told Fuhrman that I thought the time of death was about 10:00 p.m.," he says. "If he didn't put it in the book that means he didn't agree with it. I wouldn't have gone as far as 1:00 a.m." At my request, Baden reexamined the more complete autopsy notes available from the case file. He noticed in the notes a fluid in the stomach that Connecticut's medical examiner Wayne Carver had testified in Michael's trial was possibly blood that had drained from her throat wound down into the stomach. "That's not blood," he tells me. "It's described by Gross as black fluid. Blood resembles coffee grounds in the stomach. It's coffee or Coca-Cola." Baden says that since Martha was last seen at 9:50 p.m., and that the stomach absorbs fluids quickly, in about 30 minutes, he can now provide a more exact estimate of when Martha died. "I think 10:00 or 10:15 or so would be a very appropriate time of death," he says. Referring to Fuhrman, he adds, "The police are not trained to determine time of death. The medical examiner is."

Fuhrman's story, and the prosecution's theory, supposed that Michael killed Martha in a jealous rage toward his "nemesis," brother Tommy. Their hypothesis required that 15-year-old ADHD-afflicted Michael (admittedly drunk and stoned) demonstrate the sangfroid of a criminal mastermind: murdering her savagely, and then having the clarity to clean himself up, dispose of the murder weapon, and take an active role in maintaining a conspiracy that remained drum-tight for nearly 30 years.

The theory of an intricately organized Skakel conspiracy is comical to anyone who knows the family; neither Fuhrman nor Dunne did. Some members of the Skakel clan may be impulsive and even reckless. Several Skakels made a series of disastrous decisions about how to handle this case. But none of them is a murderer or conspirator. They are deeply religious and lack the moral bankruptcy to carry personal loyalty to the level of depravity—much less the organizational discipline and the cohesiveness to either form or perpetuate such a conspiracy.

I have spoken to all the Skakels about the murder, and they are as confused as various investigators have been over the years about who committed the crime. I have heard different Skakels speculate about the possible guilt of a diverse list of suspects. (Interestingly, most of them told me they have long believed that the strongest evidence points to former Skakel gardener Franz Wittine.) All of the Skakels want to see Martha's killer in jail. None of them ever imagined that Michael would be charged with, much less convicted of, the crime.

But none of them would lie to protect Michael. Even when Sherman instructed Julie to lie under oath about her memories of that evening, she refused with the full support of her brothers. At the trial, Andrea Shakespeare (Renna) testified that the night of the murder, before being driven home by Julie after dinner, she was "under the impression" that Michael was still in the Skakel house after the older boys had left for the Terrien/Dowdle home—highly ambiguous and uncertain testimony that nonetheless gave jurors room to doubt Michael's alibi. According to Julie and Stephen, on the morning that Julie was to testify at Michael's trial, Sherman assembled the two of them; Sherman's legal assistant, Jason Throne; and his son, Mark Sherman, who is also a lawyer, at Julie's home. Sherman told Julie, "You have to say that you remember that the boys were still at the house when you took Andrea home." Julie replied, "I can't. That's not true." Sherman admonished her, "You have to. It's the only way." Julie again refused. Stephen later found her weeping outside the courthouse. According to Stephen, she was devastated by the prospect that her refusal to lie might put Michael in jail. Stephen told me that he found Sherman's young assistant, Throne, and begged him to get Sherman to back off. "I told him, 'You can't do this. She's going to have a nervous breakdown.'"

Sherman denies that he ever told Julie to lie. "We would never have asked her to perjure herself," he told me. "I just asked her to add two and two and come up with four, not five or seven." He explained to me that the Skakels were difficult witnesses, refusing to testify even to obvious facts unless they had clear memories. He cited the example of Rush Jr., who clearly remembered Michael being at the Terrien/Dowdles' but refused to testify that Michael was in the car that went to the house: 27 years later, he had no clear memory of who was in the car. John Skakel refused to testify about any of the events that night, because he had no independent memories of the details of the evening. John would agree only to testify that he told the truth to the police in 1975; the police report records his saying that Michael was in the car and at the Terrien/Dowdle house. "They were impossible to deal with," Sherman told me. The children's rigid Catholic scrupulousness might have worked against Michael: post-verdict interviews quoted jury members as saying they regarded the Skakels' memory gaps not as the product of rigorous honesty but as obfuscation.

By May 1998, Garr was reduced to answering questions about what the press was treating as Fuhrman's investigation. He had been fully eclipsed. Judging by his actions, he must have, at that point, made the sinister calculation that the only way to recover the reins was to pretend the idea for Michael's indictment was his own. He relaunched the case based almost entirely on Fuhrman's repackaging of Sutton's worst-case scenario. The same case that Garr had previously dismissed as Sutton's "theories and speculation" was now courtroom ready. It was Garr's job to prep Benedict. "I'm in the process of bringing the new State's Attorney up to date, and once that's completed we'll sit down and make some decisions," he told the *Boston Herald* on May 18. "A grand jury is certainly being discussed."

In June, it happened. Superior Court Judge George Thim agreed to hear this case constructed of strands of lies and innuendo, pasted together with the flop sweat of a cop fighting to regain possession of his career case. Garr would soon show himself to be capable of stooping to unspeakable lows to win. He was seriously wounded and embarrassed, though there was one small consolation: Benedict never did call Fuhrman to testify.

Dunne's objective since 1991 was to link the Martha Moxley murder to a "Kennedy cousin," whether it was Will Smith, John Kennedy, Tommy Skakel, or Michael Skakel. Describing the day of Michael's guilty verdict, Dunne crowed in *Vanity Fair,* "The whole courtroom stared at [Michael], transfixed by his humiliation. This trial has ruined a once proud family. Their besmirched name will outlive them all." In *Vanity Fair's* December issue Dunne made the wild claim (which he repeated on *Larry King Live*) that he had information from a mysterious source that four other Skakels were involved in cleaning up the crime scene with Michael. Dunne continued to make an industry out of the Moxley murder. He parlayed his role in the case into a new Court TV series he hosted: *Dominick Dunne's Power, Privilege and Justice.*

Fuhrman also did well: the USA Network in fall 2002 aired a highly fictionalized docudrama based on Fuhrman's *Murder in Greenwich,* lionizing Fuhrman for his role in solving the Moxley murder. In perhaps the case's biggest irony, Fuhrman, fresh from being played by a *Law & Order* actor and leading a media mob to unjustly convict Michael, wrote a book called *The Murder Business: How the Media Turns Crime into Entertainment and Subverts Justice.*

Len Levitt and Frank Garr also parlayed Michael's conviction into career gold. Rupert Murdoch's star editor, Judith Regan, printed their book *Conviction* in 2004 after other publishers rebuffed the project—by then the fourth book on the Moxley murder. Levitt friend Bernard Kerick, another notoriously crooked cop, opened Regan's door to Levit. (Two years later, public revulsion forced Murdock to fire Regan when she published O.J. Simpson's "fictional account" of how he committed the murder of Nicole Brown Simpson and Ron Goldman.)

Dunne said he had "contempt for the behavior of the Skakel family" because they came from privilege and abused it. Fuhrman echoed him: "[The Skakels] lived a privileged existence" and they "frequently abused that privilege." But the capacity to write, to publish, and to hold public attention are privileges that Dunne, Fuhrman, and Levitt abused. The media have duties, too.

PART V

The Witnesses

CHAPTER 14

The Model

Loose tongues are worse than wicked hands.

—Yiddish Proverb

I do not know precisely when Garr began despising the Skakel family, but in 1998, just after Fuhrman announced that he had "solved the crime," Garr began pursuing the Skakels with the relentlessness of the French inspector Javert in *Les Miserables*. Taking his cue from Fuhrman and Dunne, his former archenemies, Garr now took his sights off Kenny Littleton and locked them on Michael Skakel. To prepare for his new crusade, Garr read the most scurrilous literature he could about the Skakel and Kennedy families.

His friend Levitt describes a rendezvous with Garr in his Bridgeport redoubt: "The small, windowless cubicle where he was sequestered . . . had a bookshelf that was empty, save for three books that indicated his resolve—some would say his obsession—with the Moxley case," and, for that matter, with my family. The three books that Levitt saw were: *A Season in Purgatory*, Dunne's novel; *The Other Mrs. Kennedy*, a similarly inaccurate vicious anti-Kennedy screed posing as a biography of my mother, Ethel Kennedy (the author of the cut-and-paste hatchet job was a *National Enquirer* hack named Jerry Oppenheimer); and *Senator*, a revenge project by Richard Burke, a former aide to my uncle Senator Edward Kennedy, who scribbled this diatribe during a cataclysmic mental breakdown that ended with his arrest by the FBI for shooting bullets into his own car, to feign an assassination attempt. Both of the latter were published by St. Martin's Press, which is notoriously biased against the Kennedys and correspondingly light on fact-checking. Taken together, those three works of fiction meshed the Skakels and Kennedys into an ugly expression of the worst kind of entitlement, arrogance, and abuse of wealth and power. That twisted confection perfectly characterizes the bigoted vision of the Kennedys and Skakels that Garr would bring to the Moxley case. "I hate the Skakels," he told Levitt. I can't blame him. I would hate the Skakels and the Kennedys too if those three books composed my entire library.

After gorging himself on this brand of vitriol, Garr still faced the problem of evidence. Following 20 years of investigation, police had no fingerprints, no DNA, no forensic evidence, no documents, and no witnesses linking Michael to the crime. There was a good deal of physical evidence, but none tied to Michael. The only way to win such a case is with a confession. Garr didn't have one, so he needed to gin one up. He began trolling for witnesses who could flesh out the Dunne-Fuhrman speculations.

As Garr's devoted scribe, Levitt chronicles his friend's far-flung quest for confession witnesses with unabashed admiration. He describes Garr "cajoling, threatening, harassing, and bringing witnesses to testify against Michael." But first Garr needed someone to cajole, threaten, and harass.

Garr deployed a farsighted ploy. Fishermen call it "chumming." He discovered that false statements about Michael that his office leaked to the *New York Post* and supermarket tabloids triggered a cascade of tips to the State's Attorney's office. His fabricated *New York Post* story reporting concocted entries from Martha's diary had already triggered a wave of tabloid frenzy, and once Dunne and Fuhrman successfully pegged Michael as a "Kennedy cousin," every rotten tidbit about the Skakels was tuna to the scandal sheet sharks. Supermarket shoppers like the *National Enquirer* have long paid top dollar for Kennedy stories. "Checkbook journalism" incentivizes sources to fabricate slanders for cash. Following Michael's indictment in January 2000, lurid, salacious, and often wildly inaccurate descriptions of the Moxley killing wallpapered most supermarket checkout lines. So there was already a feeding frenzy. Garr just needed to churn it. At this point, Garr was technically collecting evidence for the grand jury proceedings, which in America are officially sealed; those who violate grand jury secrecy can be charged with criminal contempt. But in this case, stories were not hard to come by. Garr's office was hemorrhaging.

In December 1998, the doorbell rang at author Richard Hoffman's North Cambridge, Massachusetts, home. Garr was at the door, with a colossal Massachusetts state trooper. Hoffman invited them in and Garr got right down to business: he wanted all the materials that Hoffman had acquired for the purpose of ghostwriting Michael's memoir. Waving a piece of paper in Hoffman's face, Garr said he had a subpoena and Hoffman must turn over the documents. Hoffman offered the men coffee. "Okay, Mr. Hoffman. We can do it the easy way, or we can do it the hard way," Garr threatened. Hoffman was intimidated. "Why 'the hard way'?" asked Hoffman. "I'd invited him in, offered him coffee." Within 45 minutes Garr was gone, having seized Michael's book proposal, all the tapes of his interviews, and various Skakel family ephemera, including personal letters and vacation photos that he promised to promptly return to their owners. Garr promised that Hoffman's materials were safe with him; they were bound for a grand jury proceeding and therefore sealed by force of law.

Garr was lying; he had no subpoena. The document he was waving was a Connecticut grand jury summons for Hoffman to appear. Garr had no legal right to any of the materials. Since Garr didn't get Hoffman to sign a consent to seize the property, the whole operation was illegal—technically theft. (Despite numerous pleas, my cousins have been unable to recover many of their personal materials, including mail, tapes, and photos.)

Two days later, Hoffman was shocked to read virtually identical articles in the *Boston Herald, Greenwich Time,* and *New York Post* quoting extensively from his book proposal. He called Garr. "What the fuck?" Hoffman complained. "You said this was a confidential grand jury investigation, and now it's all over the newspapers and people are talking about it on television?" Garr answered disingenuously, "It's a big office, Rich. You can't keep track of everything, and people who know journalists get their hands on things." Garr added, "I'm not about to put them all against a wall and try to find the leak." Hoffman suspected Garr was lying. "It was a crock of crap," Hoffman says. "Obviously this was part of his strategy to begin with."

Every Kennedy is painfully familiar with the attention seeker who fashions a chance encounter with a celebrity into a disparaging anecdote. With each embellishment, the story grows and puts down roots until it becomes part of the landscape of the storyteller's personal history. Michael's newfound notoriety made him a magnet for such characters.

Geranne Ridge, at 34, was a ditzy, self-described "part-time model" and "function coordinator" from Braintree, Massachusetts. During a gossipy phone call in the fall of 1997, she told her equally whimsical friend, aspiring fashion photographer Matt Attanian, that Michael Skakel was at a party—that she alone remembers—in her South Boston apartment—which Michael never visited. The phantom party occurred on a spring night in 1997, a period during which her friend, Marissa Verrochi, who knew Michael, was crashing on Geranne's pull-out couch. Geranne claims that she overheard Michael saying, "Ask me why I killed my neighbor." That is the exact wording of a chin-to-ankle sign Michael was forced to carry for two months at Élan. Stories about that sign leaked by Garr, from the Hoffman transcripts, had been crack to the supermarket rags. Geranne's recounting sounded suspiciously identical to the lurid and wildly inaccurate version of the Moxley murder recently featured in the *National Enquirer,* a periodical that Geranne acknowledged reading regularly. To her friend Attanian, on the other end of the line, Geranne's report sounded like Michael had confessed to Ridge and a room full of Verrochi's college friends.

Like a bee pollinating flowers, Attanian, himself a busy gossip, shared the story with friends, neighbors, and strangers, one of whom worked for the Massachusetts State Police. Before Attanian knew it, Garr was on the phone pressuring Attanian to tape his friend. "If this was your little sister who got killed, wouldn't you want someone like you to come forward?" Attanian recalled, with some bitterness, that the detective promised that if he taped Geranne Ridge, Garr wouldn't ask for anything further. It was another lie: Garr and Benedict would later subpoena Attanian.

Garr also visited Geranne at her family catering business to question her directly about the story, without revealing that his source was Attanian. Geranne had recited so many different versions of the yarn to so many people that she didn't realize her photographer friend had dropped the dime. Following Garr's interrogation, she called Attanian, who didn't pick up. Geranne left a distraught message on his home answering machine: "Hey, it's me," she said. "I just left. Um it didn't go very well at all." Geranne unleashed a featherbrained account of the details of the interview. "[Garr] said to me at the end, 'Geranne, you're saying you've only been with Michael Skakel once. Why would three people tell me you were with him on three different occasions and he admitted to the murder of Martha Moxley? We're talking about a very brutal case, a very tragic case. And I've worked on this for 20 years, and if it takes 20 more years I'm going to continue working this case.' He was so fucking tough. I was shaking. Mom said I didn't quiver or anything. I did a really good job I guess. I said, 'I'm sorry, I can't help you in any other way.' I said, 'I've only met Michael for 30 minutes and um, you know, I was in and out of the conversation' and Martha Moxley did come up and I said that, jokingly, he mentioned, you know, the murder. I said that, um, 'you know it was mostly in jest and I really can't help you anymore and I'm sorry.'" Her agonizing talkathon marched onward, inexorably, until Attanian probably wished his recorder would mercifully run out of tape. In listening to the recording, my consolation was the thought that Geranne's gifts for obfuscation and empty-headed whining about the dull yet somehow dramatic details of her daily life must have driven Garr nearly insane.

Garr's notes confirm Ridge's recollection except that Garr never mentions Geranne's statement that Michael was joking about the murder. "Marissa Verocchi did stay in my apartment for three weeks," she told Garr, according to a transcript of his interview, "and during that visit, which was pretty unpleasant for me considering I'm 34 and she was 21 and, you know, quite immature. And she had people in and out from B.U. and on one occasion Michael Skakel was there. He was only there for 45 minutes [she says this time] and there were about eight other people there and I was in and out of the room. But I really don't know anything. You know what I mean? I wasn't really privy to the conversation. I was in my bedroom kind of disgusted that she had so many people over and didn't even ask." Over and over Ridge reiterated to Garr that she wasn't in the room and heard nothing of substance. "As far as hearing anything about the murder or anything like that, I really have to be honest with you," she said. "I didn't." Repeatedly Garr pressed her. "That is not what I have been told," he said. But Ridge didn't falter. As she would later testify under oath, she was telling Garr the absolute truth. Regardless of whether Michael had stepped foot in her apartment, she'd heard nothing.

Attanian called her back, confused. Geranne's summary of her story to Garr on his answering machine was far more mundane than the tale she had previously told him. "I don't think you should have lied," Attanian scolded. "I didn't really lie," she replied. "I said, I only heard half the conversation. I said, you know, he told us about wearing the poster around his neck and um, you know, that he hit her with a golf club." Geranne was freaked out. Who would have told cops about her gossiping? Was her phone bugged? "I shouldn't even talk about it on the phone," she told Attanian. "They're not tapping your phone, Geranne," said Attanian, who was recording the conversation.

Ridge alternated between saying that she'd been in her room and heard virtually nothing and adding tantalizing new details that she'd never before shared.

RIDGE: I didn't say anything about masturbating in the tree or anything.
ATTANIAN: What do you mean 'masturbating in a tree'? You never talked about . . .
RIDGE: You didn't hear about that?
ATTANIAN: No.
RIDGE: Oh yeah, this is the real story. John Doe was watching this particular girl at her bedroom window, changing. And he was up in a tree, masturbating, 'cause he liked her. She went and had sex with his brother Tommy the same night while he was outside smoking pot and doing LSD and acid and really big-time drugs. After he found out that John Doe's brother had sex with this girl, he got so violent and he was so screwed up, he did that to her.
ATTANIAN: Wow. And he told you he did that?
RIDGE: Yes. But I didn't get into all of that detail . . . I didn't lie, but I didn't like, you know totally blow my mouth off either.

In the midst of the conversation, Ridge received a call from her doctor, and promised Attanian she'd call him right back. Back on the line, she complained to Attanian that the doctor refused to prescribe any more Compazine, a strong antipsychotic medication she claimed had been prescribed for nausea. The doctor refused even after Ridge told her how stressed she was feeling due to her involvement in the Skakel case!

ATTANIAN: You told her that?

RIDGE: I'm pissed . . . I did tell her. I said, 'Confidentially, I have been in-volved in this duh-duh-duh-duh case and . . .'

ATTANIAN: Why are you telling her that?

RIDGE: Everything's confidential with her.

ATTANIAN: Geranne, you're telling everybody. . . . You told Rose [a mutual friend] too, right?

RIDGE: I did tell Rose. Rose, I know, would never say anything.

ATTANIAN: You'll tell her tonight?

RIDGE: Yeah, but I won't use any names or anything.

Ridge told Attanian that not only was she worried about being dragged into this trial, she was also concerned about another possible trial.

RIDGE: You know what I'm afraid of now? There was this thing in the *Herald* yesterday. Ronald Borino, you know the attorney I dated? How I decorated his whole entire apartment, from towels to marble?

ATTANIAN: Yeah, well, who gives a shit?

RIDGE: Well, he stole nine million [dollars] from the treasury and it said that they were waiting for Rick Arrighi and Ronald Borino to admit they were involved, and they haven't. And he spent at least one million renovating his waterfront condo with a quote 'friend.' What if I get called now for that? All his friends know that I was the one who decorated that.

ATTANIAN: So you didn't do anything wrong. . . . Geranne, are you talking out of your ass? Geranne I think you're talking out of your ass. . . . Are you sure all the shit you're telling me isn't, like, repeated from Marissa?

RIDGE: Like what stories?

ATTANIAN: That night about what that guy told you and everything?

RIDGE: No . . . he was here, honey. But I was in and out of the room and I only heard, I didn't hear, like the whole, I mean, I missed a lot of the conversation.

All through the conversation, Attanian expressed a newfound skepticism about the stories his friend had told him so vividly. "Well, Geranne, your story keeps changing," he said. Any reasonable person with access to Ridge's taped conversations would immediately understand that she was spinning a yarn for attention. Her fairy tales were inconsistent. She couldn't keep track of which ver-sion she'd already told Attanian. Listening to the tape, you can feel her giddiness, her thriving on the teasing, the scolding, the drama. Even while adorning her fable with salacious new details, she is simultaneously backtracking—claiming she wasn't in the room to hear much of anything.

Everybody knows a Geranne or two. And under cross-examination in Michael's trial, Geranne admitted that her desire for "notoriety and fame" caused her to fabricate the story. "I did make stuff up, trying to appear to be knowledgeable, from things I heard from Marissa and from magazines," she testified. Why would she lie to her friend Attanian? "Because he was so inquisitive about the case; he wouldn't let it die," she testified. "He was always bragging about who he knew and I had done some modeling and he is a part time photographer and he was talking about famous models he knew and so forth."

Of course, Garr and Benedict realized that she knew nothing. They nevertheless called her as one of three star witnesses who claimed they heard Michael "confess" to Martha's murder.

Michael never visited her home. To this day, he has never met Geranne Ridge. In June 1997, when Geranne claimed Michael confessed at her party, Michael was in Russia, helping to establish the Alcoholics Anonymous program in the Russian prison system with a well-established American group. On cross-examination, Ridge admitted concocting the story. Neither Ridge nor Garr could produce a single witness who could place Michael at her apartment. Besides Verrochi, Ridge could not name any of the eight people whom she claimed had attended the imaginary party in her apartment. Verocchi testified that she had no memory of the evening. Ridge told Attanian that Michael was drunk and was excusing himself to the bathroom often, presumably to snort cocaine, "apparently having fallen off the wagon," as Benedict put it in his closing. I can attest that both Benedict and Ridge were lying about this. Michael had at that point been 15 years sober. "If I were doing cocaine," laughs Michael, "you would have heard about it on the Weather Channel. It would have been a typhoon and it wouldn't have blown over till I was dead."

Ridge was a nightmare witness for the prosecution. She drank 12 full glasses of water on the stand and repeatedly shot pleading looks at her attorney desperate for evacuation. Her testimony was worse than useless—but Benedict's ulterior motives for calling Ridge soon became clear. Summoning her to the courtroom allowed Benedict to play her recorded conversation with Attanian, exposing jurors to the juicy calumnies she'd read in the supermarket tabloids. Benedict produced no evidence to support Fuhrman's wild theory that Michael committed the crime out of filial jealousy. But there it was in the tabloids. Those sensational fabrications had, of course, been leaked to the *Enquirer,* the *Star,* and the *Globe,* by Garr's office. Ridge became the prosecution's vehicle for getting his otherwise-inadmissible speculations before the jury.

Unbelievably, it got worse. When Sherman cross-examined Geranne about the sources of her information, she confirmed that her primary source for the libels she'd shared with Attanian were, in Sherman's words, "*Star, Globe, Enquirer*—those kinds of things." In specifying the tabloids, Sherman walked into Benedict's trap. Geranne's attorney had brought to court one issue of each of these rags to illustrate the pedigree of Ridge's concoctions. However, none of the three scandal sheets that Ridge's attorney carried into court featured a specific story about Michael masturbating in a tree. Benedict, therefore, asked Judge Kavanewsky to admit the tabloids into evidence, as a way of impeaching Ridge. Benedict said that he wanted to show that she was lying about lying. The impeachment purpose didn't hold water: Ridge had testified, under oath, that she had read other tabloid stories about the case. Those other tabloid stories included the masturbation tale. These particular tabloids were compendiums of "Kennedy scandals"—Chappaquiddick and Will Smith's trial and my 1980 arrest for heroin—all flashed with opprobrious headlines about the Kennedys. Most courts would have overruled Benedict's motion in a microsecond. Almost any appellate court in the country would consider a decision to allow a jury to be exposed to that kind of prejudicial poison reversible error. But Kavanewsky must have intuited that the Connecticut appellate courts would bend over backward to not reverse the jury verdict in this highly publicized case. Public outrage about the O.J. Simpson acquittal was pervasive, and Kavanewksy was a prosecutor's judge. Instead of laughing Benedict out of the courtroom, Kavanewsky asked mildly if Sherman had an objection.

All first-year law students with an evidence course under their belt would have been on their feet with the obvious objections to this material: "Irrelevant," "Immaterial," "Hearsay," or "Potential for prejudice outweighs its probative value." Sherman rose. Somewhere in his alcohol-addled memory, those objections were fighting their way through the fog, but it was all too much for him. He had already given up on the case. "I will object, Your Honor," he began. "I can't think of the grounds, but it just bothers me to put this stuff in evidence. I mean, the *Star,* the *Globe,* the *Enquirer,* I just can't believe we would degenerate to have a jury check out . . ." He trailed off, and sat feebly down. Unbelievably, Judge Kavanewsky allowed the tabloids into evidence, providing jurors with the most irrelevant, venomous reading material imaginable. "They are not being admitted for the truth of what they contain," Kavanewsky instructed jurors disingenuously. "Only in connection with this witness's testimony that she collected them as sources of information." Typical of the three, the *National Enquirer* teased in a cover story: "Kennedy Family Secrets Exposed: Cousin blows lid off 25 years of cover-ups." That tabloid story highlights the most scurrilous and inaccurate ignominies about my family.

Unless Ridge was a time traveler, she hadn't passed information from that particular *Enquirer* to Attanian; the *Enquirer* published the issue on March 19, 2002, several months after Ridge's taped call. Filling the jurors' heads with prejudicial misinformation about our family was the essential tactic in the prosecution's strategy: Benedict needed to inspire in the jury such a revulsion toward the Skakel family, and my family, that the jury would overlook the dearth of evidence. Garr had skillfully controlled the press narrative: his selective leaks helped create the tabloid frenzy. Now prosecutors had inveigled the most poisonous of those slanderous scandal sheets into the sacrosanct jury room.

Astonishingly, in a post-trial brief, Benedict would refer to Geranne's admittedly invented fantasies as "one of three direct confessions" Michael made to the crime. The other two "direct confessions" are even less plausible than Ridge's: the string of events that would carry Garr to John Higgins and Greg Coleman began in 1996.

CHAPTER 15

The Bully

What are you willing to give me to betray him to you?
And they weighed out thirty pieces of silver.

—Matthew 26:15

As part of his media strategy to reinvigorate the 20-year-old investigation, Garr arranged for NBC's *Unsolved Mysteries* to film a segment on the Moxley murder and to provide a telephone hotline for informants. The show publicized Mrs. Moxley's $50,000 reward in the hope of eliciting leads. On February 15, 1996, Garr escaped the Connecticut winter for a three-day jaunt to Los Angeles to field hotline calls. He thought he'd hit pay-dirt with a call from a Phil Lawrence in Florida. In his summary of their brief chat, Garr wrote that Lawrence's 1977 to 1979 Élan bid overlapped with Michael's. "Mr. Lawrence reports, during group therapy, Michael Skakel admitted responsibility for this murder," Garr wrote. "Michael claimed to have been under the influence of alcohol, and that he had used a golf club during the commission of the crime. . . . Present during this group therapy session was owner and Executive Director of Élan, Joseph Ricci. According to Mr. Lawrence, Joseph Ricci tape-recorded these admissions." Garr's notes painted Phil as a promising witness. Nevertheless, it took Garr a month to call him after returning to Bridgeport. It was very uncharacteristic for Garr to procrastinate on tips he considered hot. But at that point, Garr still believed Littleton or Tommy was the perpetrator. Expediency had not yet refocused his attention on Michael. In any case, the tip wasn't so hot, it turned out. Phil either changed his story, or Garr had let wishful thinking color his recollection of the hotline call. In their taped interview, Phil said he had not witnessed any confession. "It was common knowledge that it happened . . . that he had committed the murder,"

Phil told him. Garr drilled down. How had it become common knowledge? "I think he admitted it in one or two groups." Phil said he hadn't been in the group, and could not provide any names of any other residents who might have overheard a confession. Maybe Ricci had heard it, Phil posited. "He had a lot of private meetings with Joe Ricci," Phil said, trying to be helpful. "I know the way Joe Ricci operates. . . . I guarantee you he has recordings of those confessions. I'd bet you anything. I'd bet the moon." But when Garr pressed hard about where he heard the confession, Phil went squishy. "I can't remember," he said. "And I've been asking myself that. I can't say for sure one way or the other." Garr asked about the thrice-daily group therapy sessions at Élan. "Do you think it was during one of these sessions that he made these admissions, or was it just general chitchat in the dorms when he said these things?" Garr probed. "Well," said Phil, "we weren't really allowed to have chitchat in the dorms. It had to be in a group." At this point, Garr should have learned something essential about Élan: the institution was so repressive, that there really was no such thing there as casual chatting between residents. Garr would have to will himself to forget this.

One of the few names Phil provided Garr was Alice Dunne. When Garr reached Alice, she told him definitively that this confession never happened in any group. "I kept saying it over and over again to Frank Garr," Alice says. Nevertheless, Garr persevered, hoping that Phil's hunch had been accurate. Garr tracked down and interrogated a legion of former Élan residents, none of whom could remember any confession.

Garr was an aggressive prospector. Diane Hozman, a Californian therapist, was an Élan alum in whom Michael had confided during his confinement. When Diane heard that Garr was investigating the crime, she contacted him, she told me, to help clear Michael. Garr flew Diane to Connecticut four times, once with her son and another time with her boyfriend. She felt Garr was bullying her into saying that Michael confessed. "I felt they were desperate to blame Michael," she told me. "Garr took everything I said out of context to make it fit into his puzzle. He definitely didn't want to hear anything good about Michael. I'm sorry I even talked to Garr." The night before she was to testify, Diane reiterated to Benedict that Michael had never confessed. Benedict and Garr sent her home without calling her to the stand.

After the *Unsolved Mysteries* episode aired in February 1996, *People* magazine featured the $50,000 reward in a follow-up story. Élan alumni passed that article around. That June 1996, the Moxley family announced that they were hiking the reward to $100,000. The following Halloween, eight months after Garr's *Unsolved Mysteries* Hail Mary, a former Élan resident, Chuck Siegan, called the detective. Chuck told Garr that his friend John Higgins had heard a bona fide confession from Michael. According to Chuck, Michael said, "I did it."

Garr reached Higgins by phone in early 1997. Higgins asked if Garr was recording the call. Garr said no. As usual, he was lying. "So ya know, what you say to me right now stays between you and me," he reassured Higgins. "Talking to you right now, is there any way I can be subpoenaed to give you this information?" Higgins asked. "No," Garr lied again. During the conversation, Higgins contradicted Chuck. He swore there'd been no confession. He gave his word. "I live and die by the truth," Higgins told him. "I never ever lie."

Higgins, then 34, hadn't fared as well as Michael after Élan. Police had arrested him six times, for theft, battery, criminal damage to property, and pot possession. His last bust was three years before his conversation with Garr. Courts convicted him in three of those cases. He was living in Lisle, Illinois, a Chicago suburb, near two Élan friends, Chuck Siegan and Harry Kranick. He hadn't heard Michael confess. However, he did recall a conversation they'd had on a porch in Élan. Garr had forgotten that casual conversations did not happen at Élan. There were no other witnesses. And Higgins could not recall the year. It could have been at any time between 1978 and 1980. Higgins was on "Night Owl duty" with Michael—conducting occasional bed checks to assure that nobody escaped. While the others slept, a weeping Michael spontaneously confided details about the Moxley murder. "He remembers being in his garage," Higgins told Garr. "He remembers having a golf club, he remembers being in tall pine trees, and he remembers waking up back in his house and his big dilemma at the time was he doesn't know if he did it or not. . . . And that was the only time we ever discussed it." Over and over, Garr asks Higgins to repeat everything he knew. Even though he claimed the conversation with Michael lasted two hours, Higgins was only certain of three details. "He [Michael] remembers being in his garage . . . going through golf clubs, going through a golf bag," Higgins said. "He remembers a party," Higgins said, though he could not say whether the party was in the day or the evening. "He remembers running through the woods," Higgins said. "When he leaves the garage, he's in the woods. His house is in the woods or something." Higgins did not know anything more about these woods. "He said he remembers pine trees." That was all Higgins could recall. Garr told Levitt this was when he knew Higgins was telling the truth. "Only Michael could have known about the pine trees," Garr said. "No way Higgins could have known that on his own. He had to have heard that from Michael." Garr was either lying to Levitt or delusional; by then, the fact that Martha was found under a pine tree was common knowledge, reported hundreds if not thousands of times on TV, in national tabloids, and in newspapers. Garr pushed Higgins to dig deep for some recollection of Michael confessing.

GARR: I want you to be up front with me in everything he told you.

HIGGINS: Well, I pretty much got you everything that he told me. I mean he never specifically told me that he killed anybody. I mean, he never said that specifically.

GARR: Are you sure?

HIGGINS: Yeah. I'm certain of it.

Garr asked why Higgins had kept this conversation a secret for so long, knowing that there was an unsolved murder.

GARR: Why didn't you call us? Why not Greenwich Police or some authority?

HIGGINS: Well, actually Harry Kranick called me. He told me that the whole thing was in *People* magazine. He told me that they were offering $50,000 for information leading to the arrest of the murderer of this Moxley girl.

GARR: It's been increased to $100,000.

HIGGINS: Oh that's special.

With this fresh in mind, Garr again coaxed Higgins to comb his memory for a confession.

GARR: It's really important now, at last, to come out with everything, okay, to tell the whole thing. . . . And I know there's more and I want you to feel free to tell me the whole story.

HIGGINS: The amount of things I remembered . . . I told you.

GARR: But you know, there's more. I mean, is that a fair statement?

HIGGINS: Um, no. I don't know that there's more.

GARR: Well, I mean, I think you know more, and you're just a little hesitant to share it all with me. Is that a fair statement?

HIGGINS: No, I would not say that's a fair statement.

GARR: In other words, you've told me everything you know?

HIGGINS: If, believe me, if I had a confession from him, I'd give it to you.

Garr then slowly and deliberately provided Higgins the exact details and language that Higgins would need to remember if Higgins decided he needed the reward money. "My information is that along with what you've told me, Michael did, at one point, only once, tell you that 'I killed her,'" Garr said. "And I got that from a couple different places. Michael told you one evening, 'Ya know, I did,' and he never mentioned it again to you."

Garr told Higgins that he would call him back in a few days. "Obviously, you want to think about it," Garr told him. "You probably want to talk to somebody about it, but the bottom line is, that there is more, and we got to get it out."

It's challenging to contrive any interpretation of these words other than that Garr was suborning perjury. If Michael had indeed confessed that night, Higgins had much to gain and nothing to lose from reporting it to Garr in their first conversation. He was not implicating himself in any crime and he stood to make $100,000. So why not spill? The only reason could possibly be, as he told Garr over and over, Michael had made no confession.

On its face, Higgins's story was obviously contrived. The only four details that Higgins distinctly recollected Michael telling him were all inaccurate. There had been no "party" on October 30. There was nothing resembling "woods" on the Skakel property. There was no golf bag laden with clubs. The Skakel clubs were scattered on the lawn or collected in a barrel near the mudroom door. Most damning, the Otter Rock Drive house had no garage. The property once had a three-car garage, but in 1969, following his wife's cancer diagnosis, Rucky retrofitted the building as a nursing suite. In reality, Higgins concocted the entire Élan conversation. The conversation, Michael says, never happened. Furthermore, Higgins was a notorious bully and one of Michael's primary tormentors. He was the last person to whom Michael would confide.

"The idea of me confiding in John Higgins, when we were on Night Owl duty together, is insane. Higgins was a Night Owl; I was not. I never had a single conversation with him. Higgins was a sadist. He would relish kicking people when they were down. He was always the one hitting the hardest in the boxing ring. He loved inflicting pain. The only time I spoke to him the entire time I was there was when I asked the mob he was leading to stop killing me. He and Coleman and Harry Kranick, and two others, stuffed my head in a toilet, trying to drown me. Then they banged my head against a steel bed frame repeatedly until they knocked me unconscious. Then, they dropped me on the stage where I slept for the next six days. I wasn't allowed to speak at all. They threatened to kill me if I spoke. I had to piss in my pants because I couldn't ask to go to the bathroom. I wouldn't talk to him. I never spoke to him. I hated him. He tortured me. It made me sick when they rehabilitated him during the trial. It was all lies. I was utterly powerless."

"Higgins was a total psycho," Kim Freehill told me. "He was very, very sadistic, a twisted guy that would do anything to cover his ass and be in Joe Ricci's good graces." Higgins testified that, on the night of the supposed confession, one of his duties was to report to Ricci anything that happened on his watch. Information was currency at Élan. Extracting personal dirt from inmates to expose vulnerabilities was a richly incentivized feature of its predatory culture. Ricci awarded inmates with status and privilege when they successfully mined secrets. "Higgins was someone who would do anything to gain points with Ricci," says Kim. "He would not have long withheld this information."

The claims by Higgins and by Greg Coleman that Michael had confessed while at Élan and that they then kept his secret are, according to other Élan witnesses, incredible. Referring to Higgins's and to Coleman's testimony, Élan's

Joe Ricci, as I've said before, told *Time* magazine that, "The notion of Michael's confession is just preposterous. I was there, and I would know." The facility had only a hundred students, and if Michael had confessed, "two things would have happened," Ricci said. "Everybody in the facility would have known and talked about it. And we would have called our lawyers to figure out our obligations. Neither happened." Unfortunately for Michael, Ricci died immediately before the trial, so the jury never heard his testimony. Ricci did talk to the press outside Michael's pre-trial privilege hearing using almost the same language.

Alice Dunne, a counselor at Élan during Michael's residence, scoffed at the idea that Michael would have shared personal thoughts with Higgins, who wielded a baseball bat during Night Owl duty. "I don't think Higgins would have been someone he would have confided in," she said. Higgins "had a reputation for not being truthful." Another Élan inmate, Sarah Peterson, recalled that Higgins "seemed to really like making Mike Skakel's life miserable."

So that weekend, Garr gave Higgins the time to consider the minuscule risk of a perjury charge against the $100,000 in reward money.

Garr called Higgins's wife over the weekend. There are no records of what Garr said or promised her. On Monday, Higgins and Garr spoke again. Higgins had suddenly experienced a change of heart. He told Garr that he'd just been informed that, because of some persistent shoulder problems, he could no longer work as an auto mechanic. "I'm pretty much shit out of luck as far as being a mechanic goes," he told Garr. "Basically, I don't have a job anymore." Garr offered encouragement, a winking reference perhaps to the hundred grand. "You gotta make some plans," he told Higgins. After several more minutes of buttering him up, Higgins gave Garr what he needed.

HIGGINS: Well, at the end of the conversation Michael was just obviously destroyed and he was just sitting there crying and he was probably crying for five minutes or so, and then he said that he killed her. He said, "I killed her."

Higgins was regurgitating the precise lie that Garr had fed him three days earlier.

GARR: What did you say?
HIGGINS: I don't think I said anything to him, and he just, I mean, that was the only words he said about it. He said, "I killed her," and ya know, I probably gave the guy a hug.

Garr told Levitt that the hug was what convinced him that Higgins was telling the truth. "You don't make up a detail like that," Garr lied, admiring Higgins's embroidery. Despite Garr's best prodding, over the next hour Higgins refused to gild the lily. "I sense there might be a little bit more that maybe isn't coming," Garr said. "There must be more to the conversation, even fragmented as they may be, there had to be more, to link them all together." But, all Garr's pointed coaching could not persuade Higgins to further garnish his perjury.

Higgins refused to sign a formal statement, take a polygraph, or allow the police to tape his phone calls with Garr, but Garr recorded him anyway and used the tape to force him to testify at the trial. Higgins later admitted lying to Garr about Michael's confession. When Garr told Higgins that he had him on tape, Higgins went ballistic. However, faced with the subpoena that Garr had promised would never come, he testified against Michael. Fellow prosecution witness Alice Dunne recalls seeing Higgins and the five other Élan witnesses at the hotel where Garr had stowed them all in Norwalk. "We'd hang out there and we couldn't leave," she said. During their conversations, the *People* magazine article and the reward money were the group's persistent preoccupation. After Higgins testified, Michael and Stephen and their group spotted Higgins running down the street away from the courthouse.

Following the trial, Garr, Higgins, and Chuck Siegan had a falling out. At Michael's *habeas corpus* hearing in 2013, Siegan testified that Higgins and he were close friends and business partners for a decade following their discharge from Élan. The two had had "hundreds of conversations," many of which centered on their experiences at Élan. Higgins, he said, had never mentioned Michael's confession. Higgins's recollection only kicked in when Harry Kranick told him of the reward money. Higgins, Siegan testified, was "not a very truthful person." Eight months after Siegan's testimony, Higgins died, at 50, in his sleep. He lived just long enough to collect $10,000, his paltry share of Dorthy Moxley's bounty.

CHAPTER 16

The Junkie

Lying is a medical feature of addiction.
—Bill Teutenberg, Certified Addiction Counselor

Frank Garr's proudest recruit was a mendacious rogue named Greg Coleman. Coleman guarded Michael after his third escape attempt from Élan. In September 1998, Coleman told the one-man grand jury that Michael had introduced himself to Coleman by saying, "I'm going to get away with murder and I'm a Kennedy." It's hard for me to decide which is less plausible: the spontaneous homicide confession, or the notion of Michael Skakel boasting "I'm a Kennedy." Predictably, this doubly improbable statement became tabloid fodder and poisoned public sentiment against Michael. Coleman's recollection is similar to a *National Enquirer* headline shortly after Michael's arrest, which quoted Michael as telling fellow Élan inmate Harry Kranick, "I killed that chick . . . it got me excited." Kranick emphatically denied that he ever heard Michael Skakel make this or any of the similarly sensational statements attributed to him by the media; otherwise Garr would certainly have made him testify. Judging by his behavior, Coleman himself never expected to testify.

Coleman waited 23 years to report Michael's extraordinary confession. Then one Sunday afternoon in 1998, 37-year-old Coleman made an anonymous call to a local NBC affiliate. He was either at home alone with his wife, or in the seedy Rochester, New York, motel room, the doghouse he occupied when his wife evicted him for some behavior attendant to his heroin addiction. It's difficult to peg down the slippery details because every time Coleman opened his mouth, either to police or on the stand, the particulars changed. Watching MSNBC, Coleman caught a segment featuring Mark Fuhrman updating the Moxley investigation. High on heroin and crack, as he would admit later,

Coleman called Channel 10 with new information about Michael Skakel. "The first words he ever said to me were, 'I'm going to get away with murder. I'm a Kennedy.'" The station notified the Connecticut Police after tracking Coleman through caller ID.

To his fellow inmates, Coleman was as repugnant a low-life scoundrel as ever attended Élan. "Scumbag" is the word Alice Dunne uses to describe him. In 1978, Coleman, age 16, arrived at Élan to dodge jail time for a Rochester burglary. His hefty size and merciless fists quickly made him a Ricci favorite. Coleman led the mob stomping of Kim Freehill that nearly killed her, his blows causing her to lose control of her bladder and bowels before a helicopter medevaced her out of Élan. "He was a very sick guy," Kim tells me. "A total degenerate drug addict. The only reason he even got involved in saying anything at all was for money for heroin." After Élan, he did hard time in Attica and bids in diverse mental institutions.

During a lifetime of malevolence, violence, and relentless addiction that he fed by lying, larceny, and thieving, Coleman did win one fan: Frank Garr. Garr understood that Coleman was an unrepentant drug fiend, universally despised and mistrusted by those who knew him. Virtually anyone close to Coleman became the victim of his endless chicanery. But Garr, nevertheless, trusted him. "He was a great big teddy bear of a guy with enormous problems, but he was one of the most believable guys I ever talked to," Garr told Levitt. "He was sick, physically and probably mentally because he had this monkey on his back. But that didn't mean he wasn't telling the truth." Among addiction treatment professionals, lying is a universally recognized element of the pathology of addiction. "All addicts lie," says Bill Teutenberg, an ex-addict and 30-year veteran addiction counselor at the Caron Foundation. In the beginning, addicts lie because they have to, but it becomes ingrained in their behavior. "They lie when they're happy, and when they're sad; when they're high, and when they're jonesing. They lie because it's daylight saving time. They lie just to stay in practice. Chronic habitual dishonesty is so much a feature of the disease that effective treatment of addiction always begins with teaching the discipline of rigorous honesty."

In his paean to Coleman's decency, Garr curiously failed to mention to Levitt the name John Regan Jr. Not long after Coleman's television interview, Regan, a Rochester attorney, got a call from the Connecticut prosecutor's office, seeking contact information for Coleman. If the caller was not Garr, it was someone working closely with him. As attorney for Coleman's wealthy parents, Jack and Mary, Regan found himself frequently bailing Coleman out of hot water. "Why are you looking for him?" Regan asked, assuming that Coleman was in another jam. The caller said he was intending to use Coleman as a witness before the grand jury seeking to charge Michael with murder. Regan was incredulous.

"You're not seriously considering using Gregory on a grand jury to accuse some-one of murder?" he asked. Regan told the caller a little bit about his personal experience with Coleman. "It would be fair to say that no one in their right mind, knowing Gregory, would put the slightest confidence in his contentions concerning the supposed admissions of Michael Skakel," Regan wrote in a 2008 sworn affidavit. "Gregory was known to his family and me as an incorrigible drug addict who had served time in prison. During the time I was active in rep-resenting the Coleman family . . . I formed the opinion that Gregory regularly engaged in dishonest, deceitful, and criminal behavior in order to obtain money from his father." The caller professed to be unconcerned. "We got plenty of other evidence," he told Regan. "We're going to get this guy."

In the meantime, Vito Colucci, Mickey Sherman's primary investigator, was doing his own reconnaissance on the prosecution's star witness. Rochester area cops knew Coleman well. Colucci tracked down Inspector Paul Kaseman of the Ogden Police Department. "Are you sure this guy is going to be one of the main witnesses?" asked an astonished Kaseman. "He has zero credibility," Kase-man said showing Coleman's long rap sheet to Colucci. The last time Kaseman had seen Coleman, his abscessed dope-fiend arms were oozing from pustulated lesions. Major Mark Gerbino, then head of the Rochester Police Department's homicide division, told Colucci he was absolutely dumbfounded that any pros-ecutor would put a lowlife like Coleman on the stand, especially as a star witness in a murder case.

Coleman made it, just barely, to the grand jury. An hour before taking the stand, he mainlined all the heroin in his hotel room. "I didn't have enough," he testified afterward. "I went into the hearing, sick from withdrawal and pneumo-nia." Still, Coleman looked better than usual, thanks to a new suit, courtesy of Garr. He wore a graying Van Dyke beard and a fresh short haircut. By the fol-lowing year, at a hearing to determine if Michael would be tried as a juvenile (he was 15 when Martha was murdered), Coleman weighed 340 pounds. He was incarcerated at the time and had made two requests to Connecticut authorities for cash and a reduced sentence in return for his testimony. Benedict had sprung the bloated addict from Rochester's Monroe Correctional Facility, where he was serving eight months for criminal mischief after breaking into his estranged wife's house. Benedict put him up in style, with room service and pay-per-view.

Coleman told Benedict's one-man grand juror, George Thim, that Michael was a chatterbox, regularly dishing up murder confessions, in group therapy, and at Élan's crowded dinner tables. He'd confessed five or six times—"at least!" But at Michael's probable cause hearing the following year, Coleman swore that Michael confessed just twice, and only to him personally. "That was my recollec-tion at the time." He brushed aside the discrepancy, explaining that he had shot heroin an hour before his grand jury testimony.

Coleman explained that his memory for detail was impaired by his 25-bag-a-day heroin habit. Coleman boasted that he'd been one of Élan's "head gorillas." Michael's confession, he swore, had followed his first escape, in November 1978, just a month after arriving at Élan. Ricci had assigned Coleman to guard Michael with a baseball bat on the stage near the dining room of Élan Building #3. It was in the wee hours of the night that Michael confided in him. "I made the comment to Mr. Skakel, 'Boy, this guy can get away with murder,'" Coleman testified, referring to Ricci. "And he said, 'I am going to get away with murder because I'm a Kennedy.' And he went into telling me how he made advances to this girl where he lives and she spurned his advances and he drove her skull in with a golf club . . . in the woods." Coleman testified that he'd seen two TV shows about the crime, including the tabloid show *A Current Affair,* yet he still couldn't manage to get the details of the crime or crime scene right. Coleman swore that Michael told him he had killed Martha with a driver. "He made the comment that two days later he had gone back and masturbated on the body," Coleman testified. "That's what he told me." In fact the golf club that killed Martha was an iron, and the police removed Martha's body the next day.

The circumstances of the confession—while Michael was being guarded by a giant troll with a bad temper and a baseball bat—should have left the jury skeptical. "Coleman was saying that when I was in the corner, I was talking," Michael says. "We were not allowed to talk. If you even moved your head, you'd get punched in the face. You peed in your pants because they wouldn't let you go to the bathroom."

Furthermore, what Coleman said had happened, simply did not happen. The "I'm a Kennedy" line is an inconceivable utterance. "That's so not anything that ever came out of Michael Skakel's mouth," Alice Dunne says. "It makes the hair on my neck stand up to say it because he never, ever played that card. He just didn't. And I don't think anybody there even knew it until that general meeting when it became obvious. Michael was never walking around there like he was more special than anyone."

At Michael's reasonable cause hearing in Stamford, on June 20, 2000, Coleman was a mess. On the stand, he had trouble identifying Michael, even though he was sitting right in front of him. He was sweating and twitching, and he seemed unable to take his eyes off the clock, a symptom he attributed to heroin withdrawal. Garr had put him up at a Howard Johnson's off the interstate in Darien, guarded by a brace of state troopers. He was to testify again the following day. The troopers called Garr and told him that their star witness was in trouble, pallid, sweating, and dopesick. Garr rushed over and found Coleman splayed on the bed. "I am dying," Coleman shouted. "I have to cop. You are either going to get me drugs or I'm going back to Rochester." Garr threw him in his car and began a desperate search to get his witness high. Their odyssey ended at Greenwich Hospital, which propped him up with enough methadone to last him through his next morning's testimony.

It was no shock when Coleman died a little over a year later, in August 2001. A batch of bad heroin killed him and six other Rochester junkies in one week. Even though this meant that his star witness would be unavailable to appear at trial, Benedict told the press that he would proceed "without batting an eyelash." Benedict had good reason not to mourn Coleman's passing. His demise was a prosecutorial windfall. Judge Kavanewsky ruled that since Sherman had had an opportunity to cross-examine Coleman at the reasonable cause hearing, prosecutors could read the dead junkie's earlier testimony to the jury. Michael's attorneys would have no opportunity to cross-examine Coleman at the trial, and the jury would never view his ruined demeanor. Rather than having the bulbous, twitching, sweating Coleman on the stand at trial, Coleman's testimony instead would be performed by Chris Morano, Benedict's deputy. Morano is considerably less menacing and more presentable than Coleman. Rather than a disheveled, fidgeting dope fiend with darting eyes, the jury got to swoon at Morano, who looks like a buttoned-down leading man. Morano was the calm, coiffed, credible young lawyer that every Greenwich mother on the jury would want her daughter to marry.

Playing the role of Coleman, Morano recited the deceased addict's prior testimony to the adoring jury. His delivery was the linchpin in the elaborate, expensive but fragilely constructed case that convicted Michael.

Summarizing Coleman's testimony to the jury, Benedict pointed to Michael. "The spoiled brat smugly boasted, 'I can get away with anything' and continued to describe to Coleman how he had beaten a girl's head in with a golf club and later masturbated on her and was being hidden from the police."

After the trial, perhaps thanks to Morano's reading, jurors in Michael's case told the press they found Coleman's testimony believable, citing it as one of the primary reasons they convicted Michael.

Coleman family attorney John Regan didn't think much again about that 1998 call until he read that Michael had been convicted. "I continued to assume that there must have been a lot of other solid evidence," he wrote in his affidavit. In 2003, he was horrified to learn from my piece in *The Atlantic* exactly how crucial Coleman's evidence had been in convicting Michael. He tracked down Michael's new attorney, Hope Seeley, and offered to help free Michael in any way he could.

Long after Michael's conviction, we all got independent corroboration of Coleman's dishonesty. On the stand at the grand jury, Coleman testified that former Élan resident Cliff Grubin had been guarding Michael with him and overheard his confession. In the four years between the grand jury and trial, Sherman made no effort to locate Grubin. Michael had been in prison for three years when Colucci traveled to Ibiza, Spain, in 2005 to interview Grubin, who was running a juice bar there. At the Hotel Monte Sol, Grubin told Colucci that Coleman had invented the entire tale. Grubin had never guarded Michael. He described both Coleman and Higgins as "liars." Contrary to Coleman's testimony, Grubin said that Michael was given no special privileges at Élan. If anything, he was treated worse than the other residents. Cliff had been at the brutal general meeting when Michael was beaten savagely for eight hours. "Why would Michael confess to Coleman and then get pelted at a general meeting and not confess then?" Cliff asked.

Both Coleman and Higgins claimed that Michael had confessed to them under conditions of shocking brutality. In its closing argument, even the prosecution conceded the "concentration camp–type atmosphere" at Élan. Despite the pummeling, the beatings and the threats, humiliation, degradation, and torture, witness after witness from Élan testified that Michael never confessed to killing Martha Moxley. These included Sarah Petersen, Donna Kavanah, Dorothy Rogers, Alice Dunne, Angela McFillan, Mike Wiggins, Liz Arnold, and Charles Siegan. There were only two exceptions, John Higgins and Greg Coleman, two Élan residents who stood out among many others for the brutality of their conduct, the unreliability of their stories, and their reputations as pathological liars.

Even though Levitt would spend dozens of pages in his book recounting Garr's insistence that Higgins and Coleman were telling the truth, he now admits he put little stock in the Élan "confessions" that, according to post-verdict interviews, swayed the jurors to convict Michael. "I dismissed much of the Élan testimony regarding Michael's confessions as coerced," Levitt emailed me in May 2016. Levitt explained to me the reason he did not include in his book the dire warnings about Coleman's credibility offered by Rochester attorney John Regan Jr. In the hundreds, perhaps thousands, of hours they spent discussing the case, Levitt's soul mate, Garr, never bothered to mention the telephone call. "I don't recall Garr saying anything to me about Regan," Levitt writes.

CHAPTER 17

The Handyman

Most of the trouble in life comes from misunderstandings.
—L.M. Montgomery

I n addition to the full confessions that Michael allegedly made to Geranne Ridge, Higgins, and Coleman, prosecutors produced a category of characters to whom Michael allegedly made limited inculpatory statements that didn't rise to the level of confession. One of these was the Skakels' occasional handyman and driver Larry Zicarelli.

Long before Michael's indictment, I was already familiar with the tale told by the pistol-packing mechanic with the Italian-horn necklace. Zicarelli worked for the Skakels for a short period in the late 1970s. Stephen recalls Zicarelli as a cocky, cologne-soaked hood with rolled up T-shirt sleeves and an ill-tempered German shepherd. "He reminded me of a skinny Joe Pesci—but shorter and angrier," says Stephen. Zicarelli's wife worked in the pizza parlor on Greenwich Avenue. Stephen says Zicarelli drove and ran errands for the family. "Mostly he polished his white Corvette in the driveway and tinkered with the engine—especially when Dad was away." Zicarelli also had a dark pickup truck. He kept baseball bats in both vehicles. On Zicarelli's first day of work, he spotted a parked vintage Corvette while driving Michael to school. He asked Michael to help him steal the hubcaps. Michael declined.

Many years ago Michael told me a story with his customary honesty and humor. At age 16 he had fallen asleep in his room, clutching a dress belonging to his late mother. Michael, who had prayed for their mother's death as a way of ending her suffering, felt he had helped his mother die. He had fallen asleep clutching her dress to remember her, feel close to her, and beg for her forgiveness. A maid discovered him and reported him to Rucky. His father, who considered

Anne's artifacts sacred, went wild, beating Michael ferociously. Michael called Zicarelli and asked for a ride to his psychiatrist's office in New York City. He did not have an appointment, but he was wracked with guilt, self-loathing, and anxiety, and needed to talk. The psychiatrist was unable to see him. Zicarelli testified that during the ride to the city, Michael said "he had done something very bad and he had to either kill himself or get out of the country." On the way back to Belle Haven, Zicarelli testified, Michael tried to jump off the Triborough Bridge. Shortly after that incident, Rucky fired Zicarelli. Among other sins, Zicarelli pulled a gun on the Ixes' shepherd, Zock, when he caught the dog relieving itself on his newly washed Corvette's tire.

The prosecution offered Zicarelli's story as a confession to the Moxley murder. In fact, despite widespread press reports to the contrary, Michael never said he was the murderer—to the driver or to anyone else. After Zicarelli went to work for the Skakels, Lunney was regularly in touch with the handyman, encouraging him to report anything suspicious about the family. Zicarelli professed to be eager to help, yet he never recounted his Triborough Bridge tale to Lunney or any other police officer. The handyman never intended to come forward with the story. But in 1993, he offhandedly reported the story to his bank manager, Edwin Jones, who repeated the yarn to Garr, who pressured Zicarelli to appear against Michael at trial.

CHAPTER 18

The Barber

In the future, everyone will be world-famous for 15 minutes.
—Andy Warhol

Finally, the prosecution produced Matthew Tucciarone, a hair stylist from the Golden Touch Salon in Greenwich. Tucciarone approached Benedict two weeks before Michael's trial in 2002. Tucciarone said that after seeing Michael's picture in the paper, he remembered that in the spring of 1976, Michael, Rush Jr., and Julie had come into his salon on Greenwich Avenue. As Tucciarone clipped his curls, Michael spontaneously proclaimed to his siblings, "I'm going to get a gun and kill him." To this, according to Tucciarone, Julie scolded, "You can't do that." Michael replied, "Why not? I did it before. I killed before." Julie answered, "Shut up, Michael."

Tucciarone's memories were vivid. Michael, he testified, didn't want a full haircut, just a little trim. Tucciarone described Julie as having a ponytail and showing her navel. "Dad would have grounded her for a year," Stephen told me. "Absolutely not," Julie said when I asked her if she would ever have dressed that way. "I had short hair and Dad made me zip up like an Eskimo before I left the house. I was the last person in my class to get my ears pierced. In 1975, I still had never worn blue jeans or loafers, because Dad regarded them as too promiscuous!" Moreover, Julie testified that she, Rush Jr., and Michael would not have gone for haircuts together during that era, or at any time in their lives. Julie had her hair done at Chateau Coiffures on Putnam Avenue—usually with her cousin Georgeann Dowdle. "We never had a single haircut together," she says of her brothers. The Skakel boys went to Mike at the Subway Barbershop. No Skakel, the family told me, has ever been to the Golden Touch Salon or met Tucciarone. Coincidentally, according to Tucciarone, Michael's confession occurred on the one day of the week Tucciarone was working alone in the salon—a holiday when the entire Skakel family always left town. Tucciarone waited 26 years to tell his graphic tale: he came forward only after casually relating it to one of his customers, a Stamford sheriff, who pressed him to report it to the State's Attorney's office.

ALL OF Benedict's material witnesses—Geranne Ridge, John Higgins, Greg Coleman, Larry Zicarelli, and Matthew Tucciarone—have so little credibility that their testimony would be comical had it not helped send an innocent man to prison. Most of these witnesses had changed or retracted their stories before the trial began. In each case the witness did not initially go to the police but bragged about the story to an acquaintance or to the media, who then notified the police. How likely is it that Michael Skakel, who endured years of abuse at Élan during which he refused to admit guilt, would suddenly "confess" to these crackpots, but never to any person he knew or trusted? Benedict was far too smart to have swallowed these wild yarns, but, with a little hocus pocus, he was able to persuade the jury to believe them.

CHAPTER 19

The Friend

What you end up remembering isn't always the same as what you have witnessed.

—Julian Barnes, *The Sense of an Ending*

On June 5, 2002, the jurors deliberating Michael's fate sent a handwritten note to the judge. They wanted to review Andrea Shakespeare's testimony. Following the trial, the jurors said they considered Andrea's statements to be just as dispositive to their decision to convict as either Higgins's or Coleman's "confessions." And like other pieces of evidence in the case against Michael, Benedict knew that he was selling lies.

Very few people understand the challenges facing witnesses asked to retrieve 25-year-old memories. Think about this: most Americans know where they were on 9/11. But how many of the smaller details do you recall with accuracy even 15 years later? The terrorist attacks were memorable and traumatic for all of us, even if we were not personally touched. I lost two friends among the nearly 3,000 killed, and my downtown law office was a casualty of the attack. Imagine that every couple of years someone sat you down and interviewed you about your 9/11 experience. Each time you did your best to remember every movement of that day. Inevitably, you will add new details to your story. Unless there is video footage recording your entire day, you will never be certain whether these memories actually occurred nor whether they represent the brain's natural editing. You almost certainly would share false memories of 9/11.

On the morning of 9/11, I was in Washington, DC, in a meeting at the office of AFL/CIO President John Sweeney. I accompanied my comrade and boss, John Adams, then president of the Natural Resources Defense Council (NRDC), and a small group of my fellow NRDC attorneys. We were there to strategize with Sweeney on deploying his and other unions in the fight against President Bush's plan to drill for oil in the Arctic Wildlife Refuge. At 9:37—and I only know the exact time because I looked it up—we heard an explosion. From Sweeney's window, we could see the Pentagon in flames, and eventually, we watched SWAT teams fanning out, as fireman battled the inferno. After a harrowing period, I and a few of the New York–based NRDC contingent decided that we needed to get home. Together we traversed Capitol Hill, on foot, to a Hertz rental car location. Because the nation's airports and rail traffic were shutdown, rental cars were at a premium that day and we had to pack into a sedan with another contingent of New Yorkers in order to get home. Sitting here now, I cannot remember any of the faces of the other occupants of that car, not even of the attorneys from the meeting, even though these were people with whom I worked daily. As the years passed, I found myself remembering looking out the window of Sweeney's office and not only seeing the Pentagon burning, but also seeing the White House, its roof crawling with snipers. I'm quite certain that there's no window in Washington, DC, that has a vista of both the Pentagon and the White House, and upon reflection, I probably walked by the White House on the way to pick up the car, and saw the snipers on the roof then. But I just can't be sure.

This phenomenon of false memory is likely what happened in 1991, when Garr and Solomon interviewed Andrea. Sixteen years after the murder, she remembered something that didn't happen. Her false memory would help land Michael in jail for a crime he didn't commit.

I give Andrea benefit of the doubt that I can't give Coleman or Higgins. Andrea did lie on the stand, but not for money. I doubt she did so knowingly. To her, Michael is the equivalent of my Chuck Clusen. Chuck is an NRDC lawyer who specializes in federal public lands and Alaska. Sometimes, he works out of the NRDC's Washington offices. Other times, he works in the San Francisco office. He also spends good chunks of time in the Arctic. I consider Chuck a good friend, but I can't, for the life of me, remember if he was in DC for that meeting. And in 2017, which is 16 years after 9/11, I guarantee my memories will be no clearer. I remember John Sweeney in that meeting. I remember John Adams. I don't remember Chuck. But if Chuck called me today and told me that not only was he in that meeting, he was also shoehorned into that car back to New York, I reckon that my 9/11 memories would soon include Chuck's face, whether he was actually there or not. Memory, it turns out, is malleable and we are highly suggestible creatures.

Andrea erred when she said that Michael didn't go to Sursum Corda with his brothers. In the years following the crime, police interviewed Andrea repeatedly about the two suspects who were in the Skakel house with her that night. Over and over again, they asked her the same questions: Did you see Tommy in the house before Julie brought you home? Did you notice Martha lingering by the side door when Tommy came to the front door to pass you the station wagon keys? What do you remember about Kenny Littleton's behavior during dinner at the Belle Haven Club? Was Littleton with Tommy at the front door when Tommy passed the keys to you? Even on these familiar issues, Andrea's memories are fluid. In the early years, she said that Littleton, Stephen, and Tommy all met her at the door to give her the station wagon keys. (This is correct: Littleton had trouble opening the broken front door, and the two boys scrambled to help him.) But by the 1990s, she was adamant that it was only Tommy. So what about a new issue of inquiry? Until the 1990s, Michael was not a suspect. So for Andrea he was merely a bit player, her best friend Julie's little brother. Michael never figured in any of the questions, so naturally, he faded out of her memories. Until 1991, that is.

Garr and Solomon drove up to Massachusetts in June of that year to interview Andrea. She was by then in her mid-30s. She'd married and had three kids with Rick Renna, who worked in residential real estate. Garr and Solomon began by reviewing with her the established facts of the night of the murder. Since Andrea was in the house with Julie drinking tea and watching TV while the boys were out in the car, she demurred that she had little to offer. "I didn't see anybody after a certain point," she told the detectives. "I mean, the first time I ever heard about guys sitting in a car listening to tapes, is right now." Garr laid out the facts. "When the Dowdle boy gets in, John gets in, Rushton comes in, and they depart . . . with Michael in the car," he said. She stopped him. "I don't know why my memory serves me this way, but I thought it was Rush, Johnny, and Jimmy," she said. "But I don't even know if I saw them leave." Because no witness in 16 years had ever suggested that Michael might not have gone to Sursum Corda, the investigators were surprised. "That was our understanding of what occurred," Garr told her.

Andrea was forthright about the murkiness of her memories. "For some reason, I don't know who told me . . . I don't know if I remember it, I thought it was the three boys," she said. "Did I see [Michael] in the house? No. Did I see him leave? No . . . I thought when we were recounting our stories before today, I thought I remembered hearing stories that Michael was in the back saying goodbye to Helen . . . Not that I saw, but it's just what I heard afterwards . . . It was my assumption, and it's a total assumption that there were four people in the backyard . . . Tommy, Michael, Helen, and Martha . . . I never even heard about a Geoffrey Byrne. And I don't know whether it's a story I was told from somebody. I don't know where the information came from."

Recall that the Lincoln pulled out of the driveway around 9:25 p.m. Julie and Andrea didn't emerge from the house until 9:30 p.m. Helen, who stayed in the Skakel yard a few minutes after the Lincoln departed, never recalled even seeing Andrea that night. Until emerging from the house, Andrea was essentially in an information dead zone. Even though she didn't see any of it, 16 years later she suddenly had a weird feeling, a hunch, an impression, that Michael was one of four people in the backyard when the Lincoln left. She naturally would have heard over the years that there were four people in the yard, because there were: Helen, Martha, Tommy, and Geoff, whose very presence apparently remained unknown to Andrea for 16 years.

This interview would not become noteworthy for another four years, when Garr returned to talk to her. By then, Dunne and Fuhrman had transformed the Sutton reports into the Rosetta stone of the case. And Garr was looking to pin the crime on Michael. At this point, Garr began drilling Andrea, and in the process, clearly implanting false memories in her brain. "I must have talked to her 165 times between that day and the last time I saw her in court 11 years later," Garr told Levitt. "Each time, I would say to her, 'Andrea, just tell me why you are so sure that Michael didn't go.'"

Garr's staccato questioning on that single point is a perfect example of the "misinformation effect," according to one of the world's preeminent experts on memory, Dr. Elizabeth Loftus of the University of California-Irvine. "What happens is people get feedback after they give an initial recollection and that feedback can artificially inflate their confidence," she says. "I study how post-event information can contaminate people's memories. If somebody comes along and either tells you somebody else's version of the events or insinuates something to be true, many people will pick up on it and adopt it as their own memory."

This is not junk science. Loftus, a Stanford psychology PhD, is a giant in her field. Since she began studying memory in the 1970s, she and her students have performed more than 200 experiments involving over 20,000 people, definitively proving how exposure to misinformation can induce memory distortion. In one study, she showed participants a simulated car accident at an intersection with a stop sign. Afterward, half of the participants received a suggestion that there had been a yield sign at the junction. The recipients of the suggestion tended to "remember" seeing a yield sign. Those who had not received the bogus information were much more accurate in their recollection of the stop sign. In one study, people "recalled" a large barn in a bucolic scene that contained no buildings at all. In another, by simply including a paragraph describing a fabricated childhood memory among a written description of other actual memories—getting lost in a mall at age 5, crying, being aided by an elderly woman, and finally reuniting with family—she successfully induced 29 percent of study participants to "remember" an event that never happened.

A decade after saying she didn't know why she thought Michael had stayed behind and that she hadn't seen Michael in the house, Andrea's memory had improved immeasurably. Not only had she absorbed Garr's drumbeat interrogations, she admitted having read Fuhrman's book, which reintroduced and fortified Garr's suggestions. At trial, Assistant State's Attorney Susan Gill led her through her recollections of the Lincoln and its occupants.

> GILL: And at some point earlier that evening, was there a Skakel car parked in that side driveway?
> SHAKESPEARE: Yes.
> GILL: And after that car left, you left, correct?
> SHAKESPEARE: I left after the car left, yes.
> GILL: Was Michael Skakel in the house after that car left?
> SHAKESPEARE: Yes.
> GILL: And have you ever had any doubt in your mind about the fact that Michael Skakel was home after that car left from the side driveway?
> SHAKESPEARE: No.
> GILL: From 1975 to today, have you been certain that Michael was home after that car left?
> SHAKESPEARE: Yes.

Under Sherman's cross-examination, she went even further. In 1991, she'd had no idea that Martha and the boys had even been sitting in the car listening to music in the moments just before the Lincoln left. Now, in 2002, she remembered seeing the car.

> SHERMAN: Did you indicate to Inspector Garr that you believed that only Rushton and John Skakel drove Mr. Terrien home but you're not sure if you saw them leave?
> SHAKESPEARE: I saw them leave.
> SHERMAN: Are you sure about that?
> SHAKESPEARE: Yes.

Sherman handed her a transcript of the 1991 interview, but when confronting proof of her contrary recollections, Shakespeare insisted her new memories were more accurate.

> SHERMAN: Does that document refresh your recollection as to whether or not you told Inspector Garr in 1991 that you are not sure if you saw them leave?
> SHAKESPEARE: Yes, that's what the document says.
> SHERMAN: And, in fact, did you tell Inspector Garr in 1991 that you were not sure if you saw them leave?
> SHAKESPEARE: Yes.

SHERMAN: Is that different from your testimony today?

SHAKESPEARE: No.

SHERMAN: So you are saying all along that you are not sure if you saw them leave.

SHAKESPEARE: No, I am sure that I saw them leave.

Though testimony like this makes it a challenge, I'll continue to give her the benefit of the doubt that she didn't intentionally perjure herself. (I called Andrea to discuss her testimony, but she didn't call back.) "I am so shocked at Andrea Shakespeare," says her former best friend, Julie. "I'm just in a tizzy about her testimony that Michael did not go to the Terriens. There's no way that she knew that. She didn't even know that the boys had left."

Higgins, Coleman, and Andrea were undeniably the big three prosecution witnesses in Michael's trial. No other witnesses came close to inflicting the kind of damage they did. There was, of course, ample evidence and experts available for Michael's defense to counter every claim these witnesses made. Unfortunately for Michael, the jury heard almost none of this evidence. There's a simple explanation for this: Mickey Sherman.

Sherman proved inept in countering Andrea's ambiguous testimony that she was "under the impression" that Michael was in the Skakel house when she left. A competent lawyer would have objected to Andrea's testimony because it was speculation not based on personal knowledge. A skilled lawyer adept at destructive cross-examination would have destroyed Andrea's claims as a recent fabrication.

During Michael's *habeas corpus* hearings, Sherman testified that he had reached out to memory expert Elizabeth Loftus but opted not to call her to testify, because he thought she would be of no help. Sherman was lying. Loftus looked through her detailed work notes for me and did find that she'd indeed once consulted with Sherman on a case, but not until 2004, when he was defending Mark Mangelsdorf, a Harvard Business School graduate and corporate executive accused of a 22-year-old murder in Kansas. "He consulted with me on the Kansas case but I don't see anything about Skakel," she says. "I don't see any notes or anything." Loftus says she would have been able to contextualize Shakespeare's testimony recounting details from an evening 27 years earlier, especially given Garr's "165" interviews with her. "The weaker the memory, the easier it is to contaminate," Loftus says. "If I want to contaminate somebody's memory I just let some time pass so it can fade and it becomes more and more malleable."

Even with a crooked cop willing to suborn perjury, manufacture a confession, conceal exculpatory evidence, leak grand jury testimony, and illegally seize evidence; even with an unscrupulous prosecutor, a skillfully manipulated press corps clamoring like a lynch mob for his conviction; even with a bitter and venal family lawyer nurturing a secret vendetta and manufacturing evidence to hang him, Michael still shouldn't have lost the case. Unfortunately, Michael's family hired Mickey Sherman to defend him—possibly the worst lawyer in Connecticut.

PART VI

The Lawyer

CHAPTER 20

The Clown

A good trial lawyer, no matter what the case, no matter what the court, thinks about that case to the exclusion of everything else for whatever time is available to prepare that case. I know trial lawyers who if they have six months to try the case, will stop reading the newspaper for those six months. They don't open the mail, because it's distracting. Your mind is focused upon that trial to a degree of concentration unknown to practitioners in any other branch of the profession, and unknown to any other kind of professional. You think of nothing else! You live, sleep and breathe that trial.

—Professor Irving Younger,
The Ten Commandments of Cross-Examination

A great lawyer is someone who can at least appear to give a damn.
—Mickey Sherman, *How Can You Defend Those People?*

Initially, it appeared that Mickey Sherman would be providing the kind of gold-plated defense that would justify the staggering $2.2 million that the Skakel family scraped together to pay him. (They paid another $498,000 to lawyers subcontracted by Sherman.) On April 4, 2000, there was barely room to shoehorn all the lawyers and paralegals into Sherman's office at Sherman & Richichi. Sherman's workplace hardly reflected the glitz and glamour he invested in his suits, cars, restaurants, and ostentatious jet-set celebrity friendships. In contrast to the flashy accessories of his public persona, Sherman's law office was an unassuming, two-story colonial in a blue-collar Stamford neighborhood. With no conference room to accommodate the crowd, participants dragged chairs into Sherman's first-floor office and squeezed around his desk. Taking his cue from the successful O.J. Simpson defense, Sherman had assembled a "Dream Team" of world-class criminal trial lawyers, including celebrated defense attorney Linda Kenney Baden; prominent New Haven criminal lawyer David Grudberg; and Tara Knight, the skilled, pretty, blonde Court TV litigator, whom Mickey was dating at the time. Also in the room were three green legal assistants in their 20s whom Sherman had tapped for the grunt work: his son Mark Sherman, who was admitted to the bar two years earlier and had no criminal law experience; Stephan Seeger, aged 33, who passed the bar three years earlier; and 26-year-old Jason Throne, freshly graduated from the University of Florida law school and who had yet to pass the bar. Manny Margolis, Tommy's lawyer, was also present. (Margolis had recommended Sherman to the Skakel family.)

A self-described "Jersey girl" with a fondness for high-stakes poker and chunky turquoise jewelry, Linda Kenney Baden is one of America's top-shelf criminal defense attorneys. Point by point, in Sherman's office, she outlined the gaping holes in the prosecution's case against Michael Skakel and the evidence the defense would need to assemble in order to exploit each weakness. She had come to the meeting loaded for bear.

"We must find Theresa Tirado," Kenney Baden read from a three-inch thick notebook that contained her itemized inventory of tasks the defense would need to check off before declaring "trial ready." Locating and re-interviewing Theresa Tirado was at the top of the list. Tirado, the Moxleys' housekeeper, had reported finding a bloody handprint in the Moxley home the day after Martha's murder. Tirado's statements, combined with suspicious inconsistencies in John Moxley's alibis, his reputation for violence, and a string of odd behaviors, all added up to a winning third-party culpability defense. Kenney Baden considered it imperative to reach Tirado and confirm her story. Sherman nodded, as though taking it all in.

Michael's trial team needed to find an exact replica of the Toney Penna six-iron that killed Martha and subject it to stress-testing, Kenney Baden continued. She suggested Sherman assign his investigators to locate its twin on eBay. She was confident that testing would prove it was impossible that a boy of about 120 pounds could have broken that club. In his illustrious and storied 40-plus-year career, Kenney Baden's husband, world-renowned forensic pathologist Michael Baden, had seen many murders by golf club. However, he had never seen a club shaft snap during an attack. When two beefy mobsters wielding golf clubs beat Mafioso capo Vincent "Jimmy Sinatra" Craparotta into a state of liquefaction, on the floor of his New Jersey car dealership in 1984, the golf clubs were unscathed. "Craparotta's head broke and the cement floor cracked and chipped but the golf clubs stayed intact," Kenney Baden recounted. In testimony before a 1993 grand jury, Lucchese mob informant Philip Leonetti explained, "Marty [Taccetta] told me it's better to use golf clubs than baseball bats, because baseball bats break. . . .

Golf clubs, they do a lot of damage and they don't break." To shatter the golf club, Martha's killer would have had to be a colossus with Herculean strength.

Kenney Baden continued: The Dream Team needed to collect a slide show of contemporaneous Skakel family photos. The jurors must repeatedly see how tiny Michael was at the time of the crime. No one would believe that a kid that small would have the strength to commit the savage assault and then drag Martha's body 78 feet.

Sherman would need to retain a first-class jury consultant, Kenney Baden insisted. Jury selection is a science that ought only to be entrusted to trained experts.

Sherman would need to re-interview Elliot Gross, the medical examiner. Kenney Baden read from a long list of unanswered questions she had constructed by critically dissecting his autopsy report: the inexcusable sloppiness of record keeping, the absence of autopsy photos, the lost vaginal and anal swabs and slides, and the botched handling of the hair evidence. If presented properly, these defects alone would be sufficient to raise the reasonable doubt necessary for acquittal.

I was curious to know how many items from Kenney Baden's to-do list Sherman checked off during the more than two years between the Dream Team's Stamford meeting and Michael's trial, and what Sherman had unearthed. Vito Colucci, Sherman's primary investigator, told me that the name Theresa Tirado didn't ring a bell. He explained that he took all his marching orders from Sherman and his son, Mark. Neither one of them ever mentioned Tirado. In fact, Sherman never asked Colucci to do anything related to John Moxley.

Sherman never commissioned any scientific tests on the golf clubs. He never introduced a photo of Michael at age 15 to jurors, while allowing Benedict to introduce one of the family photos seized from Richard Hoffman's apartment that showed a big, bulked-up Michael at age 19. A prosecution witness falsely claimed it looked to be from the approximate time of the crime. Sherman didn't object.

Dr. Elliot Gross told my investigator that Sherman made no effort to re-interview him.

Most disastrously, Sherman elected to skimp on jury selection. Michael repeatedly asked Sherman to hire a jury consultant. Sherman told Michael, "We don't need one. Too expensive." Sherman fancied himself a sharp jury-picker. In his book, he advises defense attorneys to use preemptory challenges to remove any juror who is predisposed toward the prosecution. As an example, he recommends that defense attorneys avoid seating a juror who admits to regularly watching *Nancy Grace*. "No offense to Nancy—she's a good friend, and I'm a fan of hers. It just sends the message that they are probably pro prosecution." He penned that wisdom six years after Michael's trial. (Michael successfully sued

Sherman's "friend" Nancy Grace for her wildly biased reporting about him.) "Why should I begin this race from a quarter mile behind the starting block?" Sherman asks.

So, it's mystifying why Sherman would not use one of his peremptory challenges to prevent Brian Wood, a Darien cop, from sitting on Michael's jury. Most defense lawyers would deem it malpractice to allow a cop to sit on a jury in a criminal case; police understandably have a predilection to convict and the capacity to influence other jurors with inside knowledge. Furthermore, Wood had a personal beef against Sherman; one of Sherman's clients had assaulted him. Wood rode motorcycles with Lunney, the Greenwich cop who had been the original lead investigator on the Moxley homicide and who had harassed Tommy for years, and believed that one of the Skakel boys was guilty. During *voir dire,* Sherman asked Wood if, in Sherman's shoes, he would pick himself. "No," Wood replied pointedly. Sherman picked him anyway. Sherman also picked 39 year-old Laura Copeland from Stamford, who admitted during *voir dire* that her friend's mother was close to Dorthy Moxley. "That was stupid," says Seeger, who wasn't in court during much of jury selection. "Leaving Mickey alone with Jason Throne at that jury selection always scared the shit out of me," he says. "It was like, 'What are these two nitwits going to do up there?'"

Sherman was aware that he was tempting fate. "I'm sure the jury experts are lining up to roast me tonight," he wisecracked to the press, as he left the courtroom after impaneling the cop. That night, Colucci got calls from two Darien police officers he knew: "What on earth was Mickey thinking by allowing Lunney's friend on the jury?" Colucci called Sherman at 1:00 a.m. "Mick, what did you do today?" Colucci asked him, gravely. Sherman knew exactly what he was talking about. "Don't worry, guy. Don't worry," he reassured his investigator. "I know what I'm doing. You don't understand. This'll show we really won this case. Vito, I'm going to put a cop on the jury and I'm still going to win." Colucci shakes his head at Sherman's hubris. "Mickey liked pushing the envelope," Colucci said. "I was mortified when I heard about some of his selections," Seeger said. "It was swagger . . . machismo. He thought he was going to win no matter what. From a lot of people's standpoints it was a case that could not be lost. But we really overestimated Mickey."

One lawyer had no illusions about what was in store for Michael. Sherman disbanded the Dream Team shortly after that Stamford huddle in his office. The first to go was Linda Kenney Baden and her nettlesome list. It wasn't her fee that irked Sherman; Rucky had committed to paying her separately. High standards and expertise were her downfall. Sherman retained only the greenhorns: his son, Seeger, and Throne. They were cheap, but, more important, they were less likely to second-guess Sherman's seemingly odd judgments or compete with him for camera time. Sherman cautioned the rookies that he alone would deal with the press. "I was just out of law school and had never worked on a major trial," said Throne. "Mickey kept everything close to the chest. He didn't share his strategy with any of us." Media-savvy Kenney Baden, an experienced capital crime litigator, undoubtedly threatened his primacy.

As part of his ongoing efforts to organize relief projects in war zones, Stephen Skakel managed the launching of a program to provide DNA testing to identify victims at mass burial sites in Croatia and Bosnia. In 2001, six months before Michael's trial, he attended a conference on clinical and forensic testing in Dubrovnik. Kenney Baden and her husband, Michael, were there assisting in the identification effort. "I'm sorry to tell you this, but your brother's going to be convicted," Kenney Baden informed Stephen. "It was incredibly obvious to me that Mickey wasn't doing his job," she told me recently. But she also understands why the Skakels didn't fire him. "You get invested in your lawyer, even if they're doing a terrible job," she explained. "It's almost like an abusive wife situation. They cut you off from the rest of the world. You see it as your only option, your lifeline."

Sherman was great at one thing: reassuring his client that he had everything under control. Each day during the trial, Michael and his siblings gathered for meals at the Ash Creek Saloon, a few blocks from the Norwalk courthouse. Sherman met every expression of doubt with his Pollyanna refrain: "There is no way in hell that you are ever going to see the inside of a jail cell."

Despite the hopes they invested in him and his ever-confident style, it was already starting to dawn on Michael and the Skakel family how many things that Sherman promised would never happen, ended up happening. During their first meeting in early 1999 at the New York Athletic Club, Sherman assured Michael that the State would never issue an arrest warrant. By then, Michael had moved to Hobe Sound, Florida, where he was living with, and caring for, his dying father, who was then in the final throes of dementia. On January 19, 2000, the prosecutors announced Michael's arrest warrant. A couple of months after that, free on $500,000 bail, Michael sat at lunch with Sherman overlooking the 18th hole in Loblolly. "This will never go to trial," Sherman insisted. "You'll never see the inside of the courthouse." A year later, after the State announced that Michael would stand trial as an adult, he watched Sherman on the *Today* show couch, assuring Matt Lauer, "I'm not surprised. I've always thought, and I've always said, this case is going to trial." Michael was already skeptical about Sherman's slick, pitchman's bluster, but he lacked the confidence to fire Sherman even as his doubts about his representation multiplied. Michael recently said to me, "When I buy an airplane ticket, I assume the guys in the cockpit know how to fly the 747." Michael shrugged and looked glum. "Even when stuff didn't make sense to me, I just kept hoping he knew what he was doing."

A few months before Kenney Baden shared her bleak forecast with Stephen, Sherman was out on the town, partying at Giovanni's II, a restaurant in Darien, for the annual Stamford Roasters Dinner. Joe Richichi, Sherman's partner of 25 years, was the roastee. The event got big play in the *Greenwich Time*. In an unintentionally prescient gag, Sherman, who loves costumes, dressed in a convict's uniform: horizontal stripes with ball and chain. The roasters' predictably jabbed Sherman for basking in the spotlight, while Richichi labored at mundane land transactions for Connecticut mobsters. Sherman joked from the dais that he didn't have to worry about his partner stealing his makeup. His role in the partnership, he said, was to do TV interviews with Katie Couric, while Richichi handled oil tank adjustments at real estate closings.

If not for the game show scandals of the 1950s, Michael may have been spared the calamity of Sherman's defense. Sherman grew up in "the slums of Greenwich," as he termed the middle class section of town in his 2008 memoir, *How Can You Defend Those People?* A C-average student at Greenwich High, he professed dismay at narrowly losing the vote for class clown. He remained a C student at the University of Connecticut in Storrs, majoring in what he termed "having a good time." Somehow, Sherman was admitted to the University of Connecticut Law School, where he maintained his lifetime C average. Following a stint as a public defender, he worked as an assistant prosecutor in Connecticut. But practicing law never interested Sherman. Married with two young kids, and yearning for money and fame, Sherman became a professional game show contestant. "I learned that you can get on the shows if you can pass a trivia test and act like a genuine moron during the interviews and mock games," he wrote. In the mid-1970s, Sherman scored minor winnings on *Jackpot*, on *The $20,000 Pyramid*, and on *The Joker's Wild*, from which he took home $17,000. Unfortunately for Michael Skakel, the game show scandals prompted an FCC rule providing a lifetime limit of three shows per contestant. Sherman hung out his shingle as a defense lawyer specializing in drunk driving cases. Always a clown, Sherman became infamous for his courtroom gags. He appeared, for example, to defend a man charged with shooting ducks from his yacht, with two rubber duck feet protruding from his briefcase.

In 1985, he represented Hossein Vaziri, pro wrestling's Iron Sheik. The Sheik faced a third-degree assault rap following his smackdown of a Fairfield gas station attendant. By way of begging Judge Alvin Rottman for leniency, Sherman traveled to a World Wrestling Federation gig to video himself extracting testimonials from the wrestler's cronies, including Captain Lou Albano and rocker Cyndi Lauper. Snatching his microphone, the Sheik's manager, "Classy" Freddie Blassie, bellowed to a grinning Sherman, "Just a minute, you pencil-necked geek! Don't interrupt me!"

Sherman boasts of his shameless lust for fame. "I'm a media whore," he says. According to his memoir, a chance golf game with film director Barry Levinson "resulted in the fulfillment of one of my lifetime goals. (No, not to argue before the Supreme Court.) Barry wrote me into one of his movies! In *Man of the Year,* starring Robin Williams, Christopher Walken, Laura Linney, and others, I play 'Talking Head Lawyer.' In one scene I appear on Laura Linney's bathroom television set, pontificating about Robin Williams's election to the presidency. My friends and family have had to suffer through countless obnoxious instances where I've let my SAG card fall out of my wallet so people can ask me what it is."

Of course, the Skakels were in the dark about this sort of cringeworthy information when they retained Sherman. His 1991 Roger Ligon acquittal had earned Sherman his reputation as a top-notch criminal litigator. Ligon, a 42-year-old African American custodian, shot Willie Dobson, an unarmed 22-year-old, three times during an argument over a Stamford parking space. Following the second shot to his chest, Dobson cried out, "Please don't kill me." Ligon fired a third fatal shot to his head. The case looked unwinnable. The many eyewitnesses included the victim's mother. Sherman pioneered a very risky "not guilty by reason of post-traumatic stress disorder" plea wherein he cited Ligon's service as a Vietnam combat veteran. By all accounts, Sherman nailed the case, spending a week in the Marine Corps's Historical Center, poring over combat chronologies to find records of the horrific sights Ligon claimed to have witnessed, and then bird-dogging members of Ligon's unit for corroboration.

Sherman fought the case like a good trial attorney. A parade of witnesses testified to the victim's aggressiveness, to Ligon's decency, and to the horrors that Ligon witnessed in Vietnam. During a firefight near Que Son, Ligon watched a close friend immolated by napalm. When Ligon grabbed his friend's arm to pull him to safety, his buddy's cooked flesh fell from his bone. "He covered all the bases," Bruce Hudock, the senior assistant State's Attorney who prosecuted the case, told the *New York Times.* "He utilized every piece of evidence he could. He had all the tools, and he went to work on me." Not only did Sherman triumph in the case—Ligon won release—he also triumphed in a new medium. The just-launched Court TV taped and broadcast the trial. Sherman found rebirth as a self-described "TV lawyer."

Before long, Sherman was juggling appearances on *Today*, MSNBC's *America after Hours*, CNBC's *Rivera Live,* and Court TV. He landed a contract with *CBS This Morning* as the show's legal expert. "Mickey the Clown" played every TV gig for laughs: on Fox News's *The Big Story,* he wore sunglasses to match guest Duane "Dog the Bounty Hunter" Chapman; on Catherine Crier's Court TV show, he appeared in the ghost face mask from *Scream.* "It's intoxicating to do this stuff," he gushed to the *New York Times* in 1997. Life at such dizzying pinnacles gave him his first brush with Dominick Dunne and the O.J. Simpson trial. Sherman was sprawled on a pool-side lounge chair at the Las Vegas Mirage Hotel next to model Paula Barbieri when she got the call that someone had murdered the ex-wife of her boyfriend, O.J. Simpson. When Dunne called to confirm, Sherman begged him to kill the story, fearing it might dampen demand for him as an impartial talking head during the upcoming trial. Dunne banked the favor.

Sherman had parlayed his legal victory in the Ligon case into a second TV career. "We make fools of ourselves in return for limo rides and cheap doughnuts in greenrooms," Sherman told the *Greenwich Time.* Michael and I were estranged at the time he chose his lawyer. Otherwise, I might have run Sherman's won/lost record on LexisNexis and learned something that the Skakels didn't know until it was too late: the Ligon case was one of a tiny handful of murder cases that Sherman ever tried to verdict. He was a rank amateur.

Rucky had hired Sherman at the recommendation of Margolis, who recommended Sherman as a man comfortable before the cameras and in the courtroom. It was a recommendation Margolis would profoundly regret. The first letter Michael received in prison was an anguished missive from Margolis apologizing for the Sherman recommendation as "the worst decision of my life."

Sherman promoted himself as a public-relations expert who could undo the damage to the family's reputation from nearly a decade of Dunne's unanswered accusations. But Sherman's appetite for the limelight turned out to be as voracious as Dunne's—and he was an ineffective spokesman. Despite some $200,000 that Sherman billed the Skakels for time he spent with the media, both the public's and the jury's impression of Michael couldn't have been more negative. Margolis thought that the lawyer he was recommending was the hard-charging litigator who'd pulled a rabbit out of his hat for Ligon. In fact, they were getting a different guy. Sherman had been dining and drinking on that victory for nearly a decade. He was done with the hard work of litigating. He had found the spotlight, loved the high life, and wanted to be a full-time "TV lawyer." As the Skakels would gradually learn, Sherman was just a blowhard confidence man with a perma-tan and an electric smile.

The Skakel case was Sherman's ticket to stardom. "He kept saying it was going to be his last case," Colucci says. "He was going to ride off into the sunset and do television." He wasn't keeping this a secret. "This could be my last big trial," Sherman told a reporter at the time, mentioning his two Hollywood films in development. "I'm ready to retire. I think in a couple of years you'll find me in the Bahamas, surrounded by 20 girls from Scores." From the moment the Skakels hired him, he was spending more time carousing at New York's flashy hot spot Elaine's than bearing down on the law books. "Every time I telephoned him after sundown," Michael recalls, "I heard a crowd in the background with the cocktail glasses clinking." Forensic pathologist Michael Baden repeatedly bumped into Sherman in the Fox News greenroom during the run-up to the trial. Both men were frequent guests of Greta Van Susteren. "His devotion was to being on television and I think a lot less on the legal aspect," Baden says. "I'd never hear anything about the case. All I'd hear about was how many times he'd gone out to dinner with Michael Bolton. He thought he had it wrapped up. He didn't think he had to do anything."

Sherman scheduled his client consultations in Florida, booking a suite at the Breakers in Palm Beach, where oceanfront rooms go for $1,900 a night. He'd often bring his girlfriend, Tara Knight, and his Harley-Davidson, which he shipped down—on Rucky's tab—and parked on display at the hotel entrance. Sherman scheduled meetings at fancy restaurants, golf courses, and high-profile venues where he could mix recreation with billable hours. "We haven't found that he spent any significant money on investigating the case," says Michael's current attorney Hubie Santos, "but a lot of two-week stays in a suite at the Breakers in Palm Beach." Sherman rented out Cabana 1 pool-side at the Breakers and trotted Michael Skakel out like a prize ham for the gawkers.

On October 18, 2001, Sherman was in Vegas on Rucky's dime, ostensibly to interview Élan alum Annie Goodman. He took the time to address a forum for young lawyers. Michael suspects Sherman scheduled the Goodman meeting to coincide with the Continuing Legal Education (CLE) Conference, which famously doubles as a tax-deductible bacchanalia.

Less than six months from trial, Sherman was ready to party. "The good news here is that you can put your pens away," he began. "This is absolutely the entertainment section of this seminar, hopefully. I'll also bring the narcissist TV lawyer definition to a new high."

Sherman was waiting for a critical court ruling on Michael's petition to be tried as a juvenile. A positive outcome would have meant that, regardless of the verdict, Michael wouldn't have gone to jail. "I'll probably lose," he volunteered from the podium, to shocked guffaws from the junior lawyers in Vegas. (He was right.) Ethical rules strictly forbid reckless public pre-trial banter that might prejudice a pending decision. But Sherman was too giddy to stop.

"I'm only going to talk about this one case and having fun with it," he proclaimed. "I mean, too many people just look upon our jobs as absolute drudges in the trench. And for better or worse, I've never been someone like that. I certainly have fun with it. I probably have too much fun, which would probably be the primary criticism you have." Instead of an audio-visual PowerPoint presentation, Sherman showed a reel of his television and newspapers clips and photos of himself lingering near the red carpet in his Dolce & Gabbana tuxedo. He flashed a photo on the screen of himself clowning it up with actors Vince Curatola and Dominic Chianese from January 19, 2000, just hours after Michael's arrest. "This is really hysterical," he said, pointing to the picture. "That night, most of you would be in a law library researching. Instead, I went to New York with friends and went out to dinner to have fun. And the guys I was with are two of the guys in *The Sopranos,* Uncle Junior and John, who is head of the New York mob. That's the way I research my cases."

It's a pity none of the Skakels heard this speech before the trial began. It was a prescient showcase of the depraved indifference and recklessness that would get my cousin convicted of murder in a case that "couldn't be lost." Sherman scored another laugh from the barristers by making light of his professional ineptitude. "Finally we got a reasonable cause hearing," he said. "Not a probable cause hearing but a reasonable cause hearing. I have no idea what that means. When I do these news conferences outside the courthouse, people would say, 'Well, juvenile court, what happens here?' And I go, 'I don't know. I've never handled a juvenile court case.' Which didn't give my client a lot of confidence. My better line is, when I'm asked a question I don't know the answer to is, 'I don't know. You should check with a legal expert on that.'" He showed a clip from the *Law & Order* episode based on the Moxley case. ("This is the fun stuff . . . Michael becomes Michael Sarno. Martha Moxley becomes Mary Mosley. I become Barry Nathanson.")

He began a section of the talk called "What the Hell Was I Thinking" by returning to the topic of his "narcissism." If it's any sort of virtue, Sherman was at least honest in acknowledging that the Moxley murder trial, for him, was always about something much larger than Michael Skakel or justice; it was about Mickey Sherman. "You have to understand the case isn't about you," he cautioned. "It's about your client and the defense." But the publicity attending the Moxley trial had propelled him, he said, "into a fugue state and I totally forgot about that."

By the time Sherman hit Vegas, Margolis and the Skakels were already chastising him, in Julie's words, "[t]o shut his fucking mouth and stop putting himself in the news." But, he told the lawyers, glitzy fashion editor Tina Brown (a career Kennedy maligner) had made his vow of silence to the Skakels impossible to keep. "I kept getting a call from Tina Brown, the publisher of *Talk* magazine," he said. Tina, continued Sherman, "wanted to do a piece on me handling this case. And I said, 'That's kind of a gossipy publication. It's a murder trial. I don't want to piss anybody off. . . .' So she started inviting me to all the A-list parties in New York . . . [and] she says, 'I'll do the interview anywhere you want.' I go, 'Anywhere?' She says, 'Yeah.' Okay. The Academy Awards and all the cool parties and this is what happens. This is horrible. Horrible!"

But most galling, Sherman shared a few capsulized reviews on the literature of the case, written, he admitted, by friends he knew from his life as a cable TV gas bag or, as he described it in Vegas, "one of those schmucks every night on one of the shows talking about whatever bullshit case is going on, whether it's O.J. or Menendez or whatever." He asked of the crowd, "Has anyone ever read any of Dominick Dunne's books? He hates defense lawyers. He thinks that everyone's guilty. He's had some tough baggage himself. But he's a wonderful guy, true judge of character." He described the book that caused Michael to be arrested for a murder he didn't commit as "Mark Fuhrman's brilliant book, *Murder in Greenwich.*" Fuhrman, too, was a friend. "He comes to our court, these hearings, and African American people go up to him and ask for his autograph," Sherman said. "Go figure that out. Actually, he and I have become good friends 'cause we do all these TV shows together and we scream at each other and then we go out to dinner. . . . So I guess in some sense I'm hypocritical. But it's just amazing to me that the public has accepted him and, **as Mrs. Moxley says, he's a hero**" [emphasis mine].

The Skakels were appalled by Sherman's obsequious relationships with Dunne and Fuhrman. During the trial breaks, Sherman clowned and mugged for photographs with Michael's two archenemies. He partied at Dunne's house and arrived at the Norwalk courthouse with Dunne in a shared white stretch limo. His shenanigans with Dunne and Fuhrman were devastating to his client's morale. I called Sherman to complain, even though I had no authority from his client. "I can't help it," he told me. "I'm a suck up."

The day after the conviction, Sherman told me that he was going to a Court TV party for Dunne. When I questioned the propriety of his attending, he said, "We're friends. What can I say? I'm a kiss-ass." Following Michael's conviction, Sherman startled CNN staffers with an unscheduled greenroom appearance to visit Dominick Dunne and Dorthy Moxley as the three awaited separate *Larry King Live* interviews. He told Moxley that he was "happy" for her. Dunne instantly reported the remark. At Michael's sentencing, Sherman, quoting a probation report, said that Michael was "an entirely different person today than he was at 15." Both statements left public doubt that Sherman believed in his client's innocence—although Sherman protests that this was not his intent. He told me repeatedly that he was certain that Michael is innocent.

On one of the final days of trial, Sherman picked up a pen camera he kept stashed at the defense table. While court was in session, he took selfies of himself and Michael with me in the background. Wearing a goofy grin, he next snapped photos of the jury and everyone in the courtroom. It was all a big party for Sherman.

MICHAEL BECAME increasingly skeptical and critical of his attorney's erratic behavior—particularly after Sherman lost his laptop. "During the trial, Mickey's laptop was stolen from his office," Colucci remembers, by Sherman's client. According to Colucci, Sherman's erectile dysfunction thwarted his burgeoning sexual relationship with her. Embarrassed, Sherman stopped returning his jilted client's phone calls, prompting her to steal his computer. She fled with the laptop to New York. The hard drive housed Michael's trial files and strategies. As

Sherman's staff searched frantically for her across two states, she goaded them by phone. "She would kid around saying, 'Oh, I made a copy of everything.' Who knows? But I never saw Mickey so crazy before."

From his prison cell, Michael wondered if the hard drive might have ended up in the wrong hands: the Skakel trial message boards lit up with anonymous but detailed and plausible-sounding accounts from people claiming to know the woman. They swore that she'd accessed Sherman's trial notes for the prosecution team. Michael fretted that Sherman himself might have been compromised. He wonders if incriminating personal information on the computer could have been used against Sherman. Michael believes his attorney deliberately threw the trial. His theory is not farfetched. Losing the case required an almighty effort.

Still, I don't believe Sherman deliberately threw the trial. I think he crashed in the deep end after a high flight on booze, parties, and self-will run riot. Stephen says that when the family gathered each morning at Julie's house in Darien for the trip to the courthouse, a ragged Sherman often arrived seemingly directly from the previous evening's debauchery.

By the time the Skakels realized they should have moved on from Sherman and his wild behavior, they felt it was too late to change lawyers. Julie told me, "We'd already paid Sherman a million dollars, and at that point it was too much." It wasn't until they consulted with a new lawyer post-verdict that they realized how catastrophic his representation had been.

Here's a far-from-comprehensive list of the things that Sherman failed to do, in addition to ignoring all the recommendations from Kenney Baden:

1. Even before the trial began, Sherman failed to make an interlocutory appeal based on Michael's strongest legal argument—that the court no longer had jurisdiction to hear a case against anyone who was accused of a murder that took place in 1975. At that time, Connecticut's statute of limitations for second-degree murder was five years. Sherman claimed that he thought the right time for such an appeal was after the final judgment. This makes no sense. "The whole point of an interlocutory appeal," Hope Seeley, the lawyer in charge of Michael's appeal, explained, "is not to have to wait for a final judgment—or endure the expense and emotion of a lengthy trial." Monumental self-interest is the only reason that Sherman failed to file the appeal. An early victory in such an appeal would have deprived Sherman of the visibility and money he would earn at a nationally publicized trial.

   The defense seemed foolproof. The lead case was *Paradise v. Connecticut*. Seventeen-year-old Wilmer Paradise stabbed a woman to death in 1974 and wasn't charged until 1992. The State Supreme Court reversed Paradise's conviction, declaring that the statute of limitations had expired. Former Solicitor General Theodore "Ted" Olsen, acting as Michael's consulting attorney on that appeal, told Michael that it was a surefire ticket to freedom. "There is no way that the State of Connecticut can hold you on a criminal charge for which the statute has expired—after all, it's the Constitution State!" As he awaited the court's decision on the post-verdict motion, Michael met Wilmer Paradise, now the leader of a biker gang, in prison on another murder charge. "You are free, man," the former teen killer told him. "I paved the road for you—just wait." Both the biker and Ted Olsen underestimated the political pressure on the Connecticut Supreme Court to uphold Michael's conviction. After a three-week jury trial, with all its attendant national publicity, three days of deliberations, and $25 million invested in Michael's conviction, an acquittal based on a "technicality" became a political hot potato too dicey for the justices to dish up. It became less perilous for them to change the Constitution; the same Supreme Court that freed Wilmer Paradise reversed years of precedence and declared that the five-year statute of limitations no longer applied.

2. At least a year before the trial, Vito Colucci located Kaseman and Gerbino, the two Rochester cops who offered to testify that Coleman was a junkie with a long criminal record and a committed and habitual liar. Colucci recalls that "as soon as I got off the phone, I ran right down to Mickey's office and said 'Mick, you gotta call these guys. These guys know Coleman better than anybody.' Every couple of weeks I said, 'Mickey, did you call the cops from Rochester?' Mickey'd say, 'Yeah, yeah, I'll get them.' Then when we came to trial, I said, 'Did you ever call those cops from Rochester?' He said, 'Don't worry about it. We don't need them.'" After David Letterman joked on *The Late Show* that he wanted to sit on the Skakel jury, Sherman found time to write up, for a newspaper, a "top 10" list of why he would pick David Letterman for the jury. Preoccupied with such self-indulgent frivolities, he never found the time to call Kaseman and Gerbino, and failed to impeach Greg Coleman's devastating testimony.

3. Sherman also failed to get a copy of the so-called Morganti sketch. The sketch, based on Belle Haven security guard Charles Morganti's recollections of a figure seen twice near the crime scene on the night of Martha's murder, is strikingly similar to Kenny Littleton. The sketch would certainly have bolstered Michael's third-party culpability defense. Benedict and Garr are guilty of prosecutorial misconduct for not turning over the sketch in discovery. However, Sherman also is guilty of malpractice for not requesting it. Police reports specifically mentioned the sketch, but Sherman apparently never read the police reports. After the

trial, Stephen took possession of Sherman's three boxes of police files. One box contained dog-eared papers with notations in the margins. He was horrified when he opened the two other boxes. The papers inside were pristine, straight, and unwrinkled, as if they'd just been picked up from a copy center. "It was clear from their condition that nobody had ever read them," he said.

4. Perhaps in recognition of Dunne's solicitude toward Littleton, Sherman refused to allow Julie or the other Skakels to testify about the strong evidence against Littleton. When I asked Sherman during the trial why he was not aggressively questioning Littleton, he said, "He's a pathetic creature. I don't want to look like I'm beating up on him." When Sherman called Jack Solomon to the stand, Solomon appeared with a three-ring binder containing nearly three decades' worth of police information about Littleton and Tommy and a summary of the State's cases against them. The binder included evidence that linked Littleton to over a dozen serial murders. That information was vital to Michael's defense. During his cross-examination of Solomon, Sherman asked for the documents. Judge Kavanewsky chided him for his timing. "Not right now," Kavanewsky told him. "You are talking about examining the witness." Sherman never renewed this request. Sherman apparently forgot to have the binder marked as an exhibit or placed in evidence. At Michael's 2013 *habeas* hearing, Sherman claimed that Judge Kavanewsky had looked angry at his request and that he didn't renew it out of fear of further provoking him. Sherman loved to be loved and that craving was ruinous to his client.

5. Solomon's binder also contained a report, co-authored by Garr, that stated unconditionally that the police knew Michael was at Sursum Corda at 10:00 p.m. This one sentence in the report could have saved Michael: "It is known and believed that as that vehicle departed from the driveway, occupied by the SKAKEL boys (Rushton, Michael and John) along with their cousin JAMES TERRIEN, that both HELEN IX and GEOFFREY BYRNE began to walk to their homes, leaving only THOMAS SKAKEL and MARTHA MOXLEY standing in the driveway."

This statement by Garr and Solomon would have provided the "independent observation, independent conclusion" about the Sursum Corda trip that Benedict argued persuasively did not exist. Sherman understood the critical importance of this statement. He explained to the Skakels that it "married" Garr and Solomon to the defense case. Then he forgot to move it into evidence. Sherman's failure to get this document before Michael's jury was, by itself, a glaring act of malpractice.

6. Sherman didn't prep his witnesses. He never provided my cousins with copies of their statements to police before they testified. It's nearly inconceivable that Sherman could have whiffed on this one. As a law professor who has taught trial practice for 30 years, I can attest that every textbook on trial advocacy stresses the critical importance for witnesses to review every prior interview, deposition, and statement before testifying. It's an essential part of witness preparation. In a case like this, where decades had passed and memories had dimmed since the witnesses made their original statements, review was particularly crucial. Since Michael was never a suspect, the trip to Sursum Corda was an inconsequential footnote that no one had any reason to recall with any clarity. With Michael's indictment, that trip suddenly became immensely consequential. All the witnesses should have pored over those early statements with Michael's attorney. It never happened. There was virtually no witness preparation. I spoke to John, Rush, Julie, and Jimmy, all of whom testified at trial. All independently told me that Sherman had never provided them with the 25-year-old police reports, statements, or interview transcripts to review. "Mickey never talked to any of us," Julie said. "The only time I went to Mickey's office was to tell him to shut his f-ing mouth and stop putting himself in the news. I told him his job was not to get Michael Skakel in the news every other day." According to Stephen, "A couple of us did ask to go over the testimony and Mickey told us, 'Don't worry about it.' Mickey said, 'Just tell the truth.' This is how Benedict was able to make such a big deal about Johnny's testimony." In 1998, my cousin John walked into his grand jury testimony blind. Sherman never showed him a scrap of paper. Michael paid dearly for that. In 1998, the one-man grand juror, Thim, had asked John what he remembered of a drunken, stoned night 23 years earlier. Understandably, John recalled virtually nothing. As he sat in the witness stand, Benedict provided him with his very first look at a transcript of his November 14, 1975, interview with police. John acknowledged that, while he had no specific recollection of any of it, his memory had probably been better two weeks after the crime. At trial, Benedict simply had John confirm his earlier testimony.

> BENEDICT: Do you recall testifying to the grand jury that about the best you could recall about October 30, 1975, was being part of a group that had gone to Terriens'?
> JOHN: Not specifically. I know that like here, I was presented with my testimony which I hadn't seen since—I had never seen before actually.

Had Sherman done his job, a review of his earlier statements would have reflected his recollection that his brother was in the car. Instead, Benedict made John look like he was dissembling—a fumbling performance bound to underwhelm the jury.

> BENEDICT: Is that your testimony today, that based on your recall here in the year 2002 and nothing else, that you just don't recall whether your brother, Michael, was in the car that went up to the Terriens?
>
> JOHN: That's right. I would love nothing more than to have clearer memory, but that's the way it is.

By not preparing his witness, Sherman provided an opening for Benedict to claim, as he did in his closing, that John was feigning lack of recall to avoid perjury. "Brother John missed the nail head completely when he testified . . . he somehow really can't remember everything or can't get the facts together anymore," Benedict told the jurors. "Ladies and gentlemen, for all people there are things in life that you are compelled to remember, that you have a need to keep forever straight in your mind no matter how far in the past they are, things that become indelible. When your cousin or brother is a suspect in a horrendous crime and you happened to have been involved with that person on the night of that crime, common sense tells us that you will retain the events of that night as though they were on videotape." Sherman's screw-up provided legs for Benedict's wild conspiracy theory that my cousins' initial statements to police were contrived in a family meeting in Windham in 1975, to alibi Michael. "What the evidence says the Skakels and Terriens have done . . . is intentionally suppress their memories and claim a lack of recall," Benedict said. "They spoke to the police in 1975. They were not under oath at the time. Certainly they were a lot more malleable then as 16- and 17-year-olds as they are now as adults. Certainly they are today a lot more aware of the consequences of lying."

7. Sherman careened through the trial like a drunk driver late for a guilty verdict. One of Sherman's most abysmal blunders was his failure to produce a non-family alibi witness to corroborate that Michael was at Sursum Corda on the night of the murder. Benedict exploited that gaffe as evidence of a family conspiracy. "Consider who the alibi witnesses are, all siblings or first cousins, not one single independent alibi witness." In my cousin Georgeann Dowdle's grand jury testimony four years earlier, she testified that on October 30, 1975, she was at home with her "beau," by whom she meant local restaurateur Dennis Ossorio. Sherman failed

to follow up on this crucial lead. Ossorio was now a widely respected 72-year-old psychologist, whose short relationship with Georgeann Dowdle ended decades before the trial. He had no conceivable reason to lie. Ossorio testified during Michael's *habeas* appeals, and repeated to me personally, that he came into the room and watched *Monty Python's Flying Circus* at Sursum Corda. Ossorio explained that while Georgeann was putting her daughter (from an early-life marriage) to bed, he spent time talking to Michael. Ossorio's testimony was convincing proof that Michael was miles away from Belle Haven between 9:30 p.m. and 11:30 p.m., the period during which overwhelming evidence demonstrated the crime occurred. Had Ossorio testified, jurors would have been much more likely to acquit Michael.

8. Sherman's third-party culpability defense was pathetic. Sherman was aware of the many suspects besides Kenny Littleton who could have committed the crime. He simply failed to follow any of the leads. "The theme of trial should have been all the people that are suspects here," Kenney Baden said. "There was a lot of possible suspects that simply weren't pointed out." These included John Moxley, Ed Hammond, Peter Ziluca, and Franz Wittine, none of whom were properly vetted by police. And then there was Tommy. The long police preoccupation with Tommy provided Michael with a powerful third-party culpability defense. Law enforcement's conviction that Tommy was the last person known to have seen Martha alive, combined with Tommy's lies about his whereabouts that evening, certainly could pose a source of reasonable doubt as to Michael's guilt. The Skakel family never asked Sherman to lay off Tommy. "I just told Mickey, 'Do what you gotta do,'" Michael told me. An attorney's duty is to vigorously pursue his client's acquittal. But Sherman never brought up Tommy at trial. He now says that he decided not to because he thought Tommy and Littleton provided each other bulletproof alibis, because of their time watching television together. If Sherman's choice was really the product of considered judgment, it would be a first.

9. Sherman could have called experts in memory manipulation and false confessions to obliterate the validity of any of Michael's Élan "confessions" and impeach Andrea Shakespeare's testimony. Michael relentlessly hammered this point to Sherman. Without expert testimony, he argued, people simply wouldn't understand the complex dynamics of Élan. After hearing that Michael was convicted based on things he said at Élan, therapeutic cult expert Richard Ofshe couldn't believe that Sherman hadn't called him. "At the risk of sounding immodest, I was the person in the country to go to on this," Ofshe says. "It would have

been impossible not to get to me." Following Michael's conviction, Ofshe approached Sherman at the premiere of a TV movie based on a case Ofshe had worked on—the false confession and exoneration of Michael Crowe, the 14-year-old San Diego teen accused of murdering his younger sister in 1998. "I told Mickey I thought it was ridiculous that he did not have someone who could speak with authority about what these environments are like," Ofshe says. "Without independent proof, you absolutely cannot put any stock in something that someone says in a setting like that. People would have confessed to anything there."

10. Sherman blew his summation. Considering Sherman's swashbuckling carriage and brassy self-promotion as a master of the drama and stagecraft of litigation, his closing arguments were a slow-motion train wreck. He began with an artless appeal to the jury's sympathy, using implausible imagery more appropriate coming from an underfunded public defender representing an indigent client than a highly paid lawyer for a family the jury perceived as multimillionaires. "We didn't have the high-tech delivery. You don't see the big fancy jury expert sitting at our table," Sherman said. "It's somewhat low key. It is me and three kids, and you can see we haven't given you any boutique defenses. We didn't bring in one expert. There is no memory expert; there is no dog expert."

Sherman's principal visual aid was a chart explaining the concept of reasonable doubt, the centerpiece foundation argument upon which every criminal defense lawyer in Anglo-American history has built their defense. Unfortunately, Sherman's offered a color-coded chart to calculate the percentage at which doubt becomes reasonable. A more experienced defense lawyer would have known that courts often frown upon—and routinely disallow—diagrams purporting to explain the concept of reasonable doubt. Judge Kavanewsky ruled the chart improper. Sherman was so rattled by the rejection that he neglected to make the reasonable doubt argument at all. It's astonishing. During his entire summation, Sherman never used the words "reasonable doubt."

The defense theory was that Kenny Littleton, not Michael, killed Martha. But Sherman seemed tentative, at best. Here was all the fire he could muster: "I am not here to say, you know, here is the guy who did it," he told the jury. "I am not here to persuade you that that's the guy." Sherman then soft-sold the fact that police found a hair microscopically similar to Littleton's at the crime scene: "Does that mean Ken Littleton did it?" he asked. "Damned if I know!" At the *habeas corpus* hearing, Bridgeport attorney Michael FitzPatrick, who himself had tried three death penalty cases, testified that he'd never seen anything like it. "Mr. Sherman did more damage to his client's defense than any piece of evidence that the prosecution presented," FitzPatrick told the appellate court. "These statements destroyed his third-party culpability defense. This is one of the poorest summations I have seen in my entire career."

Though Sherman suggested that there was some folksy gain in avoiding extravagances like expert witnesses and jury consultants, there's a more plausible explanation for his bare-bones strategy: Sherman would have had to deduct expert fees from his own paycheck. Up until December 2001, Sherman billed Rucky for his own hours and expenses, and for the hours of anyone else hired to work the case. Four months before trial, with the cost of Michael's defense spiraling out of control and the Skakels running aground financially, Sherman agreed to revisit the fee structure. In a letter to Michael dated December 5, 2001, Sherman proposed a much simpler payment plan. "My proposal to you is that I shall no longer bill you by the hour or for any legal fees, disbursements, or expenses or cost relating to your defense," he wrote. "I will accept a lump sum of $450,000, which I believe is a fair sum." He promised that the Skakels would not be nickeled and dimed any longer. This fee would cover everything he'd need to mount Michael's defense: experts, lawyers, investigators, expenses, everything. Rucky sold the Windham house to pay Sherman's bill. Rather than deposit that sum in the Skakel's client account, Sherman dumped it straight into the firm's operating account—essentially his own checking account.

He did not use the money to hire Ofshe or Loftus. Loftus charges $500 per hour for her time, plus travel expenses. Had Sherman done so, Michael may have kept his freedom and watched his son grow up. The month Sherman got his big check, he paid $54,000 cash for two new Jeeps for his grown children. They toured Greenwich in these trophy cars bought with Skakel money. Stephen has an encyclopedic knowledge of the case, but he didn't know this fact. A couple days after I shared it, he admitted it nearly caused him to drive his fist through a wall. Sherman promised to provide monthly statements on how he spent the $450,000, but he never provided the Skakels with any accounting. Following the trial, with Michael in prison for a crime he didn't commit, news items reported that the Skakels were stiffing attorneys who had worked for Michael's defense. Sherman wasn't paying his subordinates or subcontractors. Stephen wanted to throttle Sherman. He had to personally locate the court stenographer's house, show up on her doorstep, and drop off a check to obtain the trial transcripts Michael's appeals team desperately needed. Sherman had shafted her as well.

AT 10:30 a.m. on June 7, 2002, in Norwalk, after three days deliberating, jurors announced they had reached a verdict. As they filed in, the jurymen averted their eyes from Michael, looking instead toward Dorthy Moxley. "In file number FST CR00-135792 T., *State of Connecticut v. Michael Skakel*, what say you, Mr. Foreperson, is he guilty or not guilty of the crime of murder?" Kavanewsky asked. "Guilty," the foreman replied. A marshal cuffed Michael. Michael's brother David reached out to touch him. The marshal pushed him away. When Kavanewsky asked the lawyers if they had anything to say before he dismissed the jurors, Michael spoke up. "I'd like to say something," he said. "No sir!" Kavanewsky barked. In the time it took for jurors to read the verdict, Michael had become the most despised category of people in our society—a convicted murderer. As Garr, Benedict, and the Moxleys celebrated, Sherman addressed the cameras in front of the courthouse. "This is certainly the most upsetting verdict I have ever had or will ever have in my life," he declared. "But I will tell you that as long as there is a breath in my body, this case is not over as far as I'm concerned." By then, Michael was already en route to the prison, where they stripped him naked upon arrival for a cavity search. "What must Georgie be thinking?" was all Michael could think about. "I was supposed to be home hours ago to feed him." He would see his son, George, then 3, only a handful of times over the next 11½ years.

That night, Sherman and Benedict joined Dunne and Dorthy and John Moxley on *Larry King Live* for a cloying display of mutual admiration. It was a sickening kind of theater, both men pretending that Benedict had won the case fair and square on its merits. At least some of them knew the truth: Sherman had simply blown it through sheer incompetence. By then the Skakels understood what Sherman was: a colossal fraud. King asked Benedict to assess Sherman's courtroom performance. "Mickey gave an excellent argument, did a tremendous job confronting each and every witness," Benedict said. "I just don't think he had the evidence to pull off an acquittal." Later, King asked if Sherman thought that Benedict's closing won the case. "I don't know that the prosecutor's close won this," Sherman said. "And I think Jon doesn't believe that either. I think he did a hell of a job and I was the first one to shake his hand when he gave that argument. I agree with Jon Benedict when he says, it's evidence that wins it, and the people's perception of evidence. It's not the arguments themselves." Sherman offered a predictable response when King asked him what he and Michael had spoken about following the verdict. "Michael being Michael was very consoling to me," Sherman said. "I was a wreck. Still am a wreck. And Michael was saying, 'Don't worry. It's going to be okay.'"

During Michael's first weeks in prison, Sherman came to see him twice. "I screwed up on the jury selection," he told Michael. "Next time we'll pick a better jury." On his first visit, he gave interviews in front of Newtown's Garner Correctional Institute to reporters, whom someone had alerted. The prison guards made it painfully clear to Michael that they were angry at Sherman's showboating antics. Sherman's second visit only came after Michael's siblings called him and asked him why he hadn't gone back; Newtown was only an hour away from Greenwich. After that visit, Michael never saw Sherman again during his 11½ years behind bars.

Two months after the verdict, Sherman stared mournfully from Fairfield County's newsstands; his full-length portrait graced *Greenwich* magazine's cover. Sherman posed on a beach on Long Island Sound, wearing a black suit with a navy blue T-shirt underneath, a funereal token to Don Johnson's *Miami Vice* look. "Skakel Verdict Haunts His Lawyer Mickey Sherman" read the headline. Mickey offered no real mea culpa. All of his powers as an attorney, he said, couldn't overcome the perception that Michael was a "spoiled brat"; his conviction had been a *fait accompli* from the moment Michael wore the "ascot" to his arraignment. In Sherman's 2008 memoir, he barely mentioned Michael's case, but he did get back cover blurbs from Dunne and Nancy Grace, the two most vocal members of the pitchfork brigade.

In March 2011, Sherman reported to a minimum-security federal prison camp in Otisville, New York, to begin serving a one year and one day sentence on charges of tax evasion. He'd failed to pay $420,710 in taxes for 2001 and 2002, the years the Skakels were paying him. He'd had years of warnings before being sent away; the IRS had been trying, and failing, to collect taxes from Sherman since 1997. Rather than pay what he owed, he spent more than $20,000 a year on dues and expenses at Stamford's Rockrimmon Country Club. He paid $120,000 annually to finance his ex-wife's mortgage on their Stamford mansion. In just the year 2000, he paid almost $100,000 for her American Express bill. He heeded none of the many IRS warnings to curb his spending. According to a government sentencing memo, Sherman's tax attorney "told the revenue officer that there was a better chance of a Martian landing than getting the defendant Sherman to make estimated tax payments." Three years before Sherman pleaded guilty, he watched his partner Joe Richichi fork over $1.4 million in back taxes and penalties to the IRS and receive his own 16-month tax evasion prison sentence. (Richichi died of cancer in 2014.) Richichi's prison bid didn't scare Sherman straight. "How can an experienced criminal defense lawyer, who some might consider to be reasonably intelligent, have screwed myself up so bad?" Sherman asked a reporter shortly after his release from prison. "I ask the same question every night at about four in the morning. I don't have an answer."

The Skakel family gave Mickey Sherman the gift for which every defense lawyer yearns: a career case representing a genuinely innocent paying client. They paid him $2.2 million to save Michael Skakel from unjust imprisonment—and a half million dollars more to his subcontracted lawyers. Sherman squandered that fortune and sacrificed Michael on the altar of his ego.

PART VII

The Ghosts

CHAPTER 21

The Killers?

I know what happened to your cousin. He got screwed. He really did.
I wouldn't wish that on anybody.

—Tony Bryant

The three-page single-spaced letter rolled out of *The Atlantic's* office fax machine early in 2003, not long after the magazine published my article about Michael's trial. My editor forwarded it to me. The writer opened with a provocative line. "Unless I've been lied to, the jury got it all wrong."

I'm accustomed to receiving letters from strangers. Over the past 60 years, I've received many thousands. Most of them come from admirers of my family. Occasionally I get hate mail, even death threats, often from people with emotional disabilities. I'm familiar with the tiny script, the wobbly letters, the stories about secret cousins and dark conspiracies. The fax from Crawford "Tres" Mills had none of these qualities. I couldn't assume his story was true, but its writer appeared solid and sane.

"I went to school with Michael Skakel," Crawford wrote. "I think we met when I was 13 and didn't see much of him after Martha Moxley was killed the next year." Crawford's prose was florid, but his references were all legitimate and verifiable. Crawford identified himself as a classmate of Michael Skakel at Brunswick. He recounted that two years earlier following Michael's arrest and while his trial was pending, Crawford's friend Tony Bryant confided in him that he had been in Belle Haven on Mischief Night in 1975. Tony claims he was with two chums from a Manhattan public high school who, that evening, murdered Martha Moxley.

"Tony's full name is Gitano Bryant," Mills wrote. "More than one Bryant has had successful fields in the NBA. Tony's brother Wallace played for the Mavericks. His cousin Kobe plays for the L.A. Lakers."

During his Brunswick years, Mills had met the men whom Tony fingered as the killers. He knew them only as "Adolph" and "Burr." Both of them subsequently confessed to Tony their roles in killing Martha. Except for his mother, Tony told no one the secret for 27 years. But Michael's indictment prompted Tony to recount his tale to Crawford. Tony wanted Crawford to take the information about Adolph and Burr to the police, but he begged Crawford not to identify him as the source. Tony was married with four young children and was living in Florida, where he was president of a tobacco company. Tony felt he needed to keep a low profile to protect his family and his business. Having brought the two murderers to Greenwich in 1975, Tony, who is African American, feared becoming a suspect himself. He had shared what he knew of the events of October 1975 with his mother soon after Martha's murder. She was particularly fearful that Tony's skin color would make him an attractive target for law enforcement.

After reading Crawford's letter, I picked up the phone. My call took him by surprise. "So, you got my fax?" With his permission, I recorded our conversation. Crawford said he had told this tale to Mickey Sherman, Jonathan Benedict, Frank Garr, Dorthy Moxley, and many others prior to Michael's trial. No one was interested. Over the next several weeks, I would track down and talk to Tony Bryant and the two men he said were Martha's killers. I confirmed and corroborated Crawford's story and became convinced along the way that Adolph and Burr murdered Martha Moxley. I turned the information over to Michael's new lawyers, who included it as the gravamen of their motion for a new trial. At least one judge was also persuaded by the evidence, which triggered a chain of events that helped lead to Michael's release on a *habeas corpus* petition 11½ years after his conviction. Crawford ultimately testified at Michael's new trial hearing, at which I also testified. The evidence against Adolph and Burr is far more compelling than any evidence the state had against Michael or any other suspect. In my opinion, that evidence suggests that the two men are guilty beyond a reasonable doubt. Yet, state officials are still focused on keeping Michael in prison, instead of catching the real killers.

TONY BRYANT attended Brunswick from 1972 until 1975, where he became best friends with Crawford Mills. The third member of their trio was another Brunswick classmate, Neal Walker, who was Michael Skakel's Belle Haven neighbor, son of Beetle Bailey cartoonist Mort Walker and brother to Martha Moxley's friend Margie Walker.

Years after the murder, Tony graduated from the University of Houston and the University of Tennessee Law School, and then moved to Los Angeles and worked briefly in the entertainment industry. Tony wrote several screenplays, including one that aired on television. The two Greenwich boys stayed in touch with Tony after college. They saw him periodically for dinner in New York and at parties in Connecticut. They chatted by phone on birthdays and holidays.

In the late 1980s, Crawford began writing a screenplay called *Little Martha* based on the Moxley murder. Crawford told me that he crafted fictional composite characters to make a statement about the town of Greenwich. Although he did not identify any of his protagonists by their real names, the script "pointed the finger" at Tommy and Kenny Littleton as the likely culprits. Tony called Crawford two weeks after the September 11, 2001, World Trade Center attacks to check up on his East Coast friend, who lived two blocks from Ground Zero. During that conversation, Crawford told Tony about his screenplay. Tony offered to read the script, telling his friend he "had some experience in the industry." Crawford sent him his latest version.

Just after Christmas 2001, Tony finished reading the screenplay and called Crawford to discuss it. During that conversation, Tony told Crawford that none of the Skakels had been involved in Martha's killing. Tony explained that he had been at the murder scene that night and he knew that Adolph and Burr had killed Martha. By this time, Connecticut had indicted Michael. His trial was four months away.

Crawford recalled Adolph and Burr from a Greenwich block party in September 1975. Both of the boys were unusually big, muscular, and tall. Crawford described Adolph to me as "psychotic." Crawford was stunned by Tony's revelation and abandoned any thought of working with Tony on the screenplay. The wrong man was about to go on trial. Crawford told Tony that they needed to go to the police with the story. Tony agreed—he wanted the truth revealed—but he feared being implicated. "Keep my name out of this," he begged Crawford. "Promise me." The second he hung up, Crawford called his father for advice. Following his dad's recommendation, Crawford called Michael's attorney. In reciting Tony's story to Sherman, Crawford withheld only Tony's name. He did tell Sherman, however, that Tony was "black and at Brunswick." Armed with that information, a minimally curious defense attorney could have quickly tracked down Tony; only two African Americans attended Brunswick in 1975. Sherman was noncommittal. At that moment, he was preening in the spotlight of the impending legal battle. Following Crawford's phone call, Sherman coyly asked Michael if he "knew a Crawford Mills." Michael replied that Mills was a Brunswick classmate, and asked why. Sherman's response was dismissive. "Oh, he's just another guy trying to capitalize on the Moxley murder . . . he's got some crazy—you know, crazy play—*Little Martha* or something." Sherman never disclosed Crawford's allegation, and never again mentioned Crawford to Michael.

With no action from Sherman, Crawford turned to Garr and Benedict. Neither seemed eager to hear evidence that might exculpate Michael Skakel on the eve of their high-profile trial. Crawford sent three letters to the prosecutor with the same information he had given Sherman. He told me that he called Benedict over a dozen times. "He wasn't interested," Crawford said. "He told me the story didn't match up with witness statements." Unless Crawford revealed Tony's name, Benedict intended to do nothing. Crawford then told Benedict that his informant was one of only two African Americans who attended Brunswick in 1975. Crawford suggested that Benedict would only need to look at a yearbook to learn his name. But Benedict displayed no interest in undertaking new investigative work. Crawford wrote letters to Mrs. Moxley and received no response. He enlisted Neal's sister, Margie, to write to Dorthy Moxley, but Margie fared no better. Crawford had hit an impenetrable barrier. He couldn't understand why no one was interested. "Mrs. Moxley had been screaming for 20 years for someone to come forward with information, but now she didn't want to hear from me," Crawford said. "No one was interested."

After their initial conversation over Christmas 2001, Crawford regularly updated Tony on his infuriating saga of official stonewalling. Crawford begged his friend to allow him to use his name, but "Tony refused to come forward and tried to make me understand how important it was to keep his name out of this story. It seemed he was endeavoring to do the right thing but only to the point where his name was left out of it." Tony's fears were not misplaced. In 2006 and in 2009, seven black and Hispanic officers sued the Greenwich Police Department for institutionalized racism, citing promotion discrimination, targeting black residents for false arrest, and routine use of racial slurs by officers. In January 2002, Crawford contacted Neal and asked him to encourage their mutual friend to step up. "I was not a great friend of Michael," Crawford told Neal, "but I feel this is an injustice, seeing him being tried for this murder that he didn't commit." Neal had been Tony's closest friend in Brunswick's Class of 1979, and Tony frequently visited Neal's home after leaving the school.

Neal, who also remembered meeting Adolph and Burr, was particularly intrigued because Crawford's story involved Geoff Byrne, with whom Neal had been very close. Neal called Tony, who fleshed out the story, and implored Tony to go to the prosecutors, but he steadfastly refused. "I might be implicated," he said. Tony cautioned Neal not to reveal his name. Short of that, he urged Neal to do everything he could to alert the authorities, "but to keep his name out of it." Neal first spoke to Tim Dumas, author of *Greentown: Murder and Mystery in Greenwich, America's Wealthiest Community.* Dumas was only mildly interested and made no effort to follow up. Neal then called Garr, disgorging Tony's story without impact on the single-minded detective. After hitting that brick wall, Neal tried, unsuccessfully, to reach Sherman. By now, Margie was also barraging Tony with pleas to come forward.

On April 8, 2002, just as Michael's trial was beginning in Norwalk, Margie visited Garr at his office in the Norwalk courthouse and told him the story in person; Benedict attended that meeting. Margie finally revealed Tony Bryant's name to them. She impressed upon both of them that "this was a real person that we knew, that had been in the neighborhood, had knowledge of the neighborhood, and it wasn't a made-up story." Neither man pursued the lead. A few weeks later, they celebrated Michael's conviction. Soon after meeting with Garr, Margie provided Sherman with a detailed background of her relationship to Tony. Sherman reacted with now-familiar indifference. Margie recounted, "I felt that they really weren't interested in hearing more about it or investigating," she told me.

Tony called Crawford after the trial began to ask who he had contacted. "He knew that some people would want to get in touch with him," Crawford told me. "I think both of us were amazed that nobody had." Even the *New York Times,* which had been following Michael's trial, wouldn't return Crawford's calls. "I felt like an idiot, like no one would listen to me," Crawford told me in 2003. "This is the first time I have heard of anyone saying they have done it, and yet no one wants to hear about it. It's been frustrating for me, and I'm sure it's been horrible for your family as well."

Crawford was then working as an audio technician at CBS. In spring 2002, the Monday following Michael's conviction, he found himself miking up Mrs. Moxley in preparation for her appearance on *The Early Show* with Bryant Gumbel. While attaching her lapel mike, he introduced himself as the guy who had been sending her all the letters about Tony Bryant. Mrs. Moxley stared at him blankly. "She didn't seem to have any knowledge of this story at all," Crawford told me. He quickly provided a thumbnail sketch of Tony's allegation. "Mrs. Moxley, I don't think Michael did it," he told her. She remained stone-faced. "I know Michael did it," she responded. Sherman also appeared on the CBS show that morning. Crawford next introduced himself to Michael's counselor, waiting his turn in the CBS greenroom. Characteristically, Sherman gave Crawford short shrift. As Sherman left the greenroom for makeup, Mrs. Moxley was angrily reporting Crawford to the show's producer. Moments later, Crawford was unemployed. Security guards ejected him from the building in the classic bum's rush.

Immediately after being fired, Crawford called Tony. It was now after the verdict but prior to Michael's sentencing. Crawford, who had lost his own job in the cause of justice, told his friend it was time to come clean. Tony replied, "I'm very sorry that happened to you, but there is no way I'm going to do that." Crawford threw down an ultimatum: "I'm going to out you." Crawford gave

Tony's name to Benedict, to Garr, to Sherman, and to Tim Dumas. He wrote a detailed, four-page summary of Tony's story and faxed it to Benedict on June 8, 2002. "I've tried to give you this information before and it doesn't fit with the way you think things went down," he wrote Benedict. "No one has ever interviewed the guy I told you about—to this day . . . I still can't find a motivation for his confessing a lie. Hey, you should at least give the guy a call." A couple days later, Benedict passed the fax along with a snarky note to Sherman. "Enclosed is the first, but most likely not the last, of post-verdict tips."

The newly unemployed Crawford even wrote a letter to Judge John Kavanewsky. He called the *New York Times* and finally talked to one reporter who had been covering the Skakel trial. According to Crawford, the *Times* reporter responded with a "very polite" yawn. Throughout the summer of 2002 Crawford continued his crusade. No one responded to his deluge of calls and letters. Then, in February 2003, his sister sent him a copy of my January–February 2003 *Atlantic* article. Crawford faxed me a one-page summary, via *The Atlantic*, on February 6, 2003. I called immediately. "I got a phone call from Mr. Kennedy out of the blue," Crawford told the court in Michael's 2007 petition for a new trial.

AFTER TALKING to Crawford, I called Tony in Florida. I had no idea if any of Crawford's story was true, but I meant to find out. When I identified myself, he exhaled, "I've been waiting 27 years for this call." Tony agreed to speak again the next day. In that conversation and in three taped conversations that followed, Tony gave me an even more detailed account of October 30, 1975, than he had to Crawford or Neal.

In my first brief call, Tony told me only that he had known Michael at Brunswick School. "Michael and I have a stormy past. I am not his best friend . . . I am not a friend trying to help a friend. What I am is a person who knows what happened." He later described himself and Michael as "adversaries." He explained that he had been reluctant to come forward, fearing repercussions to his family, who were prominent in the African American community. "I have certain relatives that would not like any type of publicity concerning this thing that happened in Greenwich and any connection to it. That would be very bad for them and, actually, very bad for me."

Tony wasn't just referring to his NBA brother and cousin. Tony's mother, Barbara Bryant, is an Academy Award–winning educational films producer and a cofounder and executive vice president of the Phoenix Learning Group, a production company for children's programming. "Tony came from a family with a lot of aspirations," Barbara's friend Esme Dick told me later. "Barbara had two or three degrees." In 1973, she cofounded Phoenix, with Heinz Gelles, a Holocaust survivor and former McGraw-Hill executive; in 1985, Barbara Bryant won an

Academy Award for producing the short film *Molly's Pilgrim,* making her the first black person and the first woman to win an Oscar in that category. "Nevertheless," he told me, "I want to do what I can to help. Because I know, I know what happened to your cousin. He got screwed. He really did. I feel really bad for him. . . . He is innocent. He is innocent. You are talking about somebody being screwed and, you know . . . I am not a very loving or caring person but I feel very bad for his situation because I wouldn't wish that on anybody."

I brought my findings to Michael's appeals team. Attorneys Seeley and Santos set me up with Vito Colucci, who had been Sherman's investigator. Colucci interviewed me and Crawford. In July 2003, Colucci called Tony and asked if he could to come down to Florida to see him. Tony was reluctant. First he agreed to a meeting date, and then he cancelled at the last minute. He consented and cancelled again. It was a nail-biter. His reticence was understandable. In our interview, Tony had placed himself in Belle Haven at the crime scene on the night of the murder, with a Skakel golf club in his hand. Finally, Colucci got him to stick to a date—August 24. Tony kept Colucci and his co-investigator, Al Dressler, waiting for hours, but he finally showed up to their Wyndham Hotel room in Coconut Grove. Dressler set up the video camera, and in a little over an hour, Tony told the entire story almost exactly as he'd told me. When Colucci probed and challenged him, he never wavered. I've seen the range of witnesses who take the stand. Tony comes off as credible. (The interview is available on YouTube, by searching "Tony Bryant interview.")

At the time of Martha's murder, Tony was 14 years old and living in New York City, where he attended Charles Evans Hughes High School. However, for the previous two school years, from fall 1973 until June 1975, Tony attended Brunswick, which had recruited him during a diversity push. His mother lived in Chicago, so Tony stayed in the Greenwich home of a family friend, Esme Dick. Dick befriended Barbara Bryant through her work as head of the Educational Film Library Association, which ran a documentary film festival. Dick's husband, Bill, was assistant principal and Latin teacher at Brunswick.

At Michael's new trial hearing, Tony's classmates recalled him as an immensely popular student who excelled in baseball and basketball and who was the school's standout football star. Crawford described Tony as a "very friendly, easy going, kind person who I don't recall ever saying a mean word about anybody." Even though he was the shrimp of his family—his older brother Wallace was seven foot one—at 13, Tony was, at six foot one, one of the biggest kids in his class. Crawford, who would top out at six foot five, was even bigger than Tony. Crawford broke down the clique barriers at Brunswick. Because of his size, he played football, but his real love was theater. He was crazy about singing and acting. He and Tony and Neal became bosom buddies. Greenwich newcomer Martha Moxley was among Tony's Belle Haven friends.

Tony was a mediocre student and a boys' boy who loved mischief. Some of his classmates called him "Stoney" because of his affection for pot. In 1973, when he was 12, Greenwich Police busted Tony for breaking into a house.

In the summer of 1975, at age 14, Tony decided that he wanted to live with his mother, who had recently relocated to a Manhattan apartment. It was too late to get into private school, so he enrolled in Charles Evans Hughes High School.

After moving to New York, Tony continued to socialize with many of his old Greenwich chums. Neal testified under oath that he, Tony, Crawford, and their friend Geoff Byrne remained particularly close and that Tony frequently took the train up to visit Greenwich. Both Neal and Tony testified that Tony often stayed overnight at their homes. Neal said that Tony had been to his house "20 to 30 times." Tony's mother confirmed that when Tony stayed in Greenwich overnight, he would visit Neal. These boys were all friendly with Martha, who frequently mentions Tony, Neal, Crawford, and Geoff in her diaries. During his trips to Greenwich, Tony would sometimes see Michael, although they were not close friends. Michael's little brother David recalls Tony as a fairly regular visitor at the Skakel house.

At Charles Evans Hughes, Tony made fast friends with two of his new classmates, Adolph and Burr. In 1975, Adolph and Burr were 15 years old, a year older than Tony, and very large for their age. Adolph, a volatile teen from the South Bronx, was African American, six foot three inches tall, and 200 pounds. Burr, who Tony reckoned to be of Asian/American Indian/Caucasian ancestry, was of similar height and build. He hailed from the Pacific Northwest and was living with his brother in the Soho section of Lower Manhattan. Adolph and Burr were inseparable. "They were like twins that were joined at the hip," Tony told me. "They were never apart. You saw one, you saw the other." Tony described Adolph as very strong and unpredictable. Both were "wild." Adolph, in particular, "was crazy; absolutely nuts." But the pair had a dangerous synergistic dynamic. "They spurred each other on. They fed off each other big time," Tony told me.

He described Charles Evans Hughes as a "tough school." Unlike Brunswick, it was not an academic stronghold. "This was a city school in New York. We are not talking about Greenwich. . . . There's no Boy Scouts at this school." Adolph, Tony said "developed a reputation not to be someone to mess with." Tony told Colucci, "Oh, you could tell. You could say a lot of kids were afraid of him, because he was big and he was explosive." And while Burr did not share Adolph's volatile temperament, he often served as the "gasoline" that fueled Adolph's "engine." Burr goaded Adolph to do things such as throwing bricks at moving cars, burglarizing buildings, and similar acts of vandal. "It was always the dare between them. They were always trying to outdo each other. And they would just push each other." Tony described Adolph as dangerously reckless, "Anything you dared Adolph to do, he would do." Then added, "There was something wrong with him. All you had to do was look at him to know it." Tony recalled that when the Charles Evans Hughes athletic coach began developing a wrestling team, Adolph was the guy he "really had pegged as being aggressive enough, having the demeanor, and having the killer instinct to be a good wrestler." Although Tony was unusually big and tall for his age and a champion athlete, Adolph, he said, "could pin me with no problem."

In one of our later conversations, I asked Tony why, if Adolph was so dangerous and mercurial, he had nevertheless associated with him. Tony responded that, as a rebellious adolescent in 1975—he was only 14—it was precisely those aspects of Adolph's persona that had attracted him. "You have to understand, at that point in our lives that was what I was attracted to. He was a rebel. He was dangerous. He was fearless, in terms of, like, doing, I mean, you could dare him to do anything and he would do it. Anything. We, you know, we were into being athletes and smoking weed and drinking beer and chasing girls."

The two accompanied Tony to Belle Haven five or six times between mid-September and October 30, 1975. Tony told me, "Imagine coming from the inner city into Greenwich in the mid-70s. That is the difference between Beirut and Cape Cod. It's the difference between have and have-nots. It's that the whole concept that we are dealing with is forbidden fruit here, big time. Big time."

Martha's diary recalls that she met Tony through Neal the previous January. Adolph and Burr first met Martha at a United Way block party on September 20, 1975. The street fair was a milestone social event in Greenwich attended by over 12,000 people. Virtually every resident of Belle Haven was there, including Martha, who described in her diary wandering the festival with Helen, Neal, Crawford, Geoff, and Michael.

From his first sight of Martha that day, Adolph became infatuated with her. Although he was too awkward to make direct overtures, he became "obsessed" with Martha. According to Tony, he "had this thing for her" and Adolph "would just say things that were just really, looking back, you would just be, oh my God, why didn't I say something, and it just, it bothers me." Tony told me that Adolph met Martha again, once or twice, at church mixers that fall. Tony was familiar with the dances from his Brunswick days, and attended them with his New York City friends and Neal, at the Sacred Heart girls' school. On at least one occasion, Martha was there. Tony explained that Adolph "would make gestures at her, but . . . he didn't have the confidence" to pursue a serious friendship with her. "He wasn't a sophisticated person. He was very immature. She was always sort of cordial, but she sort of brushed him off real kind of nicely. She would never say, 'Get out of my face.' She was really just, you know, 'Hey, we're all friends here.' She wasn't a person who would let you down hard."

On October 4, 1975, Martha recalled the dance in her diary: "Tonight was a Sacred Heart dance. I went w/ Margie & Jackie." Martha specifically mentioned seeing Neal and Tony at the dance. She wrote that two strangers were there with Tony and Neal, and one of them had approached her when she entered. "When we walked in some guy asked me to dance. It was 'Stairway to Heaven.' At the fast part he wouldn't even let go!" Tony recalled how, at that same mixer, Adolph became jealous of other boys talking to Martha. Adolph told Tony, "I don't understand why she's spending her time with those guys when she could be with me." Tony explained that while Adolph didn't know how to cultivate a relationship with Martha, he would talk about her constantly in a sexually explicit manner.

Fantasies of Martha mesmerized Adolph, whether he was in Greenwich or Manhattan. Tony recalls that he "talked about her, and that was Adolph's main focus. From the time he met her until the murder, that's what he would talk about," Tony recalled. Throughout October, Adolph's infatuation with Martha "built up with him, it built up tremendous." Adolph would make comments about Martha even when they were not visiting Greenwich. "During the week if we weren't going to Greenwich, he would sort of mention it, you know, a couple times: 'Yeah, I really like her. She's pretty, blah, blah, blah.' But if we were going to Greenwich, it would just, just really be exacerbated. I mean, just really hyped up. He loved her beautiful blond hair. He was completely, completely intrigued with this woman—I think obsessed. We just started laughing and, you know, saying, 'You need to think about something else. You need to think about somebody else that is more obtainable, because it is not going to happen. She's not even interested in you.'" But Adolph would reply, "She likes me," and vowed that it was "going to happen." Occasionally, he would use a more menacing tone, promising "I'm going to have her." Burr, in contrast, would encourage Adolph in his fantasy. "No, you can do it," Burr would say. "You can get her."

As time went on, Adolph became more explicit. Tony recalls that for a month before the murder, his expressions devolved into vulgar and graphic aspirations. "I want to fuck the shit out of her," Adolph told Tony. He predicted he would "just take her, grab her, and have her the way he wanted her." On several occasions he said he wanted "to go caveman on her." Tony said that Adolph took the "going caveman" concept from *The Flintstones* cartoon. "Going caveman" meant hitting a woman on the head, grabbing her by the hair, dragging her off to the bushes, and sexually assaulting her.

ON THURSDAY, October 30, 1975, Tony, Adolph, and Burr took the train from Manhattan to Greenwich for Mischief Night. "Greenwich is sort of famous for Hell Night, all the pranks and stuff," Tony said. During the 50-minute train ride to Connecticut, Adolph and Burr talked about "going caveman" on someone that night. They arrived at the Greenwich station at around 5:30 p.m. and hiked to Belle Haven, arriving at Neal's house at approximately 6:30 p.m. By then, it was dark outside. A hundred yards away, Martha was leaving her house for an evening of mischief. The Walkers had just sat down for dinner. Neal had homework and, as with Crawford's mother, his mother was reluctant to allow either Neal or Margie out of the house on Mischief Night. "Neal told me to come back," Tony recalled. "He said he would catch up with us later." So the boys went next door to pilfer booze. (Tony explained that "[i]n Belle Haven you can go and open up people's refrigerators in their garage and take their beer.") Tony said they took about three six-packs that night, "maybe a little more . . . and we also had marijuana." Thus provisioned, the trio hiked across the dark street to Geoff's house. Geoff, who was already friendly with Adolph and Burr, was free from the tyrannies of parental supervision: his father traveled constantly and his mother was largely inattentive. Geoff readily joined the boys in their vandalism spree. "We started going around playing pranks," said Tony. The teens drank a six-pack and smoked marijuana while they roamed Belle Haven, toilet-papering trees, smashing pumpkins, and throwing eggs.

Throughout the evening, Adolph and Burr continued to talk about meeting girls in the neighborhood. "Where are the bitches?" they asked Tony. "We've just got to get into something." Adolph pledged, "I'm not going out of here unsatisfied." The boys walked to the Belle Haven Club, at the far south end of Belle Haven near Long Island Sound, and looked for familiar cars in the parking lot. "We went to the yacht club. We didn't go in. We just looked to see who was there by the cars and stuff." At that time, the Skakel children and their tutor were just finishing dinner.

Tony and his pals ambled back toward the Skakel house, resuming their delinquent rampage and picking up reinforcements. "We picked up people all along the way. So it could have been maybe at best six people. We'd smash some pumpkins. We threw toilet paper over the lines. We set it on fire. We shaved and soaped up some windows." They would interrupt their marauding and duck into the woods or behind stone walls to dodge Belle Haven's roaming security patrol. "The policeman. I can't remember his name exactly. We would position ourselves because we knew when he made his rounds. We would sort of hide off and go up behind the walls or up into the bushes so he couldn't see."

From the Belle Haven Yacht Club they hiked back to the Skakels' property, arriving at "The Mead" around "8:30 or 8:45." The Mead, or "the meadow," as it was otherwise known, was a five-acre refuge of field, trees, and bushes on the Skakel property. The Mead meandered northeast from the Skakels' back porch and included the Skakels' chipping range, toolshed, swimming pool, tennis court, and the meadows, woodland, and a small orchard in between. Six Belle Haven houses, including the Skakel house, the Byrne mansion, and the Ix home, backed up to the Mead, where young people in the neighborhood congregated to smoke and drink without being seen by the prying Belle Haven security guard. Tony explained to Colucci that the meadow was a "collection place for kids to sit and smoke cigarettes and marijuana and drink beer" because "the parents couldn't see" back there. According to Tony, "It was a big enough space so if someone did come a bit close, you could scatter and run, and no one could catch you." At Michael's new trial hearing, Helen confirmed that Tony accurately described the Mead and its function as a neighborhood hideout for Belle Haven's young delinquents. Rucky Skakel Sr. maintained a chipping range behind his house from which guests could hit golf balls up through the Mead. Several weeks before Martha's murder, Rucky had sponsored a chipping tournament for 100 Mitsubishi Company executives. Detritus from that event remained scattered about the lawn. Michael, David, and Tommy all recall that the golf clubs, baseball bats, lacrosse sticks, footballs, and soccer gear that perpetually littered the area were moved only when landscapers mowed the lawn. Sometimes the sports gear stayed all winter. Helen confirmed that the Mead was cluttered with golf clubs, sporting equipment, toys, and even clothes.

In the days following the murder, Steven Hartig of 180 Otter Rock Drive, told Detective Lunney that he had seen a group of unfamiliar teenagers, 14 to 16 years old, congregating near the Skakel property on Walsh Lane only a short distance from Martha's driveway around 8:15 p.m., when he was returning from work in New York City. Hartig described the gang of youths "standing on the shoulder area of the dead-end section of Walsh Lane closest to the Skakel property." The teens were loitering a few feet from the Skakels' golf tee and near the boundary of the Mead where Tony places himself and his six companions at that time. Although he was a longtime Belle Haven resident, Hartig didn't recognize the teenagers. Helen, Jackie, and Martha, whom Tony recalls seeing, also spent that part of the evening in the same area around the back and side of the Skakel property, throwing toilet paper in the trees.

"When we were coming back to the Mead," Tony remembers, "there were other refrigerators that we knew on the way back, so we collected more beer. Probably, when we got to that meadow, we probably had another . . . two six-packs," Tony told Colucci, "I had a good buzz. Not slightly buzzed, I would say lightly drunk. Adolph and Burr? Lightly drunk. We had smoked some marijuana and we had also drank." The three boys spent the rest of the evening in the vicinity of the Mead stoked on weed and at least three six-packs of beer with Adolph and Burr escalating their banter about "going caveman" and expressing their resolve not to leave Belle Haven "unsatisfied."

At precisely the time Tony recalls arriving back at the Skakel Mead (8:30 p.m. to 8:45 p.m.), Michael and his family returned to the Skakel house from their Belle Haven Club dinner. The boys in Tony's group picked up golf clubs that were lying on the grass and started fooling around with them. Tony had previously told me, "I was surprised that they didn't get my prints off those clubs." As they wandered across the Skakel lawn, everyone in Tony's group grabbed a golf club. "I picked up one. Burr picked up one. Adolph picked up one. Geoff picked up one. And we were, like, goofing around. . . . I had swung it and I put mine down. I didn't even put it down; I slung it back to where the bag—there was like a bag that was sort of lying there and so I slung it back toward the bag. Adolph and Burr were using them as sort of like walking sticks."

In 1997 Michael gave a tape-recorded interview to author Richard Hoffman and recounted that at 8:45 p.m. on the night of the murder, soon after he had returned from the Belle Haven Club, he was handing cold Heinekens to his cousin Jimmy and to his brother John as they sat on the back porch overlooking the meadow, playing backgammon. Michael noticed a group of "large guys" brazenly walking through the golf tees alongside the pool. They were barely visible in the light from the house. Michael pointed out the gang to Jimmy and John with some alarm, "Hey, who are those guys?" Jimmy and John, focused on the board game, hardly looked up. "Who gives a fuck!" Jimmy said. Michael said he would have gone out alone to confront the trespassers but was intimidated by their large size. This is precisely the time window during which Tony places himself and his large friends in the Skakel yard. It's impossible to corroborate Michael's recollection, because, since that day in December 1998 when Garr illegally seized the tapes from Hoffman's house, Benedict's office has steadfastly refused to return them to either Michael or his attorneys, or even provide them copies.

Tony reported looking up at the Skakel house and thinking that there was a party. The only time that there was a large crowd at the Skakels' was around 8:45 p.m. after the six Skakel cousins, Littleton, and Andrea Shakespeare returned from the Club and before the boys left to see *Monty Python*.

Thereafter, Adolph and Burr walked around wielding their golf clubs like walking sticks, telling Tony that they had their "caveman stick," and that they were going to "grab somebody and pull them by the hair and do what cavemen do." Adolph and Burr promised each other, "I'm going to get me a girl." There were just a few people in the Mead when Tony and his posse arrived, between 8:30 and 8:45 p.m. The teenagers were talking, drinking, rolling joints, and smoking cigarettes.

Tony recalls many of the Belle Haven residents he saw that night, including Martha, who, he said, joined them in the meadow for a time. "We saw Josh [Ingals] that night. He had gotten into trouble, so he got grounded and he couldn't really hang with us that night." Tony also saw Helen Ix and Lisa Rader Edwards and a few other Belle Haven girls, and he waved to Julie, who, according to her usual practice, did not stay in the meadow to socialize. He also recalls seeing Tommy and Michael, although neither of the Skakel boys recall seeing him. When asked 27 years after the fact, Helen, Lisa, and Julie do not remember seeing him. It's quite possible he saw them without being seen. The area around the Skakel home was illuminated from the house lights and by floodlights that hung on the back porch, on the side kitchen door, and in a grove of apple trees near the pool. On October 30, it was dark by 6:00 p.m. with overcast skies. So the meadow would have appeared pitch black to the Skakel children and their pals hanging out in the driveway. They, on the other hand, would have been visible to the kids congregating in the Mead. By about 9:00 p.m., Adolph and Burr, inebriated and "out of control," began making sexually charged comments to some of the girls. Their boorish vulgarity made the girls uncomfortable. Tony, who considered himself their friend, felt awkward. Brandishing the Skakel golf clubs, Adolph and Burr worked themselves into a frenzy. Tony said, "It was loud. It was very, very rowdy. They had embarrassed some of the girls that had come into the circle. Just making comments about, just like sexual overtures and stuff. It was uncomfortable. And I knew those girls. Martha was one of the girls that was there. I think she got fed up with what was going on and she went over to a group that was sort of standing over by the Skakel house." This would have been around the time that Martha, Helen, and Geoff joined Michael and Tommy in the Lincoln Continental. Shortly afterward, Tommy and Martha would disappear for their dalliance behind the toolshed, an area Tommy recalls as dimly lit.

As the Belle Haven kids migrated away from the Mead, due to curfews or to escape their crude antics, Adolph and Burr became increasingly frustrated and out of control. "Where are the bitches?" they were now demanding. "We've just got to get into something." Tony describes their state as desperate, reckless, and dangerous. According to Tony, Adolph kept repeating, "I'm going to get me a girl!" and "I've got my caveman club" and "I'm going to grab somebody and pull them by the hair and do what cavemen do" and "I'm gonna get some of that." Tony remembers the frantic mood: "It's around 9 o'clock. I know I was buzzing. This was Hell Night and everybody is excited. The purpose of Hell Night is to do destruction to property and to vandalize and to sort of leave your mark the night before Halloween. We were wild."

Tony feared the combustible mixture of alcohol and drugs with the violent personalities of his two friends. By 9:15 p.m., he felt they were capable of "Anything. Anything. It was always the dare between those two. I mean, they were always trying to outdo each other. And they would just push each other." Tony had a loose curfew, but he said that Adolph and Burr's antics on the night of the murder made his decision to go home "a lot easier." He sensed they were headed for trouble and says, "I didn't want any part of it" if things went ugly. "Well, I had been in trouble that summer and I had gotten arrested in Greenwich for being a little hellion. So my mother told me that I had to catch the last train."

By the time he departed, Adolph and Burr were "at a fever pitch. . . . They were sort of ready to blow up." Adolph swore, "I'm not going out of here unsatisfied." Tony told them that he had to leave due to his mother's curfew. "The last train was like either 9:35 or 9:40 [p.m.]. I already had my ticket. And I asked them, you know, 'Hey, I'm leaving. Do you guys want to go with me?' 'No. No. We're going to stay the night. We're not going anyplace.'" They asked Tony, "'Are you sure you don't want to stay?' 'My mom wants me to go.' Because, you know, mom was an excuse. But I knew better. I knew that I needed to go, because this wasn't a situation I really wanted to be in. I didn't feel comfortable with being that out of control." Tony left the group at 9:15 p.m. and hitched a ride to the train station. He barely made the train to Manhattan. Adolph and Burr intended to stay the night with Geoff.

Tony's departure occurred at the same time that Michael, his brothers, and his cousin expelled Tommy, Martha, Geoff, and Helen from the Lincoln and departed for Jimmy's house. The crowd in the Mead was dwindling. The ubiquitous 9:30 p.m. curfews were clearing the area of witnesses, and Martha and Geoff had migrated to the Skakel driveway where they stood with Tommy and Helen, illuminated by the kitchen door spotlight and visible from the Mead. Adolph and Burr might easily have watched Tommy and Martha "playing flirtatiously" in the light of the Skakel driveway and then spied on the couple as they retreated to their secluded love nest behind the toolshed. Tommy and Martha's sexual encounter would have been dimly visible from the Mead. It's possible that the two lovebirds were observed by Adolph and Burr without knowing it, which could very well have enraged someone obsessed with Martha. Tommy told me that he last saw Martha as she walked across the golf tee and disappeared into the darkness just short of the apple trees on her way toward her house on Walsh Lane.

Here, the witness testimonies come together to support Tony's story. In 1975 interviews with police and in 2003 at Michael's criminal trial, Julie and Andrea testified that, at approximately 9:30 p.m. on the evening of the murder, after the Lincoln departed for Sursum Corda and Martha and Tommy were dallying around the driveway, they saw an unidentified person run past the kitchen window in the darkness. At that time, according to the police report, "All members of the Skakel party were accounted for." Julie stated that a second figure ran across the driveway and disappeared into the hedge adjacent to the driveway. It was too dark to see who it was. Although Andrea did not see the second person, she told the police that she had heard footsteps on the driveway as she was walking back to the house to get the keys. For years, detectives puzzled over these early sightings by Julie and Andrea. The girls thought it might be someone out for Mischief Night. That figure, who Julie described as a large man—bigger than any of her brothers—fits the profile of both Adolph and Burr, who may have been stalking Martha as she rendezvoused with Tommy.

Julie told me that, after dropping off Andrea, she pulled back into the driveway at 9:50 p.m. At that moment, Tommy and Martha would have been completing their sexual horseplay behind the toolshed, and Martha would be preparing to return home. Julie was hurrying to catch the last few minutes of the detective show *Ellery Queen*. As soon as she turned her headlights off, she saw a dark figure running the length of the house from right to left in a crouched position, carrying an object in his left hand. She recalls that he was large and possibly hooded. He dashed across the driveway and disappeared between the trees behind the toolshed. This would put him within a few feet of Martha and Tommy, just as Martha was leaving for home. Julie says she was so shaken by the sight of the man running that she stayed in her car for a few minutes and missed the end of *Ellery Queen*. By the time she turned on the TV in the sun room, the credits were rolling.

Martha's path home would have required her to go left onto an unlit Walsh Lane, walk 75 feet parallel to the Mead, and take a right into her dark driveway, which was framed by groves of bushes and trees on either side. The driveway would be a perfect place for an ambush by golf-club wielding attackers who had watched her from the Mead and stalked her home. Forensic investigators say that this is precisely where the assault began.

TONY FIRST learned of Martha's murder from his mother, who confronted her son after reading an article in the Saturday *New York Times* reporting the discovery of Martha's body the previous afternoon. "Don't you know this girl?" she asked him. Tony answered, "Yes, I do." Concerned that Tony would become implicated in the crime if the authorities discovered that he was in Belle Haven that evening, Bryant admonished her son, "There is no way you are going back to Greenwich." She ordered Tony not to speak with anyone about the trip to Belle Haven on the night of the murder and forbade him from returning to the neighborhood ever again.

When Tony saw Adolph and Burr at school the following Monday, the boys were swaggering. Tony said, "Adolph said some very, very, very, very damaging statements that, I mean, just blew me away." Adolph's admissions left Tony no doubt that they had committed the murder. Adolph boasted, "Well, I got mine"; Burr in a roundabout way says, "Yeah, we did what we had to do" and "We did it. We achieved the caveman," The two friends vaunted to Tony. "We've achieved one of our fantasies. . . . We got her caveman style," Adolph said. Tony told me that Adolph boasted that "he had achieved what he set out to do, you know what I mean? I asked the question, 'With who?' and then I thought better, and said, 'You know what? I don't want to know.' It was her because later on—these conversations take place over a, maybe, two- or three-month period, and each time you get more details, more details . . . because . . . it's the type of behavior, they can't stand to keep that secret. They got to share, they got to gloat." While Adolph and Burr never mentioned the victim by name, it was obvious that they were talking about Martha. "I knew exactly who they were talking about. They were talking about Martha Moxley. They were bragging. They were bragging about it. They would take me to the limit and never mention the name, but, I mean, come on. 'We grabbed her'? 'We got her'?" Tony told me the two boys took pleasure in crowing about the murder. "After school they would stop by my mom's apartment or wait downstairs for me to come out of the building and they would walk and talk and share things with me. The most graphic things. Like just going into details about things that they had done and they would say every-thing but leave out the name. 'We got her good.' I didn't have to ask the name. I knew who it was. It was, it was just that graphic and you could tell who they were talking about that, and they just wanted me to say, 'Oh, you were talking about Martha' and I would never say it. I just said, 'Um-hum, oh really? Okay.' I wouldn't say the name and I was like, they are baiting me to say the name."

According to Tony, Adolph and Burr showed no remorse for what they did that night. "They made a joke of it." He added, "They were proud of it."

At some point, Bryant confessed to his mother that Adolph and Burr were involved in the murder. His mother warned him that they were dangerous to the entire Bryant family. Barbara Bryant ordered Tony to distance himself from his two friends. "I had already been in trouble with the police in Greenwich. So what I'm thinking in my mind is I've got to get out of this situation. This is not healthy for me. That is not good for me. So I just started creating distance." The following year, Tony's mother sent him to boarding school in Texas.

In the weeks after Martha's murder, Tony awoke every morning expecting that that day the police would appear at his door and take him into custody. He worried that his role in bringing his friends to Greenwich, and his presence on the Mead that night, would make him a target for prosecution. "I was afraid of being automatically pinned in as a suspect. My family didn't have money to defend me from a lawsuit that, you know. It would be easy."

At first, he was certain his two talkative friends would be arrested any mo-ment and that when everything exploded, he needed to be a great distance from the splatter. "I did not want to become a suspect or get involved with any of that, because I said, 'They are going to find out who did it. They don't need my help.'" Tony told me, "When it first took place I said, they are going to catch who did it." He was astonished that the police never arrested Adolph and Burr and no one from law enforcement ever appeared to question him. "I mean, this is what is so amazing about this whole thing: No one ever came. No one ever asked me. No one. Miss Walker didn't even mention that I was at her house that night."

As the days, months, and years went by, the police never questioned him about his night in Greenwich. Tony tried to put his friend's murder out of his mind and focus on his family and career. When the grand jury charged Michael, Tony believed, "The case will never go to trial." When the trial began, he thought, "They'll never convict." He knew Michael was innocent; "They don't have anything on him." He felt that this was a case Michael's attorneys simply couldn't lose. He remembers thinking, "I think they got a pretty slam-dunk case here." In any case, he had told his story to Crawford and Neal and Margie. He knew they had spoken to Benedict, Garr, and Sherman, and that if anyone was interested in the truth, they could easily find him. "I am not a hard person to find," Tony says. "When I heard the verdict, I was in shock I mean, I mean, I am sitting in total disbelief of what had transpired."

Michael's conviction reinforced Tony's mistrust of the system and validated his reasons for not coming forward. Tony explained to Vito Colucci that he feared the Connecticut justice system. "And when you have suspects that have been described by other people as having been in Belle Haven and police not following up and prosecutors not following up, it sort of makes you kind of wary. They just beamed in on that one family, the Skakels. And unfortunately for Michael, they had a bull's-eye on him. Based on the evidence that they had, they were able to convict him. But he's not guilty." Tony, who had attended law school, understood the jeopardy of getting swept into the criminal process, a peril particularly acute for a black man. "I sort of understand legal process and I know how things are supposed to work. If they can convict Michael Skakel on circumstantial evidence, I think I would be an easier conviction than Michael," he said.

Tony also stated, "One of the parties, Geoff Byrne, has passed away. So that made me . . . run to the hills even worse, because I knew Geoff knew as much, if not more, than I did."

GEOFF BYRNE, 11 years and 9 months old in 1975, was yet another victim of the cascading tragedy. On the Monday immediately following Martha's murder, Adolph and Burr told Tony that they had spent the murder night at the Byrne mansion, a fact Geoff later confirmed to Tony. Tony told me that Geoff's house offered "the perfect place" for Adolph and Burr to clean up after the crime. "If you were going to do something, in that neighborhood or in that area, and you wanted to escape, and hide, and clean up and get fresh clothes and no one would ever see you, that's the only place where you could have gone. There was hardly anybody home. . . . You could stay at that house and the parents would never know," said Tony. Anyone who had ever been in the Byrne house knew this to be true. Built in 1891, the manse was a 10,000-square-foot Tudor castle with 12 bedrooms, 8 baths, and an old coal shaft used by neighborhood kids to access a secret basement-level entrance. Adolph and Burr could have counted on Geoff's accommodating nature. According to Tony, Burr and Adolph usually simply announced that they wanted to stay at Geoff's house and Geoff was grateful to comply.

Tony, who describes himself as Geoff's close friend, said, "I knew Geoff very well. Everybody loved this kid." Tony recalled, "His parents didn't keep track of him very good, and he had an older brother [Warren] who pretty much looked after him because his mom and dad were always going on some type of trip or something. He was always out there looking for affection," Bryant trailed off sadly. "He was a great guy. He was a great guy. He was one of the best kids." Michael confirmed Tony's description, remembering Geoff as a "sweet, lost, affection-starved little boy" whose parents were never home and who was raised by his brother, Warren, a chef, who was 10 years Geoffrey's senior. "Geoff was a lonely boy in a big corral," said Michael. "He seemed to be always trying to fit in, always trying to please. He would do anything to be accepted." Tony remembered that Geoff smoked pot and drank with the older kids. These qualities made it easy for Adolph and Burr to take advantage of him.

Based on what Geoff told him in the weeks after the murder, Tony reckons that Geoff was present when the murder occurred. "I am willing to bet big money on that one." But whether Geoff was present or simply allowed Adolph and Burr to hide out in his home after the murder and clean up their bloody clothes, the little boy was clearly traumatized by the events. "He came into the city a couple of times and he wasn't even supposed to be in the city. He was younger, like, two or three years younger than we were and he would just leave his house and come to my mom's apartment in lower Manhattan." But when Geoff told Tony, "I saw what happened and I need to tell you about it," Tony, who had already "put pieces together because of things that Adolph and Burr had said to me," begged off. Tony believed Adolph and Burr were about to be busted, and the less he knew about the details of their crime, the better. "I told Geoff, I am not interested. I didn't want to know."

Tony was heartbroken that he couldn't help his obviously upset friend. According to Tony, Geoff was "freaked out" to the point that he became "a different person." Geoff "had fear in his heart." Rattled, he repeatedly told Tony, "Something bad happened. They're bad guys." He warned Tony that Adolph and Burr were "out of control." "He said, 'Tony, you've got to stay clear. They are bad guys.'" As damaged as he was by what he had seen, Geoff was concerned for Tony's welfare. "They are going to get you in trouble and they are already in trouble. You just need to keep your distance." He warned Tony, "I wouldn't be surprised if the police come and question them." Sometimes when Geoff took the train into Manhattan to talk to Tony, he would also express his dismay and anger over what had happened. Tony said that Geoff sometimes blamed him for getting him mixed up with Adolph and Burr. Recalled Tony, "[He] was just like, 'How did I get to this place? How did you put me here?' And, you know, he was sort of reaching out to me to help him. And I said, 'Geoff, I can't do anything to help you. What am I going to do?'"

Just as Tony was putting distance between himself and the dangerous duo, Geoff also felt a new fear of Adolph and Burr. Tony told me, "One time Geoff came to my house and he said, 'Listen, I got to tell you something. I was in Greenwich at home on the weekend. Burr and Adolph showed up at my house uninvited.' They had let themselves in, because they never lock doors in Greenwich." They were sitting in Geoff's bedroom when he walked in, and Geoff thought for a moment that they might attack him. He was, according to Tony, "completely freaked out by it. . . . He first thought he was going to get jumped. He was like, I just felt really uncomfortable. He was very taken aback at that. I think he knew they were dangerous."

In 1980, just after Michael got released from Élan, and while he was still an active alcoholic and addict, Geoff's father approached Michael during a ski weekend in Windham, New York. Mr. Byrne was desperate because Geoff was so badly strung out on drugs. He told Michael that he was certain his son was going to die. "At that time," recalled Michael, "there was nothing I could do. I was still a user myself."

Geoff Byrne died at age 16 on December 27, 1980, six years after Martha's murder.

The Connecticut papers reported that Geoff died of an overdose, but Tim Dumas wrote that Geoff's autopsy showed him clean at the time of his death. His siblings will only say that his death was "a family tragedy." Dumas says that Geoff died by suffocation in a waterbed on the third floor of his parents' massive Belle Haven mansion. Art Byrne, Geoff's father, told Dumas that some tightly held secret about that night may have haunted Geoff and contributed to his death. "I've always been under the impression that he willed himself to die," he said in the 1990s. "Now, how much of his memory of what transpired in 1975 contributed to his . . . feelings of despair, shall we say? He never said what he thought. He never gave me an opinion, or the police an opinion, of what he thought happened."

AFTER MY initial conversations with Tony, I attempted to verify some of his claims. I tried to reach Geoff's older brother Warren, but he didn't return my calls. I found Daryl Fleuryn, Geoff's older sister. She was astonished by the story, and doubted that her 11-year-old baby brother could have been involved with these homicidal villains. She promised to call her mother, Dori, and other brother Greg.

She called back later that day. "I talked to my mom," she said. "She was absolutely shocked. She said no way, ever, were those guys there that night." Daryl said that her father was sitting on the porch when Geoff came home, and their mother saw Geoff asleep at 10:00 p.m. She'd never even heard of the guys. "And she said Geoffrey never had any black friends. He had one black friend many years later who was a Greenwich boy." Her brother told her, "There were no black kids in Belle Haven in those days." I apologized for bothering her. I was convinced Tony Bryant had been honest with me. I sensed that Daryl, who was 28 at the time of the murder, was also telling the truth—or what she believed to be true. But one of them had to be wrong. Their certainty reflected the deep commitment to flawed memories I encountered in so many other witnesses during my investigation—often in direct contradiction to historical facts.

First, I had to discover whether Tony Bryant's two phantoms were real human beings who had ever been to Greenwich, Connecticut. With the help of my friend, a White Plains Police detective, I was able to determine, using high school yearbooks and police databases, that Adolph was Adolph Hasbrouck and Burr was Burton Tinsley. I found a telephone number for Hasbrouck in Bridgeport, Connecticut, and he eventually gave me Tinsley's telephone number in Portland, Oregon. When Hasbrouck answered the phone, I identified myself as Robert F. Kennedy Jr., first cousin to Michael Skakel. I tape-recorded the conversation. Adolph told me about his life—he worked at ABC television as a technician—and he happily reminisced about good times. He knew Tony and had been with him to Belle Haven. He told me they all used to "run around the same circle at one time." Who was in this circle? "Me and Tony Bryant and Geoff, a couple of other people, Neal Walker," he said. Had he ever, by chance, been to Geoffrey Byrne's house? "Yes, I was, many times," he said. "Geoff lived right across the street from Neal." How about Geoff's parents—did he ever meet them? "Oh yes," Adolph said. "I met them a few times." I asked if he happened to be in Belle Haven on the night of the Moxley murder. "That night, we weren't up there, unfortunately," he said. Considering what happened, it struck me as an odd construction. Adolph told me that he had only recently learned about the Moxley murder. "It was a few years ago," he said. "I said, 'Yeah, how about that.' Because that was the time we all used to hang out together . . . I wondered if anybody, if Neal was involved, or connected, or have any more knowledge of that, but I never followed it up." Adolph further confirmed that he was friends with Burton Tinsley, who lived in Oregon. Although he spoke with Burton regularly, he had not been in touch with Geoff, Neal, or Tony since the 1970s.

I provided a tape recording of my conversation with Adolph to Vito Colucci. On September 2, 2003, Colucci and another co-investigator, Kris Steele, knocked on Adolph's door on Pixlee Place, a pleasant, working-class neighborhood of two-story houses in Bridgeport. Adolph started talking immediately and, over the course of approximately 70 minutes, changed his story three times with respect to his whereabouts on the day of the murder. Adolph acknowledged that he was in Belle Haven on the night of the murder, but gave three conflicting accounts of the time he was there. First, he told Colucci and Steele that he had arrived in Belle Haven on the morning of the murder but left around noontime because "nothing much was going on. . . ." Next, he recollected that he, Burr, and Tony arrived in the morning but went home between 6:00 and 6:30 p.m., "before it got dark." Finally, at the conclusion of the interview, he said that the group got there in the morning and left around 9:00 or 9:30 p.m. He said that he didn't realize that there had been a murder in the neighborhood until he showed up at the Byrne residence a few days later and the police informed him of the Moxley murder. This contrasted with Adolph telling me that he had only recently learned of the murder. When Colucci and Steele asked if he would be willing to take a polygraph, Adolph demurred, "I'd probably flunk it." He explained that he gets really nervous and that his jitters might affect his performance. Adolph also told Colucci and Steele that he had not spoken to Burton Tinsley since the previous December, of 2002. In an email to me, however, Adolph stated he had spoken to Burton in June 2003. Following the interview, Adolph called Kris Steele collect to say that he had "checked his calendar" from 28 years before and realized that he was not, after all, in Belle Haven on the night of Martha Moxley's murder. Adolph also told Steele that since their first encounters with defense investigators, he and Burr had spoken to be sure that their stories would match.

ON MARCH 3, 2003, a few days after speaking to Adolph, I phoned Burton at his Portland home. Again, I recorded the conversation. Burton told me that Adolph had warned that I might call. Burton explained that he and Adolph befriended Tony Bryant at Charles Evans Hughes High School and that they frequently visited Greenwich. "Going up there was sort of fun," he said. "New people to meet. Rich community." Burton said that he was originally from Portland, but in the early 1970s he moved to New York with his older brother, who was going to graduate school at Hunter College. Burton said he was hoping to pursue a music career in the city after Hughes High School, but by the time I found him in 2003, he said he was working as a photographer. He recalled being in Greenwich about a half dozen times to socialize with Neal Walker and Geoff Byrne. I asked him whether he had gone to Greenwich on the night before Halloween. Burton responded, "Halloween, it seems to me we were going up there. I have a hard time remembering. . . ." Burton recalled going to a party in Greenwich sometime during the week leading up to Halloween, but could not pinpoint if it was Mischief Night. "I found out about the murder in the *New York Times*. My brother and I were out in the city. We might have been going out for coffee. I don't remember the girl. My brother said, 'See, it's like a whole different world.'" Did he keep up with his Greenwich friends? "You know after the murder, we never went up there." I asked whether he knew that Geoff had committed suicide (which I then believed) a few years after the murder. Burton responded that he was not aware of that fact. "After the murder," he repeated, "we never went up there. . . ."

Burton said that he knew the Walker family well, particularly Neal. He recalled one Saturday tooling around Belle Haven with Neal. "Mrs. Walker was
really nice to us and invited us in for something to eat." Burton said that he'd
never stayed the night in Greenwich. Had he ever been to Geoff's house? "Oh,
yeah, probably three times," he said. And his parents—had he ever met them?
"I just met his dad one time in passing," he said. "I never met his mom." Then
Burton related what it was like back in those days to spend time in Geoff's house.
"He had a lot of toys and stuff for us to mess around with," he said. One day,
alone in the house, Burton, Geoff, Adolph, and Tony engaged in a shaving
cream battle. "I think he hit Tony with some shaving cream," he recalled. "Geoff
showed us how you could put an aerosol top on the shaving cream can and it
would shoot out into a stream." I recognized this trick from the Skakel family
arsenal and deduced that it must be a Belle Haven stunt. "It must have been his
father's shaving cream obviously. There were many cases of it. I felt weird about
it. The house looked like hell, you know. We weren't purposefully spraying walls.
Geoff didn't care. He said somebody else would clean it up." Next, Burton gave
a detailed description of the inside of the Byrne home, which Margie and Neal
Walker would subsequently confirm as accurate. "That house was really huge.
They had two different kitchens and it was an old historical house. There was
a servant's kitchen, if I'm not mistaken. . . ." Burton continued, "The refrigera-
tor had no handle. At the time, it was the coolest refrigerator I had ever seen."
Burton said he pulled at the door to no avail, before Geoff intervened laughing,
"'No, dummy, You just push the button.'"

Burton's memories were too intricate for someone unfamiliar with the
house. Neal confirmed that the "Byrne had two kitchens and one of the first
push-button door refrigerators." "It was a space-age job," Neal told me, "one
with no visible handle on the door. It only opened with the push of a button."
Stephen also remembered the two kitchens and the push-button refrigerator.
Margie vouched for the other details of the mansion, including the large array of
toys and the lack of supervision. Margie said that her brother, Neal, spent a lot
of time at Geoff's house because it was "a little freer there. There wasn't as much
supervision." She also recalled a secret tunnel that ran beneath the house that was
accessible through an outside door. Tony told me he believed that Adolph and
Burr had used the tunnel to access the basement when they hid and cleaned up
after committing their crime. Garr corroborated the existence of the secret tunnel at Michael's new trial hearing, testifying that the house was "enormous" and
that if you were in one area of the house, it would be possible to be unaware that
another person was in a different area.

Neal told me another thing he remembered: back in that period he got a
concerned phone call from Geoff's mother. Geoff was off at school but Adolph
was standing in front of her house, apparently waiting for him. "Geoff's mom

called me and said, 'What's the deal? Why is this guy hanging around? Could you ask him to not do that?'" Neal recalled. "So I think I talked to him and I talked to Tony and [Adolph] stopped hanging around."

Burton told me that he, Adolph, and Tony had attended a dance in Greenwich during that period. That confirmed Tony's recollection of attending the Sacred Heart Dance on October 4 with the two friends from Manhattan where Adolph got so jealous of Martha.

I asked Burton whether he ever had seen the Skakels' house or eaten there. Burton responded: "The only time that I ever heard or thought of Michael, and I never met any of them, was when Tony pointed these guys out and Geoffrey said that one of them was nuts, and I said, 'What do you mean nuts?' He said, you know, it was Michael, and he said Michael was in a pretty serious fight at . . . Brunswick School and was expelled." Prior to his expulsion, Michael had indeed had a fight with a boy named Steven Rugasse who had made fun of his mother after her death.

I brought my findings to Santos, Seeley, and Colucci. Colucci next called Burton in Portland. Burton told him that he'd been in Belle Haven on the night of the murder, but couldn't remember any specifics about when he went out or when he returned to the city. We'd hit pay dirt. Both suspects corroborated the most crucial part of the story. They clearly had been to Greenwich; knew Neal, Geoff, and Tony; and were well acquainted with the interior of Geoff's home. Moreover, they both admitted being near the crime scene on the right day. Two days later, Colucci called Burton back. He wanted to set up a time to meet in person. Burton told him that wouldn't be possible. Furthermore, Burton told him, after their conversation, he had consulted his calendar from 1975, and realized he'd misspoken. Like Adolph, he'd somehow located 28-year-old notes from when he was a teen and discovered he hadn't in fact been in Belle Haven after all. Colucci sent Kris Steele out to Portland to track Burton down. Steele was unsuccessful.

Both Adolph and Burton subsequently refused to respond to subpoenas to testify at depositions noticed by Michael's lawyers. Both men invoked their Fifth Amendment rights against self-incrimination. When Santos and Seeley deposed Tony Bryant under a subpoena on August 25, 2006, he also invoked his Fifth Amendment right not to testify.

In November 2006, veteran private investigator Mike Udvardy and his employee Catherine Harkness drove into Manhattan from their East Hartford office. The pair staked out the entrance of The Washington Irving House, at 145 East 16th Street, a 19-story doorman building on a ritzy block in Gramercy. After some time, an elderly black woman emerged. She was over six feet tall and, despite her age and a lame leg, she walked so quickly with her cane that the pair chased her for a half block before running her to ground. "Barbara Bryant?"

Udvardy called out, breathless. He asked her for a minute of her time. There on the street, she gave them 15. She opened up by venting her frustration that Tony had shared the secret story. Barbara Bryant complained "she didn't know why he was discussing it at all." She said she hadn't talked to a soul about this in over 20 years. But she didn't take her frustration out on the investigators; Harkness describes her as a "very friendly and gracious woman." According to sworn testimony from both Udvardy and Harkness, Barbara Bryant confirmed everything that Tony had told Colucci and me. Tony had indeed been in Belle Haven on October 30, 1975, accompanied by Adolph Hasbrouck and Burton Tinsley, whom she knew only as "Adolph" and "Burr." He'd told her earlier in the day that he was going to Greenwich with his two companions. She recalled that he returned the "night" of October 30, though she wasn't sure exactly what time. Tony had told her back then that Adolph and Burton stayed overnight in Greenwich. Udvardy pulled out a copy of the November 1, 1975, article from the *New York Times*. She looked it over. Yes, she said, she'd read this specific article and discussed it with her son. And during that discussion, Tony had reiterated that Adolph and Burr had stayed the night in Belle Haven.

After lawyers subpoenaed Barbara Bryant and her son to a videotaped deposition, she changed both her demeanor and her story. The Barbara Bryant that Udvardy and Harkness had interviewed on the street—sharp and friendly—appeared a different person than the woman reluctantly deposed by Seeley in a midtown Manhattan conference room on February 21, 2007. She still placed the three boys in Belle Haven on the day of the murder, but she now recalled that her son had returned home from Belle Haven while it was still light out, not at night as she had told the investigators. She couldn't specifically recall a conversation in which she told Tony to keep his mouth shut about the incident. "It's possible that it happened, but I don't remember having it," she said. She also did not recall telling her son that Adolph and Burr were dangerous and that he should distance himself from them, although she conceded that it was "possible" that she had conveyed that warning to Tony. In Barbara Bryant's statements and deposition testimony, it was clear that she disapproved of Tony's willingness to come forward with information about Martha's murder. She clearly wished to downplay any possible involvement that he may have had with the crime.

Tony, when subpoenaed, pleaded the Fifth and asserted his right to avoid self-incrimination. Had I been his attorney, I certainly would have advised him to do this. Without any assurance of immunity from the prosecution, it would have been perilous for him to put himself with Martha in Belle Haven on murder night with a golf club in his hand. Adolph and Burton, now lawyered up, also pleaded the Fifth. That action suggests that there was some basis for Tony's allegations. If they hadn't been in Belle Haven that night, why not testify? In her videotaped testimony at Michael's new trial hearing, Barbara Bryant was a changed woman. As Harkness observed on the stand, she looked comparatively "out of it." She appeared heavily medicated, slurring her words and seeming confused. Bryant admitted that the publicity surrounding her son's disclosures had made her "ill" and that she was taking several medications, including Vicodin.

DURING MICHAEL'S new trial hearing, Benedict argued that Tony had only recently hatched his story, in order to help market Crawford's *Little Martha* screenplay. Benedict dismissed Tony as a hustler parlaying a tenuous connection to Greenwich into a show business career. That characterization is not plausible; *Little Martha* is an altogether different plot scenario involving none of the characters in Tony's tale. Furthermore, there is abundant evidence that Tony's story is not recently hatched, including Adolph's and Burton's admissions and Barbara Bryant's testimony. Tony's old house mum, Esme Dick, also corroborated Tony's chronicle. Esme Dick testified that Bryant had been alluding to his narrative for decades.

Esme Dick, with whom Tony had lived for nearly three years while he attended Brunswick, testified at Michael's new trial hearing that sometime after Martha's murder but before the 1975–76 school year ended, Tony had dinner with her and her family. The conversation turned to suspects in the Martha Moxley murder, including the Skakel boys. Tony told Esme Dick that he knew the Skakels were not guilty. He told her that he was in Belle Haven on the night of the murder. Esme Dick assumed that the police had interviewed everyone who was in the neighborhood that evening, so she never informed the police of Tony's statements. Esme Dick also testified that Tony was very upset after Michael's trial and told her that Michael had been "wrongly convicted," although he did not explain why he believed that to be the case.

Unfortunately for Michael, the Court of Appeals largely bought Benedict's explanation and Michael lost his petition for a new trial. Michael did, however, win one important convert. In his withering dissent, Judge Richard Palmer questioned Benedict's speculative suggestion that Tony invented his elaborate story to enhance Crawford's screenplay on which he hoped to collaborate. Justice Palmer pointed out that this speculative, and personally risky, enterprise would have required Tony to have begun fabricating his plot to market the screenplay three decades earlier. "The Majority Opinion requires that we believe that at age 14, Bryant was planting the seeds for a false story not to be revealed until more than one quarter of a century later."

Esme Dick was not alone in witnessing Tony grappling with his impulse to tell what he knew. Hearing Tony's story jogged a memory in Michael. Not long after the murder, sometime between Thanksgiving 1975 and early 1976, Michael got an unanticipated phone call from Tony. Tony asked to come out to

Belle Haven and meet Michael that weekend. "He got very mysterious like he wanted to tell me something." Tony's request puzzled him. Michael said, "We weren't really close; I mean I liked him but he asked if he could come up and spend the night at my house. I was mystified but I said, 'Sure,' and skipped our family ski trip to Windham." It was a Friday. The two boys had dinner at the Skakel house. "I had the feeling he had something critically important to tell me," Michael recalls. "Then, during dessert, Tony seemed to change his mind about talking."

In February 2015, I was walking through the Charleston, South Carolina, airport to catch a connecting flight to the west coast. A tall, handsome black man with a big smile hailed me from a restaurant and then bolted out to greet me. He introduced himself as Tony Bryant. It was the first time we had met. We talked for so long that I nearly missed my flight. Just before I left him, I asked about that weekend he had gone up to Belle Haven to see Michael around Thanksgiving. He smiled again, "Yes, I went up there intending to tell him the story. I knew he was friends with Martha and I felt I needed to talk to someone. But then we started drinking and I got scared about talking and the moment passed." According to Michael, the two boys decided to attend a dance at the Greenwich Country Club. It was a senior mixer for Brunswick and Greenwich County Day. "We smoked a joint and got hammered in the Club's kitchen," Michael recalls. "We broke some glasses, ate cake, and stole food and someone called the police. They chased me but I was a really fast runner when I was skinny. I jumped off the second-story balcony. And I ran home in my bare feet. And I never saw Tony again." I asked Tony if he can confirm this recollection. "Your cousin has a good memory," he told me, smiling.

During my investigation, I spent considerable time reflecting about Geoff Byrne, the neglected yet beloved 11-year-old boy whose distinguishing virtue—an open, generous heart—had tripped him into an unspeakable nightmare. Adolph admitted to Colucci and Steele that he and Burton saw Geoff on the night of Martha's murder. When two *Hartford Courant* reporters confronted Burton near his Portland, Oregon, home in December 2003 and asked him if he stayed at Geoff's home on the night of the murder, he appeared "unnerved": "I have no comment," he said. "I don't think I should be talking about this right now." It's reasonable to speculate that Adolph and Burr, after clubbing Martha, and then briefly regrouping in the McGuire garage, made their way to Byrne's house, entering through the coal chute and then pressured Geoff to allow them to clean up. In her testimony at the *habeas* hearing, Margie described the Byrnes' coal chute as a "place where the boys would go and drink beer or do things that they weren't supposed to be doing." Adolph told Colucci that he visited Geoff two days after the murder—probably to take his temperature and encourage him to keep his mouth shut.

Meanwhile, Stephen began taking a fresh look at Geoff Byrne. Police first questioned the boy four or five days after Adolph says he visited Geoff for his post-murder consultation. Geoff gave police a spine-chilling account of his journey home from the Skakels after he escorted Helen to her door. "After he left Helen, and he was walking home by himself, he heard footsteps following him," the report read. "When he stopped to listen the footsteps kept coming. He then started to run and ran all the way to his house. Geoff further stated the footsteps ran after him all the way home and that he did not look back to see who was following him."

After hearing Tony Bryant's story, Stephen listened to the tape of Geoff's interview with Officer Lunney. At minute 6:33 of the tape, after Geoff detailed the harrowing flight from his pursuer, Lunney asked the 11-year-old boy the same battery of questions that he was asking all the Belle Haven kids that he interviewed. Tony's insights invested Geoff's responses with new meaning. "Do you know for sure who hit her?" Lunney asked. There was a long pregnant silence. Several seconds pass. "Huh?" Geoff finally asks. Lunney repeated the question. Geoff finally speaks, his voice quavering as if he might cry. "No," he said.

> LUNNEY: Anything else you want to tell us that maybe we haven't asked you think it might help us in some way?
> BYRNE: [another pause] I can't think of anything.
> LUNNEY: Have you pretty much been thinking about this for the past two weeks?
> BYRNE: Uh huh.
> LUNNEY: Nothing's come into your mind . . .
> BYRNE: [cutting Lunney off] No.
> LUNNEY: You have no suspicion on anybody. Nothing that we . . .
> BYRNE: Not really anymore.
> LUNNEY: Not really anymore? What do you mean anymore?
> BYRNE: No, I don't.

And at that point, the interview ended abruptly. Stephen listened to those last minutes again and again—about 12 times in a row. Something about the exchange convinced Stephen that Geoff knew more than he was saying. He also detected that Lunney suspected as much, but for some reason didn't want to push the boy. Stephen told me his neck hairs stood up. He kept thinking about Geoff's plaintive despair and his warning to Tony: "Some bad things happened with some bad guys. Tony . . . you gotta stay clear of them. They're bad guys. They're going to get you in trouble."

Then I discovered, in a yellowed clipping, more haunting words of affirmation from the tragic little boy. In October 1980, a *Greenwich Time* reporter interviewed Geoff for a story pegged to the crime's fifth anniversary. The reporter asked Geoff what he thought about the theory that Tommy had done it. Even though he and Tommy hardly knew each other, Geoff was adamant. "He didn't do it," he said. "I know he didn't do it. He's not the sort of person who could have done such a thing." Less than two months after the story ran, Geoff was dead. His defense of Tommy would be a final act of kindness.

The evidence began to pile up. Martha's diary corroborated many of Tony's stories. She certainly knew him, and had hung around with Tony and Crawford Mills. On January 6, 1975, she wrote, "Margie invited me to a party—one of Neal's friends, Tony." Then, on January 11, she wrote, "Went to Tony's party with Margie. Had a few cigs. He had a case of beer but we didn't get around to it. Met Crawford somebody, Tony, and a few others." Tony claimed that Adolph and Burr had met her at a block party on Greenwich Avenue in the fall. On September 21, she wrote, "Yesterday was the block party on Greenwich Ave. Me, Margie and Helen went shopping in Stamford all day and by the time Margie and I got down there it was 8:00. We found Jackie, Helen, Pam N., etc. and we all walked around. We finally ended up walking home at 11:30 w/ me, Margie, Helen, Jackie, Neal, Crawford, Michael, Tom and Geoff Byrne." As previously noted, Bryant claimed that Adolph became particularly obsessed with Martha after attending a church mixer. Three weeks before her murder, Martha wrote about the Sacred Heart dance, when her dance partner "wouldn't even let go."

In September 2003, the news of Tony's allegation broke. Both Benedict and Garr steadfastly refused to interview Adolph Hasbrouck, who lived just a few minutes from their office. (Neither Garr nor Benedict would agree to talk to me about him, or anything else.) Santos and Seeley announced they would be seeking a new trial based on the new information that Tony had provided. Tony became the story. News trucks surrounded his Florida home and put him in the merciless media crosshairs. "It was really rough on him," Neal told me. "For a while we were all getting calls but I think the press were hardest on him. They staked out his house and harassed him."

Over seven days in April 2007, Michael's attorneys presented their case for a new trial. Benedict turned the proceedings into a referendum on Tony's credibility. Tony, like many witnesses in criminal trials, was not blemish free. Leading up to the hearing I learned that, in 2003, the government cited his tobacco company for underreporting how much product the company was importing and levied a substantial fine. In 1993, Tony pleaded no contest to charges of being an accessory to felony larceny. The previous year, when questioned about an armed robbery that took place in Beverly Hills, Tony had claimed he'd been kidnapped. He had lied, apparently, and served six months of home monitoring. And in the late 1980s, he was hired as an attorney in Texas; subsequently, he was fired after his firm learned he hadn't passed the bar.

On April 17, 2007, in Stamford Superior Court, I was the first witness to take the stand. "Were you aware that Gitano Bryant in the State of California in 1993 was convicted of the crime of conspiracy to commit robbery which was a felony in that state?" Benedict asked me, during his cross-examination. "No," I replied. I found his tactic ironic. Tony looked like an altar boy in comparison to the prosecution's star witness, Greg Coleman, who had a long rap sheet and testified to the grand jury high on heroin.

The most compelling reason for doubting Tony's story is the argument that two six-foot black kids—Tony and Adolph—would not have escaped notice in Greenwich, Connecticut, in 1975. Of course, the best counterargument— and it's pretty dispositive—is that all three boys have admitted—against self-interest—that they were there. Neal believes that Dori Byrne and other Belle Havenites have blinkered memories when it comes to African Americans. He says that despite claims by contemporary Greenwich residents describing their town as lily white, there were plenty of blacks there. "All the neighbors have said, 'We would have seen black kids in the neighborhood; black kids would stick out like sore thumbs,' but Tony had been visiting me for a while, and he had a girl-friend in the neighborhood," Sheila said; she confirmed that her sister Andrea, who passed away in 2008, had dated Tony. Helen recalls that her close friend Janet Tyner, who lived on Oak Ridge Street, in a less-affluent part of Greenwich, "was over at my house all the time." Belle Haven residents routinely employed African Americans as live-in domestic help; William and Larry Jones lived with their mom, Ethel Jones, at the Skakel house. Larry was 17 when Martha died. Rucky's handyman, Wade Evans, an African American furloughed from prison by Grandpa George, is not mentioned in any police reports and was never ques-tioned. Police also neglected to question Tony, who gives a detailed description of his Belle Haven meanderings that night.

None of the former Belle Haven teens we spoke to specifically recall seeing Tony that day. But could we really expect anyone to recall faces from a night 32 years before, especially when seemingly every kid and adult in the neighborhood was either drunk, high, or both? "The whole town, both adults and kids at the time, were pretty out of control," Margie told me. Plus, Tony admitted that he and his friends—delinquents on a crime spree—were making vigorous efforts to avoid detection as they stole beer, smoked pot, and committed assorted acts of vandalism. He said they ducked behind trees and stone walls to dodge passing cars, hid in "spots the parents couldn't see," and that the boys would "scatter and run" when any adult got "a bit close."

The mission on Mischief Night was to commit mischief and not get caught. The M.O., even among Belle Haven kids, was avoiding detection. Anyhow, to what end would Tony lie to his mother about being in Belle Haven with Adolph and Burton? These guys also remember being there that day. They clearly had been to Geoff Byrne's house.

Santos asked Detective Lunney on the stand if Greenwich Police ever questioned Belle Haven residents about black kids in relation to Martha's murder. "No, sir," Lunney testified. But I recalled stumbling across a piece of evidence while researching my 2003 article for *The Atlantic*. Back then, long before I ever talked with Tony, the mysterious tidbit had little significance. It was a taped interview unearthed by Santos and Seeley with Margie from late 1975. For some mysterious reason, Lunney himself pointedly grilled Margie and another neighbor and friend of Martha's, Lisa Rader, about the possibility that Martha had a run-in with "colored boys." "Has she ever mentioned having lunch at the Greenwich High School with any colored boys?" Lunney asked Walker. "Ever mention . . . maybe some colored boys became annoying?" It's difficult to conceive that question as random. Something made Lunney, the chief investigator, believe that African American teens might have been involved in Martha's murder.

Possibly it was the forensic evidence from the crime scene. Tony's story would seem to have forensic corroboration, in the forms of two human hairs found by police on a forensic sheet used by police to cover Martha's body. The FBI forensic crime lab identified the first hair as "possessing negroid characteristics" and the other "possibly" having an Asian DNA profile. Adolph is African American and Tony described Burton as mixed race, possibly part Asian or American Indian. Police investigators assigned so much importance to those hairs that they extracted comparative hair samples from the only two African Americans males known to be living in Belle Haven. The FBI crime lab in Washington found that the "negroid" hair matched neither Greenwich Police Officer Daniel Hickman, nor the son of the Skakels' cook, Larry Jones, who lived adjacent to the crime scene. (Larry's older brother William was away in the military.) The police were apparently looking for a possible explanation for the presence of that hair. Investigators never identified the contributor of either of the hairs. In February 1976, Greenwich Police briefly investigated Darryl Brooks, a 19-year-old black man from nearby New Rochelle, who had been arrested a year before, suspected of murdering a young girl with a golf club.

If the Greenwich Police had been comprehensive in their search, they might have discovered the presence of Tony, Adolph, and Burr in Belle Haven that night. Police long maintained that they chronicled every second of Martha's evening, who she was with, and her whereabouts. During Michael's 2007 appeal this was the bulwark against Tony's version of the evening. If the police didn't hear about Tony and his hooligan friends visiting Belle Haven, how could it have happened? In fact, there were many Belle Haven kids out that night, whom police never bothered to question. Among them is Maria Coomara-swamy, who spent part of Mischief Night with Martha. Coomaraswamy left the Moukad house with Martha, Jackie, Helen, and Geoff shortly after 7:30 p.m., and walked north beside Martha until they parted company at the Coomaras-wamy home. Maria watched as Martha and her comrades headed toward the Skakels. Until Seeley and Santos reached out to her in 2015, police had never approached or interviewed this girl who'd been out in Belle Haven and with the victim several hours preceding her murder. As another example of the pervious police investigation, Detective Lunney testified during Michael's 2007 petition for a new trial that none of the teenagers that he interviewed reported seeing Carl Wold, who was walking his dog from 7:30 p.m. to 8:30 p.m., or another neighbor, Mrs. McBride, who walked her dog from 9:00 p.m. to 9:30 p.m. The Greenwich Police dragnet seemingly captured only a tiny fraction of Belle Haven's Mischief Night activities.

MARTHA'S MURDER is the centerpiece of a tragic parable with powerful moral lessons about the hazards of orthodoxy, the susceptibility of journalists to the seductive gravities of the mob, the corrosive power of gossip, the abuse of police and prosecutorial power, and personal lessons about courage, perseverance, and grief.

The parade of awful tragedies that proceeded from Martha's murder seems to never end. If Michael remains free, Crawford Mills will be one of the unsung heroes of this horrible drama. Crawford never stopped pushing to broadcast Tony's story. After the failure of Michael's petition for a new trial, Crawford's life crumbled. Having lost his CBS job following Dorthy Moxley's greenroom epi-sode, and with no recommendation from his old boss, Crawford was unable to find work in New York City. He began to fear what his testimony had wrought. "He felt like he was being followed or somebody was standing outside of his apartment at all hours," Neal told me. "I don't know if that's paranoia or actually somebody was there, but whichever, things got worse and worse for him. Things just went downhill for him." He moved to rural Litchfield County in Connecti-cut. On October 6, 2008, he took his own life, shooting himself in the head with a shotgun he'd borrowed from his landlord.

Crawford's death, in particular, made me stop and think about Dominick Dunne and the Moxley family and about how each one of us bears ultimate responsibility for what we do with our grief. I was fortunate to have good paradigms.

On the day that Jack Ruby murdered Lee Harvey Oswald, no one doubted that Oswald had murdered my Uncle Jack. I was a 9-year-old boy watching my parents, shattered by tragedy, and expecting then to be satisfied that the author of their agony had suffered just punishment. I was wrong. My parents and their

Kennedy siblings gained no satisfaction from Oswald's death; instead the murder only deepened their grief for their brother and for our country.

After my father's death, I watched my mother and Uncle Teddy—my father's last living brother—plea to the judge to allow his alleged killer, Sirhan Sirhan, to escape the death penalty. My mother taught us that, while our grief would never get smaller, our job was to build ourselves bigger around it; vengeance would only diminish us and widen the reverberations of misery.

The deaths of Crawford and Byrne, Tommy's ostracism, and Michael's imprisonment were all part of the spreading ripples of misery from Martha's tragic murder.

I sympathize deeply with Dorthy Moxley. I have seen up-close the agony of a mother's grief over the loss of her child. My mother lost her husband to murder and two of her sons to violent, untimely deaths in the bosom of their youth. I was with her when my father died. I stood beside her 29 years later as my little brother Michael died in her arms.

My mother told us that we needed to let go of our impulse for revenge and allow the cycle of violence to end with our family. This, she said, was the lesson of the New Testament, which swapped the savage eye-for-an-eye tribalism of the Old Testament for the ethical mandate that we turn the other cheek. But forgiveness wasn't just ethics. It was salutary. Revenge and resentments, my mother said, are corrosive. Indulging them is like swallowing poison and hoping someone else will die. By opposing the death penalty for Sirhan, we diluted those poisonous passions.

And what if, God forbid, the object of our revenge turns out to be innocent? For several decades, my father's close friend Paul Schrade, who took one of Sirhan's bullets, has argued that Sirhan Sirhan did not fire the shot that killed my father. Recent forensic evidence supports him. How would we have felt now, if our family had demanded his execution?

As someone who has seen two family members, Michael Skakel and my former brother-in-law Paul Hill, convicted of murders they didn't commit, I know how reluctantly the State reverses course on a conviction. No matter how strong the evidence of a defendant's innocence, governments only reluctantly relinquish their grip on a convicted man. Paul Hill was convicted of another "notorious" crime—the IRA's 1974 Guilford pub bombing. The frame that ensnared Paul and three other men was the subject of the 1993 film *In the Name of the Father* starring Daniel Day-Lewis. In 1991, the British courts overruled his conviction, declaring his coerced confession "improper," and freed Paul, who had by then served 16 years in 38 British prisons. In 1993, Paul met my sister Courtney, a human rights activist, at a congressional hearing on US/Ireland relations chaired by my brother Congressman Joseph Kennedy. They later married.

In Paul Hill's case, prosecutors knew beyond any doubt that Paul was innocent and had been wrongly convicted after he served only seven years in jail. Among the abundant evidence pointing to his innocence were the voluntary confessions of the elite IRA murder squad that actually committed the Guilford pub bombing, for which he was unjustly imprisoned. Despite that evidence, government prosecutors waited another decade to free Paul. The instinct of certain prosecutors is to dig in and never admit they made an error. This dynamic will be particularly disastrous in the Moxley murder, for which we now know, beyond a reasonable doubt, who actually committed the crime. The State's intransigence and stubbornness are allowing the real killers to go free.

WE ALL have a duty to see that our efforts to heal from grief do not compound the tragedy and punish the innocent. Neither Dominick Dunne nor Dorthy Moxley took that precaution. Mrs. Moxley rhas steadfastly efused to look at exculpatory evidence. She pointed the finger first at Tommy. Her intransigence cost Crawford his job and contributed greatly to Michael's unlawful conviction. We all understand when a grieving family lashes out erratically, and we forgive as best we can. The job of prosecutors, press, police, and the judiciary is to cool those passions. None of those checks and balances worked in this case. It's time to reverse the injustice.

EPILOGUE

The bedrock of our democracy is the rule of law applied by an
independent judiciary immune to the gusting winds of popular sentiment.
—Caroline Kennedy

On June 7, 2002, following a month-long trial, the jury convicted Michael of murdering Martha Moxley. Trial Judge John F. Kavanewsky Jr. sentenced him to 20 years to life in prison. I visited Michael periodically in jail. In conformance with Stephen's and Michael's requests, I will not write in detail about the various horrors that Michael encountered during his 11½ year prison bid. Both brothers are understandably fearful that the Connecticut Supreme Court could, any day, send Michael back to prison. Anything he says about guards, gangs, or other inmates, still in the Connecticut Department of Correction system, could return to haunt him with lethal effect.

Sometimes when I visited Michael, his eyes would tear up. "Get me out of this place," he would whisper. He not only missed his son, George, but all the children who gave his soul sustenance. One day he told me, "I called my brother Johnny's house. His 4-year-old daughter picked up the phone. I only had 12 minutes on the phone and this kid always used up 90 percent of my allocation. She said; 'Hi Uncle Michael. You should have seen the dog, Danny. He was running around chasing a squirrel all day then he ran over and there was a rabbit. . . .' Oh my God. That felt like I was taking in the last little bit of oxygen before my soul died. Do you understand that?"

Michael's conviction shocked his family and friends and galvanized them into supporting his appeal. With Linda Kenney Baden's help and Stephen's leadership, the Skakels retained a pair of first-class criminal lawyers, Hubert Santos and Hope Seeley, from Hartford, Connecticut.

Hope and Hubie filed a direct appeal of Michael's criminal court conviction to the Connecticut Supreme Court in November 2003. They made the argument that Mickey Sherman should have made at the outset: Michael's trial violated Connecticut's 1975-era five-year statute of limitations governing non-capital murder. Connecticut abolished the statute in 1976, but Santos and Seeley contended that the 1975 statute should still apply; Connecticut's Supreme Court had repeatedly held that the five-year statute applied for murders committed in 1975, even when the State indicted defendants after its repeal. In order to uphold the trial court verdict against Michael, the Supreme Court would have to reverse its own long-standing, black-letter precedent.

Furthermore, the court would have to override another long-standing precedent by allowing prosecutors to try Michael in criminal court, even though existing law required that Michael be tried as a juvenile, since he had just turned 15 when the murder occurred. The maximum prison term for a juvenile under this statute was five years.

In addition, Santos and Seeley appealed the verdict as tainted by Judge Kavanewsky's strange ruling allowing the jury to view copies of the *National Enquirer*, the *Star*, and other supermarket tabloids, containing inflammatory, salacious, and patently erroneous articles about Michael Skakel and about the Kennedy family. The articles were irrelevant, immaterial, and horrendously prejudicial.

Courts are meant to be bulwarks against the vicissitudes of public prejudice and passions, but even the most courageous and impartial jurist can feel the storm of popular opinion and occasionally hold up a finger to feel the direction of the breeze. The orgy of media malpractice that fed the public's revulsion of Michael also annealed judicial reluctance to release him—even in the face of black-letter law and precedent. In an opinion written by Justice Richard Palmer, the Connecticut Supreme Court ploughed down its own ironbound legal precedent, rejected every appeal, and affirmed Michael's conviction on January 24, 2006.

On August 29, 2005, Michael had filed a second appeal. Michael's lawyers asserted that newly discovered evidence (including Tony Bryant's revelations) as well as a pattern of misconduct and nondisclosure by the prosecutors and police warranted a new trial. Santos and Seeley returned to the trial court for a hearing to show evidence that they had uncovered since taking over Michael's representation. The court needed to determine whether the newly discovered evidence, had it been shown to the jury at trial, might have resulted in a different jury verdict. If so, Michael would be entitled to a new trial. The new evidence included three witnesses discovered post-conviction who directly contradicted the testimony of the State's key witness, Greg Coleman, regarding Michael's alleged confession to murder.

Michael's lawyers also showed how the prosecution team illegally concealed reams of exculpatory evidence from Michael. The hidden evidence included the secret agreement between the State's lead investigator, Frank Garr, and author Len Levitt to share expected profits from a book and movie deal about Michael's conviction. Santos and Seeley also proved that Garr had threatened, intimidated, and harassed witnesses to testify against Michael. Garr had deliberately concealed police reports from the defense team that supported Michael's alibi defense and a composite drawing strikingly similar to suspect Kenny Littleton that would have bolstered Michael's third-party culpability defense. That sketch places Littleton near the crime scene within minutes of Martha's time of death. Garr also withheld a suspect profile of Littleton linking him to over a dozen serial murders of young women and more than 12 hours of video tape and 40 hours of taped phone conversations with Littleton from 1992. Finally, Benedict and Garr illegally withheld a suspect profile of Tommy Skakel until mid-trial and a damning audiotape of prosecution witness Andrea Shakespeare.

In addition, Judge John Karazin reviewed the new evidence that I helped uncover pointing to Adolph Hasbrouck and Burton Tinsley as the real murderers. I testified at the evidentiary hearing regarding my conversations with Tony Bryant, Burton Tinsley, Adolph Hasbrouck, Crawford Mills, and others. Since they had invoked the Fifth Amendment, Bryant, Tinsley, and Hasbrouck were not available to testify. Judge Karazin admitted my 10 tape-recorded conversations of Tony Bryant and his former friends, and Tony's videotaped testimony with Vito Colucci. Neal Walker, Margie Walker, Barbara Bryant, and Crawford Mills also testified, as did Colucci.

On October 25, 2007, Judge Karazin denied Michael's appeal. In his ruling Judge Karazin concluded that the video confessions Colucci had recorded of Tony, Adolph, and Burton were sufficiently credible to be admissible. "Mr. Bryant's statements," the court concluded, "were made under circumstances which support admission, are corroborated by sufficient evidence, and are clearly against his penal interest." Nevertheless, the court concluded, in a seemingly contradictory finding, that the new evidence, while credible enough to be admitted, would not have prompted the jury to change its verdict. Michael's attorneys appealed this bizarre ruling to Connecticut's Supreme Court on January 16, 2008, arguing that this and the other newly discovered evidence should entitle Michael to a new trial.

On April 12, 2010, by a vote of four to one, the Connecticut Supreme Court upheld Karazin's decision against a stinging dissent by Justice Richard N. Palmer, who had written the original opinion preserving Michael's conviction, but who was apparently now fed up with what was clearly a rigged game. In his scathing 103-page dissent, Palmer blasted both the prosecutor and his brother judges for allowing the unjust conviction of an innocent man based upon "evidence . . . that was weak at best, especially when viewed in the light of the testimony that was used to convict [Michael Skakel], which consisted almost entirely of equivocal admissions by [Michael Skakel] and one dubious confession."

Even more importantly, Palmer argued, the actual perpetrators of the murder had now been identified. Palmer scourged Benedict and Garr for their determination to overlook compelling new evidence indicating that Adolph Hasbrouck and Burton Tinsley had murdered Martha Moxley. Palmer characterized as "contradictory" and "unprecedented" Karazin's finding that Tony Bryant's testimony was credible enough to be admissible but not credible enough to sway a jury. "I believe that the petitioner, Michael C. Skakel, is entitled to a new trial . . . the Bryant evidence is highly relevant because it identifies Hasbrouck and Tinsley as the persons actually responsible for the murder." Judge Palmer found Tony Bryant believable. "The record reveals nothing about Bryant or his background to suggest either that he is the kind of person who would provide testimony falsely implicating two innocent people in a brutal murder or that he had any reason or motive to do so," he wrote.

Finally, Justice Palmer opined that the exculpatory evidence hidden by prosecutors during the trial was alone enough to justify a new trial. "[A]t the very least, it is likely that this new evidence, when considered in light of the State's thin case against petitioner, would give rise to a reasonable doubt. . . . The likelihood of an acquittal upon retrial is enhanced by other newly discovered evidence, namely, the relationship between the lead investigator in the case, Frank Garr, and Leonard Levitt, the author of a book about the victim's murder on which Garr collaborated, and the views expressed by Garr in that book reflecting, inter alia, his strong and long-lasting feelings of antipathy toward [Michael Skakel] and the [Skakel] family."

The law requires that Michael exhaust all other appeals before invoking his constitutional right to *habeas corpus* based on a claim that he had an incompetent lawyer. With all his legal appeals now exhausted, Michael's lawyers, on May 17, 2013, filed a *habeas corpus* petition challenging his incarceration due to Mickey Sherman's rank ineptitude. On October 23, 2013, Judge Thomas Bishop, Superior Court, issued a blistering 136-page ruling granting the *habeas* appeal and freeing Michael after 11½ years in some of the most brutal prisons in Connecticut.

Judge Bishop's long opinion gave the lie to Benedict's self-aggrandizing claim that Sherman had been a worthy and valiant opponent. *Habeas* appeals are notoriously tough to win. The defendant must prove not only that trial counsel was ineffective, but that the verdict would have been different had the defense been adequate. Courts typically grant *habeas* petitions in only extreme cases, for example, where a drunk public defender representing an indigent defendant falls asleep in court during a capital trial. A successful *habeas* appeal is exceedingly rare in cases involving million-dollar defense attorneys. However, after tabulating an inventory of Mickey's catastrophic malfeasances, Bishop wrote that "Trial counsel's failures . . . were significant and, ultimately, fatal to a constitutionally adequate defense."

Judge Bishop's decision freed Michael after 11½ years in prison. Michael had seen his son, George, only a handful of times during that period. When he went in, George was 2 years old. When Michael emerged from jail, his son was a teenager. Michael has been free for nearly three years, but he does not have the life of a free man. He wears what he calls a "Lindsay Lohan bracelet" on his wrist to monitor his whereabouts. He must apply for court permission whenever he wants to leave the state. His career is on hold until the courts make a final ruling.

Since his release from prison, Michael has lived off the kindness of his family, at first boarding in a tiny guestroom in his little brother Stephen's modest Connecticut rental that Stephen shares with his girlfriend. Eleven years of litigation and imprisonment had left him destitute and beggared many of his family members. A decade earlier, Michael had sold his beloved cabin in Windham to pay his legal bills. He spends his weekends in the Adirondacks and Catskills, coaching now 17-year-old George, a downhill and grand slalom ski racer, and waxing and tuning skis before competitions. As a former US Ski Team speed skier, Michael feels that help with ski racing is one of the few tangible things he can give his boy.

In a recent vulnerable moment Michael told me, "I feel sorry for him that he is my son." His eyes were tearing as he stood in my kitchen following a 12-step meeting. With Michael's acquiescence George had just changed his last name; the boy was tired of the teasing and the public hostility. He believed that his father's blighted reputation would hinder his college admission opportunities. That afternoon, Michael told me he had been driving with George back from Lake Placid when a man pulled alongside Michael's car and recognized him. The stranger unrolled his window, gave Michael the finger, and threw a beer can. Michael kept driving. He is used to it. "I told George he could call himself Bullwinkle for all I cared. I'll love him no matter what name he chooses." Michael is a peculiar combination of being both physically tough and impervious to pain and having extreme emotional sensitivity. Stuff like this still makes him cry. But then, suddenly, he was laughing again. "George called me an hour later and asked me for money, so I guess nothing changed."

Even in the 12-step meetings that ought to be his refuge, he is discomforted by the ubiquitous whispers and stares and occasional hostility. For three years, a group of men have held semi-private weekly 12-step meetings in my home to give Michael a sanctuary where he can feel safe. Michael said the rosary thrice daily in prison. On his release he returned to his practice of daily mass and communion, but gawkers have made church visits a painful experience. Michael erected an altar in his bedroom where he can pray in solitude and peace. He recently moved out of Stephen's guest room and is currently living with and caring for an elderly aunt in Bedford, New York, on the Connecticut border.

On August 8, 2014, Connecticut prosecutors filed an appeal of Judge Bishop's grant of *habeas corpus*. That action caused me to begin work on this book. On February 24, 2016, I attended the arguments on this appeal before a six-justice panel of the Connecticut Supreme Court in Hartford.

As prosecutor Susan Gill recited a cruel battery of calumnies and lies about Michael, I scribbled a passage from the Old Testament and handed it to Michael:

> *He was despised and rejected—a man of constant sorrows, acquainted with deepest grief. We turned our backs on him and looked the other way. He was despised, and we did not care."*

—Isaiah 53:3

Michael scrawled a note back to me, "I'm familiar with the sorrow. Having someone to shoulder the burden with me has cut its weight in half. Thanks for your friendship—and for all the laughs."

As I write this, six Connecticut Supreme Court justices are deciding whether to uphold or strike down Judge Bishop's decision. If they strike it down, Michael will go directly back to jail to complete his 20-years-to-life sentence. If, in the best scenario, the justices uphold Judge Bishop's decision, State prosecutors will decide whether to retry Michael Skakel for Martha Moxley's murder. John Smriga, the Fairfield County State's Attorney who succeeded Benedict in 2009, will choose how to proceed.

With his new lawyers and the exculpatory evidence now in hand, and the evidence of Adolph Hasbrouck's and Burton Tinsley's likely culpability already judged admissible, prosecutors would have almost no chance of convicting Michael in a new jury trial. With Benedict retired and Garr disgraced, perhaps the Connecticut State's Attorney will decide to prosecute the likely perpetrators of the Moxley murder and finally bring Martha's killers to justice.

Using the evidence I have cited in this book, prosecutors have sufficient cause to indict Burton Tinsley and Adolph Hasbrouck for Martha Moxley's murder.

They also have enough evidence to prosecute Frank Garr and Jonathan Benedict for suborning perjury and illegally concealing evidence. Benedict committed overt acts of prosecutorial misconduct of the kind that got North Carolina prosecutor Mike Nifong removed from office, disbarred, and imprisoned in the Duke Lacrosse case.

Garr suborned perjury, a felony. In addition, he has admitted to obeying Benedict's illegal orders to actively conceal police reports and witnesses that would have demonstrated Michael's innocence. Together the pair illegally conjured a conviction out of smoke and mirrors. Because of their crimes, my cousin lost over a decade of his life—and his son's entire childhood. It's time for Garr and Benedict to pay for their crimes and for Martha Moxley's murderers to finally face justice. We shall see how committed the Constitution State is to the rule of law.

INDEX

A

Adams, John, 205
Albano, Lou, 220
Appeal, denial, 275–276
Arnold, Liz, 138, 200
Attanian, Matt, 181–183, 185–186
  Ridge conversation, 183–184

B

Baden, Linda Kenney, 216, 231, 273
  recommendations, Sherman nonusage,
    226–233
  Sherman, impact, 218–219
Baden, Michael, 7, 28, 173, 216, 222
  notorious/infamous crime prosecution,
    approach, 20
Bailey, F. Lee, 163
Baker, Mary, 111–112, 114
  Littleton conversations, police tapings,
    116–117
  Solomon/Garr interview/interaction,
    115–116
Baran, Jr., Stephen (Skakel authorization
    revocation), 93
Barbieri, Paula, 221
Belle Haven Club, 4, 41, 55, 79, 83, 87–88,
    96, 103, 105–106, 207, 249–250
Belle Haven, description, 3
Belle Haven Yacht Club, 249
Belmont Hill, 104, 110
Benedict, Jonathan, 5, 8, 13, 62
  confidence, absence, 17
  disgrace, 278
  Margie Walker visit/story, 243
  multimedia display, problems, 31–33
  one-man grand jury, convening, 170
  Peeler case, failure/loss, 20–21
  phony confessions, 23

  political pressure, 171
  prosecutorial misconduct, 25
  scenarios, 23–34
  tapes, splicing, 34
  theory, solidity (absence), 30
  trial summation, 22
Bennison, Daniel, 155
Bethpage Polo Club, 41
Billings, LeMoyne, 40
Bishop, Thomas, 13, 276
Bjork, Cynthia, 56–57
Blassie, "Classy" Freddie, 220
Bohemian Grove, 44
Boroski, Jane, 120
Brannack, Ann, 36–40
Brannack, Joseph, 37
Brisentine, Robert, 118
Brooks, Darryl, 269
Brosko, Ted, 87, 166
Browne, Donald, 17–18, 94, 159
  job, quitting, 19
  payoff, Dumas speculation, 169–170
Brown, Tina, 157, 224
Brunswick School, 4, 79, 91–92, 100, 104,
    105, 108–109, 135, 137, 239–265
  Greenwich County Day, senior mixer, 265
Brush pile search, 64, 67–68
Bryan, Jamie, 148
  Purposely Prejudicial Analysis, 148–149
  Worst Case Scenario report, 62, 149
Bryant, Barbara, 244, 262–263
  subpoena, 263
Bryant, Kobe, 240
Bryant, Tony, 79
  Adolph/Burr distance, mother's insistence,
    255
  Belle Haven meanderings, police
    questioning (absence), 268

Bryant, Tony, *(continued)*
Colucci interview, 245
Fifth Amendment, 263–264
Gitano Bryant (full name), 239–240
justice system fear, 256
Kennedy meeting, 265
life, background, 240–241, 245–246
Mead departure, 253
secret, 240–241
subpoena, 263
Bryant, Wallace, 240, 245
Buckley, Jr., William F., 44
Burgess, Thornton, 38
Burke, Richard, 179
Byrne, Dori, 258, 268
Byrne estate
coal chute, Walker description, 265
description, 256
Byrne, Geoffrey "Geoff," 3, 25, 242, 246, 256
Bryant description, 256–257
death, 258
life, ruin, 271
Lunney interview, 266
Stephen Skakel examination, 265–266
traumatization, 257–258
Byrne, Warren, 257, 258

C

Cahoon, Linda, 120
"Caller, The," 147–148, 150
protection, 151
Caron Foundation, 196
Carroll, Steve, 55, 58–59, 69
interview, 63–64
Skakel cooperation, 86
Carver, Wayne, 28
Catholic Society Opus Dei, 40
Cavello, Ralph, 126
Cave Mountain, 82–83
Chapman, Duane "Dog the Bounty Hunter," 221
Charles Evans Hughes High School, 246, 260
Chateau Coiffures, 203
Chianese, Dominic, 223
Citizens Energy Corporation, 49–50
Clinton, Bill, 165
Clusen, Chuck, 206
Coleman, Greg, 268
addiction, 195–197
Attica/mental institutions, 196
confession claims, 192–193, 195, 201
credibility, absence, 204

death, heroin (impact), 199
epithets, 196
Garr recruit, 195
lying, reputation, 21
memory, drug addiction impairment, 198
sadism, 139–140
star witness, problems, 197–198
Colored boys, Martha run-in, 269
Colucci, Vito, 7, 197, 200, 217–218, 200, 222, 225, 250, 256, 259–265
interview, 245
potential witness discoveries, 227
Condit, Gary, 157–158
Connecticut v. Adrian Peeler (Benedict loss), 20–21
Connolly, Mark, 155
Conspiracy
Benedict theory, 23–25
witnesses, involvement, 24
Conviction (Levitt), 21, 100, 147
Coomaraswamy, Peter, 60, 73–74, 79
Copeland, Laura, 218
Cortese, Vinnie, 66–67, 70
Couric, Katie, 220
Craparotta, Vincent "Jimmy Sinatra," 216
Crowe, Michael, 232
Cuomo, Andrew, 81
Curatola, Vince, 223
Czaja, Paul, 92

D

Danehower, Richard, 60
Darrow, William, 112
Davidson, Gerald, 138–139
Dead Man Talking (Hoffman), 15, 33
Devlin, John, 7, 28
Dick, Esme, 244, 245, 248, 264
Diehl, Debbie, 133–134
DNA
recovery, absence, 11
tests, usage, 20
Dobson, Willie, 221
Dominick Dunne's Power, Privilege and Justice, 175
Dowdle, Georgeann, 5–6
grand jury testimony, 230–231
perjury, possibility, 25–26
Skakel account confirmation, 13, 24
Wittine attack, 78
Dowdle, James "Jimmy," 4–5
perjury, possibility, 25–26
Dowdle, John, 84

Dream Team (criminal trial lawyers),
    216–217
  disbanding, 218–219
Dressler, Al, 245
Drucker, Bonnie, 69
Dumas, Timothy, 55, 68, 120, 128
  Greentown, 19, 242
Dunne, Alice, 139, 143, 189, 198, 200
Dunne, Dominick, 224–225, 272
  alcoholism/drug addiction, 156–157
  Bryan files, release, 150
  campaign, impact, 96
  *Dominick Dunne's Power, Privilege and
    Justice,* 175
  falsehoods, 17–18, 33, 57–58, 86
  Levitt story, 161–162
  Moxley interaction, 160–161
  objective, 175
  Other Mrs. Kennedy, The, 179
  Season in Purgatory, A (Dunne), 18, 161,
    164, 179
  Smith rumor, 115, 159–160

E

Edwards, Lisa Rader, 251, 269
Élan School
  abuse, exposure, 47, 140–141
  behavior-modification program,
    controversy/discredit, 138
  Michael Skakel attendance/abduction, 46,
    48, 50, 77, 100, 136–138
  psychological domination, 141–142
  punishments, 139–140
Evidence, disappearance/misuse, 60–61
Exculpatory DNA tests, usage, 20
Exculpatory evidence
  disclosure, legal requirement, 25, 121
  new trial impact, 276
  prosecution team illegal concealment, 21,
    274

F

False confessions, expert examination
    (Sherman production failure),
    231–232
False memory, 206
Family Educational Rights and Privacy Act, 93
Fay, Red, 43
Fifth Amendment, usage, 262
Fitzgerald, F. Scott, 37–38
FitzPatrick, Dan, 61
FitzPatrick, Michael, 232–233

Fleischli, Edward, 8, 59
Fleuryn, Daryl, 258–259
Fordice, Rushton, 37
Foster, Vince, 165
Freedom from Chemical Dependency
    (FCD), 47
Freedom of Information Act, 96, 145
Freehill, Kim, 138, 140–142
Fuchs, Barrington, 75
Fuhrman, Mark, 11, 13, 17
  blame, 167–168
  Carroll, interaction, 87
  felony perjury, 163
  Morano/Galluzzo meeting, 170–171
  Murder Business, The, 175
  Murder in Brentwood, 164
  Murder in Greenwich, 19, 28, 50, 156,
    164, 170, 225
    Garr dismissal, 169
  racism, 163–164
  theory
    Benedict advancement, 22, 172–173
    problems, 172

G

Galesi, Francesco, 44
Galluzzo, Dominick, 170
Garibaldi, Giuseppe, 75
Garr, Frank, 5, 15, 17, 242
  case, relaunch, 174–175
  chumming, 180
  disgrace, 278
  Hale disagreement, 94–95
  hatred, 16
  impact, problems, 20
  interviews, 69–71
  Levitt
    hagiography, 21–22
    interaction/friendship, 114–115
    life, background, 113–114
    Margie Walker visit/story, 243
  media strategy, 188
  police report concealment, 275
  political pressure, 171
  Sheridan meeting, 147
  subpoena, possession (falsehood), 181
  threats/intimidation/bribery, 274–275
Georgetown University Homecoming,
    Revcon bus (usage), 12, 26
Gerbino, Mark, 197
  Colucci discovery, 227
Gillman, Anne, 95

Gill, Susan, 23, 209, 278
Goldberg, Lucianne, 158, 165
Golden Touch Salon, 203
Goldman, Ron, 175
Golf club(s)
  murder weapon, 89
  stress testing, 216–217
  usage, 11–12
Goodman, Annie, 223
Gorman, Mr./Mrs. Charles, 9
Grace, Nancy, 11, 235
Graham, Walter "Wally," 37
Great Lakes Coal and Coke Company (Great
    Lakes Carbon) (GLC), 37–38,
    42–45, 82–83
  attorney, Skakel estate arrival, 88–89
  control, 169
  management, change, 44–45
Green, Howard, 135
Greentown (Dumas), 19, 242
Greenwich Police (Greenwich PD)
  cover-up, Fuhrman perpetuation, 166
  crime scene management/evidence
      collection problems, 60
  curiosity/confidence, problems, 59–60,
      64, 67
  Dunne chastisement, 57–58
  Fuhrman attack, 165–166
  institutionalized racism, lawsuit, 242
  investigation problems, 7, 9, 12, 55–59
  Moxley murder, time determination, 7
  search
    comprehensiveness, absence, 269–270
    warrant, absence, 86–87
Gross, Elliot, 7, 28, 60, 216
  autopsy, 28
Grubin, Cliff, 199–200
Grudberg, David, 216
Guandique, Ingmar, 158
Guilford pub bombing, 271
Gumbel, Bryant, 243

H

Habeas corpus petition
  Connecticut appeal, 278
  filing, 276
Hale, Gerald
  Garr disagreement, 94–95
  Moxley recruitment, 94–95
Hammond, W. Edward, 55, 87, 231
  police questioning, 62–63
  polygraph, 57, 59–60

  room, search, 55–56, 59
Harkness, Catherine, 262–263
Hartig, Steven, 250
Harvey, John, 63–64, 66–67, 70
  brush pile search, confirmation, 67–68
Hasbrouck, Adolph, 240–243, 246
  Benedict/Garr interview refusal, 267
  Bryant description, 247
  control, loss, 252–253, 257
  Fifth Amendment, 262
  golf clubs, selection/usage, 250–251
  infatuation (Moxley), 247–248
  Kennedy conversation, 259
  life, background, 259
  Mischief Night, 248–249
  polygraph, denial, 260
  statements, damage, 254–255
  story, changes, 259–260
  swagger, 254–255
  vulgarity, increase, 248
Hennessy, Roland, 64
Hickman, Daniel, 11–12, 60, 269
Higgins, John, 189
  arrest, 190
  confession claims, 192–194, 201
  credibility, absence, 204
  Garr interview, 190–192
  Night Owl, 192–193
  sadism, 139–140
Hill, Paul, 272
Hoffman, Richard, 4, 10, 170, 180
  Dead Man Talking, 15, 33
  interviews, 15, 32
  photos, seizure, 217
  prosecution witness, 17
Holifield, Larry, 59, 67
  interviews, 70–71
"Horse Whisperer, The," 157–158
Howard, Ken, 107
How Can You Defend Those People? (Sherman),
    220
Howe, William, 37
Hozman, Diane, 189

I

Innocence Project, The, 20
Interlocutory appeal, Sherman failure,
    226–227
International Institute for Alcoholism, 50
In the Name of the Father, 271
Ix, Cissie, 22–23, 78–79, 84
  Bryant observation, 251

police statement, 107
Rucky friendship, 81–82
Rucky story, 152
Ix, Helen, 3, 22, 61, 80
   testimony, 8, 13, 31

J

Jachimczyk, Joseph, 7, 27–28
Jones, Edwin, 202
Jones, Ethel, 11, 268
Jones, Larry, 268
Jones, Millard, 11–12, 60
Jones, William, 268

K

Karazin, John, 275
Kaseman, Paul, 197
   Colucci discovery, 227
Kavanah, Donna, 200
Kavanewsky, John, 71, 121, 171, 186, 199,
     228, 232, 234
   Crawford letter, 244
   Skakel sentencing, 273–274
Keegan, Tom, 63–64, 109, 166
Kennedy, David, 15
Kennedy, Edward, 49, 125
Kennedy, Ethel, 168
Kennedy family
   operation, description, 14–15
   Skakel family, gulf, 35–36
Kennedy, Jack, 43, 270
Kennedy, Jean, 40
Kennedy, Joe, 49–50, 55–56
Kennedy, Joseph, 41, 271
Kennedy, Max, 46
Kennedy, Michael, 15, 46
Kennedy, Robert, 44
Kennedy, Rose, 41
Kennedy scandals, 186
Kennedy, Ted, 168, 169
Kerick, Bernard, 175
King, Larry *(Larry King Live)*, 17, 157, 159,
     175, 225, 234
Knight, Tara, 216, 223
Knopp, Mark, 71
Koch, Bill, 45
Kovacs, Tom, 126
Kranick, Harry, 190, 191, 194
Krebs, Willis "Billy," 98–99
   Skakel innocence, belief, 148–149
Krizack, Rocky, 110, 120

L

Lacrosse, Duke, 25
Lang, Joel, 86
Lauper, Cyndi, 220
Lawford, Peter, 158
Lawrence, Phil, 188–189
Lee, Henry, 12, 57–58, 98, 128
   testimony, 31, 60
Leonetti, Philip, 216
Lesse, Stanley, 24, 94, 152, 172
Letterman, David, 227
Levinson, Barry, 220
Levitt, Leonard, 7–8, 18, 58, 275
   Conviction, 21, 100, 147
   FOIA, usage, 96
   Garr, interaction/friendship, 114–115
Levy, Chandra, 157
Lewinsky, Monica, 165
Lewis, Sean (letter), 51
Liddell, Virginia, 70
Ligon, Roger, 221, 222
Little Martha (Crawford), 241–242, 264
Littleton, Ann, 110
Littleton, Kenneth "Kenny," 3–4, 17, 68–69
   alcohol rehabilitation, attempt, 111–112
   Dunne solicitude, 228
   Garr conversation, 118
   immunity, 21
   life background, 104–105
   Lunney/Brosko interview, 105–106
   Morall interviews, Garr/Benedict
     withholding, 121–122
   murderer, Solomon belief, 18–19
   Murphy perspective, 106
   perjury, possibility, 25–26
   police arrests, 108, 110–111
   polygraph exams, 109, 118–119
     failure, 110
   sexual abuse, 119
   sodium amytal interview, refusal, 110
   sodium pentothal test, offer, 111
   Solomon suspect, 115
   statement, 87–88
   testimony, 9, 13
Littleton, Wayne, 110
Lock, John (David Moxley recruitment),
     94–95
Loftus, Elizabeth, 208, 210, 233
Lowell Whiteman School, 135
Lungren, Dan, 163–164
Lunney, James, 7, 12, 59, 69, 166
   Byrne interview, 266

Lunney, James, (continued)
  questions, 75
  searches, 87
  Wittine statement, 79

M

Maher, Ted, 157
Manchester, James, 107
Mangelsdorf, Mark, 210
Margolis, Manny, 93, 97, 142, 216
  judgment, alteration, 149
Markham, Dean, 44
Marr, James "Bunny," 85
Max (Belgian shepherd), location, 80
McCarthy, Dick, 96, 99, 143–144
McCormack, William, 24, 152, 172
McFillan, Angela, 200
McGlynn, Joe, 55–56, 67
McGuire, Sheila
  body discovery, 12, 13, 30, 56–57, 62–63
  murder-night drama, report, 59
McKenzie, Jim, 87
Mead, The, 12, 249–251
  kids, congregation, 252–255
Meerbergen, John, 108–109
Meese, Ed, 111
Memory
  false memory, 206
  manipulation, expert examination
      (Sherman failure), 231–232
  weakness, contamination capability,
      210–211
Merton, Thomas, 40, 42
Metropolitan Blind Brook Club, 41
Mills, Crawford, "Tres," 239
  Bryant secret, revelation, 240–241
  hero, 270
  information, Sherman noninterest,
      241–242
  Kavanewsky letter, 244
  Little Martha, 241–232, 264
  New York Times contact, 244
  death, 270
Mischief Night (Hell Night), 3, 7, 56, 63,
      67, 239
  activities, police dragnet (ineffectiveness),
      270
  Hasbrouck/Tinsley, arrival, 248–249
  mission, 268–269
  Wittine questioning, 79–80
  Ziliuca absence, 75–76
Misinformation effect, 208

Morall, Kathy, 118, 121–122
Morano, Chris, 170, 199
Morganti, Charles, 106–107, 121
  sketch copy, obtaining (Sherman failure),
      227
Moukad house, 4, 270
Moxley, David, 3, 17, 87
Moxley, Dorthy, 3, 63, 218
  Dunne, interaction, 160–161
  polygraph test, 71–72
  public plea, 16–17
  sympathy, 271
  testimony, 7–8, 11, 66
Moxley, J. David, 64
Moxley, John, 3, 104, 231
  evening (October 30), description,
      66–67
  Littleton meeting, 120
  polygraph test, 68
  testimony, 9
  Worst Case Scenario, 62
Moxley, John (Skakel pre-dawn meeting),
      63–66
Moxley, Martha, 3, 73
  Adolph infatuation, 247–248
  bludgeoning/ambush, 4, 6, 67
  body
    crime scene management/evidence
        collection problems, 60
    discovery, 3, 7–8, 12
    dragging, Benedict supposition, 30–31
  community search, 11–12
  death, estimation, 7
  diary, 126–128
    Benedict/Garr tampering, 80
  golf club, usage, 11–12
  Gross autopsy, 28
  Sacred Heart diary entry, 247–248
  Skakel children shock, 90
Mudroom, activity, 10
Murder Business, The (Fuhrman), 175
Murder in Brentwood (Fuhrman), 164
  fiction, work, 169
Murder in Greenwich (Fuhrman), 19, 28, 50,
      156, 164, 170, 225
Murdoch, Rupert, 125
Murphy, Jim, 25, 58, 64, 66, 99
  Rucky meeting, 96–97
  Skakel innocence, belief, 148–149

N

Nifong, Mike, 25

Nixon, Richard M. (Skakel support), 43

O

Ofshe, Richard, 231–233
Olsen, Theodore "Ted," 227
Oppenheimer, Jerry, 179
Ornato, Mike, 68
Ossorio, Dennis, 23, 230–231
 testimony, 13
Oswald, Lee Harvey, 270
Other Mrs. Kennedy, The (Dunne), 179

P

Palmer, Richard, 264, 275
Paradise v. Connecticut, 226–227
Pederson, Norman, 109
Pennington, Lou, 68
Petersen, Sarah, 200
Pickerstein, Harold, 95
Police reports
 Benedict concealment, 25
 Garr concealment, 275
Proctor, James, 57
Prosecutorial Discretion, 19–20
Prosecutors, job/role, 20

R

Ramsey, John/Patsy, 157
Rancheros Visitadores, 44
Reagan, Ronald, 44, 161
Regan, Jr., John, 196, 199
Renna, Rick, 207
Representative democracy, Skakel
  perspective, 42
Revcon motor home, 84
 socialization, 11
 usage, 26
Reynolds, Ann, 45
Reynolds, Mary Ellen, 146, 172
Ricci, Joe (Élan School founder), 138–143,
  188, 198
Richichi, Joe, 220
Ridge, Geranne, 181, 201
 Attanian conversation, 183–184
 credibility, absence, 204
 Garr questioning, 182–183
 Sherman cross-examination, problems,
  185–186
 story, fabrication, 185
Roberts, Monty, 158
Rogers, Dorothy, 200
Roosevelt, Christopher, 92–93

Roosevelt, Franklin D., 42, 92
Rosen, Alvin, 152–153
Rottman, Alvin, 220
Ruby, Jack, 270

S

Sacred Heart, Moxley diary entry, 247–248
Saemann, Frieda, 69–70
Safra, Edmond, 157
Salerno, John, 69–70
 Garr/Holifield interviews, 70–71
Salerno, Marie (Garr interview), 70
Santos, Hubie, 25, 102, 223, 245
 appeal, filing, 273–274
 habeas corpus petition, filing, 276
Scheck, Barry, 20
Schlesinger, Arthur, 40
Season in Purgatory, A (Dunne), 18, 161, 164,
  179
 fiction, work, 169
Seeger, Stephan, 21, 23, 216, 218
Seeley, Hope, 199–200, 226, 245
 appeal, filing, 273–274
 habeas corpus petition, filing, 276
Serenity Project, The, 47
Shakespeare, Andrea (Renna), 4, 6, 24, 161,
  174
 dropoff, 253–254
 false memory, 206
 Garr/Solomon interview, 207
 Gill questioning, 209
 memory, murkiness, 207
 misinformation effect, 208
 Sherman cross-examination, 209–210
 statement, 87–88
 testimony, jury review, 205
Sheridan, Margot, 49–51
Sheridan, Tom, 82–83, 93–94
 allegations, fabrication, 146–147
 confidentiality, breach, 151
 Garr meeting, 147
 manipulation, 141–146, 151
 treachery, impact, 96, 98, 135–136
 vandalism, 154
Sherman, Mark, 174, 216
 reasonable doubt, explanation, 232
Sherman, Mickey, 5, 13, 17
 Baden recommendations, 226–233
 blunder, 230–231
 bluster, 219
 client consultations, scheduling, 223

Sherman, Mickey, *(continued)*
  Continuing Legal Education (CLE)
    Conference, 223–224
  criminal trial lawyers (Dream Team),
    216–217
    disbanding, 218–219
  expenses, excess, 235–236
  false confessions, expert examination
    (usage failure), 231–232
  fame, lust, 220–221
  fees, deduction (avoidance), 233
  How Can You Defend Those People?, 220
  inconsistencies, 67
  indifference/recklessness, 224
  ineptness, 210
  interlocutory appeal, failure, 226–227
  jury selection, skimping, 217–218
  Kavanewesky chiding, 228
  lead, pursuit (absence), 31
  life, background, 220–221
  memory manipulation, expert examination
    (usage failure), 231–232
  Morganti sketch copy, obtaining (failure),
    227–228
  non-family alibi witness, production
    (failure), 230–231
  objections, absence, 33–34
  Rucky hiring, 222
  self-interest, 226–227
  Skakel family
    payments, 215
    perception, 225
    skepticism, 225–226
  Skakel prison visit, 234–235
  summation, failure, 232–233
  third-party culpability defense, weakness,
    231
  trial incompetence, 60
  Vegas arrival, 223–224
  witness nonpreparation, 229–230
Siegan, Chuck, 189, 190, 194, 200
Simpson, Nicole Brown, 175
Simpson, O.J., 15, 17, 22, 157, 163–164,
  175, 221, 224
  acquittal, 19, 167, 186
  defense, success, 216
Skakel, Anne Reynolds, 4, 78–79
  brain cancer, 83–84
Skakel brothers, devilments (price), 44
Skakel children, 40–41
  Lunney/Brosko interviews, 87
  perjury, possibility, 25–26

police interviews, 12–13
  Sheridan perspective/impact, 136–137
Skakel conspiracy, theory, 173–174
Skakel, David, 3, 12, 101
  testimony, 8–9
Skakel estate
  chipping range, 249–250
  description, 39–40
  Lunney searches, 87
Skakel family
  Garr pursuit/hatred, 179
  Kennedy family, gulf, 35–36
Skakel, George, 36–39, 42
  death, impact, 82, 84
Skakel, George Henry, 273
  birth, 50–51
Skakel, Jimmy, 40
  Great Lakes Carbon management, 44–45
Skakel, John, 3, 101
  hypnosis, usage, 9
  testimony, Benedict (attack), 229–230
Skakel, Jr., George, 42–43
Skakel, Jr., Rush, 3–5, 101
  departure, 5–6
  drunkenness, 9
Skakel, Julie, 3, 29
  Andrea dropoff, 253–254
  hypnosis, usage, 6–7, 9–10, 64–65
  Kennedy perspective, 43–44
  Moxley pre-dawn meeting, 64–66
  perjury, 174
  shadow sighting, 6, 88
Skakel, Michael, 3
  academic problems, 135
  account, Dowdle confirmation, 13
  appeal, denial, 275–276
  arrest, 133
  commotion, 9–10
  confession, absence, 16
  darkness, fear, 10–11
  DNA samples, offer, 60–61
  drug treatment program, post-traumatic
    stress syndrome, 15
  dyslexia, 134–135
  Élan School beatings, 142–143
  Élan School confessions, fabrication,
    189–194
  freedom, 276–277
  Fuhrman blame, 167–168
  habeas corpus appeal, 24, 102, 231
  habeas corpus hearing/trial, 4, 13, 25, 194,
    210, 228

Hoffman interviews, 15, 32
indictment, 171
innocence, Murphy/Krebs belief, 148–149
Kennedy brothers, falling out, 50
Kennedy cousin, falsehood, 35
Kennedy knowledge, 15
life, improvement, 46–47
masturbation, Lee testimony, 31
murder admission, voice (usage), 31–32
murder suspect, public focus, 14–15
police surrender, 125–126
post-Moxley murder behavior, 128–129
post-prison rehabilitation, 277–278
post-traumatic stress syndrome, 15, 100
post-trial evidence, accumulation, 267
prison
    release, 276–277
    Sherman visit, 234–235
prosecutorial disparagements, falsehoods, 49
release, *habeas corpus* petition, 240
Santos/Seeley appeal, filing, 273–274
sentencing, 273
Sheridan, impact, 136, 142–146, 154
sobriety, 47–48
sodium amytal test, 152
Sursum Corda location, non-family
    alibi witness (Sherman production
    failure), 230–231
tapes, Garr illegal seizure/leak, 15, 17
trial, 15–16
    exculpatory evidence, prosecution team
    illegal concealment, 274–275
    five-year statute of limitations violation,
    227, 274
    whereabouts (Solomon report), Sherman
    nonusage, 228
Skakel, Pat, 45, 46, 129
Skakel, Sr., Rushton "Rucky," 4, 24–25
    anger/beatings, impact, 83–85
    consent-to-search form/access,
    approval, 87
    cooperation, Carroll perspective, 86
    cover-up, mastermind, 26
    death, 154–155
    frontal lobe dementia, 152–153
    Great Lakes Carbon management, 44–45
    Ix friendship, 81–82
    Sheridan, impact, 82–83
Skakel, Stephen, 3, 75
    relief efforts, 100, 219
Skakel, Tommy, 3, 17
    alibi provision, Littleton (impact), 102–103

behavior, medical explanation, 85–86
Carroll/Lunney pressure, 91–92
childhood bullying, 100
children/marriage, trial (impact), 102
DNA samples, offer, 60–61
innocence, Garr/Benedict belief, 101–102
Krebs interview, 98–99
Lesse psychological exams, Rucky
    request, 94
life, ruin, 271
Lunney, impact, 95–96
murderer, Dunne accusation, 18
polygraph, 90–91
psychological profile, police request, 93–94
sodium pentothal interview, request,
    93–94
Smith, Liz, 159
Smith, Steve, 42, 168–169
Smith, William Kennedy, 18, 34, 115, 159
Solomon, Jack, 18, 95, 113, 166
    binder/report, Skakel whereabouts
    (confirmation), 228
    Sherman contact, 228
    Sherman cross-examination, 228
    Time Lapse Data report, 120
Spitz, Werner, 7, 28
Sproul, Gloria, 80
Stahl, Leslie, 34
Statute of limitations, violation, 227, 274
Steele, Kris, 259–260
Stolman, Abraham, 60
Subway Barbershop, 203
Summation, Sherman failure, 232–233
Sursum Corda, 5–6, 92, 168
    alibi, 26
    brothers, exit/return, 9, 29
    Michael Skakel, exit, 22, 24
Sutton Associates
    founding, 58
    investigation, cessation, 69
    Rucky payments, 144
    Skakel Sr. hiring, 5–6, 24–25
    Sutton Report, commission, 145–146
    worst-case scenario, 175
Sweeney, John, 156
    NRDC strategy session, 205–206
Sweeney, Margaret "Nanny," 9, 24, 85, 117

T
Taccetta, Marty, 216
Ten Commandments of Cross-Examination, The
    (Younger), 14, 215

Terrien, Georgeann, 5, 92
Terrien, James, 25
Terrien, Paul, 161
Testimony with benefits, 20
Teutenberg, Bill, 196
Thim, George, 170, 175, 197, 229
Third-party culpability defense, Sherman
    weakness, 231
Throne, Jason, 174, 216, 218
Tinsley, Burton "Burr," 240–243, 246
  control, loss, 252–253, 257
  Fifth Amendment, 262
  golf clubs, selection/usage, 250–251
  Kennedy conversation, 260–262
  life, background, 260
  meeting, impossibility, 262
  memories, intricacy, 261
  Mischief Night, 248–249
  statements, damage, 254–255
  swagger, 254–255
Tirado, Theresa
  Carroll interview, 63–64
  search, 216–217
Toney Penna 4 iron
  murder weapon, 89
  stress testing, 216–217
Tripp, Linda, 165
Tucciarone, Matthew, 203
  credibility, absence, 204
Tyner, Janet, 268

U
Udvardy, Mike, 262–263
U.S. Supreme Court, Brady decision, 171

V
Van Susteren, Greta, 222
Vaziri, Hossein, 220
Verocchi, Marissa, 181–182, 185
Vinci, Will, 153–154
von Bulow, Claus, 157
Vrechek, Nancy, 64–65

W
Walker, Jean, 56–57
Walker, Margie, 79, 80, 240
  Byrne coal chute description, 265
  story, 243
Walker, Mort, 240
Walker, Neal, 79, 85, 104, 240–247, 259
  Adolph/Burr, meeting, 242
  Tinsley knowledge, 261

Weicker, Gary, 71
Weicker, Lowell, 71
Weitzen, Hyman, 172
Werner, Lou, 44
Wetenhall, Jackie, 4, 5, 58, 80
Wetenhall, Jane, 58
Whitby School, 92–93
Whitcomb, Richard, 109–110
Wiggins, Mike, 200
Windham conspiracy, 26–27
Witnesses
  Garr threats/intimidation/bribery,
    274–275
Witnesses, Sherman nonpreparation,
  229–230
Wittine, Franz "Frank," 3, 24, 77, 174, 231
  attacks/molestations, 78
  background/thefts, 77–78
  job, quitting, 80
  Mischief Night activities, police
    questioning, 79–80
  polygraph test, 80
  statement, 79
Wittine, Paula, 77–78, 80
Wold, Carl, 270
Wold, Jean, 57
Wood, Brian (Sherman challenge, absence),
  218

Y
Yard, sports clutter, 79

Z
Zador, George, 71
Zicarelli, Larry, 201–202
  credibility, absence, 204
Ziluca children, Lunney questioning, 75
Ziluca, Gina, 76
Ziluca, Nancy, 75
Ziluca, Peter, 69, 73–74, 126, 231
  addiction, impact, 74–75
  Coomaraswamy description, 73–74
  Mischief Night absence, 75–76
  Moxley girlfriend, emotional/psychic
    investment, 74
  person of interest, 74
  problems/arrests, 76
Zock (Australian shepherd)
  barking, 8, 28–31, 98
  Zicarelli gun threat, 202
Zoito, Joseph, 110

princetn